P9-DFM-917

Advance Praise for *Angles of Ascent*

"Charles Henry Rowell presents us with the most thoroughly engaging and inclusive anthology of contemporary African American poetry to date. It is a generous, wide-ranging book of precursors and heirs, of contending black aesthetics, generational waves, so many fiery voices extending American poetry, enlightening history, so many angles of ascent."
—Edward Hirsch, author of *The Living Fire: New and Selected Poems* and *How to Read a Poem: And Fall in Love with Poetry*

"A dazzling compilation that does justice to the rich variety and eloquent achievement of African American poetic voices since the dismantling of segregation, *Angles of Ascent* provides ample cause for celebration and reflection. This expansive, much-needed collection of post-1960s poetry is a compelling testimony to the aesthetic power and visionary practice of writers in full command of formal poetics informing creative interminglings of private emotion and personal experience with social worlds and global publics."
—Thadious M. Davis, author of *Southscapes: Geographies of Race, Region, and Literature*

"With thirty years of critical discernment at his fingertips as founder and editor of *Callaloo*, Charles Rowell has harvested an inspired collection of contemporary African American poets, whose rich diversity of subject and craft represents the innovative directions taken after the Black Arts Movement manifestos of the 1960s, as Rowell smartly contextualizes in his informative introduction. Whether studied systematically as a textbook by students and scholars or perused serendipitously at leisure by lay readers, this anthology provides a superb survey of the contemporary landscape of African American poetics."
—Marlon B. Ross, author of *Manning the Race: Reforming Black Men in the Jim Crow Era*

"In a stunningly rich panorama, *Angles of Ascent* charts the state of African American poetry today. Cleverly organized around the 'waves' of black writing that have emerged over the past forty years, Rowell's anthology demonstrates the multiple directions the tradition has taken in the wake of, and at times in rejection of, the prescriptions of the Black

Arts Movement in the 1960s. Like its predecessors in previous decades—from *The Book of American Negro Poetry* in the 1920s to *Understanding the New Black Poetry* in the 1970s and *Every Shut Eye Ain't Asleep* in the 1990s—*Angles of Ascent* will be known as the definitive collection of African American poetry and poetics from the vantage of its moment."

—Brent Hayes Edwards, author of *The Practice of Diaspora*

Angles of Ascent

A NORTON ANTHOLOGY OF
CONTEMPORARY AFRICAN AMERICAN POETRY

EDITED BY

Charles Henry Rowell

W. W. NORTON & COMPANY
NEW YORK • LONDON

Copyright © 2013 by Charles Henry Rowell

All rights reserved
Printed in the United States of America
First Edition

Permission credits appear after biographical notes

For information about special discounts for bulk purchases, please contact
W. W. Norton Special Sales at specialsales@wwnorton.com or 800-233-4830

Manufacturing by R R Donnelley, Harrisonburg, VA
Book design by Brooke Koven
Production manager: Anna Oler

Library of Congress Cataloging-in-Publication Data

Angles of ascent : a Norton anthology of contemporary African
American poetry / edited by Charles Henry Rowell. — 1st ed.
p. cm.
Includes index.
ISBN 978-0-393-33940-6 (pbk.)
1. American poetry—African American authors. 2. American poetry—
21st century. I. Rowell, Charles H.
PS508.N3A86 2012
811'.54080896073—dc23
2011042967

W. W. Norton & Company, Inc.
500 Fifth Avenue, New York, N.Y. 10110
www.wwnorton.com

W. W. Norton & Company Ltd.
Castle House, 75/76 Wells Street, London W1T 3 QT

1 2 3 4 5 6 7 8 9 0

I dedicate this volume
to
three of my friends and colleagues

Janis P. Stout
Karan Watson
&
Shona Jackson

who,
from my first meeting each,
respected and supported
the work
I do.

He strains, an awk-
ward patsy, sweating strains
    leaping falling. Then—

    silken rustling in the air,
the angle of ascent
    achieved.

—ROBERT HAYDEN, "For a Young Artist"

Contents

Preface   xxiii

Writing Self, Writing Community: An Introduction   xxix

♦ PART 1 ♦
PRECURSORS

Modernists, 1940s to 1960s

Gwendolyn Brooks (1917–2000)   4

    The Sundays of Satin-Legs Smith   4

    Riot   9

    Boy Breaking Glass   10

Robert Hayden (1913–1980)   12

    For a Young Artist   12

    Elegies for Paradise Valley   14

    A Letter from Phillis Wheatley   18

Melvin B. Tolson (1898–1966)   21

    from Harlem Gallery   21

        Chi   21

The 1960s and Beyond

THE BLACK ARTS MOVEMENT

Amiri Baraka (1934–)   30

    Black Art   31

    In Memory of Radio   32

An Agony. As Now.   33

A Poem for Black Hearts   35

AM/TRAK   36

Mari Evans (1923–)   42

I Am a Black Woman   43

Nikki Giovanni (1943–)   45

Nikki-Rosa   45

Ego Tripping (there may be a reason why)   47

Bobb Hamilton (1928–1998)   49

Poem to a Nigger Cop   49

David Henderson (1942–)   51

Downtown-Boy Uptown   51

Calvin C. Hernton (1932–2001)   54

The Distant Drum   54

Haki Madhubuti (1942–)   55

But He Was Cool, or: he even stopped for green lights   55

Larry Neal (1937–1981)   57

Malcolm X—An Autobiography   58

Carolyn Rodgers (1940–2010)   61

how i got ovah   61

Breakthrough   62

Sonia Sanchez (1934–)   66

Homecoming   66

Malcolm   67

blk / rhetoric   68

A Poem for My Father   70

Poem No. 3   70

Towhomitmayconcern   71

A. B. Spellman (1935–)   72

I Looked & Saw History Caught   73

Edward S. Spriggs (1934–)   74

For Brother Malcolm   74

The 1960s and Beyond

OUTSIDE THE BLACK ARTS MOVEMENT

Gerald Barrax (1933–)   76
    Eagle. Tiger. Whale.   77
    King: April 4, 1968   78
Lucille Clifton (1936–2010)   80
    lazarus   81
    leda 1, 2, 3   82
    far memory   84
Jayne Cortez (1936–)   88
    Solo Finger Solo   89
    In the Morning   90
Michael S. Harper (1938–)   93
    The Yellow Dishes   93
    Yaddo, Mrs. Ames & Black Men   95
    Coliseum Pool, 1960 (Dream)   96
    Don't Explain: A Ballad Played by Dexter Gordon   98
June Jordan (1936–2002)   100
    What Would I Do White?   101
    Current Events   101
    Adrienne's Poem: On the Dialectics
        of the Diatonic Scale   103
Bob Kaufman (1925–1986)   104
    from Jail Poems   104
    Battle Report   106
    I Have Folded My Sorrows   107
    Walking Parker Home   108
    African Dream   109
Etheridge Knight (1931–1991)   110
    The Violent Space (or when your sister
        sleeps around for money)   110
    The Idea of Ancestry   112
    Hard Rock Returns to Prison from the Hospital
        for the Criminal Insane   113
    Belly Song   114

Audre Lorde (1934–1992)   118
- Coal   119
- To My Daughter the Junkie on a Train   120
- Fishing the White Water   121

Clarence Major (1936–)   123
- On Watching a Caterpillar Become a Butterfly   123
- The Great Horned Owl   125
- Clay Bison in a Cave   126
- Territorial Claims   127

Colleen J. McElroy (1935–)   129
- Paris Subway Tango   130
- Crossing the Rubicon at Seventy   131

Ishmael Reed (1938–)   133
- I Am a Cowboy in the Boat of Ra   134
- The Pope Replies to the Ayatollah Khomeini   136

Ed Roberson (1939–)   138
- Sit In What City We're In   138
- Eclogue   142

Ntozake Shange (1948–)   146
- my father is a retired magician   146
- nappy edges (a cross country sojourn)   148

Primus St. John (1939–)   150
- The Cigar Maker   150
- Trap a Congo   151
- Catch and Release   152

Lorenzo Thomas (1944–2005)   153
- Onion Bucket   153
- Downtown Boom   154

Alice Walker (1944–)   156
- Revolutionary Petunias   157
- On Stripping Bark from Myself   158

Sherley Anne Williams (1944–1999)   159
- *from* Letters from a New England Negro   159
  - Mrs. Josiah Harris / August 25, 1867   159
  - Miss Ann Spencer / August 30, 1867   161
  - / October 22, 1867   162

/ November 24, 1867   163

/ February 15, 1868   164

Al Young (1939–)   166

The Song Turning Back Into Itself 3   167

Ravel: Bolero   168

A Dance for Ma Rainey   169

◆ PART 2 ◆
HEIRS

First Wave, Post-1960s

Ai (1947–2010)   174

Hoover, Edgar J.   175

Conversation   178

The Curious Journey of Ulysses Paradeece

After a Hurricane   179

Cyrus Cassells (1957–)   184

Sally Hemings to Thomas Jefferson   184

Wild Indigo, Because   188

The White Iris Beautifies Me   188

Wanda Coleman (1946–)   190

Ars Poetica   191

Bedtime Story   192

American Sonnet (17)   193

American Sonnet (54)   193

Toi Derricotte (1941–)   195

Holy Cross Hospital   195

The Weakness   198

Invisible Dreams   199

The Minks   203

Melvin Dixon (1950–1992)   205

Climbing Montmartre   205

Paring Potatoes   206

Turning Forty in the 90's   207

Heartbeats   208

Rita Dove (1952–)   211
    Nestor's Bathtub   212
    History   213
    The Fish in the Stone   213
    Daystar   214
    Heroes   215
    American Smooth   216
    Hattie McDaniel Arrives at the Coconut Grove   217
    The Bridgetower   219
Cornelius Eady (1954–)   221
    Photo of Miles Davis at Lennies-on-the-Turnpike,
        1968   221
    Crows in a Strong Wind   222
Christopher Gilbert (1949–2007)   223
    She   223
    Absentee Landlord   224
    Touching   225
C. S. Giscombe (1950–)   227
    The Northernmost Road   227
    The 1200N Road, Going East   230
Jewelle Gomez (1948–)   231
    My Chakabuku Mama (a comic tale)   232
    El Beso   234
Angela Jackson (1951–)   236
    The Love of Travellers (Doris, Sandra and Sheryl)   237
    Two Trains   238
    Ida Rewrites   238
Gayl Jones (1949–)   240
    Deep Song   240
    Foxes   241
    Composition with Guitar and Apples   245
Patricia Spears Jones (1951–)   250
    Wearing My Red Silk Chinese Jacket   251
    Thanksgiving   254
Yusef Komunyakaa (1947–)   256
    Venus's-flytraps   257

My Father's Love Letters 258

"You and I Are Disappearing" 259

Facing It 260

Blue Light Lounge Sutra for the Performance Poets
at Harold Park Hotel 261

Lingo 263

[The jawbone of an ass. A shank] 265

The Devil Comes on Horseback 265

Requiem 266

Nathaniel Mackey (1947–) 268

Song of the Andoumboulou: 16 269

Glenn on Monk's Mountain 275

Sound and Severance 277

Thylias Moss (1954–) 282

The Day Before Kindergarten: Taluca, Alabama, 1959 283

Timex Remembered 285

One for All Newborns 287

Mulberry Breath as Proof of the Wave in
Form of Question 288

The Culture of Near Miss 290

Me and Bubble Went to Memphis. 292

Harryette Mullen (1953–) 294

Unspoken 294

All She Wrote 296

Black Nikes 296

[if your complexion is a mess] 297

[Of a girl, in white] 298

Marilyn Nelson (1946–) 299

Mama's Promise 299

Daughters, 1900 301

Second Wave, Post-1960s

Elizabeth Alexander (1962–) 304

The Venus Hottentot (1825) 304

Boston Year   308

The Blue Whale   309

Thomas Sayers Ellis (1963–)   311

Sticks   311

View-Master   313

Bright Moments   315

All Their Stanzas Look Alike   317

Mr. Dynamite Splits   319

First Grade, All Over Again   321

Godzilla's Avocado   324

Forrest Hamer (1956–)   327

Lesson   327

In the Middle   328

from Goldsboro Narratives, #4, #7, #28   329

Kendra Hamilton (1958–)   332

The Science of Wearing a Dress   333

Belle's Promenade: Nassau Street, Princeton   334

Myronn Hardy (1972–)   336

Undertones   336

On a Bench: My Life   337

The Headless Saints   339

Making Stars with Jacob Lawrence   340

Terrance Hayes (1971–)   342

What I Am   342

At Pegasus   343

Derrick Poem (The Lost World)   345

Touch   346

Wind in a Box   347

Major Jackson (1968–)   349

Don Pullen at the Zanzibar Blue Jazz Café   349

Some Kind of Crazy   351

from Urban Renewal   353

viii. Block Party   353

xvi.   354

xxi.   354

Honorée Fanonne Jeffers (1967–) 356

The Gospel of Barbecue 356

Fast Skirt Blues 359

Hagar to Sarai 360

The Wife of Lot Before the Fire 361

A. Van Jordan (1965–) 363

Regina Brown Hears Voices, Kills Son

Week Before Christmas, December 18, 1996 364

from 367

The Flash Reverses Time 368

Black Light 369

from Thought Clouds 372

Mixed Couple, 1908 373

Discovering the Camera 374

Carl Phillips (1959–) 376

Blue 377

X 378

Leda, After the Swan 379

As from a Quiver of Arrows 380

Fretwork 382

Speak Low 383

Civilization 384

Reginald Shepherd (1963–2008) 386

Orpheus Plays the Bronx 387

How People Disappear 388

Skin Trade 389

Icarus on Fire Island 391

Homeric Interim 392

Patricia Smith (1955–) 394

Prologue—And Then She Owns You 395

She Sees What It Sees 397

Up on the Roof 397

Don't Drink the Water 398

Sharan Strange (1959–) 400

Childhood 400

Froggy's Class 401

Last Supper 403
Natasha Trethewey (1966–) 405
   Flounder 405
   Limen 407
   Bellocq's Ophelia 407
   Letter Home 408
   Elegy for the Native Guards 410
   Pastoral 411
   Incident 411
   Myth 412
Kevin Young (1970–) 413
   Letters from the North Star 413
   Eddie Priest's Barbershop & Notary 414
   The Game 415
   For the Confederate Dead 417
   Crowning 419

Third Wave, Post-1960s

Jericho Brown (1976–) 422
   Track 1: Lush Life 422
   Prayer of the Backhanded 423
   Track 4: Reflections 424
   Track 5: Summertime 425
Michael Sibble Collins (1959–) 427
   Six Sketches: When a Soul Breaks 428
   Poetry 430
   Bryan, Texas Procession 431
Kyle Dargan (1980–) 434
   Search for Robert Hayden 435
   Microphone Fiend 436
   Palinode, Once Removed 437
   Man of the Family 438
Camille T. Dungy (1972–) 439
   What to Eat, and What to Drink, and
      What to Leave for Poison 440
   Cleaning 443

To Put Things Right 444

Vievee Francis (1963–) 445
  Amarillo 446
  Horse in the Dark 446
  Smoke Under the Bale 448
  Still Life with Summer Sausage, a Blade,
    and No Blood 448

Alena Hairston (1974–) 449
  [The tyranny of pig boys] 449
  [The fathers worked their hands to meat] 450
  [Edges in the rhododendron] 451
  [Their greatgreatgranddaddies] 452
  [Daughters of four generations] 452
  [Because we love wrong] 453

Janice N. Harrington (1956–) 454
  The Warning Comes Down 455
  Falling 458
  Fire 459

Tyehimba Jess (1965–) 461
  blind lemon taught me 461
  leadbelly sings to his #1 crew 462
  martha promise receives leadbelly, 1935 464
  mistress stella speaks 465

Ruth Ellen Kocher (1965–) 466
  Meditation on Breathing 467
  The Window Cleaner Writes to the
    Astronaut's Husband 468
  gigan 63 469

Dawn Lundy Martin (1968–) 471
  Negrotizing in Five or How to Write a Black Poem 472
  The Undress 473
  The Symbolic Nature of Chaos 477
  from Discipline 480

Constance Merritt (1966–) 482
  Lying 483
  The Mute Swan 483

Woman of Color	484
Self-Portrait: Lilith, Eve	485
Fred Moten (1962–)	488
gayl jones	488
johnny cash/rosetta tharp	489
μετοικε	490
elizabeth cotten/nahum chandler	492
frank ramsay/nancy wilson	495
John Murillo (1971–)	496
Sherman Ave. Love Poem	497
Enter the Dragon	497
Practicing Fade-Aways	499
Gregory Pardlo (1968–)	501
Double Dutch	501
Copyright	503
Shades of Green: Envy and Enmity in the American Cultural Imaginary	505
Four Improvisations on Ursa Corregidora	506
Written by Himself	507
giovanni singleton (1969–)	509
el corazón—toward an ars poetica	510
from ascension	510
Day 33	510
Day 36	511
Day 41	511
Day 48	512
Tracy K. Smith (1972–)	513
Drought	513
Self-Portrait As the Letter Y	515
Theft	518
When Zappa Crashes My Family Reunion	523
The Nobodies	524
Duende	527
Amber Flora Thomas (1972–)	530
Chore	531
Dress	532

Swarm 533

The Killed Rabbit 534

Lyrae Van Clief-Stefanon (1971–) 536

Garden 536

Lost 539

Bop: The North Star 540

Crystal Williams (1970–) 542

This Parable, This Body 542

Extinction 544

Enlightenment 545

Ronaldo Wilson (1970–) 547

Brad Pitt, Kevin Bacon, and the Brown Boy's Mother 547

Serena Williams, Whiteness, and the Act of Writing 549

On the C Train the Black Object Ponders
Amuzati's Family Eaten in the Congo 551

Biographical Notes 553

Permission Credits 591

Acknowledgments 605

Index 607

Preface

THE CENTRAL PURPOSE OF *Angles of Ascent* is to introduce readers to contemporary African American poetry—that is, the many engaging collections new black artists have been producing since the demise of the Black Arts Movement in the late 1970s. As an effort to account for the extraordinary development of the literary poetry of that significant movement, *Angles of Ascent* looks at once to the immediate past and then to the present and beyond. But, again, the focus of this anthology is contemporary African American work—poems created during the last three decades, the 1980s through 2010. And yet this anthology reminds us that, although much of post–Black Arts Movement poetry in *Angles of Ascent* might appear to be different from the work that precedes it, contemporary African American poets have neither forgotten nor rejected out of hand the aesthetic, cultural, and sociopolitical traditions out of which their predecessors worked. *Angles of Ascent* should be read, then, as the first installment toward an accounting for the ideational and aesthetic achievements of contemporary African American poets.

As a professor of American literature and the Editor of *Callaloo*, I have had, for more than thirty years, the privilege of observing and participating in the development and trajectory of African American poetry in the United States. In other words, I have been an outsider and an insider, a reader and an arbiter, of some of North America's most provocative and engaging poetry created by the last three generations of African Americans. These cultural positions have afforded me the privilege of making a number of discoveries, two of which are contraries. The first discovery is the infinite range and bottomless depth of the African American imaginary, both ancestral and individual, and the linguistic energy and agility that embodies it when it is appropriately mined. The second discovery, which is indeed unfortunate, is the underappreciation of contemporary poetry in the United States, especially the literary poetry created by black Americans. The first discovery I have tried, over the years, to represent in the pages of the literary quarterly *Callaloo*—and now in the selections that constitute the main of *Angles of Ascent*. Because the reading culture of the United States privileges books over periodicals as resourceful objects, I am, via the working anthology *Angles of Ascent*, attempting to address my second discovery by bringing together, for the first time in book form, selected poems by eighty-six poets. Ultimately, this anthology, I hope, will serve as a source of engagement and information, of pleasure and education.

General readers and specialists are largely unaware of the ever-growing numbers of prize-winning black poets who are active in institutions of higher education and in literary and cultural collectives. Mass media and other popular venues have readily made available popular poetry, but— like classical jazz and European classical music, for example—the work of contemporary poets has not been adequately promoted either by our educational institutions or by our venues of popular culture. It will not come as a surprise to those Americans who remain vigilant of the politics of power over the historically marginalized groups (such as women, gays, and people of color) that African American poets—in spite of the numerous poetry prizes and high praises for their new volumes—continue to remain invisible to the public at large. If *Angles of Ascent* will make any impact, it will, let us hope, help address this serious cultural problem, and it will do so by making available, for the first time under one cover, some of the most ideationally engaging and aesthetically pleasing poems that black literary poets have created since the 1980s.

Angles of Ascent gives readers a representative dimension of African American linguistic productions, an omnifarious gathering of contemporary African American poems that offer a broad vista on the different literary scenes from the 1950s to the present. Arranged in chronological order, *Angles of Ascent* features eighty-six poets. To assist readers in navigating through this rich gathering of lyrical texts, I have divided *Angles of Ascent* into two distinct parts: Precursors and Heirs. Part 1, Precursors, is a sampling of poems by three major poets from the 1950s—Gwendolyn Brooks, Robert Hayden, and Melvin B. Tolson; poems by a small number of poets from the Black Arts Movement of the 1960s; and writing by poets who began their careers during the 1960s, but who wrote outside the Movement (and some who continue to write into the twenty-first century). The poems in the first two groups are literally samplings, and their inclusion merely suggests to the reader two of the immediate and influential backgrounds against which the contemporary poets write. For example, the work of poets of the 1950s represents twentieth-century black writers' impulse toward Modernism, against which 1960s Black Arts poets rebelled and attempted to codify what they called the Black Aesthetic. Poets such as Amiri Baraka, Sonia Sanchez, Larry Neal, and Haki Madhubuti, who shaped the Northern urban phenomenon called the Black Arts Movement, "the sister of the Black Power concept," argued against Tolson's impulse toward the academic and Hayden's lyrical gaze into the past, for example. The poets who argued for an art following the dicta of the Movement demanded that black writers must create work "of and for black people." Lucille Clifton, Etheridge Knight, Ed Roberson, Sherley Anne Williams, Audre Lorde, and Michael Harper are some of the poets in the third group represented in Part 1. Although some of them are contemporaries of the Black Arts poets of the 1960s, they wrote outside the Movement; they did not write poetry that subscribed to the dicta of the Black Aesthetic. Some of the poets of this third group—Clarence Major, Ed Roberson, and Primus St. John, for example—are still creating extraordinary poems that are significant forces on the American literary scene. In the collections of those who wrote simultaneously with but outside the Black Arts Movement, we find a bridge or transition between the poets of the 1950s and those represented in Part 2.

The poets and poems in Part 2, Heirs, are the focus of *Angles of Ascent*, for they represent—in number, artistry, and kind—a heretofore unacknowledged flowering in the development of African American poetry. They are, indeed, an American phenomenon that signals an extraordinary future for American poetry. The poets in Part 2 represent what I describe as three significant waves of African American poets. The writers in the first wave—Rita Dove, Nathaniel Mackey, Thylias Moss, Toi Derricotte, and Yusef Komunyakaa, for example—began emerging near the close of the 1970s and the early 1980s, at the end of the Civil Rights Movement and in the wake of the death of the Black Power Movement. Natasha Trethewey, Kevin Young, Elizabeth Alexander, and Carl Phillips are some of the poets in the second wave after the 1980s. That they could not write as they do without the example of the poets in the first wave is readily obvious to readers of *Angles of Ascent*. From the third wave, we hear the new voices of Tracy K. Smith, Gregory Pardlo, Alena Hairston, Vievee Francis, and Tyehimba Jess, poets who are examining, extending, or building on what they find useful in the work of Ai, Toi Derricotte, Marilyn Nelson, Terrance Hayes, Thomas Sayers Ellis, Major Jackson, and many other poets in English and other language groups. Together these three waves, whose reading habits are national and international, portend a very positive future for African American poetry.

While the overall organization of this anthology is chronological, the reader should remember that the arrangement of poets within certain groups or categories does not follow chronology based on their ages. Within particular sections, I have arranged poets in alphabetical order, according to their last names. For example, Gwendolyn Brooks (1917–2000) opens the anthology, as well as the section in which she is located; she precedes Melvin B. Tolson (1892–1966), who was twenty-five years her senior. Second, I have also placed poets in certain sections in the anthology according to the dates they began their significant publication. Dawn Lundy Martin (1980–) and Kyle Dargan (1980–), for example, were born after Michael Sibble Collins (1959–) and Janice N. Harrington (1956–); I placed them all in the same group because their significant publication histories begin around the same period. In *Angles of Ascent,* publication history trumps autobiographical history.

Instead of the traditional biographical note, I have substituted the poet's poetics as a headnote. Some of the poets wrote statements at my request, while others allowed me to use sections of their essays, interviews, or poetry collections as their poetics. I hope these statements will prove useful to readers who desire to illuminate their reading of certain poems by exploring the aesthetic landscape from which particular poets write or wanted to write. If the different statements of poetics tell us anything about the poets' practices, then readers of the poets in Part 2 of this anthology will further discover the infinite variety among poets who began writing during the 1980s, for example, as opposed to those who, as young men and women during the 1960s, were writing from the prescriptive ideology of the Black Aesthetic. The interests in poetry of these two groups of poets are distinctively different from each other. The poetics of the poets represented in this anthology further demonstrate for the reader the ranging variety in contemporary African American poetry. In short, the poetics statements are essentially a resource, intended as a tool, to enhance reading.

The title of this anthology is not an accident. "Angles of ascent" riffs on Robert Hayden's own work and pays tribute to Hayden, a master artist who left behind an extraordinary gift in the pantheon of North American poetry. Recalling his poem "For a Young Artist" and the 1975 collection of his poems, the title *Angles of Ascent* acknowledges Hayden's indelible impact on contemporary African American poets who are richer in knowledge and practice for having had the privilege of reading his poems. Then, too, like the people from whom they derive, black American poets are, like the "hawk-haunted fowl" in Hayden's poem, beginning their ascent; contemporary African American poets, writing against the backdrops of community and ancestral memory, are individually ascending the heights of art by creating a new poetry which is, in artistry and ideational imperatives, a testament of the human will to prevail and triumph.

I have tried in this anthology to give readers a representative gathering of contemporary poems that African American literary poets have created and are still creating, so as to share with readers the lyrical genius that is now at work and still to come. Writers who are not included in an anthology may be absent because they rejected the editor's invitation, or because they refused to give the editor permission to reprint their work. Sometimes, too, the high costs of permissions determined whether a poem could be included in the anthology. Ultimately, however, anthologies are representations of their respective editors—their aesthetic, creative, and critical sensibilities.

It is my hope that readers will receive *Angles of Ascent* as a necessary project that will extend their literary and cultural education, as well as provide them a glimpse into the future of U.S. American poetry as expanded, enriched, and refined by marginalized artists. In *Angles of Ascent*, general readers and specialists in literary and cultural studies will find various readings of humanity from the diverse voices of modern and contemporary African American poets.

—*Charles Henry Rowell*

Writing Self, Writing Community

An Introduction

PROLOGUE

CONSTANCE MERRITT WRITES *of how poems begin in "Lying," her medita-tion on how the poem, as artifact, is sometimes conceived when one is alone in one's interior world—perhaps when one is asleep, perhaps when one is awakened in the early morning hours by "truth turning" on one's inner private landscape, where the external world is but a presence:*

> in a quiet room a woman works
> arranging words, a world
> where she might live
> it changes little day
> to day but the mind is changed
> as light changes, as the leaves turn
>
> and whatever holds that space inside her
> it is so much harder, vaster, colder
> than this near mortal, however breathing, however loved.

That intimate world is what Vievee Francis speaks of when she declares that "it is ... [the] interior that I and so many poets of this age are mapping." And she, like Constance Merritt, goes on to tell us why there is extraordinary value in rendering unto her readers the precious finds of that interior world. "A proscriptive poetry of the external (no matter how necessary) is too limiting in its scope, ultimately allowing more reaction against than creation toward. It is not enough to call out what is happening to us, without an equal measure of what is occurring within us. Further, if we do not map our interiors, fully and continually," Vievee Francis rightly contends, "it is too easy for theorists to dismiss our voices as absent, artless, mere polemic." The origin of poetry is also personal for Amber Flora Thomas, who, revealing the sources and subjects of her poems, writes, "I suppose I see the poem as a bowl in which all of my experiences are poured; however, I must pick and choose only a few to leave in at a time; leave in too much and the poem will not make sense. Sometimes I see an infinite number of connections between all of my experiences and I want these connections to be understandable in a poem, but the reader can't be expected to follow such huge leaps, so I continue to shrink and shape my poems until they contain a single thread of feeling or thought. Sometimes a single image or action is enough to support an entire poem; however, I find the solitary images do amount to longer narratives the more I write." The voices speaking in this Prologue are the latest of the contemporary poets, the third wave, new poets who formally began their careers as artists during the first decade of the twenty-first century.

※

How different are the concerns of these new poets from those of their much earlier predecessors, who seldom if ever shared with their readers the process of writing poetry. Unlike their earlier predecessors (Gwendolyn Brooks, Jay Wright, Robert Hayden, Audre Lorde, and Etheridge Knight, for example), these new poets consider it important to give voice to their processes of writing, as does Jericho Brown, for example, when he tells us that he thinks "of writing, first, as a process of listening to some series of sounds that enter my mind and, second, as a process of embodying those sounds. I try and leave as much as I can to instinct, intuition, and reflex—even in the final stages of revision. Because I'm so interested in both music and voice, I find myself trying to figure the personality of the sounds as I am composing." The process is at once different and similar for each poet. For Tracy K. Smith, "One of the most exciting moments during the creation of a poem is when the poem itself begins to make suggestions to me. At times it's simply a matter of tapping into a sonic pattern that, if pursued, can lead in an unexpected direction. And sometimes it's an urge to turn a corner and allow myself to say something that will constitute a major contextual leap in the poem. For me, those types of shifts and junctures are sources of energy that keep the poem from feeling too pedestrian and that keep me fully engaged in—and surprised by—the process of composition." And then there is Dawn Lundy Martin, who confesses to us that for her, "The poem is compelled into existence by the very thing that prohibits its speech. Here the body is bent over awkwardly. There is a critical alliance with alienation; and what it means to say, 'I am' or 'I will be' or simply 'I': all this around the loathed body (its markers of 'race,' its methods of entry)—its piecemeal effects, its attendant gestures and speech; the will and persistence of things in the face of linguistic atheism." However different or similar the process of creation may be for each poet, many of the poets of this generation would agree with giovanni singleton, who views "writing as an act of paying attention. My aspiration is to transcend appearances in order to see clearly the essence of things." What these new poets say about writing and how they write constitutes the beginning of a new discourse on African American poetry, which, as its openness suggests, will neither prescribe nor imprison current or future voices as they invent a new American poetry. Gregory Pardlo, for example, describes how he is "both thrilled and terrified when the poem begins, seemingly of its own volition, to run afoul of the dogmas of heritage and identity, the narratives I was raised to believe in, because that suggests I am coming close to my truer rhythms and impulses of mind—the argument I am making regarding the person I care to be, my self-creation, a process that implicates my relationship to beauty and to being." Gregory Pardlo brings us back to the recognition that the most recent African American poets as artists do not place at the center of their poetry, for example, traditions associated with race and racial politics, and the heritage and histories of struggle that come with them. These new poets are beneficiaries of poststructuralist thinking which provides them other lenses to view themselves and the world before them. From that looking anew comes a new discourse different from, but still akin to, those of the precursors. If it does anything, the critical thinking and creation that this generation of poets is beginning will in turn serve as an invaluable foundation upon which their heirs may continue to develop a rigorous discourse that America has never before seen.

❧

These are only a few of the representative critical voices of the new poets, the third wave of contemporary African American poets—direct descendants of those courageous black artists who, beginning their writing careers during the late 1970s and early 1980s, dared to walk the way of a world much different from that constructed and proclaimed by the architects of the Black Arts Movement. In other words, the works of these new poets are the direct results of what such poets as Yusef Komunyakaa, Ai, Cyrus Cassells, Rita Dove, Thylias Moss, Toi Derricotte, Harryette Mullen, Nathaniel Mackey— the first wave—dared write, which is whatever they wanted and in whatever forms and styles they desired, as the influence of the Black Arts Movement was first entering its decline.

I

> First fight. Then fiddle....
> —GWENDOLYN BROOKS

At no time in the history of African American poetry has there been such a large number of working literary poets as there suddenly developed shortly after the end of the Civil Rights Movement and the decline of the Black Power Movement. That these two national movements made an indelible impact on generations of black American writers should come as no surprise to the student of African American poetry. Even casual reading of the history of black American literature reveals that major currents in the collective past of African Americans always affected—if not determined—the directions and content of the poetry, fiction, drama, and nonfiction prose that African American writers created before the late 1970s. One would suspect, then, that these twentieth-century movements remained influential even into the twenty-first century, and continue to be two of the major forces that contribute to the developing legions of established and emerging black American poets writing and publishing at the end of 2011.

Like earlier events dedicated to social, economic, and political struggles of African Americans, the Civil Rights Movement and the Black Power Movement had as their common goals "Freedom" and "Liberation." The rise and preeminence of the Civil Rights Movement (from the 1950s through the 1970s), the most successful multiracial social and political struggle in twentieth-century North America, was a response to the Black South's need for the basic human and civil rights that other citizens of the United States took for granted and exercised. Led by Dr. Martin Luther King Jr. and others, the Civil Rights Movement, which formed an alliance with progressive white Americans, was carefully organized and unquestionably triumphant in its challenge to the White South's racist ideologies and practices, especially its state-sanctioned racial segregation, its legal methods that restored and maintained the majority of black people in the region to positions reminiscent of those that they were forced to occupy before the Civil War.

The Black Power Movement (1960s and 1970s) was, on the other hand, a Northern urban phenomenon, a Black Nationalist campaign that responded in part to what its architects argued as the failures and misguided efforts of the Civil Rights Movement. In contrast to the multiracial unity on which the earlier advocates of civil rights insisted for the Black South and the rest of America, the leaders of the Black Power Movement, viewing the political and social circumstances of African Americans nationwide as informed by negative white racial politics, turned black people's attention inward in terms of the individual as a member of a racial group. Advocates of Black Power called for a radical reordering or reconstruction of the individual and of the group in terms of a *Blackness* that ran directly counter to the internalized tenets of *Whiteness*, which black people had inherited from the days of enslavement—and had continued to live by. Advocates of the Black Power Movement asserted that white slave masters (and their descendants in America into the twentieth century) successfully achieved and maintained physical and psychological hegemony over black Americans in order to control, exploit, and dominate black people as a group. This hegemony over black Americans was achieved through assorted nefarious means—political, economic, and social—that determined whether black people lived or died. White people and the public and private institutions over which they declared ownership, directorship, or control instilled in black people a persistent sense of inferiority, self-disrespect, and self-hatred—all of which ran counter to the traditional worldviews and ways of life of their African ancestors. Advocates of Black Power in the United States argued that the liberation of black people, therefore, depended first of all on the reconstruction of their individual and group selves; liberation depended on self- and group-affirmation, a new political consciousness that required a critical understanding of the group's past and a deconstruction of the group's position and circumstances in American society. What would inevitably follow, the advocates of Black Power thought, would be black people's efforts to liberate themselves and reconstruct their lives in terms of *Blackness*, as it was described and prescribed by the architects of the Black Power Movement.

Although their approaches and ideologies were markedly different from each other, the goals of the Black Power Movement and those of the Civil Rights Movement were ultimately the same and yet different: for the advocates of Black Power it was the *liberation* of African Americans by African Americans, while *freedom* for all Americans together was the battle cry of the Civil Rights Movement. With *liberation* and *freedom* as their respective mantras, these two movements were decisive, bold, and influential events that affected almost every facet of North American life, including the history and development of African American cultural productions—for example, poetry (and other forms of creative literature) in the United States.

The demands of both movements ultimately helped to garner for black people access to public resources from which they had never been allowed to benefit. In particular, they now had access to those vital resources that earlier African Americans and their immediate and long-passed ancestors had helped to create but were, by laws in the South and by general social practices in the North, denied use. The fallout from those demands also affected private venues in which the presence of progressive whites dominated or predominated: following the examples that the new laws required of administrators of predominantly "white only" public institutions, progressive white leaders began to "open doors" to African Americans. In fact, private white institutions that used public funds ultimately had to follow the new practices required of their public counterparts or lose their public funding. One of the most important cultural effects of President Lyndon B. Johnson's signing the Civil Rights Act of 1964 is its making available access to educational institutions, especially admission to colleges and universities, where most contemporary African American poets would eventually study creative writing as undergraduate and graduate students. In other words, what those black students as aspiring creative writers and literary critics studied in English departments and creative writing programs made a significant impact on the development and directions of African American literature and literary studies. Black students' access to the education, practices, encouragement, support, and contacts they found in higher education proved invaluable when some of them went on to enroll in MFA writing programs and in challenging writing workshops. The world of craft development was a new landscape to not a small number of African American writers, who, until the 1970s, knew little of it as a pursuit for formal studies and of the advantages it afforded writers. Unfortunately, administrators at historically black colleges and universities (HBCUs), which were always underfunded, have always viewed as unaffordable luxuries courses in creative writing with established writers as permanent faculty. Students attending HBCUs who wanted to study creative writing would seldom, if ever, have the privilege of studying with a widely published writer until they enrolled in a major, predominantly white institution. Since the 1970s, however, creative writing as a course of study continues to make a significant impact on African American poetry.

Another positive dimension was added to American higher education when advocates of the Black Power Movement directed their efforts toward the academy and critiqued its limiting Eurocentricity. In fact, it was the Eurocentric nature of higher education that advocates of the

Black Power Movement were responding to when they demanded that not only should more black students be recruited to study at predominantly white institutions, but that black faculty and black administrators should also be recruited and employed. This demand allowed the black intelligentsia in general and black writers in particular to profit from the educational resources of white institutions, to serve as role models for black students, and to transform certain facets of higher education into the images and visions of African Americans. Black educators who were employed as professors of English and black writers who later became teachers in creative writing programs and workshops were very positive transformative forces in their respective curricula, in their faculty politics, and in the general visions of their departments and programs. It was inevitable that with a great number of African Americans enrolling in predominantly white institutions of higher education, those academic centers would begin to reflect, if not to invest in, some of the interests of the new population that had been banned from the nation's most resourceful sites—institutions, buildings, cultural centers, libraries, etc., which, in one way or another, black people themselves had long helped to plan, construct, develop, and maintain.

Moreover, the Eurocentric nature of higher education was more directly challenged when advocates of the Black Power Movement demanded that black studies courses and programs be instituted as permanent academic components of higher education, thus offering aspiring writers (poets in particular) academic opportunities to discover facets of black culture, history, and literature which they had never before encountered in their academic studies. The infusion of this new knowledge into the education of black and non-black students would eventually affect how they had long been taught to view the history, culture, and literature of the United States. What is more important in this literary context is that black studies offerings began to affect how black students viewed themselves as individuals and how they viewed their communities' historical relations to the United States at large. A casual reading of contemporary African American poetry, placed beside that of their predecessors, readily reveals the new creators' self-concept, as each of them writes self against the backdrop of community, whose history and current circumstances are a persistent, though muted, presence. Hence a new discourse—a discourse constructed from the interior landscape of the poet and the distant and immediate world external to it.

Before the 1970s, when a new group of African American writers began their careers, black American poets faced a major dilemma: to follow, on the one hand, the dictates of their communities, which was to commit their poetry to the defense of their common social and political struggles, to write poetry that directly protested against the instruments of racial domination and exploitation or poetry that effected change in the people and the society in general; or, on the other hand, to listen to the dictates of white publishers, who controlled the publication process, and to white readers, who comprised the majority of people reading poetry in the United States. Over the years the dictates from white communities ranged from demanding that black poets follow the traditions and new writing trends set by white writers—including the stereotypical paradigm invented by the Plantation School of Southern writers who were apologists for slavery—to demanding that black poets follow the modernist modes of T. S. Eliot and Ezra Pound and not use black materials, which whites did not view as containing "universal subjects." Unlike other writing communities in the United States, African American writers—from the eighteenth century onward—suffered burdens imposed on them by two groups of dictators, one black and one white, dictators who imposed burdens no creative writer should ever be asked to assume.

One need not struggle to discern the impact of these two groups' demands on black poets and other writers: it created a divided mind, which proved harmful to African American writers as artists. As I will later attempt to demonstrate, Melvin B. Tolson, like other African American writers, was fully aware of this destructive problem. From the eighteenth century, when Phillis Wheatley published her *Poems on Various Subjects, Religious and Moral* (1774), to the 1970s, when Ai, Toi Derricotte, Marilyn Nelson, Nathaniel Mackey, and Yusef Komunyakaa published, respectively, their early books—*Cruelty* (1973) and *The Killing Floor* (1979); *The Empress of the Death House* (1978); *For the Body* (1978); *Four for Trane* (1978); and *Dedications and Other Darkhorses* (1977) and *Lost in the Bonewheel Factory* (1979)—members of black communities expected African American writers to commit their art to the political and social struggle of African Americans, to use their art, for example, as instruments to help free black people from white oppression; white publishers and white readers, on the other hand, expected African American writers to create texts they desired, an expectation which varied with the times. During the post-Civil War era, white publishers and readers demanded texts from black writers that followed the stereotypes designed by the white architects of the infamous Plantation Tradition, a White South mode of propaganda that attempted to defend its enslavement of black people and to justify its secession from the United States. It is this same demand that imprisoned the genius of Paul Laurence Dunbar. In his poem "The Poet," Dunbar complains about the denigrating plantation instrument, the White South's "literary" invention of so-called "plantation Negro dialect," which white publishers and white readers demanded that black writers also use in their literary creations:

> He sang of love when earth was young,
>   And Love, itself, was in his lays.
>   But, ah, the world, it turned to praise
> A jingle in a broken tongue.

Dunbar's "broken tongue" is "plantation Negro dialect," a malicious white invention that had no true relationship to rural Black South speech or to the collective character of black people. Like the minstrel tradition, of which it was an integral part, "plantation Negro dialect" was a white creation, a political distortion deployed in fiction and poetry to defend the Old South, whose very foundation rested on the enslavement and exploitation of black people. As he wrote his sermon poems in the vernacular manner of the unlettered and uneducated black preacher, James Weldon Johnson, as he tells us in the preface to his *God's Trombones* (1929), realized that "To place in the mouths of the talented old-time Negro preachers a language that is a literary imitation of Mississippi cotton-field dialect is sheer burlesque." As a result, Johnson did not, in *God's Trombones*, use "plantation Negro dialect," which he viewed as

> a quite limited instrument. Indeed, it is an instrument with but two complete stops, pathos and humor. This limitation is not due to any defect of the dialect as dialect, but to the mould of convention in which Negro dialect in the United States has been set, to the fixing effects of its long association with the Negro only as a happy-go-lucky or a forlorn figure.

His judgments on the dialect here and his discussions—in his preface to *The Book of American Negro Poetry* (1922)—of the needs of African American poets at the end of the first three decades of the twentieth century were invaluable advice, which the poets heeded. By the early twentieth century, "the poem in the modern vein" of T. S. Eliot and Ezra Pound became the model whites expected of black poets. These two conflicting demands—to write a literature that defends and uplifts the black race or to write a literature prescribed by those people who have always been perceived as the enemy of black people—created in the black poet a divided self which does not merely inhibit the creative imagination: these demands literally arrested the writing abilities of the poet.

The divided self of the poet as artist is the subject that Melvin Tolson takes up in "Chi," a pivotal poem in *Harlem Gallery* (1965), and it is the very problem that the new poets, who began their literary careers during the 1970s, recognized and rejected; thus they set out as individual poets in their own individual directions. Contrary to what critics have argued from their literal readings of "Chi"—and other poems in *Harlem Gallery*—Tolson uses metaphors, not the facts of the divided self, to describe a problem of black writers, as represented by Hideho Heights, Tolson's Harlem poet who wears a mask which recalls that of Paul Laurence Dunbar's poet:

> He didn't know
> I knew
> about the split identity
> of the People's Poet—
> the bifacial nature of his poetry:
> the racial ballad in the public domain
> and the private poem in the modern vein.

Rather than having the right to assume the role of the poet as the artist with the freedom to create whatever he or she desires—the African American poet—Tolson further demonstrates in "Chi," was forced to walk the line between two worlds:

> Poor Boy Blue,
> the Great White World
> and the Black Bourgeoisie
> have shoved the Negro artist into
> the white and not-white dichotomy,
> the Afroamerican dilemma in the Arts—
> the dialectic of
> to be or not be
> a Negro.

Because they know who they are as Americans and because each of them elected his/her individual path as artist (as informed by the past and by the general principles of the art of poetry), contemporary African American poets, unlike Tolson's generation and earlier, have the privilege of avoiding the problems of their predecessors. Ironically, the struggles of their immediate predecessors as civil rights workers and as black nationalists indirectly catapulted contemporary poets to this major moment in African American literary history: black writers, using resources that other American writers also rely on, are free to create as they wish. With that permission has come an extraordinary development in African American poetry, one that is the beginning of something profoundly new and positive for American poetry in general. Anachronistically speaking, it is as if the African American literary past, from the late eighteenth century up to the last quarter of the twentieth century, were scripted to the fourth sonnet in the cycle "The Children of the Poor" (1949) by Gwendolyn Brooks:

> First fight. Then fiddle. Ply the slipping string
> With feathery sorcery; muzzle the note
> With hurting love; the music that they wrote
> Bewitch, bewilder. Qualify to sing
> Threadwise. Devise no salt, no hempen thing
> For the dear instrument to bear. Devote
> The bow to silks and honey. Be remote
> A while from malice and from murdering.
> But first to arms, to armor. Carry hate
> In front of you and harmony behind.
> Win war. Rise bloody, maybe not too late
> For having first to civilize a space
> Wherein to play your violin with grace.

After the incalculable sacrifices, the long struggles, and the sociopolitical challenges of their ancestors as artists and advocates of freedom and respect for all under the Declaration of Independence, the U.S. Constitution, and post-mid-nineteenth-century progressive laws, contemporary African American poets have declared a space, however incomplete, to create as they please. Instead of engaging their poems as instruments in the sociopolitical struggles of African Americans, contemporary black American poets are now writing self against the backdrop of community.

II

> ... to play your violin with grace
> —GWENDOLYN BROOKS

The poets who dominated the African American literary scene during the 1960s and the 1970s are those who subscribed to and wrote poems that reflected the dicta of the Black Aesthetic, which was derived, in part, from the ideology of the Black Arts Movement, the cultural wing of the Black Power Movement. But the poets of the next generations, who have ascended great heights on the North American literary scene, are not direct aesthetic and ideational descendants of the poets of the Black Arts Movement; they are more akin to Robert Hayden and the poets contemporary to the Movement who wrote outside the Black Aesthetic—e.g., Lucille Clifton, Clarence Major, Jay Wright, Ed Roberson, Michael Harper, and Audre Lorde. In fact, the work of major post–Black Aesthetic poets does not bear any of the traces of the poetry whose authors devoted their art to the social and political ideology of the Black Arts Movement, which was committed to the Black Power concept.

These younger new poets, who began publishing during the late 1970s, did not decide to protest against the work of the dominant group of their immediate ancestors, for they generally respected and admired the positive social and political influence of their predecessors. However, as artists coming in the aftermath of the Black Arts Movement, this younger generation of poets had aesthetic and ideational interests of their own that did not include the prescriptive agenda of the Black Aesthetic. Unlike the African American writers who preceded them, this younger generation of writers had the privilege of deciding to write poetry that reflected their individual lives, their own families, and the communities they know. As a result of the progressive achievements of both the Black Power Movement and the Civil Rights Movement, these new writers are the first African Americans to be free of outside political and social dicta from blacks and whites commanding them on what and how to write. They are the first generation of black writers who, en masse and by example, asserted the right to commit themselves to their art, rather than commit their art to Black America's political, social, and economic struggles. Continuing the struggle for freedom that began with enslavement and culminated in the Civil Rights Act of 1964 and in Black Power liberation efforts of the 1960s and 1970s, the legions of ancestors of this new generation of poets of the late 1970s—and after—have extended to contemporary African American artists permission to create as they think appropriate.

Without negative public words for the advocates of the Black Aesthetic, the new poets of the late 1970s and beyond, relishing and using with care the literary freedom they inherited, decided from the very first to write poetry that reflects their lives and the world as they, individuals, wish to represent them. As post–Black Aesthetic poets, they do not allow themselves to be bound by social and political preachments that would limit them as artists. And yet, as they write themselves, they write their communities, entities with particularized and collective histories that frame their lives as individuals and as members of a group, with interests that are aesthetic as well as social, economic, and political. These new poets know that their freedom to write as they wish is a hard-won privilege, the result of ancestral struggle and sacrifice and death. With this knowledge always before them, each of these contemporary black poets, relishing the play and work mated with writing, are ever mindful of the grave responsibilities that come with the writing of self and community. Perhaps it is these ancestral responsibilities that drive their acts of composition—ultimately, their angles of ascent.

In their insistence on writing for all readers of English language; in their use of a variety of human experiences, past or present, including intimate facets of their own lives and of figures they invent or discover in casual reading or organized research; in their freedom to read texts of and beyond North American literatures and cultures and use from that reading whatever their need or desire; in their right to experiment with any literary or other cultural form that a poem demands, these three successive groups of contemporary poets—three waves of them, in fact—recall the examples of such earlier poets as Clarence Major, Alice Walker, Ed Roberson, Audre Lorde, and Gerald Barrax. That is, the poets, who began their writing careers during the 1970s and early 1980s and after, write poems that are more akin to Lucille Clifton's *Good Times* (1969), Michael Harper's *Dear John, Dear Coltrane* (1970), and Al Young's *The Song Turning Back into Itself* (1971) than, for example, to Amiri Baraka's *A Poem for Black Hearts* (1967), Nikki Giovanni's *Black Feeling, Black Talk* (1968), Don L. Lee's *Don't Cry, Scream* (1969), or Sonia Sanchez's *Homecoming* (1969). In other words, Ai's *Cruelty* (1973) and *The Killing Floor* (1979), Yusef Komunyakaa's *Dedications and Other Darkhorses* (1977) and *Lost in the Bonewheel Factory* (1979), Marilyn Nelson's *For the Body* (1978), Nathaniel Mackey's *Four for Trane* (1978) and *Septet for the End of Time* (1983), and

Toi Derricotte's *The Empress of the Death House* (1978) and *Natural Birth* (1983)—as debut volumes of post–Black Aesthetic poets clearly signaled that the black poetry to come would be very different from that prescribed by advocates of the Black Arts Movement.

Perhaps what marks these new poets as different from most of their black predecessors—but similar to Robert Hayden, Michael Harper, and Lucille Clifton, for example—is that they do not write about being black per se; their *Blackness* is not the theme of their poems, but instead it informs them. Contemporary African American poets use what they know, imagine, or experience to raise questions that plague all humanity—and who they are frames what they write. Some of them seldom, if ever, use facets from what some readers might be inclined to call "black life in America," as in the example of Ai, who once confessed that she writes "about scoundrels; my specialty is generally scoundrels." Marilyn Nelson does not elect to wrap her Blackness around the mother figure speaking in "Mama's Promise." The poem neither demands nor requires it, but it does require that Nelson keep our focus on an inevitable reality no mother can protect her child from: that birth is ultimately death.

> It's not so simple to give a child birth;
> you also have to give it death,
> the jealous fairy's christening gift.

In "The Minks," Toi Derricotte speaks of the violence that is the deprivation of the living being—human, animal, or animate thing—of its "natural" or "normal" existence by imprisoning it or placing it in captivity. Reading "The Minks," sensitive, close readers with ranging and discerning intellects and associating imaginations can hardly escape being reminded of the Middle Passage, the African Diaspora (particularly enslavement and Jim Crow), the North American Reservation (including the Trail of Tears and the European settlers' agenda of genocide), and the American prison complex. Toi Derricotte does not need to mention black Americans or Native Americans and the forms of captivity that have, over the centuries, arrested their development for the benefits of North American oppressors; she does not write a poem about being black in America. But as Derricotte writes about human cruelty and vanity, she writes against the backdrop of her community's history—in this case, against the particularities of one family's life. In other words, the new black poets, post–Black Aesthetic poets, write of self, not of "what it means to be black in America." The issue of "the Afroamerican dilemma in the Arts" that Melvin Tolson raises in *Harlem Gallery* is now a problem of the past. African American poets know who they are, and they affirm the vast and complex African American past and its variegations which they often use in their poems.

The new or contemporary poets have, in fact, set new directions for African American poetry, as Rita Dove also did in her debut volume, *The Yellow House on the Corner* (1980), which includes the allegorical "Upon Meeting Don L. Lee, in a Dream." In that poem, Rita Dove—unlike other artists who elect to debunk traditions, schools, or movements created immediately before them—neither assaults nor dismisses Lee (Haki Madhubuti) or the Black Arts Movement. In one of her *Callaloo* (Summer 2008) interviews, Dove "acknowledges the pivotal importance of the Black Arts Movement"; she, like many other contemporary African American poets, knows that the Movement "was an ingredient in the crucible in which I had been formed." Therefore, she "never meant for that poem ["Upon Meeting . . ."] to be interpreted as an angry retort or rejection." In the same *Callaloo* interview, Dove continues:

> It's [the poem is] an allegorical rendering of what happens when two artistic generations collide. It's not meant to be patronizing, and though the arrogance of youth may color some of the interactions in the allegory, I'm simply declaring that I found a different path, one determined by my very own aesthetic sensibilities.

The poem also meant that "now it was time," Dove asserts, "for me to move in my own direction." She is not the only African American poet who moved in her/his own direction. All of them, in fact, did just that: they, as creators, moved in their own directions, and they are still doing so.

Like Rita Dove and other post–Black Aesthetic poets, Yusef Komunyakaa also moved in his own direction; his poetry is neither an extension nor an affirmation of the poetry of the Black Arts Movement. In an unpublished statement about the meaning of the Black Arts Movement to him as an artist, he writes: "For me, the Black Arts Movement was very important, because it was a psychological foundation and sounding board in which to depart from." But he goes on to tell us that

> Growing up in the South, having closely observed what hatred does to the human spirit, how it corrupts and diminishes, through a gut-level logic I unconsciously disavowed any direct association with the Black Arts Movement. As a graduate student at Colorado

State in the mid-1970s, I said to Gwendolyn Brooks, "Ms. Brooks, what is art?" She didn't miss a beat when she said, "Well, art is that which endures." That night, in the midst of silence and loneliness, I thought about how members of the Black Arts Movement had badgered Robert Hayden and Gwendolyn Brooks at Fisk University in 1966. Since that moment of infamous shortsightedness, some of us who followed the visionary Robert Hayden dared to call and respond to a world of extended possibilities which also resides in the poetry of early Amiri Baraka and Bob Kaufman. We knew the pitfalls of tribal warfare existentially; we were ready to embrace certain commonsense aspects of modernism that allowed at least an illusion of psychological liberation. In many ways, the Civil Rights Movement had intellectually prepared us for this necessary juncture in African American creativity. For the first time, some of us believed we could do anything if a system of aesthetics were at the center of our vision; I think Hayden had conveyed this principle to us through his work and life. An internal dialogue is possible through metaphorical inquiry that is highly political and enduring, an inquiry that continuously reinvents itself. We wanted a poetry that would speak to and for the whole person.

Komunyakaa's final sentence—as politely as it is rendered—is obviously a critique of the Black Aesthetic and the poetry derived from it. Ultimately, it was "an aesthetic" that—by prescribing for poets what they were to write, how they were to write it, and to and for whom they were to write—policed artists. "We wanted a poetry that would speak to and for the whole person," writes Komunyakaa, not a poetry that was an answer to someone else's restrictive or narrow social and political requirements. Komunyakaa, like the majority of the black literary poets of his generation, "dared to call and respond to a world of extended possibilities," the examples of which he found in the poetry of Bob Kaufman, the early LeRoi Jones (Amiri Baraka), and, especially, in the vision of Robert Hayden. The example of Robert Hayden reflected the poet's assertion of his own freedom to write poems that addressed the world at large on issues he himself thought significant to explore in poetry, and for his doing so, Hayden was severely assaulted at the First Black Writers' Conference at Fisk University in Nashville, Tennessee, in April 1966, a well-known narrative that needs no rehearsal here.

The meaning of the Black Arts Movement to Rita Dove is not unlike that of Yusef Komunyakaa's—that is, they, like many other poets of their generation, wanted to write poems that reflected their individual selves: Komunyakaa, the Southerner who had witnessed close-up the important work of the Civil Rights Movement in his native Bogalousa and elsewhere in Louisiana; and Dove, the Northerner in Akron, Ohio. As Dove says in her *Callaloo* (Summer 2008) interview, she realized too that to write poetry that truly reflected herself and thus her background, she could not follow the example of the poets of the Black Arts Movement:

> . . . as I wrote more and more . . . I realized that the blighted urban world inhabited by the poems of the Black Arts Movement was not mine. I had grown up in Ohio—and though my parents started out together as lower-middle class, for most of my childhood and adolescence I enjoyed the gamut of middle class experience, in a comfy house with picket fences and rose bushes on a tree-lined street in West Akron, miles from the stench of the rubber factories on the working-class east side where my father had been raised. I was a Girl Scout and a member of the National Honor Society; my high school was 40% black, without major racial tensions (even now, our class reunions are multi-culti love fests!).
>
> As an artist, then, I had a choice: to reject my world and appropriate a different one simply by writing as others expected of me, or to be true to myself. Certainly, timing played a crucial role in my artistic development, because by the time I started to write seriously, when I was eighteen or nineteen years old, the Black Arts Movement had gained momentum; notice had been taken. The time was ripe; all one had to do was walk up to the door they had been battering at and squeeze through the breech. So I don't consider myself particularly brave or defiant: I was simply there at the right moment. The predominant powers had become less dismissive of African Americans, and the wider world was ready for nuance. I could develop artistically without undue outside pressure; and even though I'd get the occasional slap of the wrist because my poetry was, for some people, "not black enough"—hell, I've never understood what that means!—I didn't have to fit into The Program. The Program had run its course and, after some political victories that served the purpose, stumbled into dead ends, artistically speaking.

Like Komunyakaa's statement about the Black Arts Movement, the central position in Rita Dove's assertions about the Movement is a concern that runs counter to the interest of the Black Aesthetic: that the individual poet has the right as well as the need to write first out of the self. To do so, of course, does not mean that one forgets one's community or the history of one's group; rather the main of contemporary African American poets write self against the background of community and its history. The youthful self shaped by Dove's West Akron, Ohio, world, along with the myriad national and international experiences she would later acquire; the Southern world that shaped Komunyakaa, along with such horrific experiences as the Vietnam War, are part of what he calls the "whole person" and what Dove wanted to do: "to be true to myself." Neither of these two poets nor the contemporaries of their generation would agree with Ron Karenga's Black Aesthetic contention in "Black Cultural Nationalism" that "all [Black] art must reflect and support the Black Revolution, and any art that does not discuss and contribute to the revolution is invalid. . . ." The poems that Komunyakaa and Dove produced at the beginning of their respective writing careers and have since continued to create do not follow Ron Karenga's Black Arts Movement dicta; Komunyakaa and Dove, like their contemporaries and the waves of poets who have followed them, speak to humanity at large about thinking, remembering, and living in modern and postmodern societies.

To focus on the examples of Rita Dove and Yusef Komunyakaa as signals marking new directions in African American poetry during the late twentieth century is not to ignore the extraordinary work of their contemporaries: for example, Ai, whose refinement and extension of the dramatic monologue as a form that examines moments in the lives of myriad figures, high and low, the Western world over; Nathaniel Mackey, whose epic lyricism, woven of complex cosmologies and music, takes us to places "where there / was wasn't music but music was / there"; Thylias Moss, whose experimentations with language and mixed media take us beyond our own imagination; Melvin Dixon, whose representation and demythification of travel and gay male living remain a model in the literature; Brenda Marie Osbey, whose lyrical narratives of haunting women take us through a magical geography of the imagination and place; Toi Derricotte, whose treatment of the intimacies of childbirth might be the first African American book of poems focusing on the subject; Harryette Mullen, whose experimentations with language and music extends the reaches of language poetry; and C. S. Giscombe, whose poetry of geography and maps is a quest for place, which, ultimately, is identity. The aesthetic and ideational achievements of the contemporaries of the first wave of contemporary African American poets, for example, are not only extraordinary; they are also vital and exponential contributions to the growth and development of contemporary African American poetry. The focus on Rita Dove and Yusef Komunyakaa here is, however, natural, for they became the visible national figures associated with the new directions of African American poetry; and in the eyes of critical readers, some of their early collections have become watersheds for contemporary American poetry.

Rita Dove and Yusef Komunyakaa, in fact, were always quite visible in the eyes of the two new waves of poets that follow them, younger poets who early on found the two older poets and their contemporaries—like much older poets such as Robert Hayden, Audre Lorde, Lucille Clifton, and Michael Harper—to be accessible models they could learn from. After all, the fairly large productions of Rita Dove and Yusef Komunyakaa are not without variety in form, style, and subjects. Although their contemporaries continue to make invaluable contributions to the development of poetry, it is Rita Dove and Yusef Komunyakaa who, by example, lead the charge for changes in the directions of poetry writing in African American literary communities. What we have, as a result, are two engaging and evolving waves of younger poets who are extending what the older generation of post–Black Aesthetic poets, the first wave, set in motion.

With the aesthetic achievements of their immediate predecessors whose indelible imprints on American poetry are not unseen, and with various literary and educational opportunities and publishing outlets now available here in the United States, the two waves of younger poets continue to demonstrate what is possible for African American artists. They continue meticulously to build on what they find in the poets of the first wave, as well as in the work of the predecessors of that wave.

EPILOGUE

Without the fetters of narrow political and social demands that have nothing to do with the production of artistic texts, black American poets, since the Civil Rights Movement and the Black Power Movement, have created an extraordinary number of aesthetically deft poems that both challenge the concept of "the American poem" and extend the dimensions of American poetry. Such is not, however, the only distinguishing feature of contempo-

rary African American poetry. Following the examples of predecessors like Robert Hayden, Melvin Tolson, Audre Lorde, Lucille Clifton, Clarence Major, and Michael Harper, these new poets learned early that to read the United States—its literature, its history, and its other cultural productions—is not enough. To be an artist during these times one also needs, they learned, to extend one's reading practices to include the myriad cultural productions of other worlds beyond one's own. And by doing so, Nathaniel Mackey, Harryette Mullen, Thylias Moss, for example, have helped to transform African American poetry into a cosmopolitan affair.

❧

In a Callaloo *(Spring 1995) interview with Christopher Funkhouser, Nathaniel Mackey alludes to his reading practices, which entail a full range of American poetry and music, especially jazz, and also international writers:*

> A couple of Caribbean writers have been very important to me, Wilson Harris and Edward Kamau Brathwaite. Other Caribbean writers as well, like Aimé Césaire, and other writers, a range of writers. If I start naming them I'll name all day. There was a period when, for example, the new novelists of France, Alain Robbe-Grillet, Nathalie Sarraute, and others—I read their work quite attentively. I was a big fan of a Polish writer named Witold Gombrowicz. I remember reading and re-reading his novels. You know how it is: you read and you read and you read and some stuff you re-read.

The ranging internationalism of contemporary African American poets' reading practices further reveals itself not only in the various subjects the poets have elected to tackle but also in the architectonics of the poetry. A student of literature immediately discerns how Rita Dove's virtuosity with a variety of literary forms is part of the achievement of Sonata Mulattica *and how Yusef Komunyakaa's wide reading habits led him to experiment with the dramatic verse play,* Gilgamesh, *as an interpretation of the* Epic of Gilgamesh. *Ai's claim on the dramatic monologue has, of course, transformed the genre into an American speech act, an experimentation on which the literary achievement of Ai as artist partly rests. One wonders just how much reading informs Thylias Moss's* Limited Fork Theory. *The ranging reading practices of contemporary black American poets have, without a doubt, afforded them a variegated landscape on which to produce poetry. Yet they are mindful of African American literary traditions and are informed by various concerns for and myriad questions about modern and postmodern humanity.*

☙

Like her contemporaries, Harryette Mullen is judicious in her observation that too many critics have limited African American poetry by two bound- aries: music and oral culture. While we all can agree that black music and black speech acts have been—and continue to be—significant to the work of some black American poets, contemporary African American poetry is not defined by music and speech. In a Callaloo *(Summer 1996) interview, Harryette Mullen, who is interested in black speech acts, cogently states that*

One of the texts that has been inspiring to me is the work of Mel- vin Tolson, *Harlem Gallery*. Tolson is seen as a belated and deriva- tive modernist by some people, because he comes after Pound and Eliot and so forth, and he seemed to be responding to them and wanting to make his work reflect what they were doing in poetry. He saw possibilities that he hadn't thought about before, so he went about very systematically changing how he wrote and making it allusive and very complex. And one of the results is that Tolson's work is not being taught or read very much. So one of the questions or problems for me is the kind of aesthetic turf that exists for black writers, and how black writers who do not fit into the notion of what black turf is can sometimes be overlooked or forgotten or go unread, because people require interpretive strate- gies related to their notion of the black canon, or what it means to be outside of the black canon. There are certain examples, like Bob Kaufman, Melvin Tolson, or LeRoi Jones (before he became Baraka) or Stephen Jonas. Robert Hayden, even. Robert Hayden usually does get included in anthologies, but people sometimes talk about Robert Hayden as being in some sense on the edge of a black tradition, because the black tradition is being constructed as based in orality, and as concerned with a Black subjectivity in language that is speech-like.

In the same Callaloo *interview, Harryette Mullen, explaining why the allu- sive method is important to her poetry, also comments on her experiments with language—experiments that extend the dimensions of African Ameri- can poetry:*

It's important to me because I wanted the poem to be interesting and complex, as I think experience is, language is; language has that capacity. I was interested in concentrating, distilling, and condensing aspects of orality and literacy.... I am more interested in a transformation of the oral into something that draws together different allusive possibilities in one utterance, which is something that writing can do better than speech. I'm interested in taking a speech-based tradition and transforming it through the techniques that are available to me in writing.

She goes on to tell us her ambitions for her writing:

I want to push my work, and those are ways that I have found to push it beyond transcription, beyond the mimetic reproduction of speech or the oral tradition. I'm trying to transform the materials of orality into text and into a very dense and complexly allusive writing practice. You can also heighten paradox and contradiction when you compress together things that come from very different registers or different lexicons; they jostle each other so there's more tension. Yet there's more elasticity in the utterance.

Harryette Mullen's interest in "allusive writing practices" and experiments with language recall the work of Thomas Sayers Ellis, Dawn Lundy Martin, and other younger poets, who obviously know Mullen's work and benefit from it. In other words, the aesthetic positions of the poets of the first wave do indeed inform the poetry and poetics of those of the two waves that follow them. Post-Black Arts Movement poets are in conversation with each other and with the work of their predecessors, past and present, but—and this I underscore—contemporary African American poets do not confine their reading and writing practices to the literature, culture, and history of the United States of America. As a result of their ranging imaginary, the landscape from which they think and create is global.

❧

Like their predecessors who came immediately after the Black Arts Movement and who rejected its confining concept of the Black Aesthetic, the next two waves of contemporary African American poets, while recognizing the achievements of all of their ancestors, early and recent, write toward future memory and create a poetry that further extends the reaches of African American poetry in forms and ideas.

At this point, some readers might be inclined to ask this question: What distinguishes these younger poets from their predecessors? For one thing, while these two younger waves of poets do have distinguishing features, they also, as I have before stated, extend and synthesize the voices of their predecessors. Some of the new poems of Tracy K. Smith, for example, recall the mystical, prophetic, seer-like voices one hears in the poetry of Jay Wright and Nathaniel Mackey. The concept of the poem as a lyric space with linguistic precision and carefully crafted imagery is what Natasha Trethewey, no doubt, learned from reading Rita Dove, but Trethewey's impulse to look to the past and inscribe some of its erased, forgotten, ignored, and/or distorted moments and figures echoes the projects of Brenda Marie Osbey and fiction writer Ernest J. Gaines, who, looking at life in the South, ask questions about the human will toward dignity and grace. Like that of other poets, Trethewey's own imaginary is the source of her poetic work, but it is also dependent on her uses of libraries and other archives. That is, many of her poems are willed acts of restoration. Then there is another kind of poetry that Fred Moten and Thomas Sayers Ellis write. In fact, the poetry of Fred Moten, which he describes as a mode of inquiry, appears in many ways to be something all its own, yet one immediately detects how much his poetry, like some of that of Honorée Jeffers and Tyhemba Jess, is shaped by black American music traditions, whose uses long ago began a tradition in African American poetry and other literary forms. In this, Fred Moten and Thomas Sayers Ellis are similar: their poetry depends in part on sound, especially talk and the linguistic play in talk, but also on music as structured and stylized sounds. Every "sound," says Moten in one of his poems, "is a small action and broke world." But Moten's poetry is also informed by critical theory's impulse to deconstruct the moment and critique its uses. Ellis likewise experiments with sound; sound, in fact, determines the shape and form of his poems, some of which may be read as performances, dependent, in part, on the human voice and certain forms of popular culture. Ellis also experiments with language as sound and script by deliberately destabilizing the poem as a fixed artifact. That is, all inheritance and extension and refinement. But where lies the difference?

The poetry of Carl Phillips is an exemplum of difference in African American poetry. Unlike other African American poets, Carl Phillips probes subjects

seldom addressed in African American literature. Of course, a few other black poets—Melvin Dixon, Audre Lorde, and Reginald Shepherd, for example—have explored issues of sexuality in their poetry. Carl Phillips, however, takes the subject another step: to write about sex or sexuality, he says, is to investigate morality. No other black gay poet has used sex or the body with the originality and newness that one finds in Carl Phillips's poetry, where an unfamiliar syntax disrupts readers' familiar way of reading the world by disorienting them. His is, more importantly, a syntax that at once becomes a way for language to enact his subject. And his subject is the conflict between animal instinct and what we are told is moral, but what we are told is moral is not fixed. In fact, in the world of Carl Phillips's poetry nothing is fixed. He wants his readers to know that his poems "live in a realm of flexible morality." "From the very beginning," he tells us in his poetics, "I've been most concerned in my poems with the tension between how we conduct our bodies and how society says we should conduct our bodies, and more generally with the tension between a chosen and an implied notion of morality. Who is to say what is normal, what is acceptable?" Perhaps what makes the poets of the last two waves different from those of the first wave is that they, like Carl Phillips, dare ask questions in their poems that their predecessors would/do not. The collective public and private visions of the younger poets challenge the old verities and render them uncertainties. After all, this wave of poets is creating in the wake of the ascendancy of critical theory and its effects on all of our lives. And these poets have learned—and they "teach" their readers— to take nothing for granted.

❧

These younger poets also have the advantage of learning from the Black Arts Movement and from the efforts, direct and indirect, that their predecessors have made for and against it. These poets also have the advantage of learning from the whole range of twentieth-century African American poets—Melvin Tolson, Robert Hayden, Gwendolyn Brooks—and from the distinguished poets who followed immediately after the Black Arts Movement. In other words, these younger poets are fully aware that they are heirs of a rich literary tradition, but they are also aware that they are free to study and learn from other U.S. American literary traditions and from other poets of the world. Then, too, as their work demonstrates, the contemporary poets selected here continue to exercise freely their rights, and are beginning to build a tradition as hybrid as that which the jazz masters created, one which disregards geography, race, culture, class, and those other boundaries which do violence to human beings in the West. And, like John Coltrane, Thelonious Monk, Charlie Parker, Duke Ellington, Mary Lou Williams, and many other jazz musicians, these poets are prepared to use whatever they find and deem appropriate to create poems. Their respect for and use of difference, and their responsible exercise of literary freedom—perhaps this is what makes them American, in fact more American, as poets, than those who have traditionally monopolized the term, wrapped themselves in it, stamped it on their foreheads, and sought to dominate the poetic space that belongs to all of us.

—Charles Henry Rowell

PART 1

Precursors

MODERNISTS, 1940s TO 1960s

Gwendolyn Brooks

(1917–2000)

N<small>O, I HAVE NOT</small> abandoned beauty, or lyricism, and I certainly don't consider myself a polemical poet. I'm just a black poet, and I write about what I see, what interests me, and I'm seeing new things. Many things that I'm seeing now I was absolutely blind to before, but I don't sit down at the table and say, "Lyricism is out." No, I just continue to write about what confronts me.... I get an idea or an impression or I become very excited about something and I can hardly wait till the time comes when I can get to the paper. In the meantime I take notes, little bits of the idea I put down on paper, and when I'm ready to write I write as urgently and directly as I possibly can. And I don't go back to mythology or my little textbooks. I know about the textbooks, but I'm not concerned with them during the act of poetry-writing.

The Sundays of Satin-Legs Smith

Inamoratas, with an approbation,
Bestowed his title. Blessed his inclination.

He wakes, unwinds, elaborately : a cat
Tawny, reluctant, royal. He is fat
And fine this morning. Definite. Reimbursed.

He waits a moment, he designs his reign,
That no performance may be plain or vain.
Then rises in a clear delirium.

He sheds, with his pajamas, shabby days.
And his desertedness, his intricate fear, the
Postponed resentments and the prim precautions.

Now, at his bath, would you deny him lavender
Or take away the power of his pine?
What smelly substitute, heady as wine,
Would you provide? life must be aromatic.
There must be scent, somehow there must be some.
Would you have flowers in his life? suggest
Asters? a Really Good geranium?
A white carnation? would you prescribe a Show
With the cold lilies, formal chrysanthemum
Magnificence, poinsettias, and emphatic
Red of prize roses? might his happiest
Alternative (you muse) be, after all,
A bit of gentle garden in the best
Of taste and straight tradition? Maybe so.
But you forget, or did you ever know,
His heritage of cabbage and pigtails,
Old intimacy with alleys, garbage pails,
Down in the deep (but always beautiful) South
Where roses blush their blithest (it is said)
And sweet magnolias put Chanel to shame.

No! He has not a flower to his name.
Except a feather one, for his lapel.
Apart from that, if he should think of flowers
It is in terms of dandelions or death.
Ah, there is little hope. You might as well—
Unless you care to set the world a-boil
And do a lot of equalizing things,
Remove a little ermine, say, from kings,
Shake hands with paupers and appoint them men,
For instance—certainly you might as well
Leave him his lotion, lavender and oil.

Let us proceed. Let us inspect, together
With his meticulous and serious love,
The innards of this closet. Which is a vault
Whose glory is not diamonds, not pearls,
Not silver plate with just enough dull shine.
But wonder-suits in yellow and in wine,
Sarcastic green and zebra-striped cobalt.
With shoulder padding that is wide
And cocky and determined as his pride;
Ballooning pants that taper off to ends
Scheduled to choke precisely.
                              Here are hats
Like bright umbrellas; and hysterical ties
Like narrow banners for some gathering war.

People are so in need, in need of help.
People want so much that they do not know.

Below the tinkling trade of little coins
The gold impulse not possible to show
Or spend. Promise piled over and betrayed.

These kneaded limbs receive the kiss of silk.
Then they receive the brave and beautiful
Embrace of some of that equivocal wool.
He looks into his mirror, loves himself—
The neat curve here; the angularity
That is appropriate at just its place;
The technique of a variegated grace.

Here is all his sculpture and his art
And all his architectural design.
Perhaps you would prefer to this a fine
Value of marble, complicated stone.
Would have him think with horror of baroque,
Rococo. You forget and you forget.

He dances down the hotel steps that keep
Remnants of last night's high life and distress.
As spat-out purchased kisses and spilled beer.

He swallows sunshine with a secret yelp.
Passes to coffee and a roll or two.
Has breakfasted.
       Out. Sounds about him smear,
Become a unit. He hears and does not hear
The alarm clock meddling in somebody's sleep;
Children's governed Sunday happiness;
The dry tone of a plane; a woman's oath;
Consumption's spiritless expectoration;
An indignant robin's resolute donation
Pinching a track through apathy and din;
Restaurant vendors weeping; and the L
That comes on like a slightly horrible thought.

Pictures, too, as usual, are blurred.
He sees and does not see the broken windows
Hiding their shame with newsprint; little girl
With ribbons decking wornness, little boy
Wearing the trousers with the decentest patch,
To honor Sunday; women on their way
From "service," temperate holiness arranged
Ably on asking faces; men estranged
From music and from wonder and from joy
But far familiar with the guiding awe
Of foodlessness.
    He loiters.
        Restaurant vendors
Weep, or out of them rolls a restless glee.
The Lonesome Blues, the Long-lost Blues, I Want A
Big Fat Mama. Down these sore avenues
Comes no Saint-Saëns, no piquant elusive Grieg,
And not Tschaikovsky's wayward eloquence
And not the shapely tender drift of Brahms.
But could he love them? Since a man must bring
To music what his mother spanked him for
When he was two: bits of forgotten hate,
Devotion: whether or not his mattress hurts:
The little dream his father humored: the thing
His sister did for money: what he ate

For breakfast—and for dinner twenty years
Ago last autumn: all his skipped desserts.

The pasts of his ancestors lean against
Him. Crowd him. Fog out his identity.
Hundreds of hungers mingle with his own,
Hundreds of voices advise so dexterously
He quite considers his reactions his,
Judges he walks most powerfully alone,
That everything is—simply what it is.

But movie-time approaches, time to boo
The hero's kiss, and boo the heroine
Whose ivory and yellow it is sin
For his eye to eat of. The Mickey Mouse,
However, is for everyone in the house.

Squires his lady to dinner at Joe's Eats.
His lady alters as to leg and eye,
Thickness and height, such minor points as these,
From Sunday to Sunday. But no matter what
Her name or body positively she's
In Queen Lace stockings with ambitious heels
That strain to kiss the calves, and vivid shoes
Frontless and backless, Chinese fingernails,
Earrings, three layers of lipstick, intense hat
Dripping with the most voluble of veils.
Her affable extremes are like sweet bombs
About him, whom no middle grace or good
Could gratify. He had no education
In quiet arts of compromise. He would
Not understand your counsels on control, nor
Thank you for your late trouble.
                              At Joe's Eats
You get your fish or chicken on meat platters.
With coleslaw, macaroni, candied sweets,
Coffee and apple pie. You go out full.
(The end is—isn't it?—all that really matters.)

And even and intrepid come
The tender boots of night to home.

Her body is like new brown bread
Under the Woolworth mignonette.
Her body is a honey bowl
Whose waiting honey is deep and hot.
Her body is like summer earth,
Receptive, soft, and absolute . . .

Riot

A riot is the language of the unheard
—MARTIN LUTHER KING

John Cabot, out of Wilma, once a Wycliffe,
all whitebluerose below his golden hair,
wrapped richly in right linen and right wool,
almost forgot his Jaguar and Lake Bluff;
almost forgot Grandtully (which is The
Best Thing That Ever Happened To Scotch); almost
forgot the sculpture at the Richard Gray
and Distelheim; the kidney pie at Maxim's,
the *Grenadine de Boeuf* at Maison Henri.

Because the Negroes were coming down the street.

Because the Poor were sweaty and unpretty
(not like Two Dainty Negroes in Winnetka)
and they were coming toward him in rough ranks.
In seas. In windsweep. They were black and loud.
And not detainable. And not discreet.

Gross. Gross. *"Que tu es grossier!"* John Cabot
itched instantly beneath the nourished white
that told his story of glory to the World.
"Don't let It touch me! the blackness! Lord!" he whispered
to any handy angel in the sky.
But, in a thrilling announcement, on It drove
and breathed on him: and touched him. In that breath
the fume of pig foot, chitterling and cheap chili,
malign, mocked John. And, in terrific touch, old
averted doubt jerked forward decently,
cried, "Cabot! John! You are a desperate man,
and the desperate die expensively today."

John Cabot went down in the smoke and fire
and broken glass and blood, and he cried "Lord!
Forgive these nigguhs that know not what they do."

Boy Breaking Glass

*To Mark Crawford
from whom the commission*

Whose broken window is a cry of art
(success, that winks aware
as elegance, as a treasonable faith)
is raw: is sonic: is old-eyed première.
Our beautiful flaw and terrible ornament.
Our barbarous and metal little man.

"I shall create! If not a note, a hole.
If not an overture, a desecration."

Full of pepper and light
and Salt and night and cargoes.

"Don't go down the plank
if you see there's no extension.
Each to his grief, each to
his loneliness and fidgety revenge.
Nobody knew where I was and now I am no longer there."

The only sanity is a cup of tea.
The music is in minors.

Each one other
is having different weather.

"It was you, it was you who threw away my name!
And this is everything I have for me."

Who has not Congress, lobster, love, luau,
the Regency Room, the Statue of Liberty,
runs. A sloppy amalgamation.
A mistake.
A cliff.
A hymn, a snare, and an exceeding sun.

Robert Hayden

(1913–1980)

Every poem i write is for me, in Whitman's phrase, a "language experiment" and a process of discovery. I value form and rhythm as having an organic relationship to the theme of a poem. I am as much concerned with the sounds and textures of words as I am with their meanings. I write slowly and painstakingly; often work on a poem several years, revising even after publication. Irony together with symbolism modified by realism are, I suppose, characteristic features of my poetry.

For a Young Artist

Sprawled in the pigsty,
          snouts nudging snuffling him—
a naked old man
          with bloodstained wings.

          Fallen from the August sky?
Dead? Alive?
          But he twists away

from the cattle-prod, wings
          jerking, lifts his grizzled head,
regarding all
          with searching eyes.

Neither smiles nor threats,
dumbshow nor lingua franca
were of any use to those
trying for clues to him.

They could not make him hide
his nakedness
in their faded hand-me-downs.

Humane, if hostile and afraid,
they spread him a pallet
in the chicken-house.
The rooster pecked his wings.

Leftovers were set out for him;
he ate sunflowers
instead and the lice crawling his feathers.

Carloads of the curious paid
his clever hosts to see the
actual angel? carny freak?
in the barbedwire pen.

They crossed themselves and prayed
his blessing;
catcalled and chunked at him.

          In the dark his heavy wings
open and shut, stiffly spread
          like a wooden butterfly's.

          He leaps, board wings clum-
sily flapping, big sex
          flopping, falls.

          The hawk-haunted fowl
flutter and squawk;
          panic squeals in the sty.

He strains, an awk-
ward patsy, sweating strains
    leaping falling. Then—

    silken rustling in the air,
the angle of ascent
    achieved.

Elegies for Paradise Valley

I

My shared bedroom's window
opened on alley stench.
A junkie died in maggots there.
I saw his body shoved into a van.
I saw the hatred for our kind
glistening like tears
in the policemen's eyes.

II

No place for Pestalozzi's
fiorelli. No time of starched
and ironed innocence. Godfearing
elders, even godless grifters, tried
as best they could to shelter
us. Rats fighting in their walls.

III

Waxwork Uncle Henry
(murdered Uncle Crip)
lay among floral pieces
in the front room where
the Christmas tree had stood.

Mister Hong of the
Chinese Lantern (there
Auntie as waitress queened it
nights) brought freesias, wept
beside the coffin.

Beautiful, our neighbors
murmured; he would be proud.
Is it mahogany?
Mahogany—I'd heard
the victrola voice of

dead Bert Williams
talk-sing that word as macabre
music played, chilling
me. Uncle Crip
had laughed and laughed.

IV

Whom now do you guide, Madam Artelia?
Who nowadays can summon you to speak
from the spirit place your ghostly home
of the oh-rièntàl wonders there—
of the fate, luck, surprises, gifts

awaiting us out here? Oh, Madam,
part Seminole and confidante
("Born with a veil over my face")
of all our dead, how clearly you
materialize before the eye

of memory—your AfroIndian features,
Gypsy dress, your silver crucifix
and manycolored beads. I see
again your waitingroom, with its wax
bouquets, its plaster Jesus of the Sacred Heart.

I watch blue smoke of incense curl
from a Buddha's lap as I wait with Ma
and Auntie among your nervous clients.
You greet us, smiling, lay your hand
in blessing on my head, then lead

the others into a candlelit room
I may not enter. She went into a trance,
Auntie said afterward, and spirits
talked, changing her voice to suit
their own. And Crip came.

Happy yes I am happy here,
he told us; dying's not death. Do not grieve.
Remembering, Auntie began to cry
and poured herself a glass of gin.
Didn't sound a bit like Crip, Ma snapped.

V

And Belle the classy dresser, where is she,
who changed her frocks three times a day?
-    Where's Nora, with her laugh, her comic flair,
        stagestruck Nora waiting for her chance?
Where's fast Iola, who so loved to dance
she left her sickbed one last time to whirl
in silver at The Palace till her fell?
        Where's mad Miss Alice, who ate from garbage cans?
        Where's snuffdipping Lucy, who played us 'chunes'
on her guitar? Where's Hattie? Where's Melissabelle?
    Let vanished rooms, let dead streets tell.

Where's Jim, Watusi prince and Good Old Boy,
who with a joke went off to fight in France?
        Where's Tump the defeated artist, for meals or booze
            daubing with quarrelsome reds, disconsolate blues?
Where's Les the huntsman? Tough Kid Chocolate, where
is he? Where's dapper Jess? Where's Stomp the shellshocked,
clowning for us in parodies of war?

Where's taunted Christopher, sad queen of night?
And Ray, who cursing crossed the color line?
Where's gentle Brother Davis? Where's dopefiend Mel?
Let vanished rooms, let dead streets tell.

VI

Of death. Of loving too:
Oh sweet sweetjellyroll:
so the sinful hymned it while
the churchfolk loured.

I scrounged for crumbs:
I yearned to touch the choirlady's hair,
I wanted Uncle Crip

to kiss me, but he danced
with me instead;
we Balled-the-Jack
to Jellyroll

Morton's brimstone
piano on the phonograph,
laughing, shaking the gasolier
a later stillness dimmed.

VII

Our parents warned us: Gypsies
kidnap you. And we must never play
with Gypsy children: Gypsies
all got lice in their hair.

Their queen was dark as Cleopatra
in the Negro History Book. Their king's
sinister arrogance flashed fire
like the diamonds on his dirty hands.

Quite suddenly he was dead,
his tribe clamoring in grief.
They take on bad as Colored Folks,
Uncle Crip allowed. Die like us too.

Zingaros: Tzigeune: Gitanos: Gypsies:
pornographers of gaudy otherness:
aliens among the alien: thieves,
carriers of sickness: like us like us.

VIII
Of death, of loving,
of sin and hellfire too.
Unsaved, old Christians
gossiped; pitched

from the gamblingtable—
Lord have mercy on
his wicked soul—
face foremost into hell.

We'd dance there, Uncle
Crip and I,
for though I spoke
my pieces well in Sunday School,

I knew myself (precocious
in the ways of guilt
and secret pain)
the devil's own rag babydoll.

A Letter from Phillis Wheatley
London, 1773

Dear Obour
            Our crossing was without
event. I could not help, at times,
reflecting on that first—my Destined—
voyage long ago (I yet
have some remembrance of its Horrors)
and marvelling at God's Ways.

      Last evening, her Ladyship presented me
to her illustrious Friends.
I scarce could tell them anything
of Africa, though much of Boston
and my hope of Heaven. I read
my latest Elegies to them.
"O Sable Muse!" the Countess cried,
embracing me, when I had done.
I held back tears, as is my wont,
and there were tears in Dear
Nathaniel's eyes.
      At supper—I dined apart
like captive Royalty—
the Countess and her Guests promised
signatures affirming me
True Poetess, albeit once a slave.
Indeed, they were most kind, and spoke,
moreover, of presenting me
at Court (I thought of Pocahontas)—
an Honor, to be sure, but one,
I should, no doubt, as Patriot decline.
      My health is much improved;
I feel I may, if God so Wills,
entirely recover here.
Idyllic England! Alas, there is
no Eden without its Serpent. Under
the chiming Complaisance I hear him Hiss;
I see his flickering tongue
when foppish would-be Wits
murmur of the Yankee Pedlar
and his Cannibal Mockingbird.
      Sister, forgive th'intrusion of
my Sombreness—Nocturnal Mood
I would not share with any save
your trusted Self. Let me disperse,
in closing, such unseemly Gloom
by mention of an Incident
you may, as I, consider Droll:
Today, a little Chimney Sweep,
his face and hands with soot quite Black,

staring hard at me, politely asked:
"Does you, M'lady, sweep chimneys too?"
I was amused, but dear Nathaniel
(ever Solicitous) was not.

     ·   I pray the Blessings of our Lord
and Saviour Jesus Christ be yours
Abundantly. In His Name,

            Phillis

Melvin B. Tolson

(1898–1966)

NOW THE TIME HAS COME for a New Negro Poetry for the New Negro. The most difficult thing to do today is to write modern poetry. Why? It is the acme of the intellectual. Longfellow, Whitman, Milton, Tennyson, and Poe are no longer the poets held in high repute. The standard of poetry has changed completely. Negroes must become aware of this. This is the age of T. S. Eliot, who just won the Nobel Prize in Literature. If you know Shakespeare from A to Z, it does not mean you can read one line of T. S. Eliot! . . . Imitation must be in technique only. We have a rich heritage of folklore and history. We are a part of America. We are a part of the world. Our native symbols must be lifted into the universal. Yes, we must study the techniques of Robert Lowell, Dylan Thomas, Carlos Williams, Ezra Pound, Karl Shapiro, and W. H. Auden. The greatest revolution has not been in science but in poetry. We must study such magazines as *Partisan Review*, the *Sewanee Review*, *Accent*, and the *Virginia Quarterly*. We must read such critics as Crowe Ransom, Allen Tate, Stephen Spender, George Dillon, and Kenneth Burke.

from Harlem Gallery

Chi

Despite his caricatures
of poets and poetasters,

Hideho's joy was Hasidic
among the lives and works of the Masters—
old and new.
He himself was a sort of aged Istanbul
with a young Beyoglu.

He didn't know
I knew
about the split identity
of the People's Poet—
the bifacial nature of his poetry:
the racial ballad in the public domain
and the private poem in the modern vein.

I had overheard the poet say:
"Reverend Eli, in a foxhole
with the banzai in my ears,
one day
I collapsed from battle fatigue.
You know why?
Since I was unable to dig
the immortality of John Doe,
fears
(not Hamlet's . . . not Simon Legree's),
my fears
of oblivion made me realistic:
with no poems of Hideho's in World Lit—
he'd be a statistic!"

Poor Boy Blue,
the Great White World
and the Black Bourgeoisie
have shoved the Negro artist into
the white and not-white dichotomy,
the Afroamerican dilemma in the Arts—
the dialectic of
to be or not to be
a Negro.

From the grandeur that was dusky Rome,
one night I brought Hideho home,

dead drunk,
in a Zulu Club taxicab.
As he lay on the sofa,
ashy-black like a stiff on a slab
in a Harlem morgue,
I chanced to see,
in the modern idiom,
a poem called *E. & O. E.*
(A sort of Pasternakian secrecy, I thought.)
I was again the kid startled by the kettledrum
on the withers of a cavalry horse.
(Cry havoc, Poor Boy Blue.)
That he had been
a bistro habitué,
an expatriate poet of the Black Venus
in the Age of Whoopee—
Clotho had kept hid until then.

For the skeptic
on Lenox Avenue,
for the goof
on Peach-tree Street—
here was the eyesight proof
that the Color Line, as well as the Party Line,
splits an artist's identity
like the vertical which
Omar's *Is* and *Is-not* cannot define.
The face
of no man escapes the common gable roof
of this time, nor the lights and shadows in the design
of that place.

Why should a man,
in an age of anesthesiology,
seek relief
in the bark of the toothache tree?
Yet,
depressed like ondoyant glass,
Hideho Heights,
the *Coeur de Lion* of the Negro mass,
in *E. & O. E.* rationalized:

"Why place an empty pail
before a well
of dry bones?
Why go to Nineveh to tell
the ailing that they ail?
Why lose a golden fleece
to gain a holy grail?"

The Hideho Heights that Afroamerican Freedom, Inc.,
glorified
had recognition marks—plain
like the white tail of an antelope;
in the subterrane
of this poem, however,
the protagonist aped the dubiety
of a wet cake of soap.

. . .

Yet,
in front of the ramshackle
theatre that had graduated into
the Ethiopian Tabernacle,
like sandstone into gneiss,
Hideho had left "Bishop" Gladstone Coffin
tongue-tied as a puking slop-bowl gobbler with a con head
that had a Napoleonic forelock, but a naked monkey ass
behind.
Jailed for disturbing the peace, he had said
later, to the liquored-up Zulu Club Wits:
"A man's conscience is home-bred.
To see an artist or a leader do
Uncle Tom's asinine splits
is an ask-your-mama shame!"
The Jamaican bartender had staked off his claim:
"The drinks are on the house, Poet Defender!"
A sportsman with ruffed grouse
on the wing over dogs, the poet had continued:
"Integrity is an underpin—
the marble lions that support
the alabaster fountain in

the Alhambra."

.   .   .

In the poem, *E. & O. E.*,
The poet's mind kept shuttling between
the sphinx of Yesterday and the enigma of Today,
like the specter of Amphion in Thebes
'twixt fragments of requiems and stones of decay.

Time!
Time?
The poet's *bête noire*, I thought.
We everyday mortals
wrought
on the cis-threshold of the sublime
are concerned with *timing*,
not with *time*.

I remembered the wisdom
of a grand duchess of the burlesque shows,
whose G-string gave repose
to no man's imagination.
"It's all in the timing,"
said Rose La Rose,
Mister Minsky's tigress in heat.
Just as sound,
not spelling,
is the white magic of rhyming
in the poet's feat,
the timing
of a parson's spiel,
of an H-bomb,
of a golfer's swing,
of a curator's budget—
makes the gallery ring!

I
(conscious of my Judas role)
jumped
when Hideho's foot

                    plumped
                against the floor;
              but in a second flat
        the broken-down flat vibrated again with the snore
             of a mine pump's suction hole.

           I cudgeled again the eyesight proof:
                   "I am no ape
                  of Benares. I have won
                    no Monthyon
                  prize. Though I
        have cut a G clef and a belletristic S,
                    naked on
             roller skates in Butte Montmartre,
                sweated palm to palm
                to the down beats of
                   the tom-tom,
                 in Sorgue's studio
               with the Black Venus,
        and, a leaning question mark upon
        a blue white metal bar, drunk piccolo
             with Salmon, Apollinaire,
             MacOrlan, and Picasso—
                 yet, out of square,
                 I have not said,
              'Hippoclides doesn't care.'"

                  My unbelief
           as I climbed the Peak of Teneriffe
                  in the poem
                 . . . grew . . .
                  indistinct
                 . . . grew . . .
                  invisible,
        like the veins between the stem and margin of a leaf:

                   "Beneath
                 the albatross,
               the skull-and-bones,
               the Skull and Cross,

the Seven Sins Dialectical,
    I do not shake
    the Wailing Wall
    of Earth—
    nor quake
    the Gethsemane
    of Sea—
    nor tear
    the Big Top
    of Sky
with Lear's prayer,
or Barabas' curse,
    or Job's cry!"

THE 1960s AND BEYOND

THE BLACK ARTS MOVEMENT

Amiri Baraka

(1934–)

THERE ARE CERTAIN THINGS I write now that echo earlier things, and certain things that have been transformed altogether, that have changed into their opposites. I was always, from the first poem that I ever had printed, concerned with national oppression—what it did to me mentally, spiritually, what it turned people into, what one's reaction to national oppression was, etc. Being black has certainly remained a constant; but my ability to explain the sources and origins of national oppression has deepened.

1978

My writing reflects my own growth and expansion, and at the same time the society in which I have existed throughout this longish confrontation. Whether it is politics, music, literature, or the origins of language, there is a historical and time/place/condition reference that will always try to explain exactly why I was saying both how and for what.

1990

So *Digging* means to present, perhaps arbitrarily, varied paradigms of this essentially Afro-American art. The common predicate, myself, the Digger. One who gets down, with the down, always looking above to see what is going out, and so check *Digitaria*, as the Dogon say, necessary if you are to dig the farthest Star, *Serious*.

2009

Black Art

Poems are bullshit unless they are
teeth or trees or lemons piled
on a step. Or black ladies dying
of men leaving nickel hearts
beating them down. Fuck poems
and they are useful, they shoot
come at you, love what you are,
breathe like wrestlers, or shudder
strangely after pissing. We want live
words of the hip world live flesh &
coursing blood. Hearts Brains
Souls splintering fire. We want poems
like fists beating niggers out of Jocks
or dagger poems in the slimy bellies
of the owner-jews. Black poems to
smear on girdlemamma mulatto bitches
whose brains are red jelly stuck
between 'lizabeth taylor's toes. Stinking
Whores! We want "poems that kill."
Assassin poems, Poems that shoot
guns. Poems that wrestle cops into alleys
and take their weapons leaving them dead
with tongues pulled out and sent to Ireland. Knockoff
poems for dope selling wops or slick halfwhite
politicians Airplane poems. rrrrrrrrrrrrrrrrrrrr
rrrrrrrrrrrrrrr . . . . tuhtuhtuhtuhtuhtuhtuhtuhtuh
. . . . rrrrrrrrrrrrrrr . . . . Setting fire and death to
whities ass. Look at the Liberal
Spokesman for the jews clutch his throat
& puke himself into eternity . . . . rrrrrrrrrr
There's a negroleader pinned to
a bar stool in Sardi's eyeballs melting
in hot flame. Another negroleader
on the steps of the white house one
kneeling between the sheriff's thighs
negotiating cooly for his people.

Aggh ... stumbles across the room ...
Put it on him, poem. Strip him naked
to the world! Another bad poem cracking
steel knuckles in a jewlady's mouth
Poem scream poison gas on beasts in green berets
Clean out the world for virtue and love,
Let there be no love poems written
until love can exist freely and
cleanly. Let Black People understand
that they are the lovers and the sons
of lovers and warriors and sons
of warriors Are poems & poets &
all the loveliness here in the world

We want a black poem. And a
Black World.
Let the world be a Black Poem
And Let All Black People Speak This Poem
Silently

or LOUD

In Memory of Radio

Who has ever stopped to think of the divinity of Lamont Cranston?
(Only Jack Kerouac, that I know of: & me.
The rest of you probably had on WCBS and Kate Smith,
Or something equally unattractive.)

What can I say?
It is better to have loved and lost
Than to put linoleum in your living rooms?

Am I a sage or something?
Mandrake's hypnotic gesture of the week?

(Remember, I do not have the healing powers of Oral Roberts . . .
I cannot, like F. J. Sheen, tell you how to get saved & rich!
I cannot even order you to gaschamber satori like Hitler or
    Goody Knight

& Love is an evil word.
Turn it backwards/see, see what I mean?
An evol word. & besides
who understands it?
I certainly wouldn't like to go out on that kind of limb.

Saturday mornings we listened to *Red Lantern* & his undersea folk.
At 11, *Let's Pretend*/& we did/& I, the poet, still do, Thank God!

What was it he used to say (after the transformation, when he
    was safe
& invisible & the unbelievers couldn't throw stones?) "Heh,
    heh, heh,
Who knows what evil lurks in the hearts of men? The Shadow
    knows."

O, yes he does
O, yes he does.
An evil word it is,
This Love.

An Agony. As Now.

I am inside someone
who hates me. I look
out from his eyes. Smell
what fouled tunes come in
to his breath. Love his
wretched women.

Slits in the metal, for sun. Where
my eyes sit turning, at the cool air
the glance of light, or hard flesh
rubbed against me, a woman, a man,
without shadow, or voice, or meaning.

This is the enclosure (flesh,
where innocence is a weapon. An
abstraction. Touch. (Not mine.
Or yours, if you are the soul I had
and abandoned when I was blind and had
my enemies carry me as a dead man
(if he is beautiful, or pitied.

It can be pain. (As now, as all his
flesh hurts me.) It can be that. Or
pain. As when she ran from me into
that forest.
                Or pain, the mind
silver spiraled whirled against the
sun, higher than even old men thought
God would be. Or pain. And the other. The
yes. (Inside his books, his fingers. They
are withered yellow flowers and were never
beautiful.) The yes. You will, lost soul, say
'beauty'. Beauty, practiced, as the tree. The
slow river. A white sun in its wet sentences.

Or, the cold men in their gale. Ecstasy. Flesh
or soul. The yes. (Their robes blown. Their bowls
empty. They chant at my heels, not at yours.) Flesh
or soul, as corrupt. Where the answer moves too quickly.
Where the God is a self, after all.)

Cold air blown through narrow blind eyes. Flesh,
white hot metal. Glows as the day with its sun.
It is a human love, I live inside. A bony skeleton
you recognize as words or simple feeling.

But it has no feeling. As the metal, is hot, it is not,
given to love.

It burns the thing
inside it. And that thing
screams.

A Poem for Black Hearts

For Malcolm's eyes, when they broke
the face of some dumb white man, For
Malcolm's hands raised to bless us
all black and strong in his image
of ourselves, For Malcolm's words
fire darts, the victor's tireless
thrusts, words hung above the world
change as it may, he said it, and
for this he was killed, for saying,
and feeling, and being/ change, all
collected hot in his heart, For Malcolm's
heart, raising us above our filthy cities,
for his stride, and his beat, and his address
to the grey monsters of the world, For Malcolm's
pleas for your dignity, black men, for your life,
black man, for the filling of your minds
with righteousness, For all of him dead and
gone and vanished from us, and all of him which
clings to our speech black god of our time.
For all of him, and all of yourself, look up,
black man, quit stuttering and shuffling, look up,
black man, quit whining and stooping, for all of him,
For Great Malcolm a prince of the earth, let nothing in us rest
until we avenge ourselves for his death, stupid animals
that killed him, let us never breathe a pure breath if
we fail, and white men call us faggots till the end of
the earth.

AM/TRAK

1
Trane.
Trane.
History Love Scream Oh
Trane, Oh
Trane, Oh
Scream History Love
Trane

2
Begin on by a Philly night club
or the basement of a cullut chuhch
walk the bars my man for pay
honk the night lust of money
oh
blow-
scream history love

Rabbit, Cleanhead, Diz
Big Maybelle. Trees in the shining night forest

Oh
blow
love, history

Alcohol we submit to thee
3x's consume our lives
our livers quiver under yr poison hits
eyes roll back in stupidness
The navy, the lord, niggers,
the streets
all converge a shitty symphony
of screams
   to come
   dazzled invective

Honk Honk Honk, "I am here
to love
it." Let me be fire-mystery
air feeder beauty."

Honk
Oh
scream — Miles
comes.

3
Hip band alright
sum up life in the slick
street part of the
world, oh,
blow,
if you cd
nigger
man

Miles wd stand back and negative check
oh, he dug him — Trane
But Trane clawed at the limits of cool
slandered sanity
with his tryin to be born
raging
shit
    Oh
    blow,
yeh go do it
honk, scream
uhuh yeh — history
        love
        blue clipped moments
        of intense feeling.
"Trane you blows too long."
Screaming niggers drop out yr solos
Bohemian nights, the "heavyweight champ"
  smacked him

in the face
his eyes sagged like a spent
dick, hot vowels escaped the metal clone of his soul
fucking saxophone
tell us shit tell us tell us!

4
There was nothing left to do but
be where monk cd find him
that crazy
mother fucker
> duh duh-duh duh-duh duh
> duh duh
> duh duh-duh duh-duh duh
> duh duh
> duh duh-duh duh-duh duh
> duh duh
> duh Duuuuuuuuuhhhhhh

Can you play this shit? (Life asks
Come by and listen

& at the 5 Spot Bach, Mulatto ass Beethoven
& even Duke, who has given America its hip tongue
checked
checked
Trane stood and dug
Crazy monk's shit
Street gospel intellectual mystical survival codes
Intellectual street gospel funk modes
Tink a ling put downs of dumb shit
pink pink a cool bam groove note air breath
a why I'm here
a why I aint
& who is you-ha-you-ha-you-ha
Monk's shit
Blue Cooper 5 Spot
was the world busting
on piano bass drums & tenor

This was Coltrane's College. A Ph motherfuckin d
sitting at the feet, elbows
& funny grin
Of Master T Sphere
too cool to be a genius
he was instead
Thelonious
with Comrades Shadow
on tubs, lyric Wilbur
who hipped us to electric futures
& the monster with the horn.

5
From the endless sessions
money lord hovers oer us
capitalism beats our ass
dope & juice wont change it
Trane, blow, oh scream
yeh, anyway.

There then came down in the ugly streets of us
inside the head & tongue
of us
a man
black blower of the now
The vectors from all sources — slavery, renaissance
bop charlie parker,
nigger absolute super-sane screams against reality
course through him
AS SOUND!
"Yes, it says
this is now in you screaming
recognize the truth
recognize reality
& even check me (Trane)
who blows it
Yes it says
Yes &

Yes again   Convulsive multi orgasmic
                    Art
                    Protest

& finally, brother, you took you were
(are we gathered to dig this?
electric wind find us finally
on red records of the history of ourselves)

The cadre came together
the inimitable 4 who blew the pulse of then, exact
The flame the confusion the love of
whatever the fuck there was
          to love
Yes it says
blow, oh honk-scream (bahhhhhhh - wheeeeeeee)

(If Don Lee thinks I am imitating him in this poem,
this is only payback for his imitating me — we
are brothers, even if he is a backward cultural nationalist
motherfucker — Hey man only socialism brought by revolution
can win)
                    Trane was the spirit of the 60's
                    He was Malcolm X in New Super Bop Fire
                    Baaahhhhh
                    Wheeeeeee . . . Black Art!!!

Love
History
    On The Bar Tops of Philly
in the Monkish College of Express
in the cool Grottoes of Miles Davis Funnytimery
Be
Be
Be reality
Be reality alive in motion in flame to change (You Knew It!)
                              to change!!
          (All you reactionaries listening
          Fuck you, Kill you
          get outta here!!!)

Jimmy Garrison, bass, McCoy Tyner, piano, Captain Marvel Elvin
on drums, the number itself — the precise saying
all of it in it afire aflame talking saying being doing meaning

Meditations
Expressions
A Love Supreme
(I lay in solitary confinement, July 67

Tanks rolling thru Newark
& whistled all I knew of Trane
my knowledge heartbeat
& he was dead
they
said.

And yet last night I played Meditations
& it told me what to do
Live you crazy mother
fucker!
Live!
   & organize
   yr shit
   as rightly
   burning!

Mari Evans

(1923–)

WHO I AM IS CENTRAL to how I write and what I write; and I am the continuation of my father's passage. I have written for as long as I have been aware of writing as a way of setting down feelings and the stuff of imaginings.

.   .   .

Writing is a craft, a profession one learns by doing. One must be able to produce on demand, and that requires great personal discipline. I believe that one seldom really perfects. I cannot imagine a writer who is not continually reaching, who contains no discontent that what he or she is producing is not more than it is. So primarily, I suppose, discipline is the foundation of the profession, and that holds regardless of anything else.

.   .   .

So when I write, I write reaching for all that. Reaching for what will nod black heads over common denominators. The stones thrown that say how it has been/is/must be, for us. If there are those outside the Black experience who hear the music and can catch the beat, that is serendipity; I have no objections. But when I write, I write according to the title of poet Margaret Walker's classic: "for my people."

.   .   .

My attempt is to be [as] explicit as possible while maintaining the integrity of the aesthetic; consequently, I work so hard for clarity that I suspect I sometimes run the risk of being, as Ray Durem put it, "not sufficiently obscure." Since the Black creative artist is not required to wait on inspiration nor to rely on imagination—for Black life *is* drama, brutal and compelling—one inescapable reality is that the more explicitly Black writers speak their truths the more difficult it is for them to publish. My writing is pulsed by my understanding of contemporary realities: I am Afrikan first, then woman, then writer, but I have never had a manuscript rejected because I am a woman: I have been rejected more times than I can number because the content of the manuscript was, to the industry-oriented reader, more "Black" ergo "discomforting" than could be accommodated.

I Am a Black Woman

I am a black woman
the music of my song
some sweet arpeggio of tears
is written in a minor key
and I
can be heard humming in the night
Can be heard
          humming
in the night

I saw my mate leap screaming to the sea
and I / with these hands / cupped the lifebreath
from my issue in the canebrake
I lost Nat's swinging body in a rain of tears
and heard my son scream all the way from Anzio
for Peace he never knew. . . . I
learned Da Nang and Pork Chop Hill
in anguish
Now my nostrils know the gas
and these trigger tire/d fingers
seek the softness in my warrior's beard

I
am a black woman
tall as a cypress
strong
beyond all definition still
defying place
and time
and circumstance
  assailed
    impervious
      indestructible
Look
  on me and be
renewed

Nikki Giovanni

(1943–)

WRITING IS ALWAYS SECONDARY. And you cannot write in a vacuum. And so the writing is always the second thing that happens. First you conceptualize it. Or you experience it. But experience is no excuse. I mean nothing is worse than somebody saying, well this is what actually happened. Nobody cares what actually happened. What you're trying to get . . . out is what does this mean? What is the larger context here? And the writing is always going to be secondary to the life. And that's what's hard to get over because people think that writing is the product. But it's not. It's the by-product. The product is the life.

.   .   .

What would *you* feel if these were your circumstances? You try as a writer to put yourself into the other person's position. Empathy. Empathy is everything because we can't experience everything. Experience is important, but empathy is the key.

Nikki-Rosa

childhood remembrances are always a drag
if you're Black
you always remember things like living in Woodlawn
with no inside toilet
and if you become famous or something

they never talk about how happy you were to have
your mother
all to yourself and
how good the water felt when you got your bath
from one of those
big tubs that folk in chicago barbecue in
and somehow when you talk about home
it never gets across how much you
understood their feelings
as the whole family attended meetings about Hollydale
and even though you remember
your biographers never understand
your father's pain as he sells his stock
and another dream goes
And though you're poor it isn't poverty that
concerns you
and though they fought a lot
it isn't your father's drinking that makes any difference
but only that everybody is together and you
and your sister have happy birthdays and very good
Christmases
and I really hope no white person ever has cause
to write about me
because they never understand
Black love is Black wealth and they'll
probably talk about my hard childhood
and never understand that
all the while I was quite happy

Ego Tripping
(there may be a reason why)

I was born in the congo
I walked to the fertile crescent and built
   the sphinx
I designed a pyramid so tough that a star
     that only glows every one hundred years falls
     into the center giving divine perfect light
I am bad

I sat on the throne
    drinking nectar with allah
I got hot and sent an ice age to europe
    to cool my thirst
My oldest daughter is nefertiti
    the tears from my birth pains
    created the nile
I am a beautiful woman

I gazed on the forest and burned
    out the sahara desert
    with a packet of goat's meat
    and a change of clothes
I crossed it in two hours
I am a gazelle so swift
    so swift you can't catch me

    For a birthday present when he was three
I gave my son hannibal an elephant
    He gave me rome for mother's day
My strength flows ever on

My son noah built new / ark and
I stood proudly at the helm
    as we sailed on a soft summer day
I turned myself into myself and was
    jesus

men intone my loving name
All praises All praises
I am the one who would save

I sowed diamonds in my back yard
My bowels deliver uranium
    the filings from my fingernails are
    semi-precious jewels
    On a trip north
I caught a cold and blew
My nose giving oil to the arab world
I am so hip even my errors are correct
I sailed west to reach east and had to round off
    the earth as I went
    The hair from my head thinned and gold was laid
    across three continents

I am so perfect so divine so ethereal so surreal
I cannot be comprehended
    except by my permission

I mean . . . I . . . can fly
    like a bird in the sky . . .

Bobb Hamilton

(1928–1998)

IN CLEVELAND, OHIO, in the ghetto, where I grew up everyone said whilst [used in his poem] in spite of all that the teachers could do to "civilize" us (smile). There are lots of other archaisms that I used until I went to college and then became self-conscious behind my degree! My neighborhood was really a [S]outhern black community moved north, and the language there was often "quaint," so to speak. What I tried to capture in the poem was the flavor of the black storefront preacher and his female congregation. When Malik was murdered, even here in New York, the impact on the old folks was very like that of a congregation that had been whipped up about the story of the crucifixion on a Sunday morning. I remember how my granny used to get when she talked about Marcus Garvey. My use of the term ["whilst"] was not pretentious but an attempt to go back, so to speak, to the way our people responded to an emotional shock as I remember it. Malcolm did have that kind of appeal to the older people—I've even seen them shout at some of his indoor speeches.

Poem to a Nigger Cop

    Hey there poleece
Black skin in blue mask
You really gonna uphold the law?
What you gonna do when you see
Your Mama

Running down 125th street with
A t.v. set tied up in a bandana trying to catch a train to
    Springfield Gardens?
    You mean to tell me you gonna
Bang your own mother?
    Bang! Bang!
I can see you now grinning
    A big black no nuts nigger
On channel number 5
Your teeth rolling across the screen
Like undotted dice
    Talking about how you "uphelt
    De Law."
While Mr. Charlie sticks his white
    Finger up your ass
And pins a little gold medal on your
    Chest!
And then you'll bust out into soft shoe shuffle
    While a background chorus sings
"God Bless America,"
With an Irish accent.

David Henderson

(1942–)

MY POETICS ARE always evolving, changing, and I even suspect some doubling back. A great thing about having work from years ago is being able to revisit that work, and since I own it, I am able to have some interesting relationships with that work I could not have under other circumstances. Right now the language of the financial bank bailout and the bankers' revolt has me intrigued with the phrases, the vocabularies they invent to describe and/or often cover their activities. There is also always an evolving language in government as there is in other sectors, public and private, that is not easy to access. But there are windows into those languages, often in media, writings, journals, and also, often in conversation, spoken words, perhaps overheard words, or collaborations or stuff from informants. And there is also the challenge of putting poetics to the political. The ability to tolerate, to withstand ordinary language within lines that accumulate and build to a power. And there is also the story. Stories that can coexist in prose somehow in poetry become something more than that traditional setup and conclusion.

Downtown-Boy Uptown

for Mary Williams

Downtown-boy uptown
Affecting complicity of a Ghetto
and a sub-renascent culture.
Uptown-boy uptown for graces loomed to love.

Long have I walked these de-eternal streets
Seeking a suffice or a member to start my count.
Cat-Walk
Grotesque Pelican manger
Trampling the trapezium to tapering hourglass
Behind the melting sun.

I love a girl then.
My 140th St. gait varied from my downtown one.
I changed my speed and form for lack of a better tongue.
Then was, love you, Pudgy:
Thin young woman with a fat black name.
It is the nature of our paradox that has us
Look to the wrong convex.

II

I stand in my low cast window looking down.
Am I in the wrong slum?
The sky appears the same;
Birds fly, planes fly, clouds puff, days ago . . .
I stand in my window.
Can I ride from a de-eternal genesis?
Does my Exit defy concentric fish-womb?
Pudgy: your Mama always said Black man
Must stay in his own balancing cup.
Roach on kneebone I always agreed.
Was this Black man's smile enjoying guilt
Like ofay?

Long has it been that I've mirrored
My entrances through silk screen.

III

Did this Tragedian kiss you in anticipation
Of blood-gush separating from your black mirror?
Did I, in my complicity-grope relay the love
Of a long gone epoch?

sometimes questions are not questions
If I desire to thrust once more, If I scamper to embrace
Our tragedy in my oblique arms! . . .

                                                                        Nevermind.

You know.
You are not stupid, Pudgy.
You look for nothing of a Sun where you live,
Hourglass is intrinsic . . . where you live.
The regeneration in your womb is not of my body.
You have started your count
I cannot.

Calvin C. Hernton

(1932–2001)

I write because I feel I am being / outraged by life. I am alone. I / am everybody. I am God. I write because / I take God into my wounds and afflict / Him and am afflicted by all of the absurd / suffering and senseless bedroom agony / of the world.

The Distant Drum

I am not a metaphor or symbol.
This you hear is not the wind in the trees.
Nor a cat being maimed in the street.
I am being maimed in the street
It is I who weep, laugh, feel pain or joy.
Speak this because I exist.
This is my voice
These words are my words, my mouth
Speaks them, my hand writes.
I am a poet.
It is my fist you hear beating
Against your ear.

Haki Madhubuti

(1942–)

AND I'VE ALWAYS FELT that I've been given a gift in terms of poetry. And the poetry has informed my life and has allowed me to get to this point. I wouldn't be here without the poetry, no doubt about that. I'm primarily a poet. But I learned from Gwendolyn Brooks, Hoyt Fuller, Dudley Randall, Margaret and Charlie Burroughs, and even Langston Hughes and Sterling Brown, to a certain extent, that essentially we can do more than we do. But in order to do that you've got to work. It takes a long time to write a good poem. It takes an awful lot of time to write a great poem, if we ever get to that point. But when you have a community that is under siege, what else do you do? Sure, I'm saying that poetry has contributed, but I think that the building of the schools and running the press and bookstores at one time also have contributed substantially.

But He Was Cool, or: he even stopped for green lights

super-cool
ultrablack
a tan / purple
had a beautiful shade.

he had a double-natural
that wd put the sisters to shame.
his dashikis were tailor made
& his beads were imported sea shells
      (from some blk / country i never heard of)
he was triple-hip.

his tikis were hand carved
out of ivory
& came express from the motherland.
he would greet u in swahili
& say good-by in yoruba.
woooooooooooo-jim he bes so cool & ill tel li gent
        cool-cool is so cool he was un-cooled by
            other niggers' cool
        cool-cool ultracool was bop-cool / ice box
            cool so cool cold cool
        his wine didn't have to be cooled, him was
            air conditioned cool
        cool-cool / real cool made me cool—now
            ain't that cool
        cool-cool so cool him nick-named refrig-
            erator.

cool-cool so cool
he didn't know,
after detroit, newark, chicago &c.,
we had to hip
        cool-cool / super-cool / real cool
  that
to be black
is
to be
very-hot.

Larry Neal

(1937–1981)

T HE BLACK ARTS MOVEMENT is radically opposed to any concept of the artist that alienates him from his community. Black Art is the aesthetic and spiritual sister of the Black Power concept. As such, it envisions an art that speaks directly to the needs and aspirations of Black America. In order to perform this task, the Black Arts Movement proposes a radical reordering of the Western cultural aesthetic. It proposes a separate symbolism, mythology, critique, and iconology. The Black Arts and the Black Power concepts both relate broadly to the Afro-American's desire for self-determination and nationhood. Both concepts are nationalistic. One is concerned with the relationship between art and politics; the other with the art of politics.

. . .

The Black artist takes this to mean that his primary duty is to speak to the spiritual and cultural needs of Black people. Therefore, the main thrust of this new breed of contemporary writers is to confront the contradictions arising out of the Black man's experience in the racist West. Currently, these writers are re-evaluating the Western aesthetic, the traditional role of the writer, and the social function of art. Implicit in this re-evaluation is the need to develop a "black aesthetic."

. . .

The new aesthetic is mostly predicated on an ethics which asks the question: Whose vision of the world is finally more meaningful, ours or the white oppressors'? These are basic questions. Black intellectuals of previous decades failed to ask them. Further, national and international affairs demand that we appraise the world in terms of our own interests.

It is clear that the question of human survival is at the core of contemporary experience. The Black artist must address himself to this reality in the strongest terms possible. In a context of world upheaval, ethics and aesthetics must interact positively and be consistent with the demands for a more spiritual world.

.   .   .

We're clearly in the Middle Passage. The Middle Passage is symbolic of our condition now. We're in the Middle Passage now rather than the Middle Passage of the past. It's a good polemic poem ["Love Song: Middle Passage"] in one sense, because I pull up images like McNamara and the ICBMs and all that shit, which I'm very glad I did. I'm very glad that those polemics, that those poems, took a stance at the time. Just the way [Pablo] Neruda takes a stance against United Fruit Company. In some poems you have to be very blunt even with the chance of being very awkward. Now there is a literary school that would flinch at that kind of bluntness, but there're certain statements that need to be made at a certain time. You take the leap and you make the statement. They may haunt you later, but you make them.

Malcolm X—An Autobiography

I am the Seventh Son of the Son
who was also the Seventh.
I have drunk deep of the waters of my ancestors
have travelled the soul's journey towards cosmic harmony
the Seventh Son.
Have walked slick avenues
and seen grown men, fall, to die in a blue doom
of death and ancestral agony,
have seen old men glide, shadowless, feet barely
touching the pavements.

I sprung out of the Midwestern plains
the bleak Michigan landscape, the black blues of Kansas
city, the kiss-me-nights.

out of the bleak Michigan landscape wearing the slave name—
Malcolm Little.
Saw a brief vision in Lansing, when I was seven, and in
my mother's womb heard the beast cry of death,
a landscape on which white robed figures ride, and my
Garvey father silhouetted against the night-fire, gun in hand
form outlined against a panorama of violence.

Out of the Midwestern bleakness, I sprang, pushed eastward,
past shack on country nigger shack, across the wilderness
of North America.

I hustler. I pimp. I unfulfilled black man
bursting with destiny.
New York city Slim called me Big Red,
and there was no escape, close nights of the smell of death.

Pimp. hustler. The day fills these rooms.
I am talking about New York. Harlem.
talking about the neon madness.
talking about ghetto eyes and nights
about death protruding across the room. Small's paradise.
talking about cigarette butts, and rooms smelly with white
sex flesh, and dank sheets, and being on the run.

talking about cocaine illusions, about stealing and selling.
talking about these New York cops who smell of blood and
    money.
I am Big Red, tiger vicious, Big Red, bad nigger, will kill.

But there is rhythm here. It's own special substance:
I hear Billie sing, no good man, and dig Prez, wearing the
    Zoot
suit of life—the porkpie hat tilted at the correct angle.
through the Harlem smoke of beer and whiskey, I understand
    the
mystery of the signifying monkey,
in a blue haze of inspiration, I reach to the totality of Being.
I am at the center of a swirl of events. War and death.
rhythm. hot women. I think life a commodity bargained for

across the bar in Small's.
I perceive the echoes of Bird and there is a gnawing in the
    maw
of my emotions.
and then there is jail. America is the world's greatest jailer,
and we all in jails. black spirits contained like magnificent
birds of wonder. I now understand my father urged on by the
ghost of Garvey,
and see a small brown man standing in a corner. The cell.
    cold.
dank. The light around him vibrates. Am I crazy? But to
    under-
stand is to submit to a more perfect will, a more perfect order.
To understand is to surrender the imperfect self
For a more perfect self.
Allah formed brown man, I follow
and shake within the very depth of my most imperfect being,
and I bear witness to the Message of Allah
and I bear witness—all praise is due Allah!

Carolyn Rodgers

(1940–2010)

S OMETIMES IT IS DIFFICULT for me to say exactly what I want to say
without giving too much to the world.

·   ·   ·

[Literature] functions as a type of catharsis or amen arena. I think it
speaks not only to the political sensibility but to the heart, the mind, the
spirit, and the soul of every man, woman, and child.

·   ·   ·

In terms of style, I like to be as modern as I am traditional, thus combin-
ing the two. I think I tend to write more as a woman than I do as a person,
but then I think I write more as a human as opposed to a person or per-
sonality; perhaps more than anything I write as a human, a woman, who
is Brown.

·   ·   ·

I put the poem on paper by sense and touch, much like a blind person
fumbling in the dark for light.

how i got ovah

i can tell you
about them

i have shaken rivers
out of my eyes
i have waded eyelash deep
have crossed rivers
have shaken the water weed out
of my lungs
have swam for strength
pulled by strength
through waterfalls with electric beats
i have bore the shocks
of water deep deep
waterlogs are my bones
i have shaken the water free of my hair
have kneeled on the banks
and kissed my ancestors of the dirt
whose rich dark root fingers rose up reached out
grabbed and pulled me rocked me cupped me
gentle strong and firm
carried me
made me swim for strength
cross rivers
though i shivered
was wet was cold
and wanted to sink down
and float as water, yea—
i can tell you.
i have shaken rivers
out of my eyes.

Breakthrough

I've had tangled feelings lately
      about ev'rything
bout writing poetry, and otha forms
about talkin and dreamin with a

special man (who says he needs me)
     uh huh
and my mouth has been open
      most of the time, but
I ain't been saying nothin but
      thinking about ev'rything
and the partial pain has been
how do I put my self on paper
the way I want to be or am and be
not like any one else in this
Black world but me

how do I sing some lyrics ev'ry most could dig but
don't always be riffin like twenty-ten othas

      ev'rybodi's faintly heard, the trouble
is I tell you, how can I
sound just like and only my self
      and then could you dig it if I could?

u see, the changes are so many
there are several of me and
      all of us fight to show up at the same time

and there is uh consistent incongruity
      do u for instance, understand
      what I mean when I say
                I am very tired of trying
and want Blackness which is my life, want this to be
easier on me, want it not to suck me in and
out so much leavin me a balloon with no air, want it
not to puff me up so much sometimes
that I git puffed up and sucked in in to the
raunchy kind of love Black orgy I go through. do
u dig what I mean when I say I want to scream forget
it all some days and then want to cry when
I walk around the street with my hurt my mind
and some miscellaneous littl brotha
who's ultimately playin with my feelins sayin
      "what's happenin beautiful Black sistuh?"

can u dig why I want to say to him
      "why should u care?" and "why would u make me
love and puff all over again" and instead i end up
smiling and sayin, "U got it littl bro"
      because
I think he needs, and he thought I needed
                           and the
be cause is the why, and that kinda style goes on
and I become trite in my dreams
and my poems fidget and why should I care that I
can't sound as original as I think my thoughts are,
but can you dig how it could
make me question my thoughts?
      how did I ever get in this mess—
      is mess this, don't u ever sit around and want
      to get very high offa somethin and cry be cause
         u   are
and then what am I supposed to tell my self
when I want to take long bus rides and cop sunsets
for the soul I'm not sure I have / would want it, and
sometimes I want to hibernate in the summer
      and hang out in the winter and nurse babies
and get fat and lay around and be pinched by my man
and just love and laugh all the time, even if the
sun don't shine
            and then the kids go to marching and
singing songs talkin bout Blackness and schools that
ain't schools and I know what they be talkin bout
    they know that I know what needs doin and what
has all or any of this or that got to do with the
fact that I want to write a POEM, a poem poem, a
      poem's poem poem on a poem that ev'ry u could
dig, just if only a littl bit
in between, underneath, on top or a-round a word
or feelin
        and not mind the fact that it might
sound faintly like some riffin u heard.
or not mind that it's not like anything
u could have been told about to understand
      but like reading breathing or sipp-savorin uh mind

an uh hung over ecstasy in what is and ain't gon be
and uh stiff won't rub off don't washout longing
    for what u never had and can't imagine how u could
long for it since u'r not even sure it is
anyhow, like u or I is and I really hope that
    if u read this u
    will dig where I'm at
    and feel what i mean / that / where
        i am
    and could very possibly
        be
        real
at this lopsided crystal sweet moment. . . .

Sonia Sanchez

(1934–)

TO ANSWER THE QUESTION of how I write, we must look also to why I write. I write to tell the truth about the Black condition as I see it. Therefore I write to offer a Black woman's view of the world. How I tell the truth is part of the truth itself. I've always believed that the truth concealed or clouded is a partial lie. So when I decide to tell the truth about an event/happening, it must be clear and understandable for those who need to understand the lie/lies being told. What I learned in deciding "how" to write was simply that most folks tend to think that you're lying or jiving them if you have to spice things up just to get a point across. I decided along with a number of other Black poets to tell the truth in poetry by using the language, dialect, idioms, of the folks we believed our audience to be.

Homecoming

i have been a
way so long
once after college
i returned tourist
style to catch all
the niggers killing
themselves with
three-for-oners

with
needles
that cd
not support
their stutters.
        now woman
i have returned
leaving behind me
all those hide and
seek faces peeling
with freudian dreams.
this is for real.
        black
      niggers
        my beauty.
baby.
i have learned it
ain't like they say
in the newspapers.

Malcolm

do not speak to me of martydom
of men who die to be remembered
on some parish day.
i don't believe in dying
thouh i too shall die
and violets like castanets
will echo me.

yet this man
this dreamer,
thick-lipped with words
will never speak again
and in each winter
when the cold air cracks

with frost, i'll breathe
his breath and mourn
my gun-filled nights.
he was the sun that tagged
the western sky and
melted tiger-scholars
while they searched for stripes.
he said, "fuck you white
man. we have been
curled too long. nothing
is sacred now. not your
white faces nor any
land that separates
until some voices
squat with spasms."

do not speak to me of living.
life is obscene with crowds
of white on black.
death is my pulse.
what might have been
is not for him/or me
but what could have been
floods the womb until i drown.

blk / rhetoric

(for Killebrew Keeby, Icewater,
Baker, Gary Adams and
Omar Shabazz)

who's gonna make all
that beautiful blk / rhetoric
mean something.
                    like
i mean
            who's gonna take

the words
        blk / is / beautiful
and make more of it
than blk / capitalism.
                u dig?
      i mean
           like who's gonna
take all the young / long / haired
natural / brothers and sisters
and let them
        grow till
           all that is
impt is them
        selves
           moving in straight /
revolutionary / lines
           toward the enemy
(and we know who that is)
             like. man.
who's gonna give our young
blk / people new heroes
      (instead of catch / phrases)
      (instead of cad / ill / acs)
      (instead of pimps)
      (instead of wite / whores)
      (instead of drugs)
      (instead of new dances)
      (instead of chit / ter / lings)
      (instead of a 35¢ bottle of ripple)
      (instead of quick / fucks in the hall / way
        of wite / america's mind)
like.   this.   is an S O S
    me.   calling.........
                calling.........
                      some / one
    pleasereplysoon.

A Poem for My Father

how sad it must be
to love so many women
to need so many black
perfumed bodies weeping
underneath you.
             when i remember all those nights
i filled my mind with
long wars between short
sighted trojans & greeks
while you slapped some
wide hips about in
your pvt dungeon,
when i remember your
deformity   i want to
do something about your
makeshift manhood.
i guess
            that is why
on meeting your sixth
wife, i cross myself
with her confessionals.

Poem No. 3

i gather up
each sound
you left behind
and stretch them
on our bed.
            each nite
i breathe you
and become high.

Towhomitmayconcern

watch out fo the full moon of sonia
shinin down on ya.
git yo/self fattened up man
you gon be doing battle with me
ima gonna stake you out
grind you down
leave greasy spots all over yo/soul
till you bone dry. man.
you gon know you done been touched by me
this time.
ima gonna tattoo me on you fo ever
leave my creases all inside yo creases
i done warned ya boy
watch out
for the full moon of sonia
shinin down on ya.

A. B. Spellman

(1935–)

ALWAYS HAVE ENVIED painters because they can work with the music turned up loud while I cannot write a word with Charlie Parker on. All of the painters who are friends of mine dance as they work. They stroke in time & review their progress with riffs in their mouths. Their work is action, music is action; action in sound integrates with action in color. I cannot do this.

I have had periods in which I have started my work in a place so far from reason that only the maddest of Surrealists live there. But this differs from the continual rearrangement of the synapses that Cecil Taylor accomplishes so easily. I have been told that I have made some poems of power, but they could barely breathe in a small jazz room like The Half-note with John Coltrane blowing wide open. I do not mean to suggest with false modesty that my poems are entirely bereft of song, but the cold matter that embodies words makes me tune my senses on reality & reason; any music in my lines follows, it does not lead. In a long-lost poem I wrote that, "like all black dancers I am played by drums & saxophones." True, but I never have been able to achieve in poetry the immediate staccato caress of bebop. The sound & rhythm that I can call to the poem may at best have a kind of swing but they are not swing.

So I cannot claim to be a jazz poet. Though rhythm & sound are important to my work, I am more a poet of the eye than of the ear; though some of my poems are conversational enough to say well, I am more a poet of the page than of the stage. My work is neither oral nor aural.

God, I envy painters.

I Looked & Saw History Caught

I looked & saw history caught
on a hinge, its two heads
like a seesaw rocking

up & down, up
& down, the eyes of the one
turned in on the Inner
College of Murder for
White Ones Especially

black & yellow beef before the
blacks of the eyes in the deathhead.
that head swings down to

ward what has been western, up
with pocketsful of shit to spread
on hectares of earth, earth
warm with the voicings of minnow
eucalyptus & cowrie, it being human

in the eye of the deathhead to people
the drumhead of history with its own
cripple progeny. thus the drumhead swings

up by the weight of death
sinking, closer to sun, grins open
to let the weather in, over clouds
of air made thick by those
opposing eyes, rotting of their own
interior commerce.
                      O let that fruithead swing
                      down to root, & may its shoots
                      spring the sweeter past

Edward S. Spriggs

(1934–)

I NEVER MAKE A BUSINESS of poetry, nor poetry into a business. I am serious about the need that poetry satisfies within me, but does not have to feed me. I do make an effort to be free of formal structures as such. My fantasy is to craft works that communicate with future generations through what I have coined as "Wemembering" poems, which I also think of as "wememetic" poems. In both instances, I contrive and channel collective memory to transmit culturally based observations and attitudes—simple or propositional—that reflect our expressed or perceived sentiments. Simply put, I want my poems to resonate beyond the context of their inspiration. Accessibility is always a concern. Inspiration is variegated, as are often the resulting poems.

Two of the highest beacons that illuminate the soupy fog of American poetry for me have been Langston Hughes and Melvin Tolson.

For Brother Malcolm

there is no memorial site
in harlem
save the one we are building
in the street of
our young minds
till our hands & eyes
have strength to mould
the concrete beneath our feet

THE 1960s AND BEYOND

OUTSIDE THE BLACK ARTS MOVEMENT

Gerald Barrax

(1933–)

PASSION IS NECESSARY in poetry, but passion alone is not enough to turn an angry, passionate young man into a poet, especially if the only passions he has are anger and hate. I once heard Michael Weaver say that he hates having to quote Ezra Pound for anything. I agree, wholeheartedly. But give him his due—Pound made some of the wisest comments on poetry ever uttered. I have three of them on every syllabus for my creative writing students and on handouts I use for workshops:

> Technique is the test of a man's sincerity.
> The mastery of any art is the work of a lifetime.
> Poetry is an art and not a pastime.

.   .   .

Going from the particular to the universal is something that happens almost organically in most poetry. If it is a good poem—which I won't stop to define right now—if it is going to appeal to someone other than the poet, if the reader can share in the experience of the poem, then it will by itself have moved from the particular of the poet to the universal of the reader. . . . There is no such thing as a subject that is too "personal" to write about because one reason people read poems is to discover and recognize experiences similar to their own. When that happens, the "personal" is the "particular" that becomes universal for the reader.

Eagle. Tiger. Whale.

I'm old enough to stand,
a boy looking at himself
in the long mirror of a chifforobe,
Black child with sandy hair
tightly curled, hazel eyes.
I haven't learned the words,
I photograph everything into my cells:
my little yellow dress with puffed pleated shoulders
and my little pearl buttons;
my little high-topped white shoes and yellow socks;
my little blue ribbon somewhere.
The room behind me is dark,
nothing in the mirror but me
as in a spotlight, yet I feel her presence,
my seventeen-year-old mother, beautiful,
leaning somewhere behind me.
　　　　　No one can explain what I've seen, a slim Black
woman lying on her back, red geyser pumping from
her open mouth, she stares into the ceiling's yellow
eye. I see her from her right, the foot of the brass bed,
my head three feet high. Someone screams "Lord God
Lord God he done shot the woman" while the soft
splash, splash. I stand so calm, seeing, until somebody
yells "Git that chile outta here." Who knows who
knows how I got there from next door, visiting Aunt
Annie over in Gadsden, for neither mother nor father
is there to tell me "Forget it."
　　　　　　　　　　　　　　　dont tell dont
tell James Albert's sister whispers in the dim coal shed.
She has hair everywhere,
the only subject, verb, object, adverb
I can put together.
It's my birthday, I come to her yard
to pick figs from their tree. James Albert's
daddy said I can, I pull a fig,
she whispers "don't tell, don't tell,"

I feel my hand disappear into the hot full-noon mouth
of Alabama's summer solstice,
lips, lips, tongue curling around, probing
the fruit from my paralyzed fist.
She changes my hands from left to right,
leaves me partially ambidextrous and stuttering
to describe it.
              Now that I've read a lot,
I've learned boxes of "reflection," "homicide," "initiation"
to put visions into,
just as we have done with *eagle tiger whale god*
with handles and edges to finger,
inert and seamless,
no desire to break in, not letting anything out.
But there is that boy who can still do this:
In the Zaire rain forest a snow leopard like a ghost leaps
and with its perfect knives
slices open this box I've made.

King: April 4, 1968

for Eva Ray

When I was a child
in the Fall the axes fell
in Alabama and I tried
to be somewhere else,
but the squeals of the pigs dying
and hogs and the sight of their
opened throats were everywhere.

I wasn't given that kind of stomach.

When I was 14, I killed
my last thing bigger than a mouse
with my Daisy Red Ryder,
a fat robin on a telephone wire,

still singing,
as my first shot went high
I sighted down and heard from where I was
the soft thud of the copper pellet in his
fat red breast. It just stopped
and fell over backwards
and I had run away
before it hit the ground, taking
my stomach with me.

I'll never know about people—
if the soft thing in the stomach can be cut out—
because I missed all the wars—
but when I learned that non
violence kills you anyway
I wished
I wished I could do it I wished I
could
do you know what it means to wish
you could kill to
wish you were given that?

But I am
me. Whatever made me made
you, and I anesthetize the soft thing
to stop squirming when
you do it brothers I shout
righton righton rightON
my heart is with you
though my stomach is still in Alabama pig
pens.

Lucille Clifton

(1936–2010)

POETRY IS ABOUT more than logic. Poetry, it seems to me—what I tell my students—comes from both intellect and intuition. One doesn't separate oneself out. It's not either/or; it's both/and again. And so if I write, I must write out of the whole of what I am. Poetry, in my opinion, is not an intellectual exercise. But it has, I think, become something like that, or it often becomes something like that. But it has to come from not just my head but from everything that I am. And it's a balancing act, just like most things. It's about balancing. Now in writing poems, of course, I have to use my intellect. But that's not all that I use. I use intuition. I even use fear, you know. I try to use everything that I am.

· · ·

One of the things I think I might have done in my life is just to try to speak for those who have not yet spoken, to try to tell the stories that have not yet been told. Maybe that's what a poet does. Maybe what a poet does is to try to keep alive the whole story of what it means to be human, to try to tell the truth. Somewhere I said that the purpose of the poet is to tell the truth. When I say truth, I don't mean fact. Not at all. In a poem, I'm not sure that fact is a biggie. I mean it's big, but it's not that big. But truth is necessary; it's big. Tell the truth about things, maybe just to see clearly, as clearly as possible. I tell students that the purpose of a poet is to see what they look at, and hear what they listen to. To go beyond the obvious. To go down deep and to bring up what's there. Nowadays people often choose poetry as a profession. As to why I'm a poet, I have no clue. Because I didn't choose it as a profession. My way of being is unique, I think, for now. I've never studied poetry, I've never had creative writing classes, and I didn't graduate from college. So I didn't take the general path. But even when I was young I knew that I wrote poems. So it was something that seemed natural for me.

lazarus

first day
i rose from stiffening
into a pin of light
and a voice calling
"Lazarus, this way"
and i floated or rather
swam in a river of sound
toward what seemed to be
forever   i was almost
almost there when i heard
behind me
"Lazarus, come forth" and
i found myself twisting
in the light for this
is the miracle, mary   martha;
at my head and at my feet
singing my name
was the same voice

second day
i am not the same man
borne into the crypt.

as ones return from otherwhere
altered by what they have seen,

so have i been forever.
lazarus.
lazarus who was dead.

what entered the light was one man.
what walked out is another.

     third day
on the third day i contemplate
what i was moving from
what i was moving toward

light again and
i could hear the seeds
turning in the grass   mary
martha i could feel the world

now i sit here in a crevice
on this rock   stared at
answering questions

sisters stand away
from the door to my grave
the only truth i know

leda 1

there is nothing luminous
about this.
they took my children.
i live alone in the backside
of the village.
my mother moved
to another town. my father
follows me around the well,
his thick lips slavering,
and at night my dreams are full
of the cursing of me
fucking god fucking me.

leda 2

a note on visitations
sometimes another star chooses.
the ones coming in from the east
are dagger-fingered men,
princes of no known kingdom.
the animals are raised up in their stalls
battering the stable door.
sometimes it all goes badly;
the inn is strewn with feathers,
the old husband suspicious,
and the fur between her thighs
is the only shining thing.

leda 3

a personal note (re: visitations)
always pyrotechnics;
stars spinning into phalluses
of light, serpents promising
sweetness, their forked tongues
thick and erect, patriarchs of bird
exposing themselves in the air.
this skin is sick with loneliness.
You want what a man wants,
next time come as a man
or don't come.

far memory
a poem in seven parts

1
convent

my knees recall the pockets
worn into the stone floor,
my hands, tracing against the wall
their original name, remember
the cold brush of brick, and the smell
of the brick powdery and wet
and the light finding its way in
through the high bars.

and also the sisters singing
at matins, their sweet music
the voice of the universe at peace
and the candles their light the light
at the beginning of creation
and the wonderful simplicity of prayer
smooth along the wooden beads
and certainly attended.

2
someone inside me remembers

that my knees must be hidden away
that my hair must be shorn
so that vanity will not test me
that my fingers are places of prayer
and are holy   that my body is promised
to something more certain
than myself

3
again

born in the year of war
on the day of perpetual help.

come from the house
of stillness
through the soft gate
of a silent mother.

come to a betraying father.
come to a husband who would one day
rise and enter a holy house.

come to wrestle with you again,
passion, old disobedient friend,
through the secular days and nights
of another life.

4
trying to understand this life

who did i fail, who
did i cease to protect
that i should wake each morning
facing the cold north?

perhaps there is a cart
somewhere in history
of children crying "sister
save us" as she walks away.

the woman walks into my dreams
dragging her old habit.
i turn from her, shivering,
to begin another afternoon
of rescue, rescue.

5
sinnerman

horizontal one evening
on the cold stone,
my cross burning into
my breast, did i dream
through my veil
of his fingers digging
and is this the dream
again, him, collarless
over me, calling me back
to the stones of this world
and my own whispered
hosanna?

6
karma

the habit is heavy.
you feel its weight
pulling around your ankles
for a hundred years.

the broken vows
hang against your breasts,
each bead a word
that beats you.

even now
to hear the words
defend
protect
goodbye
lost or
alone
is to be washed in sorrow.

and in this life
there is no retreat
no sanctuary
no whole abiding
sister.

7
gloria mundi

so knowing,
what is known?
that we carry our baggage
in our cupped hands
when we burst through
the waters of our mother.
that some are born
and some are brought
to the glory of this world.
that it is more difficult
than faith
to serve only one calling
one commitment
one devotion
in one life.

Jayne Cortez

(1936–)

POETRY AND MUSIC

I AM SENSITIVE to word sounds, and for years I have been known as a sound poet—without the presence of musicians & music. The sounds of words and languages are an important part of my poetic expression. Out of the sound comes the image or set of images, and that is the poem which becomes the center post for encounters, the point for departures and the melodic impulse for players of musical instruments. I see it, I hear it, and I put my mouth on paper and say it in collaboration with musicians, whose main concentration is spontaneity & improvisation. . . . I formed my own band, The Firespitters, in order to experiment and reveal more fully the possibilities of poetry and music. It's a natural, supernatural & surreal combination of attitudes, feelings, dreams, experiences, and abilities. I mix images; I control the punctuation and phrasing, the emphasis and repetition; I convey the variation of sounds and the complexity of ideas. The musicians respond with their interpretations and extensions. They energize the call and response process. The overall sound of the collaboration is unpredictable.

Solo Finger Solo

When evening goes down into its jelly   jelly   jelly
into drainpipe cuts and stitches and vaccinations
protruding from arms

And spirit of the five-by-five man pushes
his sweet potatoes in the air
feather daddy leaps into a falcon of tropical bird squats
rubber legs swing into off-beat onijos   onijos
then into your solo finger solo
the blues chantress jumps up and
repeats her nasal volcanic chant   calling

Count Basie   Count Basie   Count Basie

And Count Basie
you burn through this timbale of goose flesh rhythms
a drop of iodine on your starfish lips
the intonation of your kiss of melodica trilling into
a labyrinth of one o'clock jumps
into corpuscle flashes of the blues torpedo
the erupting volcano of the blues shouters   chanting your name

Count Basie   Count Basie   take 'em to Chicago   Count Basie

And Count Basie
you punctuate this strong bourbon mist of gamma globulin breath
a mixture of chords like serpentariums coiling
from the deep everglades of your body
and when the luscious screams of three-headed root doctors split
Kansas City reeds in unison with the triple tapping
double stopping   slowing grinding   loosey butt night swinging
    with
the blues chantress
erupting volcano of the blues torpedoes chanting your name

Count Basie
you reach through the bottom of the music
way down between cross rhythm vamps
below air stream of the lowest octave
into depths of a sacred drum
and Count Basie   Count Basie   Count Basie
how powerful and dignified and exquisite and
direct and sharp
your solo finger solo is

In the Morning

Disguised in my mouth as a swampland
nailed to my teeth like a rising sun
you come out in the middle of fish-scales
you bleed into gourds wrapped with red ants
you syncopate the air with lungs like screams from yazoo
like X-rated tongues
and nickel-plated fingers of a raw ghost man
& somewhere stripped like a whirlwind
stripped for the shrine room
you sing to me through the side face of a black rooster

In the morning   in the morning   in the morning
all over my door like a rooster
in the morning   in the morning   in the morning

And studded in my kidneys like perforated hiccups
inflamed in my ribs like three hoops of thunder through a screw
a star-bent-bolt of quivering colons
you breathe into veiled rays and scented ice holes
you fire the space like a flare of embalmed pigeons
and palpitate with the worms and venom and wailing flanks
and somewhere inside this fever
inside this patinaed pubic and camouflaged slit

stooped forward on fangs
in rear of your face
you shake to me in the full crown of a black rooster

In the morning   in the morning   in the morning

Masquerading in my horn like a river
eclipsed to infantries of dentures of diving spears
you enter broken mirrors through fragmented pipe spit
you pull into a shadow ring of magic jelly
you wear the sacrificial blood of nightfall
you lift the ceiling with my tropical slush dance
you slide and tremble with the reputation of an earthquake
and when I kick through walls
to shine like silver
when I shine like brass through crust in a compound
when I shine   shine   shine
you wail to me in the drum call of a black rooster

In the morning   in the morning   in the morning
gonna kill me a rooster
in the morning
early in the morning
way down in the morning
before the sun passes by
in the morning   in the morning   in the morning

In the morning
when the deep sea goes through a dog's bite
and you spit on the tip of your long knife
In the morning   in the morning
when peroxide falls on a bed of broken glass
and the sun rises like a polyester ball of menses
in the morning
gonna firedance in the petro
in the morning
turn loose the blues in the funky jungle
in the morning
I said when you see the morning coming like

a two-headed twister
let it blow   let it blow
in the morning   in the morning
all swollen up like an ocean in the morning
early in the morning
before the cream dries in the bushes
in the morning
when you hear the rooster cry
cry rooster cry
in the morning   in the morning

I said
disguised in my mouth like a swampland
nailed to my teeth like a rising sun
you come out in the middle of fish-scales
you bleed into gourds wrapped with red ants
you syncopate the air with lungs like screams from yazoo
like X-rated tongues
and nickel-plated fingers of a raw ghost man
& somewhere stripped like a whirlwind
stripped for the shrine room
you sing to me through the side face of a black rooster

In the morning   in the morning   in the morning

Michael S. Harper

(1938–)

I MEAN TO SUGGEST a shifting of zones of poetic discourse. There was something about the nature of metrics that forced an accommodation to the mechanics of the count. So much of my own music was announced to me in the auditory registers of phrasing. The world as I saw it was a cadence of song with speech elements that were fundamental to a theory of increment, a kind of progression that clarified the makings of voice in good and bad times.... I began to write poems because I could not see those elements of my life that I considered sacred reflected in my courses of study: scientific, linguistic, and literary. In the hope of creating fresh space for my majority—those years of maturity that would allow thought and action to become one—I set out on a path to document those elements of contradiction most salient to my antenna and to find a speech that would have some influence on the world.... Against this backdrop, any poetic efforts I have made over the last three decades in formal application are a barometric reading of the sanctity of family and the miseducation of the poet.

The Yellow Dishes

You taste the lemon of speech
all the way from El Paso *chile verde*

two idioms of the same tongue
two shadows in the range of Fort Bliss

one could be lying in the coffin
of a saint at Notre Dame

the Indiana of the klan
like border ruffians everywhere

whenever you hear the name Chairman
Walcott you shudder, his hexameters

of touch just out of view
as a jetty, eclipse, now horizon

in Harvard Yard near the institute
the dreadlocks of shame fall into holographs

and now astride Mt. St. Auburn's episcopal elite
you find the segment of the self

in the pulse of slave narratives
and tell the story of the self

as a modern crucifix
and reach across the *crossroads*

as a song only you can sing
delicious as the taste of lemon

"po' wayfaring stranger" on the fenway
how luscious the waterways of Rio Grande

[for Barbara 9 21 98]

Yaddo, Mrs. Ames & Black Men

I worked in the icehouse
and she complained:
late hours, bad for compost,
bad for the muse
one person removed;

he thought: I must get my own Yaddo.

Once he stood in the circle
of pine-topped trees
though he has to go to Skidmore to fire ovens

and probably would not have been invited
back
because of the hours he worked 'round the clock

There is a vantage point
at winter table above the office
that allows for every
conversation

including this one:
archival
pastoral
digital as the schematic softens

for one's face sags
during the day
the muscles relaxing

do you want a morning cast?

much laughter [MSH's Iowa BLUES & LAUGHTER]

for "character" talks back
behind the screen

but this is winter

one cannot be trusted
in the outhouse any time of day

and the icehouse
is always one person removed

keeps itself ready for late hours

more monitoring than usual
for this brand of fly in a late, bad time:

ointment too hot for salve on any wound

> *[in memory of Ed Wilson, sculptor-extraordinaire,*
> *who spent time in Iowa, knew Baltimore's worst over-*
> *lords, camped in every vestige of tradition, both head*
> *and heart, decamped in Vestal, New York: and how he*
> *loved tunes!]*

Coliseum Pool, 1960 (Dream)

With a full keyring, beach bathtowel,
and a kickboard,
he lets her into the pool
in the shallow end
which, Olympic size,
is six feet deep,
and because it is dark
takes off his sweats, sneakers
and disappears under the surface;
on his toes
he can barely breathe
in the darkness
and it is cold.

She comes to the edge;
in moonlight she could see
him clearly, but it is overcast,
and the burgers and fries
are in her throat
and her pounding heart
takes up the squat
on the beach towel,
which has his initials
on both sides of his color
scheme:
        she utters his name
which has a music
she has written
in his science notebook
with her very fine hand;

and from the surface
he calls to her;
unafraid, except for her hair,
she slides into his arms;
from this distance, inches
at neck, her arched toes
on his bobbing feet
and like him, smooth
to the coldness of the water
whose slosh is like all bathtubs
overfilled; in his ear,
in the clearest tones,
she admonishes her beautician,
and asks him, no matter what,
to keep her head dry.

This is forbidden fruit (mango);
he hears "Earth Angel" and "Gypsy
Woman" in the sockhop of his sternum
and keeps her head dry.

              for Karen

Don't Explain: A Ballad Played by Dexter Gordon

The one you hold in your arms is not `Maxine` (his living wife &
    manager)
And because you love tonal music you must listen: scrunch against
    her close-up

You are not lucid: have not written anything down: this "calendar
    event" do-wah
The chordal structures at the moment cut you as butter-knife cuts
    you: toastfully

You bleed as sacraments finally prescient in sinews, her gloss most
    delicious
Confessionals and Penance not the same in late-to-come-manhood,
    are they, altar boy?

Your Brooklyn habit of `shul` & flag@P.S. 25 jewish holidays: `you`
    `will get caught`
Staten Island Ferries canvas clover & dale: getting under her skin-
    flint, Indian scout

You remember Muriel Burwell—then Doreen loops into your `Physi-`
    `ology` textbook
You recite `William Blake's` songs: dress-ups sock-hops dishevel
    her blue stockings

`"Mrs. Germann doesn't like you: might you help me`
    `with my Lab. assignments? I have keys."`
You are in the world of Dolphy and Wardell Gray: `"Like Sonny"` &
    `"Soul Eyes"`

`Trane's tenor hums fantasies of the third rail:` you
    spell this three-some-raga-blues
remember the cadences of `"Sonny's Blues"` torn-out of `Parti-`
    `san Review` (Iowa hawkeye)

Langston's cues had a feel for lineal substitution: but no feel for
    incremental-leaping
Bird was different: praxis his woodshed free of 'territory
    bands'—Kansas City uptime

Now you have your grip—her bunches—your gardening & its truck
    without trowels
You say this slowly Citation in and out of the **Derby**: then she fell
    out: huckleberries

My mother's handmade dress just before the Comus
    dance she'd sown herself
Horace Silver's band on "Six Pieces of Silver"—it was 1958—
    annual leave, Senior Blues

When she turned into your back you were not looking: pink &
    pointed-oriole-nipples
"All the Things You Are" came rushing forth: **"teach me to
    swim"** says: MSH's lifeguard X

San Pedro/Malibu Beach I am not visiting without lunch/rowboat/
    condoms
Toliver's resonant pitch on every ring-finger: sanguine itch & then
    bootcamp, pal

June Jordan

(1936–2002)

POETRY IS A POLITICAL ACT because it involves telling the truth. In the process of telling the truth about what you feel or what you see, each of us has to get in touch with himself or herself in a really deep, serious way. Our culture does not encourage us to undertake that attunement. Consequently, most of us really exist at the mercy of other people's formulations of what's important.

But if you're in the difficult process of living as a poet, you're constantly trying to make an attunement to yourself which no outside manipulation or propaganda can disturb. That makes you a sturdy, dependable voice—which others want to hear and respond to. So, poetry becomes a means for useful dialogue between people are not only unknown, but mute to each other. It produces a dialogue among people that guards all of us against manipulation by our so-called leaders.

.   .   .

I became a poet because my father forced me to read and memorize and recite from Shakespeare's plays, the Bible, and the poetry of Paul Lawrence Dunbar and Edgar Allan Poe—all before I was five years old. This literature was completely incomprehensible to me, but I became immersed in the sounds of the language of these great writers. That, of course, was the hook that I seized in order to try and memorize this stuff so I could avoid getting beaten in the morning. The music of language became extremely important to me, and obvious to me. By the time I was seven I was writing myself. I was a poet.

What Would I Do White?

What would I do white?
What would I do clearly full
of not exactly beans nor
pearls my nose a manicure
my eyes a picture of your wall?

I would disturb the streets by
passing by so pretty kids
on stolen petty cash would look
at me like foreign
writing in the sky
I would forget my furs on any chair.
I would ignore the doormen at the knob
the social sanskrit of my life
unwilling to disclose my cosmetology,
I would forget.

Over my wine I would acquire
I would inspire big returns to equity
the equity of capital I am
accustomed to accept

like wintertime

I would do nothing.
That would be enough.

Current Events

He did not!
He did so!
He did not!
I'm telling you!

You lie!
Uh-unhh.
You're kidding me!
Cross my heart and hope to die!
Really?
No shit!
Yeah?
Yeah!
The What?
The Ayatollah Khomeini!
Getoutahere.
Square business!
The Who?
The Ayatollah Khomeini of Iran!
So?
So he said it!
Big deal.
That's what I'm saying:
Thursday
November 15th
1979
the headline reads:
IRAN SET TO
FREE WOMEN
AND BLACKS
Run that by, again!
Okay:
Thursday
November 15th
No! Not that part!
Just wait a second:
Thursday
November 15th
1979 and
this is the headline:
IRAN SET TO
FREE WOMEN
AND BLACKS:
See now
I told you it's a big deal!

How was I supposed to know?
Girl
you better keep up with the news!
Yeah, yeah:
I'm planning to!

Adrienne's Poem: On the Dialectics of the Diatonic Scale

Supposing everytime I hit this key
somebody
crumples to the ground or stops
breathing for a minute or begins to strangle
in the crib

Supposing everytime I play this chord
ribs
smash
brain-cells shrink
and a woman loses all of her hair

Supposing everytime I follow a melody
the overtones irradiate five Filipino
workers
burning their bodies
to bone

A-Flat. *A. A*-Sharp.
C. F. G. C.
Suppose my music is a hyper-
homicidal harp
and I'm just playing

Bob Kaufman

(1925–1986)

WANT TO BE ANONYMOUS. . . . I don't know how you get involved with univolvement, but I don't want to be involved. My ambition is to be completely forgotten.

from Jail Poems

1

I am sitting in a cell with a view of evil parallels,
Waiting thunder to splinter me into a thousand me's.
It is not enough to be in one cage with one self;
I want to sit opposite every prisoner in every hole.
Doors roll and bang, every slam a finality, bang!
The junkie disappeared into a red noise, stoning out his hell.
The odored wino congratulates himself on not smoking,
Fingerprints left lying on black inky gravestones,
Noises of pain seeping through steel walls crashing
Reach my own hurt. I become part of someone forever.
Wild accents of criminals are sweeter to me than hum of cops,
Busy battening down hatches of human souls; cargo
Destined for ports of accusations, harbors of guilt.
What do policeman eat, Socrates, still prisoner, old one?

3

In a universe of cells—who is not in jail? Jailers.
In a world of hospitals—who is not sick? Doctors.
A golden sardine is swimming in my head.
Oh we know some things, man, about some things
Like jazz and jails and God.
Saturday is a good day to go to jail.

6

There have been too many years in this short span of mine.
My soul demands a cave of its own, like the Jain god;
Yet I must make it go on, hard like jazz, glowing
In this dark plastic jungle, land of long night, chilled.
My navel is a button to push when I want inside out.
Am I not more than a mass of entrails and rough tissue?
Must I break my bones? Drink my wine-diluted blood?
Should I dredge old sadness from my chest?
Not again,
All those ancient balls of fire, hotly swallowed, let them lie.
Let me spit breath mists of introspection, bits of me,
So that when I am gone, I shall be in the air.

8

All night the stink of rotting people,
Fumes rising from pyres of live men,
Fill my nose with a gassy disgust,
Drown my exposed eyes in tears.

13

The jail, a huge hollow metal cube
Hanging from the moon by a silver chain.
Someday Johnny Appleseed is going to chop it down.

17

After spending all night constructing a dream,
Morning came and blinded me with light.
Now I seek among mountains of crushed eggshells
For the God damned dream I never wanted.

20
Now I see the night, silently overwhelming the day.

25
We sat at a corner table,
Devouring each other word by word,
Until nothing was left, repulsive skeletons.

29
Link by link, we forged the chain.
Then, discovering the end around our necks,
We bugged out.

Written in San Francisco City Prison
Cell 3, 1959

Battle Report

One thousand saxophones infiltrate the city,
Each with a man inside,
Hidden in ordinary cases,
Labeled FRAGILE.

A fleet of trumpets drops their hooks,
Inside at the outside.

Ten waves of trombones approach the city
Under blue cover
Of late autumn's neoclassical clouds.

Five hundred bassmen, all string feet tall,
Beating it back to the bass.

One hundred drummers, each a stick in each hand,
The delicate rumble of pianos, moving in.

The secret agent, an innocent bystander,
Drops a note in the wail box.

Five generals, gathered in the gallery,
Blowing plans.

At last, the secret code is flashed:
Now is the time, now is the time.

Attack: the sound of jazz.

The city falls.

I Have Folded My Sorrows

I have folded my sorrows into the mantle of summer night,
Assigning each brief storm its allotted space in time,
Quietly pursuing catastrophic histories buried in my eyes.
And yes, the world is not some unplayed Cosmic Game,
And the sun is still ninety-three million miles from me,
And in the imaginary forest, the shingles hippo becomes the gay
    unicorn.
No, my traffic is not addled keepers of yesterday's disasters,
Seekers of manifest disembowelment on shafts of yesterday's pains.
Blues come dressed like introspective echoes of a journey.
And yes, I have searched the rooms of the moon on cold summer
    nights.
And yes, I have refought those unfinished encounters. Still, they
    remain unfinished.
And yes, I have at times wished myself something different.

The tragedies are sung nightly at the funerals of the poet;
The revisited soul is wrapped in the aura of familiarity.

Walking Parker Home

Sweet beats of jazz impaled on slivers of wind
Kansas Black Morning / First Horn Eyes/
Historical sound pictures on New Bird wings
People shouts / boy alto dreams / Tomorrow's
Gold belled pipe of stops and future Blues Times
Lurking Hawkins / shadows of Lester / realization
Bronze fingers—brain extensions seeking trapped sounds
Ghetto thoughts / bandstand courage / solo flight
Nerve-wracked suspicions of newer songs and doubts
New York altar city / black tears / secret disciples
Hammer horn pounding soul marks on unswinging gates
Culture gods / mob sounds / visions of spikes
Panic excursions to tribal Jazz wombs and transfusions
Heroin nights of birth / and soaring / over boppy new ground.
Smothered rage covering pyramids of notes spontaneously
    exploding
Cool revelations / shrill hopes / beauty speared into greedy ears
Birdland nights on bop mountains, windy saxophone revolutions.
Dayrooms of junk / and melting walls and circling vultures/
Money cancer / remembered pain / terror flights/
Death and indestructible existence
In that Jazz corner of life
Wrapped in a mist of sound
His legacy, our Jazz-tinted dawn
Wailing in his triumphs of oddly begotten dreams
Inviting the nerveless to feel once more
That fierce dying of humans consumed
In raging fires of Love.

African Dream

In black core of night, it explodes
Silver thunder, rolling back my brain,
Bursting copper screens, memory worlds
Deep in the star-fed beds of time,
Seducing my soul in diamond fires of night,
Faint outlines, a ship-momentary fright
Lifted on waves of color,
Sunk in pits of light,
Drummed back through time,
Hummed back through mind,
Drumming, cracking the night.
Strange forest songs, skin sounds
Crashing through—no longer strange.
Incestuous yellow flowers tearing
Magic from the earth.
Moon-dipped rituals, led
By a scarlet god,
Caressed by ebony maidens
With daylight eyes,
Purple garments,
Noses that twitch,
Singing young girl songs
Of an ancient love
In dark, sunless places
Where memories are sealed,
Burned in eyes of tigers.

Suddenly wise, I fight the dream;
Green screams enfold my night.

Etheridge Knight

(1931–1991)

I UNDERSTAND POETRY and the poet as a song—as a chant; the poem and the poet are like songs. They are mystical. When you say things in a chant they take on a different meaning from what you say—and you may be saying the same words—in everyday speech. What's involved is music—a kind of arrangement of the sounds that create in you a certain feeling.... In music, a certain beat is set up and you find yourself patting your foot. These are the same rituals in poetry. That's the reason for the devices in poetry—rhyme and rhythm. They set up a oneness. If anyone is patting their feet at the same time, a ritual is being played out. Basically, I see the poet as singing in a sense that his sounds are put together in harmony or in a structure which differs from just plain talking. I see poets basically as singers, as preachers, as prophets.

The Violent Space
(or when your sister sleeps around for money)

Exchange in greed the ungraceful signs. Thrust
The thick notes between green apple breasts.
Then the shadow of the devil descends,
The violent space cries and angel eyes,
Large and dark, retreat in innocence and in ice.
(Run sister run—the Bugga man comes!)

The violent space cries silently,
Like you cried wide years ago
In another space, speckled by the sun
And the leaves of a green plum tree,
And you were stung
By a red wasp and we flew home.
(Run sister run—the Bugga man comes!)

Well, hell, lil sis, wasps still sting.
You are all of seventeen and as alone now
In your pain as you were with the sting
On your brow.
Well, shit, lil sis, here we are:
You and I and this poem.
And what should I do? should I squat
In the dust and make strange markings on the ground?
Shall I chant a spell to drive the demon away?
(Run sister run—the Bugga man comes!)

In the beginning you were the Virgin Mary,
And you are the Virgin Mary now.
But somewhere between Nazareth and Bethlehem
You lost your name in the nameless void.
"O Mary don't you weep don't you moan"
O Mary shake your butt to the violent juke,
Absorb the demon puke and watch the white eyes pop,
(Run sister run—the Bugga man comes!)

And what do I do. I boil my tears in a twisted spoon
And dance like an angel on the point of a needle.
I sit counting syllables like Midas gold.
I am not bold. I cannot yet take hold of the demon
And lift his weight from you black belly,
So I grab the air and sing my song.
(But the air cannot stand my singing long.)

The Idea of Ancestry

1

Taped to the wall of my cell are 47 pictures: 47 black
faces: my father, mother, grandmothers (1 dead), grand-
fathers (both dead), brothers, sisters, uncles, aunts,
cousins (1st and 2nd), nieces, and nephews. They stare
across the space at me sprawling on my bunk. I know
their dark eyes, they know mine. I know their style,
they know mine. I am all of them, they are all of me;
they are farmers, I am a thief, I am me, they are thee.

I have at one time or another been in love with my mother,
1 grandmother, 2 sisters, 2 aunts (1 went to the asylum),
and 5 cousins. I am now in love with a 7 yr old niece
(she sends me letters in large block print, and
her picture is the only one that smiles at me).

I have the same name as 1 grandfather, 3 cousins, 3 nephews,
and 1 uncle. The uncle disappeared when he was 15, just took
off and caught a freight (they say). He's discussed each year
when the family has a reunion, he causes uneasiness in
the clan, he is an empty space. My father's mother, who is 93
and who keeps the Family Bible with everybody's birth dates
(and death dates) in it, always mentions him. There is no
place in her Bible for "whereabouts unknown."

2

Each fall the graves of my grandfathers call me, the brown
hills and red gullies of mississippi send out their electric
messages, galvanizing my genes. Last yr/like a salmon quitting
the cold ocean-leaping and bucking up his birth stream/I
hitchhiked my way from L.A. with 16 caps in my pocket and a
monkey on my back. And I almost kicked it with the kinfolks.
I walked barefooted in my grandmother's backyard/I smelled the old
land and the woods/I sipped cornwhiskey from fruit jars with the men/
I flirted with the women/I had a ball till the caps ran out
and my habit came down. That night I looked at my grandmother

and split/my guts were screaming for junk/but I was almost
contented/I had almost caught up with me.
(The next day in Memphis I cracked a croaker's crib for a fix).

This yr there is a gray stone wall damming my stream, and when
the falling leaves stir my genes, I pace my cell or flop on my bunk
and stare at 47 black faces across the space. I am all of them,
they are all of me, I am me, they are thee, and I have no children
to float in the space between.

Hard Rock Returns to Prison from the Hospital for the Criminal Insane

Hard Rock / was / "known not to take no shit
From nobody," and he had the scars to prove it:
Split purple lips, lumbed ears, welts above
His yellow eyes, and one long scar that cut
Across his temple and plowed through a thick
Canopy of kinky hair.

The WORD / was / that Hard Rock wasn't a mean nigger
Anymore, that the doctors had bored a hole in his head,
Cut out part of his brain, and shot electricity
Through the rest. When they brought Hard Rock back,
Handcuffed and chained, he was turned loose,
Like a freshly gelded stallion, to try his new status.
And we all waited and watched, like a herd of sheep,
To see if the WORD was true.

As we waited we wrapped ourselves in the cloak
Of his exploits: "Man, the last time, it took eight
Screws to put him in the Hole." "Yeah, remember when he
Smacked the captain with his dinner tray?" "He set
The record for time in the Hole—67 straight days!"
"Ol Hard Rock! man, that's one crazy nigger."
And then the jewel of a myth that Hard Rock had once bit
A screw on the thumb and poisoned him with syphilitic spit.

The testing came, to see if Hard Rock was really tame.
A hillbilly called him a black son of a bitch
And didn't lose his teeth, a screw who knew Hard Rock
From before shook him down and barked in his face.
And Hard Rock did *nothing.* Just grinned and looked silly,
His eyes empty like knot holes in a fence.

And even after we discovered that it took Hard Rock
Exactly 3 minutes to tell you his first name,
We told ourselves that he had just wised up,
Was being cool; but we could not fool ourselves for long,
And we turned away, our eyes on the ground. Crushed.
He had been our Destroyer, the doer of things
We dreamed of doing but could not bring ourselves to do,
The fears of years, like a biting whip,
Had cut deep bloody grooves
Across our backs.

Belly Song
(for the Daytop Family)

> "You have made something
> Out of the sea that blew
> And rolled you on its salt bitter lips.
> It nearly swallowed you.
> But I hear
> You are tough and harder to swallow than most . . ."
>   —S. MANSFIELD

1

And I and I / must admit
that the sea in you
        has sung / to the sea / in me
and I and I / must admit
that the sea in me

   has fallen / in love
   with the sea in you
because you have made something
out of the sea
   that nearly swallowed you

And this poem
This poem
This poem / I give / to you.
This poem is a song / I sing / I sing / to you
from the bottom
   of the sea
      in my belly

This poem
This poem
This poem / is a song / about FEELINGS
about the Bone of feeling
about the Stone of feeling
   And the Feather of feeling

2
This poem
This poem
This poem / is /
a death / chant
and a grave / stone
and a prayer for the dead:
   for young Jackie Robinson
a moving Blk / warrior who walked
among us
   with a wide / stride—and heavy heels
moving moving moving
thru the blood and mud and shit of Vietnam
moving moving moving
thru the blood and mud and dope of America
   for Jackie / who was /

a song
and a stone
and a Feather of feeling
    now dead
and / gone / in this month of love

This poem
This poem / is / a silver feather
and the sun-gold / glinting / green hills breathing
river flowing—for Sheryl and David—and
their first / kiss by the river—for Mark and Sue
and a Sunday walk on her grand / father's farm
for Sammy and Marion—love rhythms
for Michael and Jean—love rhythms
love / rhythms—love rhythms—and LIFE.

3
This poem
This poem
This poem
This poem / is / for ME—for me
and the days / that lay / in the back / of my mind
when the sea / rose up /
    to swallow me
and the streets I walked
    were lonely streets
    were stone / cold streets

This poem
This poem / is /
for me / and the nights
    when I
wrapped my feelings
    in a sheet of ice
and stared
    at the stars
        thru iron bars
           and cried
in the middle of my eyes . . .

This poem
This poem
This poem / is / for me
  and my woman
  and the yesterdays
when she opened
  to me like a flower
but I fell on her
  like a stone
I fell on her like a stone . . .

4
And now—in my 40th year
  I have come here
to this House of Feelings
to this Singing Sea
and I and I / must admit
that the sea in me
  has fallen / in love
with the sea in you
because the sea
that now sings / in you
  is the same sea
that nearly swallowed you—
  and me too.

       Seymour, Connecticut
       June 1971

Audre Lorde

(1934–1992)

A POEM GROWS out of the poet's experience, in a particular place and a particular time, and the genius of the poem is to use the textures of that place and time without becoming bound by them. Then the poem becomes an emotional bridge to others who have not shared that experience. The poem evokes its own world.

.   .   .

I am a Black, Lesbian, Feminist, warrior, poet, mother doing my work. I underline these things, but they are just some of the ingredients of who I am. There are many others. I pluck these out because, for various reasons, they are aspects of myself about which a lot of people have had a lot to say, one way or another. My sexuality is part and parcel of who I am, and my poetry comes from the intersection of me and my worlds. There is nothing obscene about my work.... It is about revolution and change. That is what my writing serves. We are living in a sick society, and any art which does not serve change—i.e., does not speak the truth—is beside the point.... The white artistic community has very belatedly seen the handwriting on the wall, which says no society is going to finance its own reorganization and demise, or contribute to a culture bent upon radical change, not for long. I mean, Black people, Black writers, and other artists of color have known that for a very long time.

.   .   .

Now, what does my sexuality have to do with my writing? I believe in the power of the erotic. What does my blood, or my heart, or my eyes have to do with my writing? They are all inseparable.

Coal

I
is the total black, being spoken
from the earth's inside.
There are many kinds of open
how a diamond comes into a knot of flame
how sound comes into a word, coloured
by who pays what for speaking.

Some words are open like a diamond
on glass windows
singing out within the passing crash of sun
Then there are words like stapled wagers
in a perforated book,—buy and sign and tear apart—
and come whatever wills all chances
the stub remains
an ill-pulled tooth with a ragged edge.
Some words live in my throat
breeding like adders. Others know sun
seeking like gypsies over my tongue
to explode through my lips
like young sparrows bursting from shell.
Some words
bedevil me.

Love is a word, another kind of open.
As the diamond comes into a knot of flame
I am Black because I come from the earth's inside
now take my word for jewel in the open light.

To My Daughter the Junkie on a Train

Children we have not borne
bedevil us by becoming
themselves
painfully sharp and unavoidable
like a needle in our flesh.

Coming home on the subway from a PTA meeting
of minds committed like murder
or suicide
to their own private struggle
a long-legged girl with a horse in her brain
slumps down beside me
begging to be ridden asleep
for the price of a midnight train
free from desire.
Little girl on the nod
if we are measured by the dreams we avoid
then you are the nightmare
of all sleeping mothers
rocking back and forth
the dead weight of your arms
locked about our necks
heavier than our habit
of looking for reasons.

My corrupt concern will not replace
what you once needed
but I am locked into my own addictions
and offer you my help, one eye
out
for my own station.
Roused and deprived
your costly dream explodes
into a terrible technicoloured laughter
at my failure

up and down across the aisle
women avert their eyes
as the other mothers who became useless
curse their children who became junk.

Fishing the White Water

Men claim the easiest spots
stand knee-deep in calm dark water
where the trout is proven.

I never intended to press beyond
the sharp lines set as boundary
named as the razor names
parting the skin
and seeing the shapes of our weaknesses
etched into afternoon
the sudden vegetarian hunger for meat
tears on the typewriter
tyrannies of the correct
we offer mercy   forgiveness
to ourselves and our lovers
to the failures we underline daily
insisting upon next Thursday
yet forgetting to mention each other's name
the mother of desires
wrote them under our skin.

I call the stone   sister   who remembers
somewhere my grandmother's hand
brushed   on her way to market
to the ships
you can choose   not to live
near the graves where your grandmothers sing
in wind through the corn.

There have been easier times
for loving   different richness
if it were only the stars
we had wanted
to conquer
I could turn from your dear face
into the prism light makes
along my line
we cast into rapids
alone   back to back
laboring the current.

In some distant summer
working our way farther from bone
we will lie in the river
silent as caribou
and the children will bring us food.

You carry the yellow tackle box
a fishnet over your shoulder
knapsacked
I balance the broken-down rods
our rhythms pass through the trees
staking a claim   in difficult places
we head for the source.

Clarence Major

(1936–)

I'M A VISUAL THINKER. I imagine the thing before or as I am developing it on the page, and I can see it. I can see it as clearly as I can see actors on a stage. And if I don't see it clearly, I keep working at it until it becomes clear. The colors, the sounds, the smells, everything that gives it its particular life. But in writing and in painting, you don't put everything in. Even if you're a Nature painter, for example, you go to Nature for inspiration, and you change it. Nature is not perfect. It's never really been a matter of translating Nature to the canvas. It's a matter of selecting and rearranging Nature, which is what you do when you write a scene. You select the elements that are going to make that scene come alive. And anyway you could not possibly put everything in. So I think you have to have a kind of ear and an eye for those elements that add just the right touch.

On Watching a Caterpillar Become a Butterfly

It's a slow, slow process
sitting here on the porch

just watching a clumsy male
milkweed caterpillar

slowly turning itself
into a graceful butterfly while

hanging from the underside
of a withered leaf dark with life

among a pungent cluster
of other rich leaves

from this old branch
leaning over my banister

at a certain point
in its natural growth

probably caterpillar thinks it can
decide which way

it wants to go—to fly or die,
by simply taking an oath and dreaming

of having the loveliness
of, say, the male-*crow* butterfly

or having the stripes
of the tiger butterfly

or maybe stay in the *chrysalis* stage
or become a *friar* butterfly

caterpillar is a dreamer
and a natural schemer

in this changing light where
cuticle-shaped drops of fluid

glow and glow
like red nectar

changing itself
as it hangs from the bottom

of this green leaf
wedged tightly

as though bolted
with metal springs,

throwing off that light,
a light of silver-purple

outlined in gold—
golden trimmings

The Great Horned Owl

He glides, descending
to the forest floor—

his round face
like an African

mask, carved out
of soft wood.

He sails down smoothly
(his face as wide

as his shoulders
with big ears

jutting straight up
like horns)—descending

to the forest floor
where a mouse

scurries along.
And the wingspan

of the great night bird
spreads, showing

his white plumage
in this, his pale phase,

as he snatches it

he sings and dances
in the half-light,

scattering dry leaves,
spreading again

those great wings.
On the takeoff

he fans his fluffy
black-and-white tail.

Clay Bison in a Cave

Clay-tan, eyeless,
voiceless, even in a sense weightless,
in motion yet motionless still
for centuries and centuries,
stuck in this motion
of climbing, perhaps lost, these
two Paleolithic bison,
heads lifted, strained back
to the black endless sky,
as they climb toward sunny grass.
Which black sky? Which grass?

Rock-step by rock-step,
up they go, on up and up.
The black sky at the top of the cave.
The grass that is always
more a promise in a dream
than that sweet kiss
blown by water-colored wind.

Territorial Claims

While walking a narrow path
high above Boulder, looking

for a spot to sit, I paused
at a large rock

alongside a path
and there stood on the rock

(with grays and greens—
the same as her own colors)

a pregnant lizard, a skink
standing high

careful to keep her belly
lifted

from her perch, the hot surface
while she, weary of trouble, watched

me, cooly calculating
my next move

determined to protect
her inner bubble

skinny enough to go to war
with me, if necessary

so I moved off the path
far from her, making a large circle

I regained the path all the same
up

beyond her rock and again
took up my search

for a place
I could claim my own

Colleen J. McElroy

(1935–)

I THINK OF A POEM as a marriage of music and painting through the instrument of words. Poetry, like dance, involves the whole body. The artist, the dancer, the poet is constantly aware of the rhythms of the body, from heartbeat to breath to expression of self and perceptions of the outer world. The genesis of poetry was, and is, inspiration: ordinary events as well as divine inspiration, dreams as well as daily life, gossip, stories, or signifying as well as eulogies and elegies. We are all molecules in motion, meeting by coincidence the demands of the physical world. By the same token, language is always in motion, in the throes of its own dance. The poet hears the rhythms of language, the images paced to the rhythm of the story told and retold. The poem becomes, then, the sum of what pulls the reader into the movement of language, what enhances the narrative, and gives rhythm to the dreams of daily life breathing on the page. Poetry is a painterly act of what draws the dancer to the dance. The tension between what we imagine and what exists, the tension of politics, gender, race, and ethnicity, and, most of all, spirituality. The art of it all is how we represent what we see: a flower, a baby, lovers, the act of walking, the dance. Molecules in motion.

Paris Subway Tango

> somebody almost walked off
> wid alla my stuff
> —NTOZAKE SHANGE

at best you can say
your judgment was tainted
by movies and old
expectations
    Paris equals passion
    n'est pas? so why not ride
          the subway just this one
          night despite
          all the echoes of caution
          dancin : in your head
          and how even in Harlem
          you have a thousand
reasons to stay above
ground instead
of ruttin : beneath
the fabric of some city
that seems clipped
from a Romare Bearden
nightmare book
    but this is Paris
    Chagall and Degas
and men whose eyes fill
with mysteries
of North African deserts
          so the first brush
          of body against body
and you get this wild rush
of good sense fightin : desire
yellin : *I want**I don't want*
like salt messin : with perfume
    and although his face

flirts with your imagination
    his hand's dippin : into your purse
    so, baby, you fling aside all caution
lay him out with a one-two step
swingin : hip to hip
like when you used to
Arthur-Murray-in-a-hurry
    part Hustle : part Hucklebuck
    matchin : his every tightass turn
    groovin : between track and train
        like the two of you been
        practicin : M*T*V
except your purse is the cash prize
so do it, girl, cause
maybe this home-boy-arab
don't know you
ain't takin : no shit
even if you gotta tango
on this metro clear to the end

Crossing the Rubicon at Seventy

we do not know the name
of the river that roils
beneath us until we arrive
at its shores—until we give
reason to pass along or stay
there where waters sound
like uncut jewels swirling
in a tide pool—until the little
boats we've made fold like kites
in a storm—until we've come
to that point where turning mid-
stream is outside reason and staying
lays sour on the tongue—know

you have shaped a raft before
floating with the current toward
another long day's journey—know
you have yet another reason
to reinvent yourself before
you take the last route home

Ishmael Reed

(1938–)

I CONSIDER MYSELF a fetish-maker. I see my books as amulets, and in ancient African cultures words were considered in this way. Words were considered to have magical meanings and were considered to be charms. . . . Everyone thought that I had made some innovations, but the more I get into Afro-American culture, the more I find that I've really not done anything that former writers haven't.

.   .   .

It was interesting to me that before vaudevillians would go into a town they would read the local newspaper and derive their skits from that. I think that this explains much of my writing. American vaudeville is a serious mystery drama of civilization. I believe that. It is necessary to change the act from time to time, and I think I'm conscious of that when I'm writing. I want a switch, a shift, a shift in syntax, a shift in structure, a change, a surprise! Like instead of Indians invading, you're liable to get Teutonic Germans.

I am a Cowboy in the Boat of Ra

"The devil must be forced to reveal any such physical evil
(potions, charms, fetishes, etc.) still outside the body
And these must be burned." (Rituale Romanum, *published*
1947, endorsed by the coat-of-arms and introductory
Letter from Francis Cardinal Spellman)

I am a cowboy in the boat of Ra,
sidewinders in the saloons of fools
bit my forehead   like   O
the trustworthiness of Egyptologists
who do not know their trips. Who was that
dog-faced man? they asked, the day I rode
from town.

School marms with halitosis cannot see
the Nefertiti fake chipped on the run by slick
germans, the hawk behind Sonny Rollins' head
or the ritual beard of his axe; a longhorn winding
its bells thru the Field of Reeds.

I am a cowboy in the boat of Ra. I bedded
down with Isis, Lady of the Boogaloo, dove
down deep in her horny, stuck up her Wells-Far-ago
in daring midday getaway. "Start grabbing the
blue," I said from top of my double crown.

I am a cowboy in the boat of Ra. Ezzard Charles
of the Chisholm Trail. Took up the bass but they
blew off my thumb. Alchemist in ringmanship but a
sucker for the right cross.

I am a cowboy in the boat of Ra. Vamoosed from
the temple i bide my time. The price on the wanted
poster was a-going down, outlaw alias copped my stance
and moody greenhorns were making me dance;

     while my mouth's
shooting iron got its chambers jammed.

I am a cowboy in the boat of Ra. Boning-up in
the ol West i bide my time. You should see
me pick off these tin cans whippersnappers. I
write the motown long plays for the comeback of
Osiris. Make them up when stars stare at sleeping
steer out here near the campfire. Women arrive
on the backs of goats and throw themselves on
my Bowie.

I am a cowboy in the boat of Ra. Lord of the lash,
the Loup Garou Kid. Half breed son of Pisces and
Aquarius. I hold the souls of men in my pot. I do
the dirty boogie with scorpions. I make the bulls
keep still and was the first swinger to grape the taste.

I am a cowboy in his boat. Pope Joan of the
Ptah Ra. C/mere a minute willya doll?
Be a good girl and
bring me my Buffalo horn of black powder
bring me my headdress of black feathers
bring me my bones of Ju-ju snake
to get my eyelids of red paint.
Hand me my shadow

I'm going to town after Set

I am a cowboy in the boat of Ra

look out Set   here i come Set
to get Set   to sunset Set
to unseat Set   to Set down Set

          usurper of the Royal couch
          —imposter RAdio of Moses' bush
          party pooper O hater of dance
          vampire outlaw of the milky way

The Pope Replies to the Ayatollah Khomeini

My Dear Khomeini:

I read your fourteen thousand dollar
ad asking me why the Vatican waited
all of these years to send an envoy
to complain about conditions in Iran
You're right, we should have sent one
when the Shah was in power, look,
I'm in total agreement with you
Khomeini, that Christ, had he lived in
Iran under the Shah, would have led the
biggest damned revolt you ever saw

Believe me, Khomeini, I knew about
the Shah's decadence, his extravagance
his misdeeds, and how he lolled about
in luxury with Iran's loot
I knew about the trail of jewels which
led to his Dad's capture
but a fella has to eat and so when
David Rockerfeller asked me to do something
how could I refuse?

You can afford to be holier than thou
What is it, 30 dollars per barrel these days?
You must be bathing in oil
While each day I suffer a new indignity

You know that rock record they made me
do? It's 300 on the charts which is about
as low as you can get.
And I guess you read where I
had to call in all those Cardinals and
for the first time reveal the Vatican
budget?
I had to just about get down on my hands

and knees to get them to co-sign for a
loan
The Vatican jet has a mechanical problem
and the Rolls-Royce needs a new engine
The staff hasn't been paid in months
and the power company is threatening to
turn off the candles

To add to that, the building inspector
has listed us as having 30,000 code
violations
I'm telling you, Khomeini, that
so many people are leaving the church
I have this nightmare where I
wake up one day in Los Angeles and
I'm the only one left

Pretty soon we'll be one of those
cults you read about in the *San
Francisco Chronicle*
And so, Khomeini, I promise
you that when we pay off the
deficit, I won't send an envoy
I'll come visit you myself

I'd like to discuss this plan
that Patriarch Dimitrios, of
the Greek Orthodox Church, and I
just came up with

You know, we haven't spoken to
those fellows in 900 years but
when you are 2 billion dollars
in the red
You'll talk to anybody

Ed Roberson

(1939–)

YOU KNOW HOW an association in a [John] Donne poem opens world upon world of the same poem. I do that in my work with the worlds (black, white, male, educated, middle class, reclusive—yet all of them black) in which I live. Not with Donne's specific metaphysical formality; but there is an exacting formality of my own in what I do. Yet I have little reason to expect that readers get more than one world of connections when they experience my work in today's language.

I can justifiably assume that my work is not given access to or presumed to carry certain of the multiple associations to be got from a reading of a mainstream work. I can also reasonably assume that many readers think a black writer writes only from that black perspective which has nothing in it for them / nothing of them in it beyond just the intellectual value of a "perspective" . . . without ever guessing that I might occasionally have no choice but to write from their own white "black perspective" at the same time; how could they see this, peeping through closed eyes? . . . You miss some lines. I knew this soon after I began writing; it has only become that much clearer.

Sit In What City We're In

1

Someone may want
to know one day how many steps we took

          to cross one of our streets,
to know there were hundreds
in one city   streets in one direction
          and as many
as could fit between the land's contours
crossing those,
          our hive grid as plumb
as circles flanked into the insect
hexagonals,
          our stone our steel.

Others may want more
to know what steps aside the southern streets required
          to flow at last free to clear,
to know how those kept out
set foot inside, sat down, and how
          the mirrors around the lunch counter
reflected the face
to face—the cross-mirrored depth reached
          infinitely back into either—
the one pouring the bowl over the head of
the one sitting in
          at that counter

          this regression this seen stepped
back into nothing both ways
From which all those versions of the once felt sovereign
          self   locked together in the mirror's
march from deep caves of long alike   march back
into the necessary   together
          living   we are
reflected in the face to face we are
a nation facing ourselves our back turned
          on ourselves   how
that reflection sat in demonstration
of   each face
          mirror reflecting into mirror generates

a street cobbled of the heads of
our one
                    long likeness
the infinite regressions.
The oceans, themselves one,   catch their image
               hosed by riot cops down the gutter into
The sphere surface
river
                  looked into   reflects
                  one face.

2

A here and not-here division of things,
where the future is in the same
                  place as the past, is
maybe one of the African
masquerades of time   like these facing mirrors
              in which time is making faces
at you from the elemental
moment,   the faced and yet to be
                faced
in one frame   where from, where to are faces of here.
Where a few in the crowd at that lunch counter
                face their actions.

Where what dark is revealed
in the face to face   is a back to back.
                The words of that god
against us. In the glass, the face
observed, changes the looking at that face, cancels both
               their gaze to transparence, opens
around it a window containing right here
around us;   and in that window these
                same
— in the lapped frame of this one moment —
are the other one's
                world we see into in ours:

You can't smash the mirror   there but it break here.
And in it you see   that you can't see
                              your own back,
your angel of the unfamiliar, of that not like
your face . . . See.   and
                              relax that hand raised against
your impossible
hand   that reaches to give the pat, to okay   touch you
                              at the unfamiliar,   those stubs of your
back.

3

From mirror to window   glass   to thin air
Between   and finally, us with no you nor I
                              but being
— with all our world —   inside the other;
but there only in   our each part yet having
                              no displacement of the other,
just as each wishes   the self not lost, shared
being in common in each other   being
                              as different as
night and day still   of one spin.
The sphere surface
                              of this river.

To know ourselves as a god would know us
would make us gods
                              of ourselves   we are so
fused in communication we happen at once,
as if as one   gazing
                              ball pivot of critical gardens,
cocked Creations.   Here, in the glass of the city,
a godlike simply knowing doesn't determine
                              what built
raft of citizen draughts where the street runs
up the walk to the door   ocean teased apart
                              to its each drop

                              of rain.

Someone is riding a bus, too tired
for everything   except what is right;
            a god has his back against the wall
of a church in Birmingham;
the marchers take to the streets.
               Someone may want to know
what city we're in
that curves glowing over the edge
          into an earth.

Eclogue

I wonder if anyone ever thought
to tell time with them   know where their shadow
tipped on 3 o'clock   which floor   which parking spot
from a window desk   or if they ever
stood completely over their own shade's dot
that moment they had no metered footprint;
a peek-a-boo we now find ticketed
as a before and an after   an either
side of a space the zero pulls into,
its long reserve wheel of nothing there.
Yet here a gnomon of absence bears its shadow
placement on some dial of brevity and cold
about life   about the footprint we may leave
empty of light   empty of even point to it.

Here it's flat and densely packed with people
unlike the empty open of the plain;
here our expanse   the grown over dumpsite
of the meadowlands wetlands or the shore
is corps of engineered   the bulldozer-beetle's
ball of dung shines in it   and somewhere the body
hidden in our shit to fake us innocent . . .

one of our jokes sometimes　things rise and float.

　　　　　　　　　　　　　　We in the morning
catch, from the train, in the green garbage runoff,
sight of white herons and the cormorants.
When they're there in the evening, we safely
assume the world hasn't gone anywhere;
a take of bearings　the same the next morning
when we'd see the lit towers on the island
we were headed for　we see now the hour.

From the Jersey side we take a bearing, as
on mountains from the vantage of the plain,
on the towers from the vantage of the
dirt-stiffened, unyielding, tarmac of marsh
grass　gray like steel grayed a vegetable steel
from blur and the exhausts of the turnpike.

Position with regard to surrounding objects
here is unlike in the mountains which give
a bearing even from deep within them, let you
see them from inside their formation.

Climbing to the high plateau of the street
from the subway, we check the peaks downtown
or midtown　skyscrapers for direction.
Walk a few doors up the block　they parallax
eclipsed by the postcard we no more see.

　　　　　　　　　*

There was a deep well lit its entire depth
at noon on the solstice　light without shadow:

so with an in-line position with regard
to the sun　any cast line of shadow

would indicate a curve; the distance between
one and not,　an arc of circumference.

That phrase of the psalm says death's shadow is
as deep as that valley which is our grave;

its length is the same cast everywhere   as deep;
no one's is further from death than another's;

death surrounds us   is our uncurbed circumference.
We map our way with only the bearing

of surrounding life   itself borderless
uncontrolled by the surface of our self.

The bridge towers of the Verrazano
are so far apart they tilt away from
each other on the curve of the earth   factored in.

I wonder if from the distance apart
of the The Towers you could figure that reach
'round of the world with this method of shadow?

The shadow of flesh casts how deep and far
a landscape of perspective?   how round
a circumference enough to fit the living

world   does a single life turning to its labor spin?
Take each story of a building as the radius
of expansion   we make of the earth,

concentric spheres   on Turtle Island,
the hundred ten circumferences go nova

So high a reach of vision set on so short
a perspective   the world on the turtle's back:
at top, the wake of star formation   at base, the animal

god.   the jealous Need.   a stomach
of feet   trying to stand through this.

What can we say of our own that stand
in Newark say   so far adrift from a chance

to wash   that the dirt on her feet cracks
into sores the skin of her soles   and steps her in
one more shit infection she has to kick,

one more occupation of her body by
her monkey rulers she will have to throw off
into space   off her back   burned out but clear

of starring habit.   Of her destroyed sun   say
it endows the landfill   on which to build a
new development   "We are the stuff of stars," Sagan says.

Ntozake Shange

(1948–)

[What makes a poet is] a very conscious effort to be concise and power-
ful and as illusory as possible, so that the language can, in fact, bring you
to more conclusions than the one in the poem, but that that one conclu-
sion can't be avoided, even though there are thousands of others roaming
around. And there should be wit and grace and a movement from one
image to another, so that there's no narrowness to the body of your work.
That to me would suggest someone is a poet.

my father is a retired magician
(for ifa, p.t., & bisa)

my father is a retired magician
which accounts for my irregular behavior
everythin comes outta magic hats
or bottles wit no bottoms & parakeets
are as easy to get as a couple a rabbits
or 3 fifty cent pieces/ 1958

my daddy retired from magic & took
up another trade cuz this friend of mine
from the 3rd grade asked to be made white
on the spot

what cd any self-respectin colored american magician
do wit such a outlandish request/ cept
put all them razzamatazz hocus pocus zippity-do-dah
thingamajigs away   cuz
colored chirren believin in magic
waz becomin politically dangerous for the race
& waznt nobody gonna be made white
on the spot   just
from a clap of my daddy's hands

& the reason i'm so peculiar's
cuz i been studyin up on my daddy's technique
& everythin i do is magic these days
& it's very colored
very now you see it/ now you
dont mess wit me
                    i come from a family of retired
sorcerers/ active houngans & pennyante fortune tellers
wit 41 million spirits critturs & celestial bodies
on our side
                    i'll listen to yr problems
                    help wit yr career   yr lover   yr wanderin spouse
                    make yr grandma's stay in heaven more gratifyin
                    ease yr mother thru menopause & show yr son
                    how to clean his room

YES YES YES   3 wishes is all you get
          scarlet ribbons for yr hair
                benwa balls via hong kong
                    a miniature of machu picchu

all things are possible
but aint no colored magician in her right mind
gonna make you   white
        i mean
                this is blk magic

you lookin at
         & i'm fixin you up good/ fixin you up good n colored
& you gonna be colored all yr life
& you gonna love it/ bein colored/ all yr life/ colored & love it
love it/ bein colored/

nappy edges (a cross country sojourn)

     st. louis/ such a colored town/ a whiskey
black space of history & neighborhood/ forever ours/
     to lawrenceville/ where the only road open
to me/ waz cleared by colonial slaves/ whose children never
moved/ never seems like/ mended the torments of the Depression
the stains of demented spittle/ dropped from lips of crystal women/
still makin independence flags/
     from st. louis/ on a halloween's eve to the veiled prophet/
usurpin the mystery of mardi gras/ made it mine tho the queen
waz always fair/ that parade/ of pagan floats & tambourines/
commemoratin me/ unlike the lonely walks wit liberal trick or
treaters/ back to my front door/ bag half empty/
     my face enuf to scare anyone i passed/ a colored kid/
whatta gas

         1)   here
             a tree
             wonderin the horizon
             dipped in blues &
             untended bones
             usedta hugs drawls
             rhythm & decency
             here a tree
             waitin to be hanged

     sumner high school/ squat & pale on the corner/ like
our vision/ waz to be vague/ our memory
of the war/ that made us free to be forgotten

becoming paler/ a linear movement from south carolina
to missouri/ freedmen/ landin in jackie wilson's yelp/ daughters of
the manumitted swimmin in tina turner's grinds/ this is chuck
berry's town/ disavowin misega-nation/ in any situation/ & they let
us be/ electric blues & bo diddley's cant/ rockin pneumonia &
boogie-woogie flu/ the slop & short-fried heads/ runnin always to
the river

/ from chambersbourg/ lil italy/ i passed everyday
at the sweet shoppe/ & waz afraid/ the cops raided truants/
regularly/ after dark i wd not be seen/ wit any other colored/
sane/ lovin my life/
in the 'bourg/ seriously expectin to be gnarled/
hey niggah/ over here/
& behind the truck lay five hands claspin chains/
round the trees/ 4 more sucklin steel/

hey niggah / over here
this is the borderline/
a territorial dispute/

hey/ niggah/
over here/
cars loaded wit families/ fellas from the factory/ one or two
practical nurses/ black/ become our trenches/ some dig into cement
wit elbows/ under engines/ do not be seen/ in yr hometown/ after
sunset we suck up our shadows/

2) i will sit here
my shoulders brace an enormous oak
dreams waddle in my lap
round to miz bertha's where lil richard
gets his process
run backwards to the rosebushes/ a drunk man/ lyin
down the block to the nuns in pink habits
prayin in a pink chapel
my dreams run to meet aunt marie
my dreams draw blood from ol sores
these stains & scars are mine
this is my space
i am not movin

Primus St. John

(1939–)

I BRING TO THE ART and practice of poetry the model of my maternal grandmother, who believed the function of racism is to deny us possibility, so don't accept that, and my maternal grandfather's negative capability—an island man easy with his fruit. I enjoy approaching tough subjects being friendly but not tame. I look forward to unexpected opportunities for childhood delight in a word or the nuance of an idea, and I usually try to make it my business to move through a poem like the man the Pointer Sisters say they like—"a slow man with an easy touch."

The Cigar Maker

He is not quite the color of coffee
steaming on the edge of her table
She can see that

He is not the taste of chocolate either
but at least as thick and sweet

He is not a sprinkling of cinnamon
over the secrets of her body

His ways are the ways of dough rising

So she gathers the moist tobacco leaves
that have come around the world
to the middle of her table

and wraps them
not so tightly that they do not draw
for this is the way he loves her

Trap a Congo

She dips the calabash
in the stew like a cat's paw
after the bush rat,
for her children.
Catching is giving in our folklore,
a bloodsong of meat's crimson lyricism
dipping back to the taste of the earth.
But *El Jefe*
he doesn't kill chickens or goats
to feed his children at all
he kills the mysteries of us he despises
the ones honoring the forest
not the trees themselves of course
but the spirits in their swaying
the ones asleep in the mangroves sometimes
or dancing once in a while on the sea's faces.
He kills us to kill our incantations
to kill our divinations . . .
What is the libation for killing twenty thousand of us?
Twenty-nine dollars apiece
Trap a congo . . .
pouring our blood from machetes like cane juice
hanging the screaming like raffia from the ceilings
rows of arms and legs like shards
heads rolling like precious stones

into the old Hidalgo legend of El Dorado.
We have been stacked on this altar
in huge numbers before
and it still doesn't seem to make white men
or men who think they can be white men, pure.

Catch and Release

Butte Creek steps out of the canyon
With all the ecstasy
Of the Florida A&M Marching Band
High stepping and juking rocks
Then rambling on to the valley floor
The way young life ought to . . .
I have hiked in for two hours
And by ten o'clock
My line is singing and dancing
To the enchantment of her beautiful
Silver-blue face
I am a shameless flirt
For her *Kokane and Rainbow*
Mountain White and Dolly Varden
I am the slut flying Green Drakes
And Stovepipes
Comparaduns and Girdle Bugs
Until I am almost as dark as the evening
And then I hike out.

Lorenzo Thomas

(1944–2005)

WHEN I FIRST BEGAN WRITING, I was an adolescent trying, as they say, to express myself. I recorded things that happened to me through either the spiritual or the practical world. I did that for quite a while until I realized that that is not a proper function for a poet. The proper function of the poet is to be a Cyrano, to be a ventriloquist, to speak not merely for one's self but for others.

. . .

I think of poetry as performance, and one studies one's craft for the purpose of being able to perform well. The individual poem is not that important—and that's the interesting thing about poetry, too. It's like music in that the practice and the artifact are the same thing. . . . So the individual poem is not going to change the world unless you believe there are magical sounds which, when uttered, have efficacy in the real world, which I believe. But then one spends one's time practicing until one is able to produce those sounds effectively.

Onion Bucket

All silence says music will follow
No one acts under any compulsion
Your story so striking and remain unspoken
Floods in the mind. Each one trying now

To instigate the flutter of light in your
Ear. The voice needling the flashy token
Your presence in some room disguised
As the summer of the leaves. Hilltops
Held by the soft words of the running
Wind. What lie do you need more than this
The normal passion. And each thing says
Destroy one another or die. Like a natural
Introducing here on this plane to Europe
The natural. A piece of furniture, smell
Taste some connection to your earth and
"Realize" nothing more than you need
Another view nothing more than you need yourself
Or that is beautiful. Or your luck that speaks.
Lifting its shoulders out the language
Of the streets. Above. The sky worried
Into its own song. Solid rhythm. She stays
Too close for a letter, scared of a telegram
The finger drum express. Impatient blues
Anxious blues. Her chemical song loud and
Bright in his dimension. This is the world.
The vegetables are walking.

Downtown Boom
Houston ca. 2001 A.D.

There are no gospel singers
Anymore

On the corners
They held down for Jesus
Valets park cars
At restaurants for fancy people
On expense accts or dates

So many times
People come up to me
And say, Billy
Hey wait a minute
You not Billy!

You can see the new ballpark
Just past the Courthouse

But which way is redemption?

Alice Walker

(1944–)

T HE WRITING OF MY POETRY is never consciously planned; although
I become aware that there are certain emotions I would like to
explore. Perhaps my unconscious begins working on poems from these
emotions long before I am aware of it. I have learned to wait patiently
(sometimes refusing a good line, images, when they come to me, for fear
they are not lasting), until a poem is ready to present itself—*all* of itself, if
possible. I sometimes feel the urge to write poems way in advance of ever
sitting down to write. There is a definite restlessness, a kind of feverish
excitement that is tinged with dread. The dread is because after writing
each batch of poems I am always convinced that I will never write poems
again. I become aware that I am controlled by them, not the other way
around. I put off writing as long as I can. Then I lock myself in my study,
write lines and lines and lines, then put them away, underneath other
papers, without looking at them for a long time. I am afraid that if I read
them too soon they will turn into trash; or worse, something so topical
and transient as to have no meaning—not even to me—after a few weeks.
(This is how my later poetry—writing differs from the way I wrote *Once*.)
I also attempt, in this way, to guard against the human tendency to try to
make poetry carry the weight of half-truths, of cleverness. I realize that
while I am writing poetry, I am so high as to feel invisible, and in that
condition it is possible to write anything.

Revolutionary Petunias

Sammy Lou of Rue
sent to his reward
the exact creature who
murdered her husband,
using a cultivator's hoe
with verve and skill;
and laughed fit to kill
in disbelief
at the angry, militant
pictures of herself
the Sonneteers quickly drew:
not any of them people that
she knew.
A backwoods woman
her house was papered with
funeral home calendars and
faces appropriate for a Mississippi
Sunday School. She raised a George,
a Martha, a Jackie and a Kennedy. Also
a John Wesley Junior.
"Always respect the word of God,"
she said on her way to she didn't
know where, except it would be by
electric chair, and she continued
"Don't yall forgit to *water*
my purple petunias."

On Stripping Bark from Myself

Because women are expected to keep silent about
their close escapes I will not keep silent
and if I am destroyed (naked tree) someone will
please
mark the spot
where I fall and know I could not live
hearing their "how nice she is!"
whose adoration of the retouched image
I so despise.

No. I am finished with living
for what my mother believes
for what my brother and father defend
for what my lover elevates
for what my sister, blushing, denies or rushes
to embrace.

I find my own
small person
a standing self
against the world
an equality of wills
I have lived to understand.

Besides:

My struggle was always against
an inner darkness: I carry within myself
the only known keys
to my death—to unlock life, or close it shut
forever. A woman who loves wood grains, the color
yellow
and the sun, I am happy to fight
all outside murderers
as I see I must.

Sherley Anne Williams

(1944–1999)

I AM NOT A VERY political person in the sense of joining organizations or espousing political philosophies—my disenchantment with the exponents of Black Power began in 1967, while a graduate student at Howard University, when a friend and Black Power advocate disparaged my writing because I wasn't writing Richard Wright. I remain, more firmly now than then, a proponent of Black consciousness, of "The Black Aesthetic," and so I am a political writer. I try to elucidate those elements in our lives on which constructive political changes, those that do more than blackwash or femalize the same old power structure, can be built.

from Letters from a New England Negro

Mrs. Josiah Harris
No. 5 The Grange Street
Newport, Rhode Island

August 25, 1867

Dear Miss Nettie,

The School is in a spinney
down behind the old Quarters
where many of the freedmen

live. The teachers, myself
included, live in the Big
House, which—thus far!—has stirred
little comment among the
local whites.

The School is the largest
public building in which blacks
and whites can safely congregate.
Sunday services are held there
and many of the freedmen
attend. Miss Esther introduced
me to several as "the
herald of Emancipation's
new day."

They murmured discreetly
among themselves, the women
smiling quickly, the men
nodding or cutting their
eyes toward me. Finally an
older man stepped forward, "I'm is
Peter, Miss Patient Herald,"
he said, pumping my hand. Then,
with great satisfaction,
"Lotsa room in the Big House.

                              Now."

Miss Ann Spencer
Lyme on Eaton
New Strowbridge, Connecticut

August 30, 1867

Dear Ann,

Caution is not so necessary
here as in some other parts
of the state, but we hear of
the "night-riding" and terror
and so are careful. Yet, Miss
Esther's bearing is such that
she is accorded grudging
civility by even
rabid Rebels and though there
was at first some muttering
at young white women teaching
"nigras," Cassie and Beryl are
likewise accepted; thus the
School escapes reprisals.

And,
if the local ladies lift
their skirts aside as I pass—
Well, perhaps I <u>should</u> smirch them.

If my cast-off clothes are
thought unsuited to my station,
my head held too high as I
step back to let the meanest white
go before me, why— What then
is a concert in Newport

or a day in Boston compared
to the chance to be arrogant
amongst so many southerners!

October 22, 1867

The girls are bold, fingering
our dresses, marveling at
our speech. They cluster around
us at recess, peppering
us with questions about the
North and ourselves. Today, one
asked why I did not cover
my head or at least braid my
hair as is decent around
white folk. We do not speak of
hair in the north, at least in
public, and I answered sharply,
It is not the custom in
the North and I am from the
North—meaning, of course, that I
am freeborn.

I know how
chancy freedom is among
us and so have never
boasted of my birth. And
they were as much stung by my
retort as I by their question.
But in the moment of my
answer the scarves worn by the
women seemed so much a symbol
of our slavery that I would
have died before admitting
my childhood's longing for just
such patient plaiting of my

tangled hair or cover now
my wild and sullen head.

November 24, 1867

There was in Warwick Neck, at
the time we lived there, a black
woman called Miss Girt whose aunt
had bought her out of slavery
in the District some fifty
years before. She was a
familiar and striking figure
in that town where there were few
negroes; of that color we
called smoothblack—a dense and
even tone that seems to drink
the light. The strawberry pink
of her mouth spilled over onto
the darkness of her lips and
a sliver of it seemed to
cut the bottom one in two.

She kept a boarding house for
negroes, mostly men who worked
at odd jobs up and down the
Coast. The white children whispered
about it—though the house
differed only in being
set in a larger plot with
two or three vacant ones between
it and its nearest neighbors.
It was the closest thing to
a haunted house the town provided
and on idle afternoons
the white children "dared
the boogey man"—though they seldom

got close enough to disturb
Miss Girt or her boarders with
their rude calls and flourishes—
and withdrew giggling and
pushing at the slightest
movement or noise.

We went also,
on our infrequent trips
to town, to see the boogey
man and sometimes heard a strain
of music, a sudden snatch
of laughter. Or watched the white
children from a distance. Once
George Adam called out, "Here She
come," sending them into clumsy
flight and us into delighted
laughter. Once Miss Girt herself
came round the corner on the
heels of their cry, "Nigger!"

"And
a free one, too," she called and
laughed at their startled silence.
They fled in disorder,
routed, so George said, by the
boldness of this sally, and,
I thought, by the hot pink in
the laughing dark of Miss Girt's face.

February 15, 1868

I know you are not wholly
knowledgeable of all I
write you, dearest Ann, yet your
own eccentricity at

times allows you to apprehend
what most would miss. And I do
not expect answers or advice.
We stand outside each other's
lives and are enchanted with this
unlikely meeting: the blue-
stockinged white lady, the smart
colored girl. I stand now
outside the life I know as
negro. Sometimes, as I try
to make sensible all that
I would tell you, I see my
self as no more than a
recorder and you a listening
ear in some future house.

Al Young

(1939–)

A POEM BEGINS with images which are intimately related to feelings. I don't like to separate the two. That's one of the things that you're forced to do when you teach. You start dissecting poems for the purpose of analysis and after a while you start to think that way. You say, "Well, I'm going to write a poem. First I'll wait for the feeling and then I'll imbue it with the proper images." What happens with me is that I generally perceive things in terms of memory through imagery. I will have a feeling about something, perhaps something from my childhood. Before the words come, the pictures and the feelings will well up inside of me. The third section of the long poem "The Song Turning Back Into Itself" perhaps illustrates what I'm saying. It is simply one of my earlier memories in Ocean Springs, Mississippi, on the Gulf Coast near Biloxi. It's an attempt to use the imagery of my memories to re-create some of the earlier memorable feelings I had. I remember my father out in the backyard sawing wood. "Consider the little house / of sunken wood / in the dusty street / where my father would / cut his fingers / up to his ankles / in fragrant coils / of lumber shavings / the backyard of nowhere." This was the kind of life we were living there. Extremely poor. But in a strange kind of way they're very happy memories.

The Song Turning Back Into Itself 3

Ocean Springs Missippy
you don't know about that
unless youve died in magnolia
tripped across the Gulf
& come alive again
or fallen in the ocean
lapping up light
like the sun digging
into the scruffy palm leaves
fanning the almighty trains
huffing it choo-choo
straight up our street
morning noon & nighttrain
squalling that moan
like a big ass blues man
smoking up the sunset

Consider the little house
of sunken wood
in the dusty street
where my father would
cut his fingers
up to his ankles
in fragrant coils
of lumber shavings
the backyard of nowhere

Consider Nazis & crackers
on the same stage
splitting the bill

Affix it all to
my memory of Ma
& her love of bananas
the light flashing
in & out of our lives

lived 25¢ at a time
when pecans were in season
or the crab & shrimp
was plentiful enough
for the fishermen
to give away for gumbo
for a soft hullo
if you as a woman
had the sun in your voice
the wind over your shoulder
blowing the right way
at just that moment in history

Ravel: Bolero

Unraveling Ravel is no longer a secret;
it's all how you plop yourself
in the Spanishness of all this French
kissing in public

Dance!
That's what they say—the flute,
the muter of emotions older than time,
can dance itself.
Clarinet me that one,
Mister Tromborrorooney.

Ay, the clean, brown plains and slopes
of Spain forever Spain forever gallant
forever picaresque.

Saxophone says: I got your pictures;
I got my angles on all of this
and you're all full of steam—

Love is neither now nor
has it ever been tender;
it's castanets; it's the gypsy
of forever who takes you for a ride,
          my friend,
and hits you up for keeps.

A Dance for Ma Rainey

I'm going to be just like you, Ma
Rainey this monday morning
clouds puffing up out of my head
like those balloons
that float above the faces of white people
in the funny papers

I'm going to hover in the corners
of the world, Ma
& sing from the bottom of hell
up to the tops of high heaven
& send out scratchless waves of yellow
& brown & that basic black honey
misery

I'm going to cry so sweet
& so low
& so dangerous,
Ma,
that the message is going to reach you
back in 1922
where you shimmer
snaggle-toothed
perfumed &
powdered
in your bauble beads
hair pressed & tied back

throbbing with that sick pain
I know
& hide so well
that pain that blues
jives the world with
aching to be heard
that downness
that bottomlessness
first felt by some stolen delta nigger
swamped under with redblooded American agony;
reduced to the sheer shit
of existence
that bred
& battered us all,
Ma,
the beautiful people
our beautiful brave black people
who no longer need to jazz
or sing to themselves in murderous vibrations
or play the veins of their strong tender arms
with needles
to prove that we're still here

PART 2

Heirs

FIRST WAVE, POST-1960s

Ai

(1947–2010)

I WRITE ABOUT SCOUNDRELS; my specialty is generally scoundrels. If somebody's done a bad thing, I just talk about it. I don't prettify it or anything. My characters, a lot of them are disgusting—what they've done in the past. Somebody described them once as "last-ditch attempts at justification." And sometimes that's what my characters or my personae are doing: they're saying, "Yes, I did this and that thing, and perhaps it was evil. It was bad—maybe it was even evil—*but* this is why I *did* it. You don't know the circumstances surrounding it." And this is the telling; they're almost retelling what happened from *their* point of view. . . . I use "bad words" whenever I feel the need, you know, I just put 'em in there—*if* it's true to my character. I always like to think that I'm doing things that are true to character. And I hope that, when I'm dealing with violence, for example, that it's not gratuitous, that it's coming out of character that requires that. . . . I usually start with character, rather than a concept or an idea. If I do want to deal with an idea, I must create a character, in order to work from there, from that angle.

Hoover, Edgar J.

1

I'm the man behind the man
behind the man
and I have got my hands
in everybody's pockets.
I know who's been sticking his plug
in Marilyn Monroe's socket.
The shock it would give,
if everybody knew what King Arthur Jack
won't do to keep his rocket fueled.
I have files on everyone who counts,
yet they would amount to nothing,
if I did not have the will to use them.
Citizens must know their place,
but so must the President,
who simply decided one day
to hock his family jewels to the Mob.
They call me a cruel sonofabitch
just to aggravate me,
but my strength is truth.
I have the proof
of every kind of infidelity
and that makes me the one free man
in a country of prisoners
of lust, greed, hatred, need
greater than the fear of reprisal,
all the recognized sins
and all those unrecognizable,
except to me and God. Maybe God.

Sometimes my whole body aches
and I lie down on the floor,
just staring at the ceiling,
until I am feeling in control again,
my old confidence surging back
through me like electricity

and I get up, Frankenstein, revived
by the weakness of others
and as unstoppable as a handful of pills
that might kill you on a night like this,
like the night when Marilyn kissed it all goodbye.
It only came up roses after her show closed.
Too bad she had to row, row her boat
in lava lake.
They said they would make her a star.
Now far out in space,
her face big as a planet,
she looks down
on the whole pathetic, human race, wasting time,
as it shivers and shakes
down the conga line
behind Jack, Bobby, and me too.
When the voice on the phone
cried *"We're through"* and hung up,
she took an overdose,
trusting someone to save her,
but now she whispers,
"Honey, don't trust anybody
and never, ever fuck the head of state."

2
I had a head bald
as a licked clean plate
and a face . . .
Nobody ever said grace at my table,
yet, the god of judgment hovered over my head.
He led me down
dark halls to motel rooms,
where a locked door
and heavy perfume
could neither conceal, nor contain
the fumes of love that proclaimed
another fallen angel by his name.
Martin Luther King, Jr. preaches freedom,
but it means slavery for the white man.
It hands our keys to the robbers

and says, please, don't take anything.
Look at him on his knees
before pussy's altar.
Tomorrow with his wife beside him
he won't falter, as he shouts
from the pulpit about equality.
His words are a disease sweeping
through the colored people.
I can stop it if I choose.
I can release the tapes, the photographs
and end the so-called peaceful revolution,
but my solution is to sabotage discreetly,
to let someone else take the blame,
the Klan, or even another smoke,
who's younger and not broken in by privilege.
Someone like that Malcolm X,
that showstopping nigger,
who respects no boundaries
and hates the white man,
because he understands him.
He doesn't want to vote,
he doesn't want to tote that bail
in the name of integration.
He wants to sail back into blackness
and I say let him.
There is no such thing as freedom
and there never will be,
even for the white man.
The X-man knows it is eat, or be eaten
and Grandpa Hoover
has the biggest teeth.

3

They all wanted me
to take the A train to anonymity,
those who would seduce their own mothers,
after an audience with the Pope.
The Holy joke I call him.
I'd like to get a tape, or two,
of that crew in Rome.

A two-way mirror
somewhere in the Vatican, the camera rolling,
while some Cardinal is jerking off
over a silver bowl,
until his Vesuvius erupts again and again.
But I digress.
Now Lyndon Johnson and a negress,
that *is* delicious,
something best served on a platter.
Save it until after the elections
when it really matters.
I'm so scattered lately.
I feel like shattering all my Waterford crystal.
Ask me anything you want, but don't touch me.
I keep my pistol loaded.
Don't say I told you. Do.
I want the lowdown sonsofbitches
who betray me to know
I'm on to them like a fly on shit.
I will not rest,
until I spit in their mouths
and piss on their faces. The fools.
J. Edgar Hoover runs this country.
J. Edgar Hoover rules.

Conversation

for Robert Lowell

We smile at each other
and I lean back against the wicker couch.
How does it feel to be dead? I say.
You touch my knees with your blue fingers.
And when you open your mouth,
a ball of yellow light falls to the floor
and burns a hole through it.
Don't tell me, I say. I don't want to hear.

Did you ever, you start,
wear a certain kind of silk dress
and just by accident,
so inconsequential you barely notice it,
your fingers graze that dress
and you hear the sound of a knife cutting paper,
you see it too
and you realize how that image
is simply the extension of another image,
that your own life
is a chain of words
that one day will snap.
Words, you say, young girls in a circle, holding hands,
and beginning to rise heavenward
in their confirmation dresses,
like white helium balloons,
the wreaths of flowers on their heads spinning,
and above all that,
that's where I'm floating,
and that's what it's like
only ten times clearer,
ten times more horrible.
Could anyone alive survive it?

The Curious Journey of Ulysses Paradeece After a Hurricane

"It's your imagination," said Mama Paradeece.
"You can't feel nothing below your knees."
"That may well be," I answered,
"but I still feel something tickling me."
She said, "son, doctor done cut off your legs,
you may as well accept it now and go on."
"Anyhow, you don't listen to mama.
You never did, smoked that dope,
run out on your wife and kids,

now look at you
laid up, black and alone,
ain't got nobody, homeless, penniless and old."
I said, "Mama, I ain't black, I'm Creole like you."
She said, "that ain't the way the world sees you
might as well get used to it, I did,
anyway, your white blood ain't going to save you today."
"What you talking about?" I asked.
But Mama Paradeece had disappeared,
leaving me alone
in the hospital hallway
After awhile, the wind howled like a dog,
walls shook, lights went out
and it took all my strength
to raise up and look down the hall
where I seen water pouring through the doorway
and a nurse's aide wading toward me,
a strange look on her face.
She said, "Mr. Paradeece, I'll get you out somehow,"
but I could see she didn't know what to do
so I said, "save yourself, cause they done black tagged me.
I'm hopeless and that's the truth
it's no use trying to rescue me,"
but she said, "take this old man."
"What is it?"
"Ain't you never seen a life jacket before? It's from my boat.
My husband brought it to me, but he drowned,
'cause I couldn't hold him.
Now I got to go."
As she waded away with a sigh and a faint goodbye,
I knew I was going to die,
so I closed my eyes.

Lord have mercy, I'm still alive. I thought,
as I floated into the street beside the body of someone familiar,
but I couldn't quite remember who,
then it came to me. It was the nurse's aide,
now bloated and as dead as Mama Paradeece.
How long had I slept, I wondered,
holding on to the lifejacket,

as I bumped up against a tree whose branches snagged my robe
and tore it off me,
but I held on to the lifejacket anyway
and kept on drifting down the street.
I heard somebody call to me,
but I couldn't open my mouth without swallowing water.
I couldn't let go of the tree either
so I just held on until it got stuck on something
and broke me free.
I kept going, when a water moccasin swam up to me
I swear I heard him speak.
He said, "do you believe in Jesus?"
And I said, "occasionally. You gonna bite me?"
"What happened to your legs?" He asked.
"I got diabetes, doctor had to amputate below my knees."
"Why you want to live then?
Why don't you let me put you out of your misery?"
That's when I heard a shriek
as a big old bird, look like a hawk, or something
sank its beak down on that snake.
I couldn't help myself, I screamed
and the filthy water liked to drown me
when suddenly two arms wrapped around me
and pulled me up onto a porch.
When I caught my breath,
I saw a man with a flashlight bending down to look at me.
"That a dress you got on?" I asked.
"See," he said to a chihuahua in a fruit basket,
"what happened to this old man,
lost his legs in this cruel storm."
"Naw, they gone a long time before this," I whispered.
but I don't think he heard me.
"Come on, old fellow, we got to get you a beer. How's that sound?"
I nodded, as he held a beer can to my mouth
and I just about choked.
"Ain't you got no water?"
"Not to drink," he answered.
"Lemme rest a minute, then I'll take me another drink," I told him.
"What do you think is gonna happen to us now?"
"We gonna survive, pop," he said,

"otherwise we going to die. Either way, I'm dressed for it."
I said, "I guess you are."
then I slept and when I woke, it was daylight
and he was smoking a cigarette and holding the dog on his lap.
He was wearing a camouflage t-shirt, jeans, combat boots and a hat
that said, Vietnam Veteran.
"Funny," I said, "you don't look old enough for Vietnam."
"It's my dad's cap," he said. "He's dead now. Alcohol."
"That's sad," I told him,
but he just said, "water's rising." "We better head up to the roof."
"I'll carry you," he said, putting the dog in a leather pouch he wore
strapped across his chest
and lifting me onto his back.
Somehow we made it and there we sat three days
without food, or water
when at last, we heard a helicopter.
He stood up and waved his t-shirt over his head
as the sound grew louder and louder.
"Well, goddamn," he shouted, as the chopper
flew right over us.
"I second that," I told him. "It's no use, is it?" I said,
but miraculously, a row boat floated up beside us.
He climbed in first then, half-carried, half-dragged me
into the boat. Didn't have no paddles,
so we just floated wherever the water took us,
using our hands to push things aside.
until a few cans of pork and beans floated toward us
and a loaf of soggy bread which we ate,
not worrying about germs, worms, or anything
but food, food, food. He had a Swiss Army knife
which he used to open the beans
and then we had us a feast.
After that, I fell into another deep sleep
and when I woke, the boat was on fire,
I mean the oil in the water was
as the dog barked and struggled to get away
biting the man something awful
as he struggled to hold onto it, but finally, the dog got free
and jumped right into the flames

I tried to paddle with my hands, but I was afraid they would catch on
    fire
so I stopped, watching helplessly as the man followed the dog into
    the water
whereupon he himself was engulfed in flames,
leaving me alone with the awful smell of burning flesh in my nostrils
and the vision of a man on fire to carry to my own grave.
Who would save me now, I thought, as the boat suddenly floated away
from the flames and into the path of a larger boat
where strong hands lifted me onto the deck.
"Thank you, sir, oh, thank you," I murmured,
thinking I had seen him somewhere before as he disappeared
behind a stack of boxes of food and emergency kits.
"Who is that man?" I croaked
and a voice answered,
you've been saved by an actor come all the way from Hollywood
and I said, "good God,"
as I passed out again.

Now, I'm in Tucson, at the Villa Del Sol Rest Home.
I have my own room and a pair of prosthetic legs
the actor gave me
and sometimes, I use them, but I don't go anywhere,
I just stand in my room, staring out the window at all that sunshine,
wondering why Mama Paradeece doesn't come to see me anymore,
yet relieved too.
I don't miss the scolding and arguing,
the holding on to nothing but the emptiness
that was her after death interference in my life.
I've done enough of that.
Now all I want is to sit back down in my wheelchair
and spin it around on the dime of a time
I heard the sirens wail
and looked into the one-eyed storm,
then set sail without direction
but reached my destination anyway.

Cyrus Cassells

(1957–)

M Y POETRY HAS always been a mirror of my myriad travels and spiritual quests. My work is mystical, multicultural, and international in spirit; my five books have been very much concerned with issues of justice, war, conscience, the healing of trauma, as well as the restorative power of romantic and erotic love. I strive hard to make the language in my poems precise, musical, and memorable. My friend, the Paris-based American poet Ellen Hinsey, once said, "Poetry is an independent ambassador for conscience: it answers to no one, it crosses borders without a passport, and it speaks the truth." With my poetry, I like to think of myself as an intrepid African American ambassador working freely and fearlessly in the world.

Sally Hemings to Thomas Jefferson

for Barbara Chase-Riboud and
for my family, reputed to be the
direct descendants of
Hemings and Jefferson

Je m'appelle Sally:
How simply my first French lesson
Returns to me,
The stern and exacting gaze of my tutor,
Monsieur Perrault,

And your rich, commanding voice
—The voice of one
Both demigod and father:
Tell me Sally, what did you learn?
Master, I learned to say
My name.
Now, years later, I repeat the French,
As if to yield
All that I am,
And open the locket to find,
Cached in the tiny, gold-lined womb,
A lock of your red hair:
It happens, your face
Looms again in my lifetime.
If I could go to the doorway,
And stand, waiting for you
As you take the hall, your leonine figure
Assembling in the longest mirror
As in my eyes.
But you are dead, Thomas Jefferson,
And I can only sit,
Motionless, my heart pounding
At your phantom,
For today I learned
The census-taker made me white
To absolve you of the crime
Of having loved a slavewoman.
So I burned our correspondence
—The diaries and *billets-doux* an ash
Clinging to my skirts,
A smoke in my hair. Each word
A swatch of myself, a forbidden history:
The Hôtel de Langeac, the Palace of Marly,
The Capitol, Monticello—
Now I am robbed of everything,
Even of my color.

I was fifteen when you took me,
Your daughter's nursemaid;
You brushed my cheek

With your red-plumed chest,
Whispering *Martha, Martha*
—Piercing me with the name
Of your dead wife, my white half-sister
Whom I resembled.
I was so frightened by you then,
So overawed and unbelieving
Of your love.
I would stand before my mirror,
Cupping my breasts
In my two hands, amazed: no fledgling
But a woman—
Je t'aime, Sally, Je t'aime,
I heard you say,
And in Paris I mislaid
My slavery.
So home to Monticello, I met
My mother's loving, though accusatory face,
And knew I should have chosen freedom.

* * *

The battlecries,
Your glittering words of revolution
Have been recorded,
But in a secret wing of Monticello,
Against your will, I marked
The dreams and follies of our seven children,
The shocked faces of our foreign guests.
But O what I could not capture
Was your silence

As all the country crowned me
Black Lillith, Sooty Chatelaine.
In your pain and ravaged pride,
You clung to me.
Love me, stay with me, you whispered.
They say a man cannot free what he loves:
Is it your truth, your story,
I hear in these words?
Love me and remain a slave?

* * *

In the recurrent dream,
I stand on the steps of Monticello,
And see what blinds me:
Our children like hunted deer,
In a dead run—our children
You could never acknowledge.
I recall pausing on the Pont de Neuilly,
And absently dropping
A key into the Seine,
As I watched the word *enceinte*
Darken your gaze:

Return with me to Virginia,
You pleaded, a great man,
Lonely in your aegis,
But I refused, knowing I was unfettered
As long as I remained in France.
You would love me;
We would return to Paris,
And my child would be given
Freedom at adulthood
—A perilous, vouchsafed freedom, surely,
To pass from slavery
Into a forged whiteness
That begs amnesia.
I looked into your eyes, two sapphires
Set in a human face,
And met a suffering so vast, what else
But to take your hand
And whisper, *Yes* . . .
My love and master, I need to believe
I would choose this way again,
Though as property
I had no choice
'Cept to give myself
But I, Mademoiselle Sally,
Gave you my heart,
And returned to slavery.
Nothing could free me from you.

Wild Indigo, Because

When rice was our nemesis
and callous-making cotton,

and the onus
of a Satan-hot tobacco

seemed to stain
our very souls,

beyond the spirit-choking
pest houses of Sullivan Island

(*our* Ellis Island),
beyond the dust and ragtag

squalor of slave row,
we found a dew-soaked,

purplish blue
in the needed time—

imagine,
in a siren patch

behind the blacksmith's—
a God-sent and doe-wild blue.

The White Iris Beautifies Me

Not the white of hard-won cotton,
or of pitiless snow—

I've found a whiteness
that gives me its glory;

it blooms
in Master Bellemare's garden,

and though it is, by all counts,
untouchable,

quiet as it's kept, I've carried it
into the shabbiest of cabins,

worn it as I witnessed
the slave-breaker,

the hanging tree;
in dream-snatches

it blesses me, and I become
more than a brand,

a pretty chess piece:
at the mistress's bell,

always prudent and afraid,
wily and afraid—

And when the day comes,
my rescuing flower's name

will become my daughter's;
a freeborn woman,

I swear,
she will never be shoeless

in January snow.
Bold iris,

she will never fear sale
or the bottom of the sea.

Wanda Coleman

(1946–)

C IRCA FALL OF 1957, six weeks before my eleventh birthday, I became terribly ill. It is an experience I have never forgotten—a milestone. During it, I came to understand aspects of myself and my parents I had never considered or understood. We lived in the West, Los Angeles, and our Black enclaves, dotting postwar Southern California, were relatively tiny compared to a Harlem or South Side. In that hostile vastness where the smiles were double-edged, it was difficult to get a firm grasp on the negatives that weighed so mightily on our lives—the constraints and evils of racism as the strong battled—lucky to save their own hides, let alone others'—and the weak succumbed. I listened to the countless arguments and discussions as my parents, their friends, and associates bled into one another. Their youth, their beauty, their hopes wasted in fruitless struggling. Inspired by the world of classical music, opera, and concerts, I had hoped to raise myself above this madness as a violinist—to shine with such virtuosity that I would transcend all that misery on a sea of quarter notes. I dreamed that I would transform them as well—take them with me—fulfill their aspirations through my genius as a soloist. That would not happen. I had contracted a form of encephalitis the doctors called "African sleeping sickness," which affected my motor skills and dulled my ability to play. My fingering became thick and clumsy; tremolos eluded me. By age thirteen, I resigned myself, and Mother sold my instrument for gas money. My creativity had to go somewhere, but where? I could sing— but Billie Holiday, Sarah Vaughan, and Marian Anderson had vocal skills I could never equal. It was important to me to be an original. An avid reader, I had long bristled at the absence of life as we fought to live it in the most lauded texts of Western literature. That decided me. I would put

the world of my parents into books as poems and stories. My world too.
I've done my best to become a virtuoso as a writer.

Ars Poetica

he came down the mountain
with a full growth of beard, smiling
the new MS taut in his mitts
precious gold of months of solitude/thought/work
he'd done it—conquered the bitch muse
made a nympho of her
begging at his boots to be taken
he felt proud. proud as any man who can
wear pain well
he showed it to his old lady, the black chick
who'd had a hard life. a woman with little mercy
in her heart and less in her vocab
he unwrapped his dream carefully, cautioned her
to wash her hands before touching a single page
after a guttural sound from her throat
she obliged, angry at having her
chores in the kitchen interrupted
he sat her down and read each event. when he
finished, cast eyes to reel in her expression
"how do you like it?"
she watched his hope dance. "that what you went away fo?
it real nice for some poetry"
"is that all you can say about it?"
"no. i could say more"
"well say it—for god's sake, say it!"
she took off the sanitary napkin she was wearing
and plopped it on the page
"needs more blood in it"
and went back to the kitchen

Bedtime Story

bed calls, i sit in the dark in the living room
trying to ignore them

in the morning, especially Sunday mornings
it will not let me up. you must sleep
longer, it says

facing south
the bed makes me lay heavenward on my back
while i prefer a westerly fetal position
facing the wall

the bed sucks me sideways into it when i
sit down on it to put on my shoes. this
persistence on its part forces me to dress in
the bathroom where things are less subversive

the bed lumps up in anger springs popping out to
scratch my dusky thighs

my little office sits in the alcove adjacent to
the bed. it makes strange little sighs
which distract me from my work
sadistically i pull back the covers
put my typewriter on the sheet and turn it on

the bed complains that i'm difficult duty
its slats are collapsing. it bitches when i
blanket it with books and papers. it tells me
it's made for blood and bone

lately spiders ants and roaches
have invaded it searching for food

American Sonnet (17)

i am seized with the desire to end

my breath in short spurts. shoulder pain
the world lengthens then contracts
(in deep water—my sudden swimming. the surface
breaks. thoughts leap. the Buick bends
a corner. an arc of light briefly sweeps the dark walls)
everywhere there are temples of stone
and strange chantings—ashes angels and dolls
i forget my lover. i want a stranger—
to shiver at the unfamiliar touch of the one
who has not yet touched me

a furred spider to entrap my hungers
in his silk. with virulent toxin
to numb my throat

American Sonnet (54)

dearest cousin,

　　forgive this ruined narrative begging the first
element of creation. last time i was here i was here.
now i wonder what, exactly, are the components of my
invisible spectrum? sun-ra rising.

　　i went for a reading of palms to rediscover
disappointment. "better an almost-was," said the gypsy,
"than a never-was." her peculiar conjure left me staring at
my naked brown feet for hours. when reverie broke it was
near dawn, mist had occluded the volcano and i found
myself old, alone sans shelter from the ever-blessed heat.

this note is sent perchance you've wondered what
befell one adventuresome one solongago lost, this missive
in an empty ron rico bottle set adrift on a sea of flute
music—this repetitious rendering of pain—for on my
one-palm island dwells no such beast as joy.

Toi Derricotte

(1941–)

MUCH OF WHAT HAPPENS in my writing takes place underground, out of consciousness. It is a process that takes many years during which I am, more or less, completely out of touch with what's happening. Memories, perceptions, feelings, and intuitions stew around in there, decaying and remixing, and when I am ready to host them, they surface, but not as individual experiences, as whole constellations, a black universe with a network of unknown stars.

Sometimes I can catch that moment with a string of words that might eventually be a poem. Most times, however, I must live in this difficult process for many years. Surfacing involves a personal confrontation with some truth that I have not accepted. It also demands formal changes in my poetry. For me a book is not a collection of poems; it is an embodiment of a distinct process.

Holy Cross Hospital

*In my ninth month, I entered a maternity ward set up for
the care of unwed girls and women in Holy Cross Hospital.*

couldn't stand to see these new young faces, these
children swollen as myself. my roommate, snotty,
bragging about how she didn't give a damn about the
kid and was going back to her boyfriend and be a

cheerleader in high school. *could we ever "go back"?*
would our bodies be the same? could we hide among the
childless? she always reminded me of a lady at the bridge
club in her mother's shoes, playing her mother's hand.

i tried to get along, be silent, stay in my own corner.
i only had a month to go—too short to get to know them.
but being drawn to the room down the hall, the t.v. room
where, at night, we sat in our cuddly cotton robes and
fleece-lined slippers—like college freshmen, joking
about the nuns and laughing about due dates: jailbirds
waiting to be sprung . . .

one girl, taller and older, twenty-six or twenty-seven, kept
to herself, talked with a funny accent. the pain on her face
seemed worse than ours . . .

and a lovely, gentle girl with flat small bones. the
great round hump seemed to carry *her* around! she never
said an unkind word to anyone, went to church every morning
with her rosary and prayed each night alone in her room.

she was seventeen, diabetic, fearful that she or the baby
or both would die in childbirth. she wanted the baby, yet
knew that to keep it would be wrong. but what if the child
did live? what if she gave it up and could never have another?

i couldn't believe the fear, the knowledge she had of
death walking with her. i never felt stronger, eating
right, doing my exercises. i was holding on to the core,
the center of strength; death seemed remote, i could not
imagine it walking in our midst, death in the midst of
all that blooming.

she went down two weeks late. induced. she had decided
to keep the baby. the night i went down, she had just
gone into labor so the girls had two of us to cheer about.
the next morning when i awoke, i went to see her. she
smiled from her hospital bed with tubes in her arms. it
had been a boy. her baby was dead in the womb for two

weeks. i remembered she had complained *no kicking*. we
had reassured her everything was fine.

meanwhile i worked in the laundry, folded the hospital
fresh sheets flat three hours a day. but never alone.
stepping off the elevator, going up, feeling something,
a spark catch. i would put my hand there and smile with
such a luminous smile, the whole world must be happy.

or out with those crazy girls, those teenagers, laughing,
on a christmas shopping spree, free (the only day they
let us out in two months) feet wet and cold from snow.

i felt pretty, body wide and still in black leotards
washed out at night. my shapely legs and
young body like iron.

i ate well, wanted lamaze (painless childbirth)—i
didn't need a husband or a trained doctor—i'd do it
myself, book propped open on the floor, puffing and
counting while all the sixteen-year-old unwed children
smiled like i was crazy.

one day i got a letter from my cousin, said:

> *don't give your baby up—*
> *you'll never be complete again*
> *you'll always worry where and how it is*

she knew! the people in my family knew! nobody died
of grief and shame!

i *would* keep the child. i was sturdy. would be a better
mother than my mother. i would still be a doctor,
study, finish school at night. when the time came, i
would not hurt like all those women who screamed and
took drugs. i would squat down and deliver just like the
peasants in the field, shift my baby to my back, and
continue . . .

when my water broke, when i saw that stain of pink blood
on the toilet paper and felt the first thing i could not
feel, had no control of, dripping down my leg, i heard
them singing mitch miller xmas songs and came from the
bathroom in my own pink song—down the long hall, down
the long moment when no one knew but me. it was time.

all the girls were cheering when i went downstairs, i was
the one who told them to be tough, to stop believing
in their mother's pain, that poison. our minds were
like telescopes looking through fear. it wouldn't hurt
like we'd been told. birth was beautiful if we believed
that it was beautiful and good!

—*maternity*—*i had never seen inside those doors.*
all night i pictured the girls up there, at first hanging
out of the windows, trying to get a glimpse of me . . .
when the pain was worst, i thought of their sleeping faces,
like the shining faces of children in the nursery, i held
onto that image of innocence like one light in the darkness.

The Weakness

That time my grandmother dragged me
through the perfume aisles at Saks, she held me up
by my arm, hissing, "Stand up,"
through clenched teeth, her eyes
bright as a dog's
cornered in the light.
She said it over and over,
as if she were Jesus,
and I were dead. She had been
solid as a tree,
a fur around her neck, a
light-skinned matron whose car was parked, who walked on swirling
marble and passed through

brass openings—in 1945.
There was not even a black
elevator operator at Saks.
The saleswoman had brought velvet
leggings to lace me in, and cooed,
as if in service of all grandmothers.
My grandmother had smiled, but not
hungrily, not like my mother
who hated them, but wanted to please,
and they had smiled back, as if
they were wearing wooden collars.
When my legs gave out, my grandmother
dragged me up and held me like God
holds saints by the
roots of the hair. I begged her
to believe I couldn't help it. Stumbling,
her face white
with sweat, she pushed me through the crowd, rushing
away from those eyes
that saw through
her clothes, under
her skin, all the way down
to the transparent
genes confessing.

Invisible Dreams

> *La poésie vit d'insomnie perpétuelle.*
> —RENÉ CHAR

There's a sickness in me. During
the night I wake up & it's brought

a stain into my mouth, as if
an ocean has risen & left back

a stink on the rocks of my teeth.
I stink. My mouth is ugly, human

stink. A color like rust
is in me. I can't get rid of it.

It rises after I
brush my teeth, a taste

like iron. In the
night, left like a dream,

a caustic light
washes over the insides of me.

.   .   .

What to do with my arms? They
coil out of my body

like snakes.
They branch & spit.

I want to shake myself
until they fall like withered

roots; until
they bend the right way—

until I fit in them,
or they in me.

I have to lay them down as
carefully as an old wedding dress,

I have to fold them
like the arms of someone dead.

The house is quiet; all
night I struggle. All

because of my arms,
which have no peace!

.   .   .

I'm a martyr, a girl who's been dead
two thousand years. I turn

on my left side, like one comfortable
after a long, hard death.

The angels look down
tenderly. "She's sleeping," they say

& pass me by. But
all night, I am passing

in & out of my body
on my naked feet.

.   .   .

I'm awake when I'm sleeping & I'm
sleeping when I'm awake, & no one

knows, not even me, for my eyes
are closed to myself.

I think I am thinking I see
a man beside me, & he thinks

in his sleep that I'm awake
writing. I hear a pen scratch

a paper. There is some idea
I think is clever: I want to

capture myself in a book.

.   .   .

I have to make a
place for my body in

my body. I'm like a
dog pawing a blanket

on the floor. I have to
turn & twist myself

like a rag until I
can smell myself in myself.

I'm sweating; the water is
pouring out of me

like silver. I put my head
in the crook of my arm

like a brilliant moon.

.   .   .

The bones of my left foot
are too heavy on the bones

of my right. They
lie still for a little while,

sleeping, but soon they
bruise each other like

angry twins. Then
the bones of my right foot

command the bones of my left
to climb down.

The Minks

In the backyard of our house on Norwood,
there were five hundred steel cages lined up,
each with a wooden box
roofed with tar paper;
inside, two stories, with straw
for a bed. Sometimes the minks would pace
back and forth wildly, looking for a way out;
or else they'd hide in their wooden houses, even when
we'd put the offering of raw horse meat on their trays, as if
they knew they were beautiful
and wanted to deprive us.
In spring the placid kits
drank with glazed eyes.
Sometimes the mothers would go mad
and snap their necks.
My uncle would lift the roof like a god
who might lift our roof, look down on us
and take us out to safety.
Sometimes one would escape.
He would go down on his hands and knees,
aiming a flashlight like
a bullet of light, hoping to catch
the orange gold of its eyes.
He wore huge boots, gloves
so thick their little teeth couldn't bite through.
"They're wild," he'd say. "Never trust them."
Each afternoon when I put the scoop of raw meat rich
with eggs and vitamins on their trays,
I'd call to each a greeting.
Their small thin faces would follow as if slightly curious.
In fall they went out in a van, returning
sorted, matched, their skins hanging down on huge metal
hangers, pinned by their mouths.
My uncle would take them out when company came
and drape them over his arm—the sweetest cargo.

He'd blow down the pelts softly
and the hairs would part for his breath
and show the shining underlife which, like
the shining of the soul, gives us each
character and beauty.

Melvin Dixon

(1950–1992)

I THINK I'VE RELINQUISHED, in a sense, a sense of imposing a story, or a theme, or an identity on the fiction or poetry that I might be writing, in order for the work itself to create this organic quality or what it is; I would also like to think that, in a sense, I am relinquishing to the outside world, by the very act of writing, how it is going to define me or perceive me as a writer, as a black writer, as a gay writer, as an American writer. I would think that it would be very presumptuous on my part to say what those categories are to me, and how I fulfill those categories, because I really don't know; I can make something up, but I don't think it would be a reflection of anything other than my delusion at this particular point.

Climbing Montmartre

Take these thousand steps, these up-running shoes,
the orange / red / brownstone rooftops
studded like Arab faces in the sun. Take
my one African eye.

Take these white steps, these ladders up-growing
from the green, the marble-head dome with eyes
the flicking cameras of tourists, the franc rusted
fountains, the postcards, the translated prayers.

Take the beaded stained glass and the false
night naked inside, the nuns singing, the
statues looking cool, the candles leaning from light.

Langston in the twenties and old Locke too,
Cullen from the Hotel St. Pierre,
Wright from rue Monsieur le Prince, even too,
Martin came to climb Montmartre.

Take the fast breathing, the up-going,
the wide plane of rooftops frozen in a Paris mist
the dignity of trodden stone descending to
subway sleepers, take my primitive feet
danced out and still.

Take the iron colored dust from *Gare du Nord*,
the pigeon feeders, the hundred smelling vendors
the fast hands, the begging. Take jazz in
twisted TV antennas and wire clotheslines, or
my lips quivering, hands watching, holding.

Take this hill into the mind as you look
all over Europe; your clogged ears can't hear
the screaming, your pointed noses snuff out
blood and urine smells, your green eyes
don't see this body drop on angry gargoyles.

Paring Potatoes

I take two from the sack,
examine their round dust bottoms
where something else has eaten
between the pipes and onions.

Roaches dig there, leaving skin
and hollow vegetable.
From one starchy tunnel
a root hangs limp. My hands

rest at the spot, a knife
ready for the food
one man can find.

In this kitchen space of two men
and brown bottom
tunnels of roaches and quick hunger
something else eats here the bleeding

pulp, the vitamin juice gone
in the crunch of roach wings,
and gouged eyes clinging
from the empty food.
My stomach eats itself hollow

like a gourd in winter
as potato eyes
rimmed with mold
watch my black paring hands.

Turning Forty in the 90's

April 1990

We promised to grow old together, our dream
since years ago when we began
to celebrate our common tenderness
and touch. So here we are:

Dry, ashy skin, falling hair, losing breath
at the top of stairs, forgetting things.
Vials of Septra and AZT line the bedroom dresser
like a boy's toy army poised for attack—
your red, my blue, and the casualties are real.

Now the dimming in your man's eyes and mine.
Our bones ache as the muscles dissolve,
exposing the fragile gates of ribs, our last defense.
And we calculate pensions and premiums.
You are not yet forty-five, and I
not yet forty, but neither of us for long.

No Senior discounts here, so we clip coupons
like squirrels in late November, foraging
each remaining month or week, day or hour.
We hold together against the throb and jab
of yet another bone from out of nowhere poking through.
You grip the walker and I hobble with a cane.
Two witnesses for our bent generation.

Heartbeats

Work out. Ten laps.
Chin ups. Look good.

Steam room. Dress warm.
Call home. Fresh air.

Eat right. Rest well.
Sweetheart. Safe sex.

Sore throat. Long flu.
Hard nodes. Beware.

Test blood. Count cells.
Reds thin. Whites low.

Dress warm. Eat well.
Short breath. Fatigue.

Night sweats. Dry cough.
Loose stools. Weight loss.

Get mad. Fight back.
Call home. Rest well.

Don't cry. Take charge.
No sex. Eat right.

Call home. Talk slow.
Chin up. No air.

Arms wide. Nodes hard.
Cough dry. Hold on.

Mouth wide. Drink this.
Breathe in. Breathe out.

No air. Breathe in.
Breathe in. No air.

Black out. White rooms.
Head hot. Feet cold.

No work. Eat right.
CAT scan. Chin up.

Breathe in. Breathe out.
No air. No air.

Thin blood. Sore lungs.
Mouth dry. Mind gone.

Six months? Three weeks?
Can't eat. No air.

Today? Tonight?
It waits. For me.

Sweet heart. Don't stop.
Breathe in. Breathe out.

Rita Dove

(1952–)

I HOPE I NEVER FEEL entirely comfortable while writing a poem; I want to experience new ground, bending what were once the rules. Obviously, with such an attitude there can be no set "poetics." As I wrote in my poem "The Fish in the Stone": The fish ". . . is weary / of analysis, the small / predictable truths"; and though he himself is set in stone—"his profile stamped," figuratively speaking, black on white—he's surrounded in the undulating, fluctuating process of truth: "the silence / moves and moves."

.   .   .

Crassly put: When I write, I am trying not to bore myself and my readers. That may sound flippant, but not to be bored as a writer means to keep challenging my own complacency, the ordinary human desire to just kick back and relax. To feel challenged as a writer means to push myself constantly, in the hopes that readers will always find something fresh and exciting in my work, something they've never seen or heard expressed in quite that way before. Like dear Emily Dickinson, I want to write poems that make you feel as if the top of your head has been taken off, with so many layers of perception sparking at once that you can't separate them anymore. That's really the only poetics I can ascribe to: to write so that both I and the reader emerge from the poem chastened, not quite sure what just happened—but deliciously, terrifyingly alive.

Nestor's Bathtub

As usual, legend got it all
wrong: Nestor's wife was the one
to crouch under
jug upon jug of fragrant water poured
until the small room steamed.
But where was Nestor—
on his throne before the hearth,
counting the jars of oil
in storeroom 34, or
at the Trojan wars
while his wife with her white hands
scraped the dirt from a lover's back
with a bronze scalpel?

Legend, as usual, doesn't
say. But this heap of limestone
blocks—look how they fell, blasted
by the force of olive oil
exploding in the pot, look
at the pattern left in stucco
from the wooden columns, sixty
flutings, look at the shards
scattered in the hall where
jars spilled from the second floor,
oil spreading in flames
to the lady's throne.

For the sake of legend only the tub
stands, tiny and voluptuous
as a gravy dish.
And the blackened remains of ivory
combs and 2,853 tall-stemmed
drinking cups in the pantry—
these, too, survived

when the clay pots screamed
and stones sprang their sockets
and the olive trees grew into the hill.

History

Everything's a metaphor, some wise
guy said, and his woman nodded, wisely.
Why was this such a discovery
to him? Why did history
happen only on the outside?
She'd watched an embryo track an arc
across her swollen belly from the inside
and knew she'd best
think *knee*, not *tumor* or *burrowing mole*, lest
it emerge a monster. Each craving marks
the soul: splashed white upon a temple the dish
of ice cream, coveted, broken in a wink,
or the pickle duplicated just behind the ear. *Every wish
will find its symbol*, the woman thinks.

The Fish in the Stone

The fish in the stone
would like to fall
back into the sea.

He is weary
of analysis, the small
predictable truths.
He is weary of waiting

in the open,
his profile stamped
by a white light.

In the ocean the silence
moves and moves

and so much is unnecessary!
Patient, he drifts
until the moment comes
to cast his
skeletal blossom.

The fish in the stone
knows to fail is
to do the living
a favor.

He knows why the ant
engineers a gangster's
funeral, garish
and perfectly amber.
He knows why the scientist
in secret delight
strokes the fern's
voluptuous braille.

Daystar

She wanted a little room for thinking:
but she saw diapers steaming on the line,
a doll slumped behind the door.

So she lugged a chair behind the garage
to sit out the children's naps.

Sometimes there were things to watch—
the pinched armor of a vanished cricket,
a floating maple leaf. Other days
she stared until she was assured
when she closed her eyes
she'd see only her own vivid blood.

She had an hour, at best, before Liza appeared
pouting from the top of the stairs.
And just *what* was mother doing
out back with the field mice? Why,

building a palace. Later
that night when Thomas rolled over and
lurched into her, she would open her eyes
and think of the place that was hers
for an hour—where
she was nothing,
pure nothing, in the middle of the day.

Heroes

A flower in a weedy field:
make it a poppy. You pick it.
Because it begins to wilt

you run to the nearest house
to ask for a jar of water.
The woman on the porch starts

screaming: you've plucked the last poppy
in her miserable garden, the one
that gave her the strength every morning

to rise! It's too late for apologies
though you go through the motions, offering
trinkets and a juicy spot in the written history

she wouldn't live to read, anyway.
So you strike her, she hits
her head on a white boulder,

and there's nothing to be done
but break the stone into gravel
to prop up the flower in the stolen jar

you have to take along,
because you're a fugitive now
and you can't leave clues.

Already the story's starting to unravel,
the villagers stirring as your heart
pounds into your throat. O why

did you pick that idiot flower?
Because it was the last one
and you knew

it was going to die.

American Smooth

We were dancing—it must have
been a foxtrot or a waltz,
something romantic but
requiring restraint,
rise and fall, precise
execution as we moved
into the next song without
stopping, two chests heaving

above a seven-league
stride—such perfect agony
one learns to smile through,
ecstatic mimicry
being the *sine qua non*
of American Smooth.
And because I was distracted
by the effort of
keeping my frame
(the leftward lean, head turned
just enough to gaze out
past your ear and always
smiling, smiling),
I didn't notice
how still you'd become until
we had done it
(for two measures?
four?)—achieved flight,
that swift and serene
magnificence,
before the earth
remembered who we were
and brought us down.

Hattie McDaniel Arrives at the Coconut Grove

late, in aqua and ermine, gardenias
scaling her left sleeve in a spasm of scent,
her gloves white, her smile chastened, purse giddy
with stars and rhinestones clipped to her brilliantined hair,
on her free arm that fine Negro,
Mr. Wonderful Smith.

It's the day that isn't, February 29th,
at the end of the shortest month of the year—
and the shittiest, too, everywhere

except Hollywood, California,
where the maid can wear mink and still be a maid,
bobbing her bandaged head and cursing
the white folks under her breath as she smiles
and shoos their silly daughters
in from the night dew . . . what can she be
thinking of, striding into the ballroom
where no black face has ever showed itself
except above a serving tray?

Hi-Hat Hattie, Mama Mac, Her Haughtiness,
the "little lady" from *Showboat* whose name
Bing forgot, Beulah & Bertha & Malena
& Carrie & Violet & Cynthia & Fidelia,
one half of the Dark Barrymores—
dear Mammy we can't help but hug you crawl into
your generous lap tease you
with arch innuendo so we can feel that
much more wicked and youthful
and sleek but oh what

we forgot: the four husbands, the phantom
pregnancy, your famous parties, your celebrated
ice box cake. Your giggle above the red petticoat's rustle,
black girl and white girl walking hand in hand
down the railroad tracks
in Kansas City, six years old.
The man who advised you, now
that you were famous, to "begin eliminating"
your more "common" acquaintances
and your reply (catching him square
in the eye): "That's a good idea.
I'll start right now by eliminating you."

Is she or isn't she? Three million dishes,
a truckload of aprons and headrags later, and here
you are: poised, between husbands
and factions, no corset wide enough
to hold you in, your huge face a dark moon split
by that spontaneous smile—your trademark,

your curse. No matter, Hattie: It's a long, beautiful walk
into that flower-smothered standing ovation,
so go on
and make them wait.

The Bridgetower

> *per il Mulatto Brischdauer*
> *gran pazzo e compositore mulattico*
> —LUDWIG VAN BEETHOVEN, 1803

If was at the Beginning. If
he had been older, if he hadn't been
dark, brown eyes ablaze
in that remarkable face;
if he had not been so gifted, so young
a genius with no time to grow up;
if he hadn't grown up, undistinguished,
to an obscure old age.
If the piece had actually been,
as Kreutzer exclaimed, unplayable—even after
our man had played it, and for years
no one else was able to follow—
so that the composer's fury would have raged
for naught, and wagging tongues
could keep alive the original dedication
from the title page he shredded.

Oh, if only Ludwig had been better-looking,
or cleaner, or a real aristocrat,
von instead of the unexceptional *van*
from some Dutch farmer; if his ears
had not already begun to squeal and whistle;
if he hadn't drunk his wine from lead cups,
if he could have found True Love. Then
the story would have held: In 1803

George Polgreen Bridgetower,
son of Friedrich Augustus the African Prince
and Maria Anna Sovinki of Biala in Poland,
traveled from London to Vienna
where he met the Great Master
who would stop work on his Third Symphony
to write a sonata for his new friend
to premiere triumphantly on May 24,
whereupon the composer himself
leapt up from the piano to embrace
his "lunatic mulatto."

Who knows what would have followed?
They might have palled around some,
just a couple of wild and crazy guys
strutting the town like rock stars,
hitting the bars for a few beers, a few laughs . . .
instead of falling out over a girl
nobody remembers, nobody knows.

Then this bright-skinned papa's boy
could have sailed his fifteen-minute fame
straight into the record books—where
instead of a Regina Carter or Aaron Dworkin or Boyd Tinsley
sprinkled here and there, we would find
rafts of black kids scratching out scales
on their matchbox violins so that some day
they might play the impossible:
Beethoven's Sonata No. 9 in A Major, Op. 47,
also known as The Bridgetower.

Cornelius Eady

(1954–)

I REALLY ENJOY the idea of the language that's inside of music itself. The idea that maybe when you hear a jazz solo, or when you're hearing a good saxophonist, or a guitarist, that you're actually hearing that person's story. They're telling you a little tale. That has always fascinated me. I try to find a way to translate or interpret what I hear in music. I just think musicians are very noble. Maybe that's giving too much of a spin to them, but I think they do really amazing and necessary work in our culture.

Photo of Miles Davis at Lennies-on-the-Turnpike, 1968

New York grows
Slimmer
In his absence.
I suppose

You could also title this picture
Of Miles, his leathery
Squint, the grace
In his fingers *a sliver of the stuff*

You can't get anymore,
As the rest of us wonder:
What was the name
Of the driver

Of that truck? And the rest
Of us sigh:
Death is one hell
Of a pickpocket.

Crows in a Strong Wind

Off go the crows from the roof.
The crows can't hold on.
They might as well
Be perched on an oil slick.

Such an awkward dance,
These gentlemen
In their spottled-black coats.
Such a tipsy dance,

As if they didn't know where they were.
Such a humorous dance,
As they try to set things right,
As the wind reduces them.

Such a sorrowful dance.
How embarrassing is love
When it goes wrong

In front of everyone.

Christopher Gilbert

(1949–2007)

T HERE IS VERY MUCH a musical influence on the poems. It's interest-
ing that when I was growing up, my first ten years were sort of blues
years because my parents listened to blues, rhythm and blues. During
my teenage years my older brother listened to jazz, and I can remember
not understanding it. I only understood later when I started writing. It
became the cadence of the poems. He listened to neo-boppish people like
Stanley Turrentine and Wes Montgomery, and neo-bop and bop is the
jazz I identify with. There's the format in the horns playing together. The
collective improvisation fits well with the kind of poems I write. Some-
times they seem linear. For some of them I didn't mean for them to happen
all at once. The thing about bop that's interesting is the hard-driving qual-
ity. There is something at issue in the music and it's critical. For poems, I
like a sort of reflective, deliberate, laid-back attitude, but I like poems that
have a critical issue, something at stake at the same time, something to be
gained by writing or reading it. With bop in particular what seems to be at
stake is the self. The musician goes after something, pursues it. Every note
is a choice that's made on the process of progression toward *now*.

She

for Carolyn Grace

When she sits at the kitchen table
while she talks her hands seem to balance

in the air faithful at the level of
her words; she is careful what she says.
The morning sun through the window strikes
her skin, shows how the faint lines in her
palms will come to deepen like corduroy
cloth to fit the weather of her age.
Still a young woman, she has to work
the graveyard shift, sleeps what is left,
then wakes to get the kids to school.
It must be morning when she dreams.
Peering into her coffee's surface
she looks back from its depth, her hands
caught holding an implement, a fossil of
her life: Alabama born, feelings
huddled north, these steel cities this cold month,
her dark soul twisting into fingers
whose motion at this brown angle
is the slow fall flight of leaves through time.
And she rises with the gesture, and
the oil in her hands is necessity's
sweat: each hand on the tabletop
a work cloth rubbing the other fine
wooden one.

Absentee Landlord

A dog's bark breaks the December
ten-degree weather, a bitter dark
space bleaching into a voweled ache
that staccatos the thin wind, fuzzes
into consciousness as a hurt.

A cry ballooning in the surface
of things, it's like the residue
of city air left in the lung,
while you search these suspenseful streets—
the houses, snowmen holding their tongues.

At the boundary between buildings
the fence rattles its steel scream,
as you peer in an iced-over window
and swear the owner must be absent
since he lets you take his absent signs

be a prophet for all that he means.
While the wind, which holds our worry,
whistles wild, while the dog barks
himself out, when you look in the glass
and feel yourself in the view as a part,

you are now the subject of this scene.
Become the symbol of what you've framed,
or else don't change. Be nothing
like the dead, be the absentee
who will not attend what he means.

Touching

Light is a distant world
though at 5 a.m. in the bedroom
window where the spider plant hovers
shining, there is a silken presence
where it traces, leaves a constellation.
I roll over and the room moves
a little closer, it is light-
like when Karen sleeps beside me
turned away but warm rubbing back
and I curve myself like hers
to hold her body for seeing
whatever is far in her.
Now I'm almost dreaming.
Words run transparent from my mouth
and almost find the edge of things.
Across the street in the park
a big hawk sails, gently flapping,

its outspread arms hugging the air
just as the sun kisses upward
to find its way through the sky.
Back here off the edge of the bed
my fingers, blind at both ends,
dangle in a void like starlight
travelled so far its source burned out.
Now a light goes off in my head as
I hold this hand that seems so far away.
I think of the monster fullback
in high school, after running over me
he dropped the ball to see was I hurt.
Where is he now, or the woman
who put the message in the bottle
I found splashing in the fouled waters
off Point Pelee. What was on her mind
writing, *kindness anywhere is still kindness,*
I'm in Cleveland, cold, alone—
wherever you are you hold this part of me.
I roll over in the glow
where sunrise goes across the bed,
knowing our age thinks light is wavelike
bundles spreading outward like ships
floating home in measured gaps toward each shore.
So part of the world waits distant.
For all I know as a man it might happen
like kelp bits drifting to no shore.
Still if there's a moment somewhere
equal to this light filling my skin,
then there is a constant I can count on
and I'll go forth and live with that.

C. S. Giscombe

(1950–)

T HE RECENTLY PUBLISHED poetry book—*Prairie Style*, 2008—is about
the Midwest, where I've lived. The book leans heavily on speech acts,
music, the inevitable geography; it's interested in the talk of black and
white Midwesterners. By "talk" I mean a number of things—the incli-
nation for speakers to qualify themselves *as* speakers and the relation-
ship of that to issues in lyric poetry, the racial dialogues of books such as
Thornbrough's *The Negro in Indiana*, love talk, Ellison's evocation of "our
little palaver," the stretch of argument, the presence of A.A.V.E. and its
reception as lazy speech, etc.

Talk's different than voice—natural voice, finding one's voice, coming
to voice, big voice, etc.—and from whatever icon or vision we make to
steady abstraction or buy off what's waiting for us.

The Northernmost Road

1
Having wanted to drive out to the edge, right out
to the mutest edge out there,
the mutest edge, the emptiest soundstage,
out to the invisibility there, out
to all that "up" there in Canada that took place up there—
Giscome, B.C. all unincorporated now up
on the Upper Fraser Rd off desolate Rte 16 to Alberta,

off the Alberta-bound road the Yellowhead (for Pierre B—, the blonde
    Iroquois who'd arrived
at the mountains there at the Alberta end, the source of the road):
    miscegenation's
the longest nuance, the longest-lasting open secret
(in old B.C., Gov. Douglas was also "a man of colour," "a West Indian
of racially mixed parentage" out at the end of a pier in Victoria,
    welcoming,
"creole," pragmatic

2

The past is a skein of rocks.
The past is watery.
The past is tree'd.
The past is a list of houses.
The past is a fat metaphor sitting down to dinner.
The road so rocky & so long (the song repeated)
the explanations got dense on their own:
the past names nothing anyplace:
sites got pre-empted:
at the river-landing the field name verges on the day name:
at the river-landing's the place where the river's "noble" in a descrip-
    tion of it there—
the river's aimless self & the portage trail are something else, one
    goes
off into the trees

2.5

A real word for the talk between Europeans travelling far afield, *our
    little palaver,*
and the Africans themselves, some story "intended to charm or
    beguile":
tell me it's creolized, tell me that it's a bridge between designations.
No story gets elucidated in the song & no one talks or waves from the
    stage: hands
& the lips too stay on the horn, that's human nature.

2.7

Names rise from locations, the metaphor comes from water (what
    water does),
is the verb for that kind of arrival, the verb for location. There's no
    remote source
to any of it & you never know how consequence will appear or seem
    to take place
here or here or here (being described as arrival)—

3

The water there goes on & on like nobody's business,
bounding water, furthering water, eating the heart
of water, water drains & edges in,
the gouge of water at the bottom-most levels,
a bridge waiting at the bottom of each hill the road descends,
centerless water but with an edge,
that trill to it, an osmotic line, jagged & minute & strange,
no word for the way blood will tell, the edge
of some line disappeared out in the water

.   .   .

5

—Giscome Road's a real road, "the path made by a moving point," the
    lips of the pavement,
the centerless inflection, the return through the same bends wch
    isn't sweet:
across a river's the way up in Canada too, the link looming in the
    trees over
the divide, but then along the helix of visible little ridges:
the long song's wordless & necessarily rolling, the long song's that
    commotion, rolling
(wordless): the long song's a series of greetings
gone astray, muted, a caravan of horns, quotidian, rolling (wordless):
the trees gave way onto an exact location of the place furthest away,
    the trees gave way

6

"Spanish" was always a euphemism, the word used
among planter families down in the Islands,
now among their descendants in Canada:
I'd wanted to drive out to the end of Giscome Rd,
out to where it hits the Yellowhead, & did so one night:
there was music on the French Service that had flamenco overtones
    to it,
the sketch of openings in an edge or series of edges, the rough drift
outward, "over the edge," no end in sight, no word for the way
music appears.

The 1200N Road, Going East

To me, image is any value in the exchange. Pleasure's accidental. In
any event, it's hard to measure and harder still to memorize, plea-
sure. Image stands in. To me, voice is that which gets stuck in the
head, effected voice, or inbetween the teeth, the hiss of love. Songs,
eating. Whatever love says it's no image, no consequence. This far
inland, the erotic's only obvious from a distance. This far inland you
need something more sexual than dichotomy.

Jewelle Gomez

(1948–)

THE BLACK ARTS MOVEMENT was the voice of (partial) change. Its male members (no pun intended) insisted that Black women were merely reflections of their masculine counterparts; workers' struggles counted, but were Native Americans entitled to reparations too? And what about those gay people? "Power to the people" was meant—apparently—for only half the people; and they held a patent on the words. But power, like freedom, is not something that can be locked up in a safe. And if it was, then I met the safecrackers: Gwendolyn Brooks, Sonia Sanchez, June Jordan, Jayne Cortez, Nikki Giovanni, Audre Lorde—they were no shadows. When they spoke fire came out of their mouths, fire that fueled not the burning down of Black neighborhoods, but the melting of the locks. Their fire lit up the cooking pots, the reading lamps, the hearths, the kilns, the generators; the furnaces of living, not dying.

Each colored woman who put her pen to paper made a real revolution inside me. They proved that words could still evoke passion and create something; that women could be our own subjects rather than someone else's objects. The passion grew with every poem—passion for making the world safer for people of color, for those living in poverty, those wanting peace, for women, for women who love women, for everyone. Art and social change grew entwined inside of me, like another element added to my DNA. I write to remind myself that the revolution is not all about me, to spotlight how futile it is to pretend each liberation is not dependent on the liberation of those around us. I write to describe what freedom is and how we might grow it, within ourselves and in our communities. I write my poems and stories to the rhythm of songs and to the remembered scent of possibility. The songs promised "a change is gonna come." And it does . . . nearer with each silence I break, with each question I ask, with each poem and story I let loose in the world.

My Chakabuku Mama (a comic tale)

My first big love was cosmically correct:
vegetarian chili, herbal tea, feng shui.

I pretended to comprehend numerology,
graphology, phrenology and the phases of the moon.

We meditated on celestial seasonings about who
should do the laundry in an equal relationship.

I slept with my head facing north abiding a vicious draught.
My shoes sat outside the door crying to be let in.

We searched together for the higher ground
through macrobiotic bushes and abstinence.

I peered into her thick transcendental glasses.
She faced the way of the Wicca.

We chanted to find our center
beneath an azure blue candle from Key food.

We never separated without talking it all out
or allowed bad vibes to invade our space.

She made breakfast on alternate Sundays
and I gave up drinking gin.

We went on camping trips every Spring.
I read dense poets and kept copious journals.

I sprinkled a pinch of salt in the four corners of each room,
and loaned all of my favorite clothes to mere acquaintances.

I never eavesdropped when she talked on the phone.
I ate fresh fruit and only argued with Con Edison.

I cut my finger nails. We played kalimba duets.
I threw out my Salems. She threw out the roach spray.

We shuddered in unison at the mention
of french fries or Table Talk pies.

I never watched TV
or listened to James Brown.

I gave up aspirin and wore 100% cotton,
had my tarot read, meditated on a tatami bed.

I learned to love brown rice and Japanese slippers,
eat raw fish and burn patchouli.

She could squeeze the names of three
Egyptian goddesses into any general conversation.

Malice and jealousy beat a hasty retreat. Our life moved forth
on a path of righteous awareness and sisterhood.

Then she left me flat. Exiting serenely
on a cloud of universal love.

El Beso
*for Angelina Weld Grimke and Akasha Hull**

> . . . Who will ever find me / Under the days?
> —A. W. GRIMKE

There is no darkness like a closed door
ornate panels, thick with filigree—soundproof,
denying time.
Your fair pen finds its mark in the coal black
circle of Boston society. Sheaves of paper-thin custom
threaten to bury you. Fashion   father   negritude
slip steadily from the pile of demands,
to land on your breast, to press you more firmly
into their muffled folds.

Behind the door you dare to leave whispers
of your precious, stolen breath, desire
for "her of the cruel lips," a fragment unrequited,
evidence of unruly passion and wild sadness
in the strain to press your mouth
to the hem of her skirt.

Who decides which mouth speaks truth,
whose lips deserve to sense the yield
of another's? It is 1920—
Uptown bands are playing
Women are dancing in starched shirt fronts
and top hats, laughing out loud with painted faces.
Abolition, the obsession of your family,

---

*Angelina Weld Grimke (1880–1958) is a lesser-known poet whose work appeared in
journals published during the Harlem Renaissance and who was the niece of the Aboli-
tionist Grimke sisters. Her many cryptic references to her love for women survive in her
unpublished letters and poems which were first written about by scholar Akasha Hull.

has come home to Harlem.
Every shape and shade build to cacophony
in the newness of freedom. Many are reborn
into the singing, glorious hints of redress
and burnished futures. But you arrive
after the sound has died down. Your legacy:
"crying want" in the muted tones—
saffron and lilac evocations of crimson secrets.

The soft rustle of days passing like crisp, fiery leaves
tumbling around our feet evoke that final soil
dropping darkly onto sturdy pine.
Still, you do not write of your heart pounding,
except in solitude.

The soft scratch on paper is the earth cracking
open, pages filled—a lock turning
light falls on "dark, dark bodies."
You, under those days: primrose and dusk
demure, glistening with hunger.
The dewy orchid taste of your full lips, a thick
scent in the air.
A look of surprise.
Mouths finally touch for all to see.

Angela Jackson

(1951–)

"WHY I MUST Make Language" (whether poem, story, or play, because everything for me is poem): For a Voice / like a star. / Shining. / With points to pierce / space. / and be / simple, superb / clarity. / Incandescent. / Some thing / a child might carry / down the black hall, / to make peace with Mystery. / Or woman / into a wooded place / where she may see / the shapes and / names of trees. / Anonymous awe be called / Glory. / Or man / might seek / in the cave / of a woman / and see the writing / on the wall, / and find some / luminosity. / Ancestors may descend / on streams of light. / Or / all look up / and listen / deep / into the night. / The wild / and civilized / Sky.

I measure my pulse in my singular African Diasporan woman way, a particular music that is mine. I hold Time still. I go into Time where the poem lives in an infinite moment. Full of momentum and power. Moving into and through the world. I believe in NOMMO, the ancient power of The Word to make material change, the transformative power of The Word to change me, all who hear and see and inhabit the poem with me, and then go further, moving out, transforming the world as "Love is an active force." The Word is an active force. The Word is Love, momentous and intimate, heady and visceral with surprise, and change, original, magical, and revivifying, wide, pushing back the narrow places. NOMMO.

The Love of Travellers
(Doris, Sandra and Sheryl)

At the rest stop on the way to Mississippi
we found the butterfly mired in the oil slick;
its wings thick
and blunted. One of us, tender in the finger tips,
smoothed with a tissue the oil
that came off only a little;
the oil-smeared wings like lips colored with lipstick
blotted before a kiss.
So delicate the cleansing of the wings
I thought the color soft as watercolors would wash off
under the method of her mercy for something so slight
and graceful, injured, beyond the love of travellers.

It was torn then, even after her kindest work,
the almost-moth exquisite charity could not mend
what weighted the wing, melded with it,
then ruptured it in release.
The body of the thing lifted out of its place
between the washed wings.
Imagine the agony of a self separated by gentlest repair.
"Should we kill it?" One of us said. And I said yes.
But none of us had the nerve.
We walked away, the last of the oil welding the butterfly
to the wood of the picnic table.
The wings stuck out and quivered when wind went by.
Whoever found it must have marveled at this.
And loved it for what it was and
had been.
I think, meticulous mercy is the work of travellers,
and leaving things as they are
punishment or reward.

I have died for the smallest things.
Nothing washes off.

Two Trains

The countryside slides away, elides trees,
sunlight rolls down like a savior.
The train shudders and hisses to a stop.
Which train?
Who is in the wrong spot?

A seat on a train is the site of a war.
Ask Gandhi, East Indian in South Africa:
Ask me, a colored schoolmarm, in skirts, hat, and gloves.

We lost the battle, and won a war.
Equally colored.

There is something about insult that burns
bodily as one is seized and dispatched
like an angry letter full of inkblots of significance.

Gandhi led his story.
I wrote mine,
in my way led my match-light.

Ida Rewrites

"I, as usual, lost what favor I had
by becoming furiously angry."

I agitate to a fault.

If I were vulgar enough
to sing the Blues
I would be the Blues

and shake hands with the Devil
and bring him to his knees.

I look Fear in the eye. I show no Fear.
I look Hate eyeball to eyeball. I do not blink.
I must, however, admit
difficulty with rivals.
Indeed so less than me
can they be called rivals?
Women!
Fellow workers for the Good!
History Tellers who omit me!

Yet I cannot hold
my peace
when holding would benefit
my cause and circumstance.

Now I must rewrite.
I must not admit

my breach.

Gayl Jones

(1949–)

S OME OF THE INFLUENCES toward narrative and storytelling in my
poetry are the medieval Spanish ballads. . . . Also the Afro-American
ballads and toasts have influenced the structural procedures of some of
those poems. . . . I'm interested particularly in the ways time, space, and
transformations of reality are handled in them, and such specific techni-
cal things as the narrative viewpoint, abrupt transitions, conflicts, uses
of irony and paradox, and certainly the characterizations in them.

.   .   .

I write poetry from the viewpoint and interest of a storyteller—the con-
cern with character and event. . . . Sometimes I've adapted stories as
poems and poems as stories. *Song for Anninho* is an adaptation of a novel
I've written called *Palmares*. But I'm drawn to the things that are now the
content of fiction, but of course which used to be the territory of poetry.

Deep Song

for B.H.

The blues calling my name.
She is singing a deep song.
She is singing a deep song.
I am human.
He calls me crazy.

He says, "You must be
crazy."
I say, "Yes, I'm crazy."
He sits with his knees apart.
His fly is broken.
She is singing a deep song.
He smiles.
She is singing a deep song.
"Yes, I'm crazy."
I care about you.
I care.
I care about you.
I care.
He lifts his eyebrows.
The blues is calling my name.
I tell him he'd better
do something about his fly.
He says something softly.
He says something so softly
that I can't even hear him.
He is a dark man.
Sometimes he is a good dark man.
Sometimes he is a bad dark man.
I love him.

Foxes

The railroad station is like a big barn.
The man is standing in a tweed coat
waiting for them, smiling.
Her boyfriend introduces them.
He puts their luggage in
the trunk of his Mercedes.
He owns a farm and has one race horse
that he calls Atlantic City
though it was born in Zion's Hill, Kentucky.
"How's Atlantic City?"

"Just fine. I'm getting him
ready for Saratoga."
She stands in the corner of the living room
looking at old photographs—
fair-skinned black women in long skirts and high-topped shoes,
dandelions in their straight black hair.
She tells a joke; the man she came with doesn't laugh,
excuses himself, goes out to the stable.
They can see him from the window
standing at the white fence, watching the horse eat grass.
"Why didn't he laugh at your joke?"
"I think he's in love with me."
"Oh."
On the shelves lining the walls are leatherbound books,
what they call "good literature."
She wonders if too much good literature can ruin you.
Ulysses. She remembers only that it was banned for being vulgar.
Wuthering Heights. She remembers a dark-browed Heathcliffe,
but can't separate the book from the movie.
He is in the kitchen making supper.
("The cook has weekends off.")
"I wish he and his wife were still together,"
her boyfriend says, back now and sitting on the couch,
arm around her shoulder. "She's some kind of woman.
Very beautiful. You'd like her. A real knockout.
Are you having a good time?"
She doesn't commit herself.
"You'd really like his wife . . . his ex-wife . . .
I don't know the whole story.
Just that she wanted out. But that's always the story, right?"

She's from New Hampshire.
This is not the Kentucky she expected to see.
Cottonfields? Jukejoints? She doesn't know what she expected.
"Are you glad you came though?"
"Yes. With you, I mean."
"Well, I like you too, girlie."

In the living room, his friend lifts a portrait
of his ex-wife. Fair-skinned like the women in

the old-time photograph. Wind-swept, holding the
reins of a horse, a girl of modern times
(and what desperations? she wonders
and whenever she sees such black women
she thinks of octoroon slaves girls.
New Orleans. She herself as dark as a brazilnut.)
He talks to the photograph,
holding the photograph in one hand,
a glass of rum in the other,
"Why do you always look at me like that?
Why do you always try to make me feel like a bastard?
I'm no bastard."

"Were you born and raised in Kentucky?"
she asks him.
(She doesn't formulate it in her head,
but really it's just that she didn't expect
to find rich black folks here,
behaving like Southern blue-bloods.)
"No, dear, I'm from New Mexico," he says.
"Do you know what my wife said when I told her I was
from New Mexico?"
"What?"
"I didn't know there were colored people in New Mexico."
He mimics her, sounding like Flip Wilson playing Geraldine.
She's sure the voice is nothing like that.
"I said, 'My dear, there are colored people everywhere.'"

"Watch out for the poison oak," he says.
"I will."
They walk in the woods near his farm.
He's picking dandelions to make wine with.
(She wonders if he will make it himself
or if the cook will.)
He carries a basket over his arm.
Her boyfriend did not want to go walking.
"Is he afraid to be in love with you?" he asks.
"I think so."
"Because you're dangerous?"
"Yes," she laughs.

"You don't look dangerous to me."
(She can't help it,
but she wonders if only women like those in his photographs
are dangerous.)
"We used to call those cigar trees," he says,
pointing up.
"I don't know what the scientific name is."
He picks a green cigar, plops it in his basket.
"You two must have some fun together though," he says.
"You must really enjoy each other at least sometimes."
"Yes."
"Where you from?"
"I was raised in New Hampshire, but actually I
was born in Amazon, Alabama."
"Colored folks everywhere," he says, and grins at her.
They sit under a maple tree.
He moves as if he knows where he is, and knows it's his.
(She's never moved that way.)
He kisses her. She frowns, but doesn't shrink from it.
He squeezes her shoulder.
"But you wouldn't take a chance with me, would you, girl?"
"No," she says, but smiles.
"Your guy?"
"Yeah."
"Just wait till you want out."
She shakes her head. "I won't." Thinks *maybe he will*
but keeps it half-thought.
"A real fox like you. Sure you will."
She doesn't feel like a fox.
She lifts up the basket, swings it
onto her arm, stands. Smell of acorns.
"Let's go back."

He pours dandelion wine into tall glasses,
hands one to her and one to her guy.
He goes to the hi-fi,
puts on Prince singing, *Little Red Corvette*.
She listens to places where horses run free,
she listens to the need to find a love
that's gonna last.

"I didn't know you could make wine this fast."
He winks at her. "Magic."

In a moment,
he's holding the picture of his ex-wife again.
"You've changed, dear," he says.
"What do you mean, how would I *know* if you've changed?
Now is that anything to say to a man?
Who else'd know if a woman's changed
but her loving man?"

He puts the photograph down,
turns to look at them,
rolling back onto his heels,
raises his glass in a toast,
"To love," he says.
She raises her glass,
tosses her head back,
and drinks the glass down,
like she imagines
a real fox would do.

Composition with Guitar and Apples

She eats breakfast
after a night of long sound.
A plate of sliced apples.
A guitar on a corner table.
A rock singer. But listen.
Her almond face on an album cover.
Lean.
Black hieroglyphic eyes.
Chocolate elbows.
Tonight they have heard her,
singing till the pipes are hollow.

Hieroglyphic eyes,
and sometimes dangerous.

Sitting at the table,
the guitar goes with her.
At night,
glued to the shoulders.

Flight from Amsterdam.
Now in an inn in Brazil
(Recife),
she sleeps and awakens
to a plate of apples.

Somewhere in Recife
she has a foster daughter
(adopted through the mails
by some parental plan
for taking care of
the world's hunger).
She has kept her identity
from the girl,
kept herself anonymous,
but has pictures
of the girl
in growing stages,
kept in folders.

Slices of apple in the fist.

"When I saw Hendrix
I know what I wanted.
Everything
but a broken guitar."

She combs her nappy hair,
twists a scarf around it.

She is a thinking woman,
but not always a thoughtful one.

There are chains in her act,
handcuffs,
whips,
but neither
the guitar nor the soul
are broken.

She is certain about the guitar.

Sometimes she is considerate.

In the yard
she walks with the woman
who owns the inn
and from whom she leases
room and board.
The woman is so-called colored
like herself.
The woman is older.
She imagines them
in other landscapes,
timescapes,
spacescapes.
The woman keeps peacocks
in her yard,
against a bewildering superstition.

"In the old days
in colonial Brazil
they thought it was
bad luck
to keep peacocks
in one's yard.
I'm superstitious,
but I like to
challenge superstitions.
I like to confront my fears.
I like to meet them."

So she confronts this fear
with the peacocks strutting.

"I like you," she says.
"I've followed your career.
I like luck.
You seem to glow with luck.
I'm drawn to luck.
It frightens and amazes me."

She does not want to know
about the peacocks,
or her own business.

The peacocks, all masculine,
show their feathers,
their treasures.

The Brazilian woman
shoos a path for them to travel.

"I do it because that's
the only way I know
to handle fear,"
she says.

She does not break the guitar.
But she breaks the melody
down into its pieces.

A plate of broken apples.
Guitar in the corner.

In the afternoon,
she will go to the school,
and stand behind the wrought-
iron railing
and peer at the girl.

In the Amazon
they have discovered gold.
She reads about it
in the papers.

"Wouldn't you like to rush off
to a gold rush,
like in the old days,
the dangers and fevers?
Don't you feel lucky?"

The rock singer smiles
and chews an apple.

"In that last engagement
I lost my voice.
I tried something
with my voice
I shouldn't have tried.
That's why I came here.
To wait until
I get my voice back.
I tried something
I wasn't ready for."

The peacocks are strutting.

"I was almost thirty
before I liked rock and roll.
My classical training.
Then I saw Hendrix."

There are peacocks in the yard.

The woman she stays with
is half woman
half peacock.

Patricia Spears Jones

(1951–)

L IKE OTHER WRITERS who grew up in communities where silence was necessary for survival, I had to find other ways to engage with language. So I started as a reader. But what was available? Besides the Bible, popular magazines (*McCall's*, *The Saturday Evening Post*, *Look*, *Life*, *TV Guide*, and always *Jet*, *Ebony*, and *Negro Digest*, later *Black World*) and my schoolbooks. Reading took me into the noise of fiction, poetry, essays, and journalism. It also provided me with a very old-fashioned education in American literature—great Negro poets (Cullen, Hughes, McKay) and nineteenth-century poets like William Cullen Bryant, and yes, I know Bryant was an abolitionist.

Growing up in a time of intense transition in a place as violently contested as was the American South in the 1950s and 1960s made me care deeply about the need to be *able to author my life*; to be able to write well. I admit to my desire for authorship; for telling my version of the world; for breaking silence. To write poetry is to make art, whether the poem is out of personal pain, political rage, or deep spiritual trekking. *I am grateful for words*.

Wearing My Red Silk Chinese Jacket

1

Children of the Pentecost like moles
burrow through this city of shadows
fleeing light.

2

There are no dialectics when the spirit
calls forth the tongues on Sunday mornings
There the Sisters converse with the blood
of all the saints
There the Brothers shift their dignity
from one foot to the other before their
bodies forget the necessity of gravity
There the smoke rises joyous as if
from the ashes of a terrible defeat
There are no dialectics when the spirit
rips open the heart of the Children of Darkness
and takes them back through the sun to home

3

Ancestress in woodblock
Her babe torn from her side by slavetraders
Their hats cocked sideways. Their eyes rapacious.
Her lips large.
Her cry clear as the sky
above the auction block
A universe composed of empty tears
Ancestress in woodblock screaming
across the Middle Passage
quaking on this makeshift stage
What has Jesus done for you?

4

Who owns the Sun?
A question for terrorists.
I got this ability to see three sides

of each issue and know that all of them
are wrong.
I sat on the Mourning Bench, but never cried.
Jesus did not want men.
Jesus did not comfort me.
Jesus took a walk across the street
went into a bar and ordered a double whiskey.
Straight up.
Jesus hung with the tough guys till they bled
him good and sealed him in some big tomb. Known
locally as the Sepulchre. It was the drunk tank.
His fast friends came and got him out of there.
But Jesus couldn't admit to liking moonshine
whiskey or the company of tattooed men. I mean,
what would the choir members think?

5

There she sits in regal nudity
No sceptre, no sash.
Her brown skin bespeaks the earthen hues
of her voluptuous body. The face kneeling at
her crotch wants her. Wants to eat her. Wants
all of the earth within her. This face forgets
to leer. This is serious. You come to these
islands to escape civilization. What do you find:
civilization? This ego cannot stand this confusion.
She is mine, ego dreams
She is mine
I paint her naked because she needs only skin
I paint her naked because she has beautiful breasts
and I want them to know where I've supped.
I paint her because I can't eat dirt and she is—as
the elements are—available.
Her smile is hers.
I take only the deliberate angles of her body
and dine
Ancestress in woodblock
What has Jesus done for you?

6

What bright women turned the spindles;
dyed the thread. Jungle colors. Who called
bebop "Chinese music." A Sunday in Chinatown
an old woman touched my jacket. Admiration.
She say to brownskinned girl in red silk Chinese
jacket
"good"
"good"
and walks off with her friend
into the metallic clatter of the traffic
I stunned
cannot twist my mind from the heart of
gospel music—how it stirred the soul's ear
and crowded the mind's eye
And when the bristling gestures of
busy waiters recall our mutual houses of contempt
I see the wonder in that woman's eye and know that
fleeing light is not always about escape.

7

The hand that rocks
The body rolls
The good lord comes down to earth, on occasion
and clasps a poor misguided man to this bosom
Makes him a minister and sets his mouth
open with words that flow like a flood in late
Spring. His charm is his hip motion when he roars
across the pulpit like a linebacker stalking prey.
The backsliders signify.
The better, stronger get on up and shout!
Soaking in holy water—drums, guitars, the choir's
rhapsodic singing and clapping
The whirling ceases
like the cry of the women and men
who separated across state lines still remembered
the family names
Brother to brother
Sister to sister

Crying in the wilderness, blessed America
Creeping through canyon constructed on the
principles of implosions
Crafty, devilish, yes
You, in your bad madness
Not even hip to history or the possibility
of good news
You there, torn up; tear it up!
Drugged, drummed down, daily eating the
crumbs from your mama's table
wearing the last dregs of an impossible
nightmare
Tell me
Tell me
What has Jesus done for you?

Thanksgiving

There are many parched lips
as the cup of human kindness empties.
So little milk, this year

the main course consists of boiled greens,
no salt, and a tantalizing meat.
It stinks.

Fat flies link a pyramid
above the rotting flesh.

On each of the round clothed tables
a bouquet of silk roses plucked by the hands
of women working in El Salvador, Sri Lanka,
the Cameroons.

I will become a vegetarian.

What of this pain? These sharp slaps
on the knee? Sleet comes
a hard, fast rain like laughter
erupting in a prison yard.

Paradise to you, bub.
But to me, a mystic's splendid guitar.

Yusef Komunyakaa

(1947–)

I WRITE EVERYTHING in longhand. Each poem is sparked by phrases and images that allow us to simultaneously glimpse memory and imagination. No topic is taboo, but a system of aesthetics has to exist. The poet is blessed and condemned to live at the apex of life and death, gazing into and out of, always beckoning to the dark and the light. At times, it seems that we've been tooled and shaped by pathos, but it is also natural to insist that poetry arrives to us from joy and love, dripping with the dew of relentless entanglement. Poetry craves a commitment of the soul, the psyche. We participate in an industry of observation; and what we witness reduces and exults us. In that way, yes, often elements of childhood tyranny define us. We still run out into the world shouting, "Where, how can that be? I don't believe you." And we trust the language of metaphor and metonymy to deliver us to reality through the pleasures of insinuation. Of course, improvisation is always at the axis of my method of writing poetry. I like how the senses attempt to take in everything at once, but of course music is at the heart of the conjuring and reliving. Finally, the poem is shaped; it is a made thing (pulsing with sensation and revelation). Form and structure come out of the music of language. The poem challenges me to discover something that is usually a feeling of tangled surprises reaching for clarity. Basic language is important to me because it keeps us honest, true to what we are made of. For me, the poem exists within the time of *now*, and sometimes it even owes something to an echo of history linking us to the past and future. When we consider systems of thinking through the symbolic, poetry is perhaps the most democratic, though it often is a matrix of accidental symbols within natural symbols. In that sense, the making of a poem is an action. Poetry embraces mystery.

Venus's-flytraps

I am five,
    Wading out into deep
        Sunny grass,
Unmindful of snakes
    & yellowjackets, out
        To the yellow flowers
Quivering in sluggish heat.
    Don't mess with me
        'Cause I have my Lone Ranger
Six-shooter. I can hurt
    You with questions
        Like silver bullets.
The tall flowers in my dreams are
    Big as the First State Bank,
        & they eat all the people
Except the ones I love.
    They have women's names,
        With mouths like where
Babies come from. I am five.
    I'll dance for you
        If you close your eyes. No
Peeping through your fingers.
    I don't supposed to be
        This close to the tracks.
One afternoon I saw
    What a train did to a cow.
        Sometimes I stand so close
I can see the eyes
    Of men hiding in boxcars.
        Sometimes they wave
& holler for me to get back. I laugh
    When trains make the dogs
        Howl. Their ears hurt.
I also know bees
    Can't live without flowers.
        I wonder why Daddy

Calls Mama honey.
   All the bees in the world
      Live in little white houses
Except the ones in these flowers.
   All sticky & sweet inside.
      I wonder what death tastes like.
Sometimes I toss the butterflies
   Back into the air.
      I wish I knew why
The music in my head
   Makes me scared.
      But I know things
I don't supposed to know.
   I could start walking
      & never stop.
These yellow flowers
   Go on forever.
      Almost to Detroit.
Almost to the sea.
   My mama says I'm a mistake.
      That I made her a bad girl.
My playhouse is underneath
   Our house, & I hear people
      Telling each other secrets.

My Father's Love Letters

On Fridays he'd open a can of Jax
After coming home from the mill,
& ask me to write a letter to my mother
Who sent postcards of desert flowers
Taller than men. He would beg,
Promising to never beat her
Again. Somehow I was happy
She had gone, & sometimes wanted
To slip in a reminder, how Mary Lou

Williams' "Polka Dots & Moonbeams"
Never made the swelling go down.
His carpenter's apron always bulged
With old nails, a claw hammer
Looped at his side & extension cords
Coiled around his feet.
Words rolled from under the pressure
Of my ballpoint: Love,
Baby, Honey, Please.
We sat in the quiet brutality
Of voltage meters & pipe threaders,
Lost between sentences . . .
The gleam of a five-pound wedge
On the concrete floor
Pulled a sunset
Through the doorway of his toolshed.
I wondered if she laughed
& held them over a gas burner.
My father could only sign
His name, but he'd look at blueprints
& say how many bricks
Formed each wall. This man,
Who stole roses & hyacinth
For his yard, would stand there
With eyes closed & fists balled,
Laboring over a simple word, almost
Redeemed by what he tried to say.

"You and I Are Disappearing"

—BJÖRN HÅKANSSON

The cry I bring down from the hills
belongs to a girl still burning
inside my head. At daybreak
    she burns like a piece of paper.
She burns like foxfire

in a thigh-shaped valley.
A skirt of flames
dances around her
at dusk.
       We stand with our hands
hanging at our sides,
while she burns
      like a sack of dry ice.
She burns like oil on water.
She burns like a cattail torch
dipped in gasoline.
She glows like the fat tip
of a banker's cigar,
     silent as quicksilver.
A tiger under a rainbow
  at nightfall.
She burns like a shot glass of vodka.
She burns like a field of poppies
at the edge of a rain forest.
She rises like dragonsmoke
  to my nostrils.
She burns like a burning bush
driven by a godawful wind.

Facing It

My black face fades,
hiding inside the black granite.
I said I wouldn't,
dammit: No tears.
I'm stone. I'm flesh.
My clouded reflection eyes me
like a bird of prey, the profile of night
slanted against morning. I turn
this way—the stone lets me go.
I turn that way—I'm inside

the Vietnam Veterans Memorial
again, depending on the light
to make a difference.
I go down the 58,022 names,
half-expecting to find
my own in letters like smoke.
I touch the name Andrew Johnson;
I see the booby trap's white flash.
Names shimmer on a woman's blouse
but when she walks away
the names stay on the wall.
Brushstrokes flash, a red bird's
wings cutting across my stare.
The sky. A plane in the sky.
A white vet's image floats
closer to me, then his pale eyes
look through mine. I'm a window.
He's lost his right arm
inside the stone. In the black mirror
a woman's trying to erase names:
No, she's brushing a boy's hair.

Blue Light Lounge Sutra for the Performance Poets at Harold Park Hotel

the need gotta be
so deep words can't
answer simple questions
all night long notes
stumble off the tongue
& color the air indigo
so deep fragments of gut
& flesh cling to the song
you gotta get into it
so deep salt crystalizes on eyelashes
the need gotta be

so deep you can vomit up ghosts
& not feel broken
till you are no more
than a half ounce of gold
in painful brightness
you gotta get into it
blow that saxophone
so deep all the sex & dope in this world
can't erase your need
to howl against the sky
the need gotta be
so deep you can't
just wiggle your hips
& rise up out of it
chaos in the cosmos
modern man in the pepperpot
you gotta get hooked
into every hungry groove
so deep the bomb locked
in rust opens like a fist
into it into it so deep
rhythm is pre-memory
the need gotta be basic
animal need to see
& know the terror
we are made of honey
cause if you wanna dance
this boogie be ready
to let the devil use your head
for a drum

Lingo

Herodotus, woven into his story,
    tells how the Phoenicians lent
        war fleets to Greece & Egypt,

how a ghost-driven flotilla
    eased like salmon up birth water
        & sailed the Red Sea,

hoping to circumnavigate Africa
    around the Cape of Good Hope
        & along Gibraltar. A blue

door opened. Diodorus
    says of the Ethiopians,
        "born under the Sun's path,"

that "its warmth may have ripened them
    earlier than other men." As if
        a ventriloquist inherited

the banter of a sailor's parrot,
    words weave with Herodotus's—
        angel food . . . sellers didn't touch

the gold . . . devil's food. The stories
    become flesh as these ghosts
        argue about what's lost

in translation, believing two images
    should spawn & ignite a star
        in the eyes of a sphinx

or soothsayer. Sometimes they do.
    There's a reason why the dead
        may talk through a medium

about how Aryans drove cattle
     along the seven rivers & left
          dark-skinned Dravidians

with tongues cut out, sugarcane
     fields ablaze, & the holy air
          smelling of ghee & soma.

These ghosts know the power
     of suggestion is more than body
          language: white list, black

sheep, white tie, black market.
     Fear climbs the tribal brainstem
          or wills itself up an apple tree,

hiding from the dream animal
     inside. The serpent speaks
          like a Lacan signifier,

posing as a born-again agrarian
     who loves computer terminals
          better than cotton blossoms

planted, then we wail to reap
     whirlwind & blessing. Each prefix
          clings like a hookworm

inside us. If not the split-tongued
     rook, the sparrow is condemned
          to sing the angel down.

[The jawbone of an ass. A shank]

The jawbone of an ass. A shank
braided with shark teeth. A garrote.
A shepherd's sling. A jagged stone
that catches light & makes warriors
dance to a bull-roarer's lamentation.
An obsidian ax. A lion-skin drum
& reed flute. A nightlong prayer
to gods stopped at the mouth of a cave.

The warrior-king summons one goddess
after another to his bloodstained pallet.
If these dear ones live inside his head
they still dress his wounds with balms
& sacred leaves, & kiss him
back to strength, back to a boy.

The Devil Comes on Horseback

Although the sandy soil's already red,
the devil still comes on horseback
at midnight, with old obscenities
in his head, galloping along a pipeline
that ferries oil to the black tankers
headed for Shanghai. Traveling
through folklore & songs, prayers
& curses, he's a windmill of torches
& hot lead, rage & plunder, bloodlust
& self-hatred, rising out of the Seven Odes,
a Crow of the Arabs. Let them wing
& soar, let them stumble away on broken feet,
let them beg with words of the unborn,
let them strum a dusty oud of gut & gourd,
still the devil rides a shadow at daybreak.

Pity one who doesn't know his bloodline
is rape. He rides with a child's heart
in his hands, a head on a crooked staff,
& he can't stop charging the night sky
till his own dark face turns into ashes
riding a desert wind's mirage.

Requiem

So,
when the strong unholy high winds
whiplashed over the sold-off marshlands
eaten back to a sigh of saltwater,
the Crescent City was already shook down to her pilings,
her floating ribs, her spleen & backbone,
left trembling in her Old World facades
& postmodern lethargy, lost to waterlogged
memories & quitclaim deeds,
exposed for all eyes, damnable
gaze & lamentation—plumb line
& heartthrob, ballast & watertable—
already the last ghost song
of the Choctaw & the Chickasaw
was long gone, no more than a drunken curse
among the oak & sweet gum leaves, a tally
of broken treaties & absences echoing
cries of birds over the barrier islands
inherited by the remittance man, scalawag,
& King Cotton, & already the sky was falling in on itself,
calling like a cloud of seagulls
gone ravenous as the Gulf
reclaiming its ebb & flowchart
while the wind banged on shutters
& unhinged doors from their frames
& unshingled the low-ridged roofs
while the believers hummed

"Precious Lord" & "Deep River"
as the horse-hair plaster walls
galloped along with the surge,
already folklore began to rise up
from the buried lallygag & sluice
pulsing beneath the Big Easy
rolling between & through itself,
caught in some downward tug
& turn, like a world of love affairs
backed up in a stalled inlet,
a knelt-down army of cypress,
a testament to how men dreamt land
out of water, where bedrock
was only the heart's bump
& grind, its deep, dark churn
& acceleration, blowzy down
to those unmoored timbers,
already nothing but water
mumbling as the great turbulent eye
lingered on a primordial question,
then turned—the gauzy genitalia of Bacchus
& Zulu left dangling from magnolias & raintrees,
already . . .

Nathaniel Mackey

(1947–)

I WRITE INFORMED by the fact that there is a strain, especially in twentieth-century poetry, which does not presume that the poem is the vehicle for representing and revealing the travails of a discrete first-person subject, with consistencies of tone and voice and perspective and with constraints upon what that voice can chart, both in literal, spatial, and temporal terms and in terms of what that single voice can believably be taken to know or to be able to utter.

It's a sense of the writing as—"ceremonial" is perhaps the word, "sacramental" is perhaps the word—with almost a priestly or a prophetic task being taken on by the poet. I'm informed by that, and there are impulses in me that tend very strongly in that direction. Those impulses are complicated by other influences, among them the fact that we do live in a secular age and in a secular culture, an age of skepticism and doubt. I'm also in touch with that. Some of the manner in which the poetry moves—because movement conveys and is a vehicle for meaning and implication as much as overt statement—some of the way in which it moves, I think, is a carrier of that anxious or not altogether settled relationship to the desire or the need for a poetry that would carry a hieratic voice or at least a desire for reaching after a hieratic voice.

Song of the Andoumboulou: 16

—cante moro—

They were dredging
the sea, counting
   the sand. Pounded
     rocks into gravel,
paid a dollar a
           day,
   sang of the oldest
fish like family,
         tight
   flamenco strings
distraught . . .

        Some
   ecstatic elsewhere's
advocacy strummed,
unsung, lost inside
     the oud's complaint . . .
The same cry taken
up in Cairo, Córdoba,
         north
     Red Sea near Nagfa,
  Muharraq, necks cut
   with the edge
         of a
broken cup . . .
        Lebrijano's
burr-throat, raspy
  as night, adamant
night, long night
       longer
  than a lifetime of
       nights . . .
Turning away what light
was outside, night

without end . . .
Muttering,
"Time," less than a
sigh, resigned
to it, would-be
Book
of Coming Forth by Day,
would-be
kef-pesh, pinkish
sun . . .
Between lips, resuscitant,
reached
where they were, no boat not
one they drowned in, dredged
it,   letterless the
book we thumbed . . .

Blocked
synonymy steeped as though
linked and unlocked,
lest it engulf them in smoke,
squat,
squint-eyed god afloat in a
saucer filled with rum.
Steeped in memory, bedrock
mischief, misanthropy,
soul
sent rousing the dead,
wrested
kiss . . .
Later to be
burned, beliefless,
ya-habibi'd
endlessly, burr-throat,
threnodist . . . Lest
it be said they saw less
than they said, lipless,
less
than a sough . . .

Sprocketed,
watch. Moot mechanical troth,
treadmill mesh. Ever to
be gone to again, lost
body
of love . . . Aspic allure,
lost-
limbed entanglement,
toxic . . .
Bitten we'd have
been
and were

* * *

Udhrite collapse, mute
school it advanced with . . .

Voice taken up into
airlessness, eked-out
insistency,
eked-out amends . . .

Strangled horse. Blistered
fist around a dove's
neck,   word brought back
from one who crossed
over,   beginning, we
would
say, to see the
light . . .

In a dark room
discussing duende. Something
they saw or they thought
they
saw. An aura he called it,
air, though they choked on
it, smoke bound in leaves,
ambulant,
sleight . . .

Conscript air, she
replied, meaning manic,
want without remedy,
endless refrain, would
it would cease,   night
not only itself but all
nights, not-ness her
muse,
no light but one star, that
one star black . . .

Flutter spoke
next, not flight, not
even feeling though they
felt it squirm its way
out
from inside . . . Panicky
butterfly, lyric escape.
Stubbly
cheeks' rough remembered
caress turned hunter, haunted
her, imminent ghost, gotten
ready,
resigned . . . Reminiscing the
few for whom the word
was enough, no longer
among them. Never the
same for him as for her,
for
them as for either, isolate,
again
the awaited blow ripped
away the wall, tore the
floorboards up

* * *

News
arrived as they were
singing. Cries of thousands
cut in on the music,

          charred bodies blown
        about, unembalmable,
                     bombed,
    these the black torsos they
        saw, no Pharaoh's
                  crypt,
    night not only itself,
                 ominous
    night . . .

No heavenly night, what
she had hoped for, later
               crept in . . .
    Child tucked in bed while
bombs fell, ya habibi echoing
      endlessly, remedyless,
complaining *Played God,*
              got
    burned . . .
          Burr spoke now,
    not subtly, flat sanity's
      enablement labored,
             let go . . .
    Took between her lips their
gruff tongues' foretaste of
      "heaven," raspy word given
back by the newly
            dead

        * * *

    Hummed.   "Tell me," so
disdainfully it stung . . .
                Raw-throated
    singer beating time with a
    dry stick . . .
           Feasted on ghost-
lore, leavings, "whither thou
goest . . ." In another house

dwelt far beyond sight. That
     they were there, anywhere
                                   at all,
          ever the heist it had
always been . . .   Brute
          pointlessness bearing
                                   down,
          blunt eminence. Dead the
          more alive they were
                                        when
     alive, less dead. "Took into
                                   my hand
a straw . . ."

                    Banged adamant head
          Spun with plugged-in harps,
                                        agitant
               oud-light,   knottedness of
          locks, disarray . . .
                              Theoretic rush, thought
          filled with blood. Dust . . . Inexistent
               water . . . Tossed rump. Rounded
          edge. Roll of the
                              earth . . .

No longer impressed, no new
     day terminus. Numbered where
abundance led. Dazed under
     a crumbling dome,
                              torn
     socket.
               Bought soul
                         yelling
     sell
          so loud
ears
     burned

Glenn on Monk's Mountain

—"mu" twenty-fourth part—

Next it was Austria we
were in. Unexpected rain
soaked our shoes,
unexpected snow froze
                    our
      feet. A bitter book
      took us there . . .
                    A bitter
book in our stomachs,
      an aftertaste on
      our tongues, a book
                    based
      on another Glenn,
                Monk's
Mountain not the Monk's we
      took it for. A book of overlay,
a book about death at fifty-one,
                          a book
      we lay awake at night reading,
       . a book we read wanting
      to wake up from . . .
                    So it
      was another Monk's
Mountain we haunted. Sat
                          upside
it crosslegged, lotusheaded,
                    humphed,
      heads encased in crystal it
      seemed . . . Bits of straw like
      unexpected snow filled the
                          sky.

Stars were bits of straw blown
about in the crystal we were
in, the rags on our backs a bolt
of black, star-studded
                                        cloth
the jukebox dressed us in
gabardine, burlap, scratched
our skin with raw silk . . .

A bit of straw caught in my eye
made it water,   water
                                        filled my
head with salt . . . Straw, ridden
by water, filled my head, my
throat, my chest,   salt filled
my head with sound. A sound of
                                        bells
not of bells but of pounded
iron, the Falasha spoken to
by Ogun . . . I played "Asaph,"
the horn's bell a swung censer,
                                        wafted
scent the furtive sound I sought . . .
Liturgical ambush . . . Fugitive straw . . .
Limbic ambush . . . Nastic address . . .
Pads and keys cried out for
climb, clamor, something yet
                                        to arrive
we called rung. Rickety wood, split
reed, sprung ladder. More splinters
the more steps we took . . . Rung
was a bough made of air, an
unlikely plank suddenly under our
                                        feet we
floated up from,   rung was a loquat
limb, runaway ladder, bent miraculous

branch, thetic step . . . Flesh beginning
    to go like wax, we sat like Buddha,
                    breath
  an abiding chime, chimeless,
                bells
 had we been
rung

Sound and Severance

   —"mu" fifty-ninth part—

 Suddenly two, they sat side by
side. He and he looked out the
  nod house door . . . They wanted
   to go back, wanted not to
                know
  what they knew, looked out at
   the receding world, eyes whiting
over, in dreams repeatedly bid
  goodbye . . . Choric escort . . .
              Chronic
  dispatch . . . Wondered what but
andoumboulouousness awaited
  them. They were waiting to be
born it seemed . . . It wasn't one
            was
  it, one wasn't enough, he nor he
   the I and I's he and he of it,
   he nor he the he and he's I and
               I . . .
Gnostic imposter each according
to the other. Falsetto. Birdbone flute.
  About to be born or about to be
 bodiless, flew, soon to find out
            which . . .

Featherless wren said to be what
   soul was, wren if not robin, picked
on, plucked, he number one's en-
   dangerment, risk he number two
now took . . . Saw one's other self it
                        seemed

   or at least one said so, he number one
he number two no end . . . A hole at
   whose edge one stood, looking in,
unspun incumbency's engine, the mo-
   ment, what there was of it, all there
                    was . . .
   But if both neither he the he of it. "Time's
tongue," he said, meaning to say, "Time
   tough." Bad leg pulsing with pain at
the hip, he and he the quintessential he . . .
                  Time's
   tongue was a scroll he unrolled and wrote
      on. *Beaked we'd be we read and*
were, book blown open by wind, he
   wrote, *winged we'd be, bereft* . . . He
                and
he read out loud in unison, a net of X's
               each
   annulling the next . . . Looked out the nod
house, looked into each face. *We'd see*
   what face was only front for, he wrote . . .
             Saw
   from before, early in life, an earlier life,
      eyes looking to see beyond sight . . .
What lay beyond, intimated by look,
what lay behind, look's far side soon
come . . . *We'd be beside ourselves*, he
              wrote,
   a succession of X's. Rapt ecstatics, we'd
   see ourselves outside . . . Faces wherever
he and he looked, each an invitation, soul

a certain bareness he and he thought . . . He
who wrote was less a he than a committee,

he and

he's X's' I and I. Time's tongue a rough rug,
part brush, part papyrus . . . Water crept under
the door . . . He and he sat side by side
braving the nod house. What was to come
all but already there . . . Quizzical hedge if

not

would-be trump if not nothing . . . Nothing.

None-

theless
near

The book bit its tail and became a
disc. Spun sonance he and he were
the proof of. What was to come lay
caught between planks . . . The
                                        floor
torn loose or begun to be, he and
he sat looking out the nod house
door . . . He and he knew nothing
if not unlikeliness, scrounged amenity
                                        what
was left were not everything lost.
Antiphonal spin toward what tore
                                loose,
prolegomena, epilogue and prologue
                                        both,
    prologue
both

The book as it turned acoustic became
a disc, *The Namoratunga Nextet*
Live at the Nod House, he and he's
eyes were in the sky ... Forehead
                                        scoured
by starlight ... Cheekmeat scuffed by
meteoric scree ... Face wanting to
be what soul was ... He and he's
eyes were rocks outside their
                                        sockets,
lids blown shut by inclement wind,
                                        cosmic
        acidity,
    drift

Thylias Moss

(1954–)

M Y WORK, MY THINKING, my understanding, my loving—anything
I do is now, and has been since October 2004, within a context
of Limited Fork Theory, an approach to existence that considers and is
part of interacting systems, on any scale, in any location, for any dura-
tion of time. Any visual, sonic, olfactory, tactile, cognitive, imaginary,
etc. system and subsystem. This approach assumes movement to and
away from connections to connect again, eventually, in all ways pos-
sible for connections to occur. In thinking about bifurcating gestures
implied in movements/behaviors/activities of components of systems, a
likelihood of entanglement emerges, a scenario emerges in which space
becomes available or expands to accommodate temporary (on some
scale) configurations that form as interaction. . . . Careful study (though
not complete, no matter how careful) of an interaction set can lead to,
as part of the outcome system, the making of a *poam* (product of an act
of making) that can resemble, for some duration of time, in some loca-
tion, what is often referred to as a *poem*. Form itself is part of what is
configured and reconfigured as momentary and circumstantial stations.
So I deal with partialities of partialities only; because I now use a lim-
ited fork, I can never trust what adheres to the tines, forming the basis
of understanding, because the spaces, the holes between tines, make it
likely that something falls through them and is not available for con-
sideration—indeed, more could fall out of availability for consideration
than what adheres to the tines. Wild and exciting things can happen in
LFT; I am only at the beginning of making and pursuing predictions in
the form of *poam*, loving that things manage to connect, however briefly,
willing to risk (not that choice is involved) apparently aggressive forms of
interaction in order to have the range of possible configurations, a range

that includes whatever exists, including the apparently blissful (that may also manifest [on some scale in some location for some duration of time] robustly).

The Day Before Kindergarten: Taluca, Alabama, 1959

I watch Daddy tear down
Mama Lelia's outhouse
with just his hands;
the snakes and slugs
didn't fret him none.
Then he takes me and Mama riding.

We stop at the store,
looks like a house,
okra right in front,
chickpeas and hollyhocks.
Me and Mama go in. The fan
don't move her hair.
She keeps her head down, stands
a long time at the counter.
Just wants some thread,
could get it herself,
there's a basketful beside her.
Clerk keeps reading.

She's hurting my wrist,
I pull away, pick up a doll.
Clerk says we have to leave.
Mama grabs me and runs
right by Daddy,
he's just coming in.

We hide in the car.
Mama smells like sour milk
and bleach.
Daddy comes out toting a sack,
clerk thought he was white.

When the store starts burning
I'm on Mama Lelia's porch
wanting to see
how the red
melts off peppermint.
I know it's like that.
One by one
each thing burns.
Pickle jars explode.
Mama Lelia asks me:
Do it look like rain?
No'm, it don't.
Ain't God good!
She laughs.

Later,
while it's still smoking
I go poking with a stick.
Ashes look like nappy
nigger hair. Smells
like when the hot comb
gets too hot
and burns Mama's neck.
This smell's so big
must have come
from a hundred necks.

Holding my doll
I look at the smoke,
could be a black man
running down the road;
then rub some ashes
on her face
'cause I ain't scared

no more
of nothing.
Maybe I should be
but I ain't.

Timex Remembered

In the middle of an argument I recall a high peak
in the South Pacific; a diver wearing
only loin cloth and watch
plunges, surfaces, thrusts his watch towards the camera
and microphone, then John Cameron Swayze takes over:
Timex, it takes a licking and keeps on ticking!

By fourth grade lickings simmered in everything
simmering. Dennis raped his sister's Patty Playpal
at her request. I locked my doll away. Olivia jumped
from a window the same day I saw a boy killed fifty yards
from a hospital, his bubblegum like a pink hole in
the street. What would he do, I asked the policeman,
without a sweet taste forever on his tongue?
I was pushed aside into silence, thereafter moved
through Glenville like a spirit.

It didn't make sense when Tomasina's mother whipped her
up and down Durkee Avenue with a peach tree limb.
Tomasina had done what her mother did, slept with a man,
someone else's man. Tomasina got a licking for her efforts,
her mother got Tomasina. And yes, Tomasina kept on ticking;
the cross around her neck moved like a metronome
when she walked.

Then there was Blondell who stole my piggybank full
of silver dollars, the only pieces of my grandmother
and her mother that I had. Blondell who stole
my innocence and couldn't even use it in her gang

that stole forty automobiles and dissected them.
She knew no other science. She popped her gum and
ticked like a bomb.

Louise thought her Navaho heart ticked too loudly
and I was so quiet she couldn't hear me above the racket
saying what I also needed someone to say.
She returned to Piñon, Arizona, in pieces
that each bore the signature of the craftsmen
who broke her with knives, bottles, and the tines
of forked tongues. *How* she said to me, *This is how*
she thought my silence said. I was praying
for the answer. Nothing ticks between us.

The lickings haven't stopped. Nowhere in the world
have the lickings stopped.
What else translates as well as the sun
setting in a bloodbath? Every heart bleeds
just keeping us alive. Oh the ticking, ticking. . . .
Sometimes that's just Old Lady Samodale trying
to grow flowers, not even thinking about race, not even
worrying about who's winning the human race, just doing
her spring cleaning, making room in her mind for flowers.
Rowdy youth ride by after a riot and tell her
the neighborhood is a ghetto now, no longer zoned
for the flowers they trample, uproot, try to smoke.
Their afros remind her of barbed wire. She knows more
about ghettos than they ever will. Her daffodils
were the goal of crayons. Sometimes the ticking
is Mrs. Samodale sinking to her knees, shaking *tch, tch, tch*
out of her head a long way from Czechoslovakia.
There's no freedom anywhere from the *Timex* watch, the
accuracy of its score.

One for All Newborns

They kick and flail like crabs on their backs.
Parents outside the nursery window do not believe
they might raise assassins or thieves, at the very worst
a poet or obscure jazz musician whose politics
spill loudly from his horn.
Everything about it was wonderful, the method
of conception, the gestation, the womb opening
in perfect analogy to the mind's expansion.
Then the dark succession of constricting years,
mother competing with daughter for beauty and losing,
varicose veins and hot-water bottles, joy boiled away,
the arrival of knowledge that eyes are birds with clipped wings,
the sun at a 30° angle and unable to go higher, parents
who cannot push anymore, who stay by the window
looking for signs of spring
and the less familiar gait of grown progeny.
I am now at the age where I must begin to pay
for the way I treated my mother. My daughter is just like me.
The long trip home is further delayed, my presence
keeps the plane on the ground. If I get off, it will fly.
The propeller is a cross spinning like a buzz saw
about to cut through me. I am haunted and my mother is not dead.
The miracle was not birth but that I lived despite my crimes.
I treated God badly also; he is another parent
watching his kids through a window, eager to be proud
of his creation, looking for signs of spring.

Mulberry Breath as Proof of the Wave
in Form of Question

Jennifer, here are some facts bred by the others:

a polar bear's fur is not white.
Each hair shaft is pigment-free and transparent
with a hollow core

that scatters and reflects visible light,
much like ice, snow, and other cold partnerships

When photographed with ultraviolet sensitivity,
polar bears appear black.

Because they give off no detectable heat,
they do not show up in infrared capture.

A scientist's infrared snapshot,
produced a single spot: the puff of air

caused by the animal's breath
so trust it. It will not lie. If it has toxins
it will give them to you. That which is airborne
overcame drag and coefficients. Air will let
almost anything pass through it   —why do you think

souls always get away? The fact that basic air
doesn't make itself conspicuous is in its favor,
                                   —most of it is nitrogen
that seldom gets attention which goes to minority oxygen
but they don't bother with trading places: I fear air

is polluted with perfection: kites, balloons; breathers
can see the gas come out: balls of our electricity float:
that's what's in us   —but there is transience

among balloons expanding into a battalion
of odd lollipops, in that same family of don't-take-candy-
from-strangers unless it's Halloween:
some balloon sophisticates
that came to Oregon, Seattle, Wyoming,
one to the open outskirts of Detroit from Japan

released in the winter jet stream
to burn when they landed   what they touched:
initially the spirit.

the actual descent like that of gift
of alien interpretations of angels
as nonhuman as our versions

    (the immortality for one
    and sufficient. usual thing):

        mulberry paper balloons, potato flour, expansive hydrogen
                in November, arrival in
                      Thermopolis, Nogales,

                          and Bly
              where a minister, his wife, five
                Sunday school pupils
        experienced fisherman's luck, catching
        the balloon, pulling it through the trees
              as they would their savior
              in form of cross that fifth of March

        preoccupation with Easter on top of war

        —through even cheap binoculars:
        a patch of mulberry paper became the whole sky:
        a scrap on the lens.

I also didn't see (till now)
how much like, turned on its side,
a chart of the eye this gift is: focal point,
the so-put-upon retina,

images falling short, going too far
requiring other names for vision:
myopia, hyperopia, utopia

with cockeyes, convergent strabismus, cross-eye:
garnishes, painting, the day's featured menu

peered at with bifocals
for a chance at recognizing everything.

The Culture of Near Miss

Because all energy went into making him breathe
dawn was not noticeable

though on the beach it was bigger than anywhere
else, awakened stars stowing away in sand,

low-tide sparkle of a cosmos the sea will take away,
subtraction is basic, the boy's body when movement

is subtracted becomes less, there is hardly any boy
left, his color drains invisibly; it leaves him

to arrive nowhere, his chest becomes a sunken basket
for white peaches (out of season)

through what he's lost, not what he's gained.

* * *

I loved Jerdy
and if my name's not here,
he won't know it was ever true
love, not that he hasn't been loved
by others

also not present, subtracted from the picture,
and even if he has been loved by others
perhaps he won't be again

unless someone falls for a picture;
that has been done (someone I know fell
for a picture of Cindy Song).

Loving Jerdy now is to love him
in the way that makes most museums mean more
to me, he's not to be touched, ideally

he's to be observed in silence, perhaps
photographed, probably without flash,
and if he's not stolen,

insulting the injury of his having been stolen from,
he can be returned to, sometimes only his outline

while he's on loan and his permanent space
has a chance to discolor.

He travels much more this way.
This way, it's not necessary for Jerdy to breathe.

He hangs.	The museum is closed
on Friday	open on Sundays.
His arms rest	on nails.
He seems as wide	as his length.
Crowds gather.	*On the beach*

his breath fell out of him like stars

When he's on loan	a pale cross is left behind

and he couldn't even see or touch the sky.

Me and Bubble Went to Memphis. I did everything I could for Bubble to have a better name, but that didn't happen. Maybe because of how the name immediately stuck to the problematic motherhood of Bubble, how she wanted to burst the bubble of her abdomen every step of the way, how she   wanted   to   stick   pins in Bubble's bubblehead, much too big for the birth canal, bowling ball down twisted
alley, hair all slick   birth
products, a dip in batter.
That was years ago. Way before
me and Bubble watched the little rascals'
                    door-size cake, white like every kitchen
door   I've ever walked through
maybe I've entered only   test
kitchens, maybe there was some doubt   about
everything being cooked up when I entered the scene,
            often dragging Bubble who was compelled
                since he couldn't be an astronaut
to wear a diving helmet   that he built himself,
strict to specifications in *Modern Mechanix*
so thrills
of lake bottoms   could be
his, lust
for bubbling bogs,   he saw
thick skinned bubbles rising out of slime,
                membranes that housed feral embryos,
                    snake-mounds
of braid above the ear over a swell of head,
        hairy hump graft
of miniature camel taking hold   in some
maddening science like the physics of going to Memphis
            with Bubble, wearing a slab of polyurethane-
coated ribs,   pageant sash slabs
pageant sash slabs of ammunition.   He
sprayed his mother's face with polyurethane too, when he
got there,   some of it splattering off
the sides of her casket   like bubbles of

bacon grease, as if to coat particles of air,
tiny globules of synthetic sleet
going up the nose   breath of
tiny bubbled tea, his air supply
          in depth of bog so thick he walked on it as he
nearly drowned   pushing his mother's casket
turned botched kite off a cliff,
scouted good ones the four days it took to get through
Knoxville   because of scouting, then
once in Memphis, collecting tin cans ten inches   in
diameter, thirteen inches deep, cookie cans destined to
become diving bells,   destined to be outfitted
with plate glass windows destined to be placed tight
          against his face, his lips pressed wider, nose
flattened, the punch of the deep,   just as long as he
didn't go too deep,   just as long as he didn't get too
near   the center of
anything, remaining in some margin, near some border, some
sideline where he could have been unnoticed had it not been
for that collection of tin can diving bells, each one over
a commandeered head like crude armor that he found out,
couldn't stop a bullet, repeat: couldn't stop a bullet, and
Bubble couldn't stop firing, monogramming execution's
polite oversized hankies with airholes.

Harryette Mullen

(1953–)

I [WANT] THE POEM to be interesting and complex, as I think experience is, language is; language has that capacity. I [am] interested in concentrating, distilling, and condensing aspects of orality and literacy. Because when you have an oral tradition and you also have writing, you don't have to put the oral tradition on the page as transcription. I think that maybe in Sterling Brown, Langston Hughes, [Paul Laurence] Dunbar, there's a way in which the oral tradition is—though this is not completely true, because there's obviously transformation in what they're doing—but they're closer to a practice of transcribing the oral onto the page. I am more interested in a transformation of the oral into something that draws together different allusive possibilities in one utterance, which is something that writing can do better than speech. I'm interested in taking speech-based tradition and transforming it through the techniques that are available to me in writing.

Unspoken

I'm holding on to you, but you're gone already,
halfway up the mountain, maybe,
in a dream I cannot climb.
I lie awake outside the door
that leads to my own dreams of houses
with bookshelves in every room.

I'm holding your body the color of walnuts—
brown shell you've left behind,
a code I cannot crack—
and wishing you talked in your sleep,
so I could listen in.

Always, when I want to know what you're feeling,
you put your hands on me:
"Here, let me show you,"
and you let your hands do the talking.
Oh yes, I like it and it feels good,
but of course that isn't what I meant.

"We don't need words for this," you tell me.
I wonder if that's what you like best
about our bodies side by side,
together and strange,
like words of two languages
trying to form a sentence.
There I go again,
talking of words and languages
while you've gone to sleep,
leaving me to find a message in your snoring.

Holding you,
I concentrate on the arcane language of your breathing.
Holding your hands in the dark,
I finger the lines of each curling palm,
as if they were a braille I could learn to read.

Finally, I put my ear to your chest,
thinking I can eavesdrop on your heart,
hoping to hear a meaningful pattern of beats—
a telegram you stop to send
on your way down the far side of that mountain.

All She Wrote

Forgive me, I'm no good at this. I can't write back. I never read your letter. I can't say I got your note. I haven't had the strength to open the envelope. The mail stacks up by the door. Your hand's illegible. Your postcards were defaced. "Wash your wet hair"? Any document you meant to send has yet to reach me. The untied parcel service never delivered. I regret to say I'm unable to reply to your unexpressed desires. I didn't get the book you sent. By the way, my computer was stolen. Now I'm unable to process words. I suffer from aphasia. I've just returned from Kenya and Korea. Didn't you get a card from me yet? What can I tell you? I forgot what I was going to say. I still can't find a pen that works and then I broke my pencil. You know how scarce paper is these days. I admit I haven't been recycling. I never have time to read the *Times*. I'm out of shopping bags to put the old news in. I didn't get to the market. I meant to clip the coupons. I haven't read the mail yet. I can't get out the door to work, so I called in sick. I went to bed with writer's cramp. If I couldn't get back to writing, I thought I'd catch up on my reading. Then *Oprah* came on with a fabulous author plugging her best-selling book.

Black Nikes

We need quarters like King Tut needed a boat. A slave could row him to heaven from his crypt in Egypt full of loot. We've lived quietly among the stars, knowing money isn't what matters. We only bring enough to tip the shuttle driver when we hitch a ride aboard a trailblazer of light. This comet could scour the planet. Make it sparkle like a fresh toilet swirling with blue. Or only come close enough to brush a few lost souls. Time is rotting as our bodies wait for now I lay me down to earth. Noiseless patient spiders paid with dirt when what we want is stardust. If nature abhors an expensive appliance, why does the planet suck ozone? This is a big-ticket

item, a thickety ride. Please page our home and visit our sigh on
the wide world's ebb. Just point and cluck at our new persuasion
shoes. We're opening the gate that opens our containers for recy-
cling. Time to throw down and take off on our launch. This flight
will nail our proof of pudding. The thrill of victory is, we're exiting
earth. We're leaving all this dirt.

[if your complexion is a mess]

if your complexion is a mess
our elixir spells skin success
you'll have appeal bewitch be adored
hechizando con crema dermoblanqueadora

what we sell is enlightenment
nothing less than beauty itself
since when can be seen in the dark
what shines hidden in dirt

double dutch darky
take kisses back to Africa
they dipped you in a vat
at the wacky chocolate factory

color we've got in spades
melanin gives perpetual shade
though rhythm's no answer to cancer
pancakes pale and butter can get rancid

[Of a girl, in white]

Of a girl, in white, between the lines, in the spaces where nothing is written. Her starched petticoats, giving him the slip. Loose lips, a telltale spot, where she was kissed, and told. Who would believe her, lying still between the sheets. The pillow cases, the dirty laundry laundered. Pillow talk-show on a leather couch, slips in and out of dreams. Without permission, slips out the door. A name adores a Freudian slip.

Marilyn Nelson

(1946–)

'M INTERESTED in historical narrative, in character, and in formal verse. I'm grateful to have been given, or to have found, some wonderful stories to tell. The stories I tell make a contribution to the popular knowledge of US history, and to interracial understanding. And my poems demonstrate to young (and older) readers some of the traditional pleasures to be taken from poetic form.

I'm interested in narrative, and in character. I enjoy writing dramatic monologue. I like telling stories to people: Life is made up of stories. Yes, I'm aware of the fact that I'm not writing "trendy" poems. I strive to be accessible, not difficult.

Mama's Promise

I have no answer to the blank inequity
of a four-year-old dying of cancer.
I saw her on TV and wept
with my mouth full of meatloaf.

I constantly flash on disasters now;
red lights shout *Warning. Danger.*
everywhere I look.
I buckle him in, but what if a car
with a grille like a sharkbite

roared up out of the road?
I feed him square meals,
but what if the fist of his heart
should simply fall open?
I carried him safely
as long as I could,
but now he's a runaway
on the dangerous highway.
Warning. Danger.
I've started to pray.

But the dangerous highway
curves through blue evenings
when I hold his yielding hand
and snip his minuscule nails
with my vicious-looking scissors.
I carry him around
like an egg in a spoon,
and I remember a porcelain fawn,
a best friend's trust,
my broken faith in myself.
It's not my grace that keeps me erect
as the sidewalk clatters downhill
under my rollerskate wheels.

Sometimes I lie awake
troubled by this thought:
It's not so simple to give a child birth;
you also have to give it death,
the jealous fairy's christening gift.

I've always pictured my own death
as a closed door,
a black room,
a breathless leap from the mountaintop
with time to throw out my arms, lift my head,
and see, in the instant my heart stops,
a whole galaxy of blue.
I imagined I'd forget,
in the cessation of feeling,

while the guilt of my lifetime floated away
like a nylon nightgown,
and that I'd fall into clean, fresh forgiveness.

Ah, but the death I've given away
is more mine than the one I've kept:
from my hands the poisoned apple,
from my bow the mistletoe dart.

Then I think of Mama,
her bountiful breasts.
When I was a child, I really swear,
Mama's kisses could heal.
I remember her promise,
and whisper it over my sweet son's sleep:

> *When you float to the bottom, child,*
> *like a mote down a sunbeam,*
> *you'll see me from a trillion miles away:*
> *my eyes looking up to you,*
> *my arms outstretched for you like night.*

Daughters, 1900

Five daughters, in the slant light on the porch,
are bickering. The eldest has come home
with new truths she can hardly wait to teach.

She lectures them: the younger daughters search
the sky, elbow each others' ribs, and groan.
Five daughters, in the slant light on the porch

and blue-sprigged dresses, like a stand of birch
saplings whose leaves are going yellow-brown
with new truths. They can hardly wait to teach,

themselves, to be called "Ma'am," to march
high-heeled across the hanging bridge to town.
Five daughters. In the slant light on the porch

Pomp lowers his paper for a while, to watch
the beauties he's begotten with his Ann:
these new truths they can hardly wait to teach.

The eldest sniffs, "A lady doesn't scratch."
The third snorts back, "Knock, knock: nobody home."
The fourth concedes, "Well, maybe not in *church* . . ."
Five daughters in the slant light on the porch.

SECOND WAVE, POST-1960s

Elizabeth Alexander

(1962–)

I TRY TO BE LIKE a radio tower, gathering signals from as many places as possible. That's how I live, and such living feeds the storehouse from which poems are made. My ears and eyes and pores are open; you never know what the poem needs so you have to slurp it all in. "It" is: other poems, from now and from the past, from next door and from across the universe; music, sung and not; voices and vernaculars; landscapes and cityscapes; bodily sensations and phenomena; gravitas and fancy; ancestral imaginings and imperatives.

I hope always to be challenged and opened by new poems. With each I start from scratch, my own stern taskmistress, moving myself towards formal resolution, and then—something jagged, open, untidy, and surprising, even within the formalities of the poem.

The Venus Hottentot (1825)

1. *Cuvier*

Science, science, science!
Everything is beautiful

blown up beneath my glass.
Colors dazzle insect wings.

A drop of water swirls
like marble. Ordinary

crumbs become stalactites
set in perfect angles

of geometry I'd thought
impossible. Few will

ever see what I see
through this microscope.

Cranial measurements
crowd my notebook pages,

and I am moving closer,
close to how these numbers

signify aspects of
national character.

Her genitalia
will float inside a labeled

pickling jar in the Musée
de l'Homme on a shelf

above Broca's brain:
"The Venus Hottentot."

Elegant facts await me.
Small things in this world are mine.

2.
There is unexpected sun today
in London, and the clouds that
most days sift into this cage
where I am working have dispersed.
I am a black cutout against

a captive blue sky, pivoting
nude so the paying audience
can view my naked buttocks.

I am called "Venus Hottentot."
I left Capetown with a promise
of revenue: half the profits
and my passage home: A boon!
Master's brother proposed the trip;
the magistrate granted me leave.
I would return to my family
a duchess, with watered-silk

dresses and money to grow food,
rouge and powders in glass pots,
silver scissors, a lorgnette,
voile and tulle instead of flax,
cerulean blue instead
of indigo. My brother would
devour sugar-studded non-
pareils, pale taffy, damask plums.

That was years ago. London's
circuses are florid and filthy,
swarming with cabbage-smelling
citizens who stare and query,
"Is it muscle? Bone? Or fat?"
My neighbor to the left is
The Sapient Pig, "The Only
Scholar of His Race." He plays

at cards, tells time and fortunes
by scraping his hooves. Behind
me is Prince Kar-mi, who arches
like a rubber tree and stares back
at the crowd from under the crook
of his knee. A professional
animal trainer shouts my cues.
There are singing mice here.

"The Ball of Duchess DuBarry":
In the engraving I lurch
toward the *belles dames,* mad-eyed, and
they swoon. Men in capes and pince-nez
shield them. Tassels dance at my hips.
In this newspaper lithograph
my buttocks are shown swollen
and luminous as a planet.

Monsieur Cuvier investigates
between my legs, poking, prodding,
sure of his hypothesis.
I half expect him to pull silk
scarves from inside me, paper poppies,
then a rabbit! He complains
at my scent and does not think
I comprehend, but I speak

English. I speak Dutch. I speak
a little French as well, and
languages Monsieur Cuvier
will never know have names.
Now I am bitter and now
I am sick. I eat brown bread,
drink rancid broth. I miss good sun,
miss Mother's *sadza*. My stomach

is frequently queasy from mutton
chops, pale potatoes, blood sausage.
I was certain that this would be
better than farm life. I am
the family entrepreneur!
But there are hours in every day
to conjur my imaginary
daughters, in banana skirts

and ostrich-feather fans.
Since my own genitals are public
I have made other parts private.

In my silence I possess
mouth, larynx, brain, in a single
gesture. I rub my hair
with lanolin, and pose in profile
like a painted Nubian

archer, imagining gold leaf
woven through my hair, and diamonds.
Observe the wordless Odalisque.
I have not forgotten my Xhosa
clicks. My flexible tongue
and healthy mouth bewilder
this man with his rotting teeth.
If he were to let me rise up

from this table, I'd spirit
his knives and cut out his black heart,
seal it with science fluid inside
a bell jar, place it on a low
shelf in a white man's museum
so the whole world could see
it was shriveled and hard,
geometric, deformed, unnatural.

Boston Year

My first week in Cambridge a car full of white boys
tried to run me off the road, and spit through the window,
open to ask directions. I was always asking directions
and always driving: to an Armenian market
in Watertown to buy figs and string cheese, apricots,
dark spices and olives from barrels, tubes of paste
with unreadable Arabic labels. I ate
stuffed grape leaves and watched my lips swell in the mirror.

The floors of my apartment would never come clean.
Whenever I saw other colored people
in bookshops, or museums, or cafeterias, I'd gasp,
smile shyly, but they'd disappear before I spoke.
What would I have said to them? Come with me? Take
me home? Are you my mother? No. I sat alone
in countless Chinese restaurants eating almond
cookies, sipping tea with spoons and spoons of sugar.
Popcorn and coffee was dinner. When I fainted
from migraine in the grocery store, a Portuguese
man above me mouthed: "No breakfast." He gave me
orange juice and chocolate bars. The color red
sprang into relief singing Wagner's *Walküre*.
Entire tribes gyrated and drummed in my head.
I learned the samba from a Brazilian man
so tiny, so festooned with glitter I was certain
that he slept inside a filigreed, Fabergé egg.
No one at the door: no salesmen, Mormons, meter
readers, exterminators, no Harriet Tubman,
no one. Red notes sounding in a grey trolley town.

The Blue Whale

swam alongside the vessel for hours.
I saw her breach. The spray when she sounded
soaked me (the lookout) on deck. I was joyous.
There her oily, rainbowed, lingering wake,
ambergris print on the water's sheer skin,
she skimmed and we skimmed and we sped
straight on toward home, on the glorious wind.

Then something told her, Turn (whales travel
in pods and will beach themselves rather than split)—
toward her pod?—and the way she turned was not

our way. I begged and prayed and begged for her
companionship, the guide-light of her print,
North Star (I did imagine) of her spout.
But she had elsewhere to go. I watched
the blue whale's silver spout. It disappeared.

Thomas Sayers Ellis

(1963–)

T HERE IS NO ONE WAY to write a poem. I have tried to teach myself, via complete literacy (not just reading text), an appreciation for all types of writing, all types of speaking, and many types of artistic expression. I believe the thing that poems want from sculpture, dance, and cinema, etc. is to reclaim the poetic. Even in its chaos or percussive prosody, the poem must appear to adhere to some sense of uniformity, some sense of its own order (not necessarily control), some combination of what Robert Hayden called "something patterned, wild and free." A pattern, any semblance of such, organizes the senses and provides the reader with a reading experience that he or she can breathe his or her own cultural stance into. The content and the container can agree or disagree, but either way they must do so together, as one. They also must, as Francois Truffaut writes about his expectations of film, "express an idea of art and an idea of life."

Sticks

My father was an enormous man
Who believed kindness and lack of size
Were nothing more than sissified
Signs of weakness. Narrow-minded,

His eyes were the worst kind
Of jury—deliberate, distant, hard.
No one could outshout him
Or make bigger fists. The few

Who tried got taken for bad,
Beat down, their bodies slammed.
I wanted to be just like him:
Big man, man of the house, king.

A plagiarist, hitting the things he hit,
I learned to use my hands watching him
Use his, pretending to slap mother
When he slapped mother.

He was sick. A diabetic slept
Like a silent vowel inside his well-built,
Muscular, dark body. Hard as all that
With similar weaknesses

—I discovered writing,
How words are parts of speech
With beats and breaths of their own.
Interjections like flams. Wham! Bam!

An heir to the rhythm
And tension beneath the beatings,
My first attempts were filled with noise,
Wild solos, violent uncontrollable blows.

The page tightened like a drum
Resisting the clockwise twisting
Of a handheld chrome key,
The noisy banging and tuning of growth.

View-Master

for you, mother, thanks

I guess
I got it
from her,

this habit
of clenching
my face
into a fist,

this brutal
looking into,

her way
of seeing things,

squinting—

one eye
clearly unable
to reach

as far as
the other.

A childhood
plagued
by headaches

from straining,

I watched
far too
much TV—

up close,

so nothing
would escape.

Then at ten
I got an
inexpensive gift,

one that held
images up

closer to
my face
like a kiss.

Imitating
the kids
who were
supposed to be
my friends,

I blinked
and blinked,

testing my
sight with it—

perfect vision
in my right eye,

but the left one
was weaker.

It backed away,

watered,
then blurred.

Farsighted!

her doctor
proclaimed,

adding windows

to our already
veiled corner
of the world.

We left linked,
two good eyes
between us,

joined by
our shared flaw.

You passing
your gift,

me making myth
with it.

Bright Moments

for Globe Poster Printing Corporation's
Byrd and Bank Street Ciceros:
Joseph, Bob and Frank

All night long the capitol glows. The Day-Glo day all night long.
Day-Glo makes the capitol glow makes the capitol glow just like
the globe. To break dawn to break dawn a bridge to cross to break
dawn. All night long all night long the Day-Glo day all night long.
Orange Blaze makes the poster glow makes the poster glow just
like the globe. Between Maryland and Virginia a bridge to cross
between Maryland and Virginia a web of wards. The Day-Glo day
all night long a bridge to cross to break dawn. To break dawn to

break dawn home rule a bridge to cross all night long. Lock this: the pocket is the sound of the capitol and the sound of the capitol is a school without walls. A Day-Glo globe all night long. A Day-Glo poster postering dawn. The light from the posters lasts longer than the shows. A bridge to cross a percussive map home. A short conversation between first gear and dawn. A web of wards a severed map home. Beneath the monuments a baptist chipboard of noise. Behind the monuments a school without walls. Formerly ten miles per side formerly ten miles per side. Day-Glo makes the darkness glow makes the darkness glow just like the globe. A hill and a river between Maryland and Virginia between Maryland and Virginia a hill and a river. Song of the District in bits and pieces, a stapled splatter, proper utensils. Da dee dee dee Da cee cee cee. A short conversation between hill and bottom. All the ugly people in the house be quiet. A web of wards a severed map home.

Song of the District in bits and pieces, sirens and synthesizers, technical difficulties. Da dee dee dee Da cee cee cee. All fat men free before ten p.m. Saturn Yellow makes the poster glow makes the poster glow just like the globe. Security to the middle of the pocket between Maryland and Virginia. A Y-shaped river, lost in the city, the staple gun's silver clip of unstitched bridges. Security to the middle of the pocket between Maryland and Virginia. Work youngin' work all week and pocket on the weekend. Before a poster disappears it works all week and pockets the weekend. Offset and screened. Twenty-two by thirty-three all week and pocket the weekdays. Before a pocket disappears it works all week and posters the weekend. Offset and screened. Twenty-two by thirty-three all week and pocket the weekend. All night long to poster dawn. Work youngin'. The Day-Glo day stapling home. Splotches of do-it fluid fluorescence, lost curfews and white marble. The light from the posters lasts longer than the shows. Welcome to Washington, a capitol city, the nation's capitol. To glow national to glow national hot pink and lavender to go national. Day-Glo makes the capitol glow makes the capitol glow just like the globe. The Day-Glo day all night long. All night long all night long. Signal Green makes the Beltway glow makes the Beltway just like go-go. The money beltway around Washington won't let glow go won't let go-go glow national. To go national to go national a lightning bolt of trouble to go national. Welcome to Washington, a capitol city, the nation's capitol, already national. All the ugly people in the house (and Senate) please be quiet!

All Their Stanzas Look Alike

All their fences
    All their prisons
All their exercises
    All their agendas
All their stanzas look alike
    All their metaphors
All their bookstores
    All their plantations
All their assassinations
    All their stanzas look alike
All their rejection letters
    All their letters to the editor
All their arts and letters
    All their letters of recommendation
All their stanzas look alike
    All their sexy coverage
All their literary journals
    All their car commercials
All their bribe-spiked blurbs
    All their stanzas look alike
All their favorite writers
    All their writing programs
All their visiting writers
    All their writers-in-residence
All their stanzas look alike
    All their third worlds

All their world series
   All their serial killers
All their killing fields
   All their stanzas look alike
All their state grants
   All their tenure tracks
All their artist colonies
   All their core faculties
All their stanzas look alike
   All their Selected Collecteds
All their Oxford Nortons
   All their Academy Societies
All their Oprah Vendlers
   All their stanzas look alike
All their haloed holocausts
   All their coy hetero couplets
All their hollow haloed causes
   All their tone-deaf tercets
All their stanzas look alike
   All their tables of contents
All their Poet Laureates
   All their Ku Klux classics
All their Supreme Court justices
   Except one, except one
Exceptional one. Exceptional or not,
   One is not enough.
All their stanzas look alike.
   Even this, after publication,
Might look alike. Disproves
   My stereo types.

Mr. Dynamite Splits

December 25, 2006

"Can I go back to the top,
Yeah
Can I start one mo 'gin
Yeah
Can I start like I did b-e-f-o-r-e
Yeah
Yeah ready, can I count it
Yeah
Can I hit it
Yeah
Hit me now!"

Long before the patriot acts
of anthems *Say It Loud, I'm Black and I'm Proud,*
Funky President and *Living in America,*
you and your Revue were

the only flames the hood could afford,
and by "hood" I mean "nation"
and by "nation" I mean "community"
and by "community"

I mean any one of the various
Black "folk" Americas
within Black America,
the Constitution's future reframers.

Your famous flames
were not the famous flames
of civil war or civil rights.
These flames were raw chicken guts

and a bewildered next-time fire
of choked chords and percussive horns
Papa lit the behinds
of new bags with.

To quote Sweet Charles, *Yes it's you*
the warm globe mourns . . .
for passing mashed potatoes and peas.
Gimme some more.

No. 1, not because of the hits
but because the roads,
like Augusta, all lead back to you.
Georgia might not-never let us bury you.

The hellish crossroads of black genius
(not geography) left you leathery as Miles.
Not the first to smack-your-bitch-up
and stick-it-to-the-man,

but the first to smack-your-bitch-up,
stick-it-to-the-man,
fine your band, tour Vietnam,
serve two drummers,

fire your band, tour Africa,
save the Boston Garden, endorse Nixon,
rehire your band, sue a rap group
and start a choir in prison.

Pre Hip Hop, you had your own emcee,
your own dancers, your own cape,
Lear jet and crown.
You graduated Super Bad.

Dr. King called it Drum Major Instinct.
Shirley Chisholm,
unbought and unbossed.
Damn right you were somebody!

"These nuts," that's what all the Camel Walks,
splits, spins and Popcorns
told those early closed doors.
Get up offa that thang.

Long live your plea please pleases,
Byrd's brotherly loyalty,
and calling-on Maceo's licking-stick.
Live at the Apollo laid legend to myth.

Before Hammer Time,
there was a time when "whatsinever" you did,
you did "to death."
Funky Broadway.

Your *eeeeeeeeeeeyow* will never rest.
You remain proud, cold bodyheat and sweat,
that muthafucka Black Caesar,
the only one who ever murdered dying.

Wasn't Jesus born today?
The Big Payback: the Angel Pneumonia
(not escape-ism) calling
the Godfather only halfway home.
What you gon' play now?

(Harlem, January 2007)

First Grade, All Over Again

[1]
When he was little
and just a boy
and called Barry,

his report cards
were shown, first,
to the one person

whose approval
mattered the most,
his mother, Ann Dunham.

Works well with others
who do not work
well with each other.

Another GOP *No,*
another honor roll of polls,
locked-in telephoto.

[2]
Barry Obama was
African-American,
African father, American mother,

but not Barack,
Barack Obama is mixed,
race-less and Black.

I have seen more photos
of Barack Obama
than I've ever seen

of my own mother.
Blame the Press,
digital photography, all

the camera-phones,
raised like Rockefellers,
above the rest of us.

[3]
My mother hates
being aimed at. "But Mom, this is
a really good camera,

a Leica." So what, it's
all German to her
and that means torture,

already half locked-up
with my brother.
Armed robbery, his war crime.

My parents broke up
the day Jimmy Carter
was inaugurated,

the last time swine
sent to wipe out drug cartels
came home to roost.

[4]
There's no way to stay
"on-subject" and do this
without high marks

for marksmanship.
Some bald class bully
taking shots at him,

saying he's not tough.
Saying he's a brown Apologist,
shaking hands with

future allies-of-color
weakens us, so let's waterboard Bo,
the biracial Water Dog.

Let's let the human eye decide
if color-blind is cultural
or regular-blindness.

[5]
Mother's Day in the White House,
Marian and Michelle.
First Granny and First Lady.

Out of vernacular-respect,
Black men often refer
to the women they love as "Mama."

This is not something
the minority expects the majority
to accept, reconciliation.

"Once a man loses his mother,
he can accomplish
damn-near anything."

I heard this on the streets
of Washington, D.C.,
right outside the office of citizen.

Godzilla's Avocado

Tonight, Prophet
is helping Noni make
"creatures," the term

    she "cooked up" for mussels.
    I am "Noni," her
    fake baby daddy,

the one she got
her style from, not her
"soft and buttery"

    bottom lip, that came
    from Mommy. Nonies see things differently.
    Waffles, brown skin.

Lady Liberty making us all healthy
holding up her green
flame of asparagus.

    Prophet's a beaneater,
    a yummy Kingpin critter.
    Run, edamame, run,

the same sun
that rises in orange juice
sets in mac and cheese.

    From a lumpy russet, swirling
    in a cosmos of miso,
    colors mash into casserole.

Kids love kitchens, the sushi chef
re-ending monsters
with embassy-precision.

    Life's raw rolls, ready
    to unravel the difficult answers
    we wrap in seaweed.

"Love is when two people
like the same food
and the same toys,

    but war is when lots of people
    dress up like salads
    and eat each other."

Messy imagination.
All meals need metaphors.
Poems, cutting boards.

An artichoke's heart does not pump ketchup.
It pumps pesto,
oily, olive clots of guacamole.

Prophet is learning
to grow things, including time,
real time, some sense

of the vitamins of radiance.
The seedling on
the windowsill, slow to trust sun.

Kids love nature, things smaller than them,
like mushrooms,
cooked into clouds.

Radiation.
Fooling time, rushing food,
hurts the body.

Pesticides are a big deal, poor bees.
The microwaves
hives fear.
Our silver age of dining.

Forrest Hamer

(1956–)

I APPROACH THE WRITING of poems the way I approach the reading of poems—with the anticipation that something waits to be discovered in language, and with the hope that I will be affected in some way I did not expect. It is the very same experience I have as a psychotherapist and psychoanalyst, encountering what others say with the anticipation of discovering something new to say in turn.

I am always trying to hear better. I work in two domains where close listening is central to what I try to do. I've come to appreciate that, in both poetry and psychoanalysis, the speaker, the spoken, and the spoken-to act upon each other so as to create an evocative space wherein thoughts and feelings evoke other thoughts and feelings, many of them formerly unconscious; as well, multiple meanings and multiple levels of meaning are suggested, as are states of mind more commonly described as creative, reflective, perhaps even aesthetic. This is the space of potential discovery.

Lesson

It was 1963 or 4, summer,
and my father was driving our family
from Ft. Hood to North Carolina in our 56 Buick.
We'd been hearing about Klan attacks, and we knew

Mississippi to be more dangerous than usual.
Dark lay hanging from trees the way moss did,
and when it moaned light against the windows
that night, my father pulled off the road to sleep.

                         Noises
that usually woke me from rest afraid of monsters
kept my father awake that night, too,
and I lay in the quiet noticing him listen, learning
that he might not be able always to protect us

from everything and the creatures besides;
perhaps not even from the fury suddenly loud
through my body about this trip from Texas
to settle us home before he would go away

to a place no place in the world
he named Viet Nam. A boy needs a father
with him, I kept thinking, fixed against noise
from the dark.

In the Middle

          I could be wrong, but I think my life is half over.
I think this because of a dream I had a few years ago about a house.
            It was my new home. Mostly. It was unfinished.

    The house was a circle resting above a story and overlooking trees.
Each room was different and each room had two doorways but no doors,
           so leaving and coming in was very easy.
      The dream conceived in my conception, cells of me
              beginning their own end.
   Showing me halfway through my house. The unfinished home.

    In a dream I had one year—more a dream about something else
          than being 39—I recognized a mere idea

was stopping me from crossing a threshold.
It was like news. It changed me in a small way.

I have an idea about aging.
It is not the same as aging; the body will do as it has been doing.
But there is now less time before death
than there is from being conceived.
It startles me I think about dying
through cliches and dreams I don't author.

In the dream about the unfinished home the rooms are warm
and quite light.
When the floorboards are done, when white paint covers the plaster,
I would bring in the furniture.
I may not need doors.

The truth is I am waiting for the next dreams.
The last one has to be perfect.

from Goldsboro Narratives

Goldsboro narrative #4
My father's Viet Nam tour near over

The young dead soldier was younger
than they thought. The 14-year-old passed
himself as seventeen, forged
a father's signature. In the army no more
than months, he was killed early
the week before a cease-fire.
The boy was someone-I somewhat-knew's
older brother and someone-my-mother-
had-taught's son, and, lying
in the standard Army casket, an American
flag draped over the unopened half,

the boy didn't look like anyone
anybody would know—a big kid his dark skin
peached pale, lips pouted. I was sure
I hadn't recognized him.

        When kids older than us
closed down one campus after another,
I thought they'd close all colleges down,
and there would be no place for me
when it was my time. It didn't seem fair.

        Capt. Howell's wife answered
the door one day, and two men
in military dress asked to come in.
She had no choice, I suppose,
but once they came into her living room,
she no longer had a husband, and
the three boys and the girl no longer
had their father. *So this is how
it happens,* I thought: two men come
to your house in the middle of the day,
ringing a bell or rapping on the door.
And, afterwards, there's nothing left
to look forward to.

Goldsboro narrative #7

Time was a boy, specially a black boy,
need to be whipped by his kin, teach him
not to act up, get hisself killt.
Folks did this cause they loved them boys.
The man laughs. And boys would do what all
they could to get out of them whippings,
play like they was getting tore up,
some play like they was going to die.
My grandmama the first one that whipped me,

and she made me go get my own switches.
If I come back to her with a switch too small,
she make me go right back and get a big one.
And she whipped me for that, too. He laughs.
I loved that woman, though. Sho did.

Goldsboro narrative #28

When folks caught on to what was happening
between Rev. Johnson and Sister Edna,
the grown-ups went back to speaking
in front of children as if we couldn't spell.
It was easy to figure out, though:
Rev. Johnson's wife didn't get happy; and,
after service, she wouldn't shake hands
with Sister Edna or any of her kin.
And Sister Edna's husband, Mr. Sam,
who never came to church, began waiting
in the parking lot to drive his wife home.

Now the age Rev. Johnson was then, I doubt
he was concerned with being forgiven.
But when I was 12 and kept on falling
from available grace, I began dismissing him
and mostly all of what he said he meant.
I went witnessing instead to Mr. Sam,
his truck idling outside the paned windows,
him dressed in overalls and a new straw hat.

Kendra Hamilton

(1958–)

YES, POETRY IS ABOUT that moment of observation—as my friend Sam Witt, a Southern poet of amazing gifts, calls it: "that stinkbug in the window with the red underwings" moment. But poetry does far more—it tosses that stinkbug, that immediately physical manifestation of the lived, into a deep well of dark water. And in following it there, we are harrowed, laid open, and ultimately, at least in my poetic practice, healed. Critically, too, poetry is not just the experience; it is a language: a language of riddling, song, spell, and incantation that itself becomes a *making*, both Apollonian and Dionysiac, of the intellect and imagination and the blood and the bone and the muck. You must take care with what you speak into the poem for you may summon a spirit: an efrit or the goddess Oshun draped in cowries and bearing honey or the archangel Michael with his fiery sword. These spirits stand with us as we chant and drum and hum our connection to that hidden world that stands beside and inside the one in which we pay our taxes and take out the trash and watch cities dissolving into madness and despair from Wall Street to Tehran. Many have said this—it is certainly not original with me—but the fundamental responsibility of the artist is to remind us of our mortality: from Homer's warriors chanting of their great deeds and everlasting fame to Thomas and Beulah dancing, weeping, laughing, and dying over three-quarters of a bewildered century. And it is everything between and beyond. For that is poetry's great power and its greatest gift: It allows us to see, to be, to live fully into our own lives and those of others, to bear witness to it all while, blessedly, relieving us of the burden of our names.

The Science of Wearing a Dress

Something there is in every woman
that wants a grand entrance, craves it.
Far more than chocolate or red moiré silk
worse than a kiss from Montgomery Clift.
She'll stand for hours grappling with perplexity
at Tootsie's two-for-one cocktail dress sale.
All around her bugle beads are snapping off
hangers with a music like computerized pinball
and women, smiling gamely or grimly,
are maneuvering their way about the racks
with a sinuous yet unapplauded grace
like that of pickup ballplayers pirouetting under a hoop.
    At moments like these what's uppermost
in her mind is not the face of the man
who asked her to the ball—but whether to rip
up the phone bill, buy those Ferragamos
half-price at Diamanté's on Main.
Ravishing shoes the color of sea foam
with stiletto heels she just knows
will strike sparks off a stone-flagged step.
    Yes, something there is in every woman
standing rooted in a dress shop
that knows the night will be hers,
that every Japanese lantern on every rooftop
in Dallas will be lit just for her
and that Susan Hayward hip snap she worked
three months to perfect will get a tryout
after all—this night—with "the one."
Though he, not being such a one as can interpret
the arcane cricket whisperings of nylons
in the ladies room, will never know
what it cost her, or how she chose to pay.

Belle's Promenade: Nassau Street, Princeton

Maundy Thursday
and a blade of wind knifes
through my light spring coat.
My feet, shod in new kid, are numb.

The sky looks like snow
but this park is filled with children:
children with chalk
and rope
skipping clapping singing
tuneless as jays
in a lane of new green:

Old Black Dinah
Sick in bed
Sent for the doctor
The doctor said . . .

A shiver of dance
steps up my spine.

Said what?

bliss   rattle

I turn a corner
find myself once more
amid the crew cuts
in rut
the cocksure
smiles and curious
eyes
I wear my distant face
but allow a dimple to wink.

In two days time,
the rails will belch
girls by the trainload, whole
chattering families for the Easter repast
and I'll take a day of rest
from that gothic folly,
the Chancellor Green.

Another turn and there it is
so ridiculous
squat and octagonal,
so beloved
its east and west wings
for all the world like flippers
on a tortoise
bearing a brick-and-marble crown
on its back.

Here, amid all my deceptions
—fatherless child
from sun-washed Cape Verde,
mama's genteel pretensions—
is also everything that's
true in my life.

The American books I pop
like chocolate drops on the tongue.
The fine bindings, incunabula,
for which I hunger as a child awaiting
Easter supper.

And no mere riches of our pretty
world can sate me.

Myronn Hardy

(1972–)

I**T IS IN THE COLLISION** of civilizations. The languages, mores, histories, narratives that are kept in the forefront, made dominant, written, or perhaps in which I'm most interested, those forced into obscurity, subservience, or seemingly erased are where my poems attempt to inhabit or negotiate. In fact, it is through these collisions whereby the Americans were formed and continue to be morphed. My poetry aims to explore these tight spaces, gaps, fissures striving to foster new breath.

Undertones

The sail had been drawn into an
albino python hung vertically for
the town to witness. The sea too
shallow to dock. The boat   its
chipped purple belly remained
somewhat distant   solitary with
only its static reflection. The fishermen
swam to shore. Dark-brown sand   their
patterned trails to the plaza for rest. One
wore a straw hat with a wide rim floppy

as fins　　the sun burned above yet
the tawny shield kept his face shadowed.
From the three buckets they showed
friends their catch　　stingrays with pale
undersides like hands. Placed on rocks
gray skins spotted　　pink　green
undertones from pieces of coral　　seaweed
eaten when there was nothing else.

They told a story of the giant squid that almost
pulled their boat under. The ink spewed took
weeks to clean　　foamy bristles against
the deck　　years of tanning until it bled.
Those young men will grow old filling
their nets. Sirens will sing　　love them
when overboard. Intoxication is warm
saltwater　　coconut air　　will-less-ness.

When all the fish were sold they toasted cold
russet bottles　　drank. Women skinned　　chopped.
The fish will fall into stews　　onions　　dendê
milk from trees over rice. Back into the sea where
the boat waited　　a day turned violet. They breathed
on small waves　　these fragile lives wrought with lore.

On a Bench: My Life

How did I believe life would change?

My choices so limited I had to conjure
something that reflected light. It's cold
in Venezia but I sleep on a bench
the sea will soon swallow.

Here in a small jacket I'm observed by a poet
wayward in his search for a canal through this mind.

Ethiopia.

Yes.

I'm from Addis Ababa. Family slaughtered by
a murder of ghosts. Some were visible with guns
others inside skin   arms   fingers   proud
lives were all they knew. This place
of cathedrals   Catholic saints but bodies
are still nailed down   carried through crowds.

Return.

Yes.

To the desert lush as cantos.
The green place where we shared bread is
all I need: my sister spinning about the room   dinner
of roasted fish   yellow lentils as my father
tells of his favorite student   my uncle in church
speaking Ge'ez.

We have prayed so many years.
We are scrolls tightly wound yet I'm the only one left.

Return.

Yes.

In this head is all I have. My warm-poor
country these feet will never touch. I hope the water I
cup   let go   will spill over my desolate land.

The Headless Saints

Agave water crests
beneath azure. Black moths

return to hills   islands waiting
to lose their vapor coronets   snow

pines. I will spool each cloud
into thread   cloth   clothes.

We will walk quietly through
town   bare soles. There is so much

to search for   paradise
in poverty's hot house.

Chop indigo   smear the juice
on cement walls   tree trunks.

Remember seas   the salt
that preserved those bodies

washing to shore. They are headless
but have learned to walk   climb

coconut palms   a green sweet harvest.
How holy they are naked   born

in a garden without unnecessary knowledge.
In a church they gather. We watch

with hands covered in the stickiest blue
(no fallen sky). A Pope has not

made us saints   we neither want
nor need one to do so but here in

this town of stars   the smooth
feet of our dead against this

burned ground   there is
enough light here.

Making Stars with Jacob Lawrence

The only cardboard we had was the box
where those red-scaled fish were frozen

whole. The grocer who owns the two
stores presented it to us when we

visited his home of cedar pillars   glass.
We drank bitter wine   ate spongy rolls

with strange cheese   discussed
the project of his country.

How the horizon blinked when I
heard water   sand in funnels.

The ashen clouds were royal with blue as I
pressed my palm to my chest.

The fish are thawing for today's lunch.
As I flatten the box   a plane   Jacob draws

seven stars   cuts each with a Japanese blade.
On metallic paper they are traced

fourteen times   cut with scissors   glued
front to back   each side a mirror. Fish-line

is attached to each so they may hang from
the sloping boughs of the grumichama.

They sway   night's unassertive
light reflects crests   craters   bounce

from one to another. Beneath
the tree   wind-spun stars   a play.

A boy missing the moon   a wandering
girl humming   friends laughing   unaware

of his elaborate sorrow. The air will hoard
this occasion in its slender history.

Terrance Hayes

(1971–)

"SHAFT AND THE ENCHANTED Shoe Factory" asks what kind of language (the shoes are a metaphor for language) should one wear into the world and do battle. That is part of what I'm interested in as a poet: how language can be worn and changed. Which is to say, I have very little interest in establishing a fixed style or subject matter. The Shaft poem is an ars poetica because it reflects my own quest for language. I'm very interested in wearing Larry Levis on one foot and Harryette Mullen on the other. Or on another day—in another poem—Gwendolyn Brooks and Frank O'Hara. Perhaps this is part of being a young poet. I hope not. I'd like to think I'd never be comfortable wearing the same shoes. Reading provides an infinite number of shoes and paths.

What I Am

Fred Sanford's on at 12
& I'm standing in the express lane (cash only)
about to buy *Head & Shoulders*
the white people shampoo, no one knows
what I am. My name could be Lamont.
George Clinton wears colors like Toucan Sam,
the *Froot Loop* pelican. *Follow your nose,*
he says. But I have no nose, no mouth,
so you tell me what's good, what's god,

what's funky. When I stop
by McDonald's for a cheeseburger, no one
suspects what I am. I smile at Ronald's poster,
perpetual grin behind the pissed-off, fly-girl
cashier I love. Where are my goddamn fries?
Ain't I American? I never say, *Niggaz*
in my poems. My ancestors didn't
emigrate. Why would anyone leave
their native land? I'm thinking about shooting
some hoop later on. I'll dunk on everyone
of those niggaz. They have no idea
what I am. I might be the next Jordan-
god. They don't know if Toni Morrison
is a woman or a man. Michael Jackson
is the biggest name in showbiz. *Mamma se*
Mamma sa mamma ku sa, sang the Bushmen
in Africa. I'll buy a dimebag after the game,
me & Jody. He says, Fuck them white people
at work, Man. He was an All-American
in high school. He's cool, but he don't know
what I am, & so what. Fred Sanford's on
in a few & I got the dandruff-free head
& shoulders of white people & a cheeseburger
belly & a Thriller CD & Nike high tops
& slavery's dead & the TV's my daddy—
        You big Dummy!
Fred tells Lamont.

At Pegasus

They are like those crazy women
    who tore Orpheus
        when he refused to sing,

these men grinding
    in the strobe & black lights
        of Pegasus. All shadow & sound.

"I'm just here for the music,"
    I tell the man who asks me
        to the floor. But I have held

a boy on my back before.
    Curtis & I used to leap
        barefoot into the creek; dance

among maggots & piss,
    beer bottles & tadpoles
        slippery as sperm;

we used to pull off our shirts,
    & slap music into our skin.
        He wouldn't know me now

at the edge of these lovers' gyre,
    glitter & steam, fire,
        bodies blurred sexless

by the music's spinning light.
    A young man slips his thumb
        into the mouth of an old one,

& I am not that far away.
    The whole scene raw & delicate
        as Curtis's foot gashed

on a sunken bottle shard.
    They press hip to hip,
        each breathless as a boy

carrying a friend on his back.
    The foot swelling green
        as the sewage in that creek.

We never went back.
   But I remember his weight
      better than I remember

my first kiss.
   These men know something
      I used to know.

How could I not find them
   beautiful, the way they dive & spill
      into each other,

the way the dance floor
   takes them,
      wet & holy in its mouth.

Derrick Poem (The Lost World)

I take my $, buy a pair of very bright kicks for the game
at the bottom of the hill on Tuesday w/ Tone who averages
19.4 points a game, & told me about this spot, & this salesman
w/ gold ringed fingers fitting a $100 dollar NBA *Air Avenger*
over the white part of me—my sock, my heel & sole,
though I tell him *Avengers* are too flashy & buy blue & white
Air Flights w/ the dough I was suppose to use to pay
the light bill & worse, use the change to buy an Ella
Fitzgerald CD at *Jerrys*, then take them both in a bag
past salesmen & pedestrians to the C where there is a girl
I'd marry if I was Pablo Neruda & after 3, 4 blocks, I spill out
humming "April in Paris" while a lady w/ a 12 inch cigar
calls the driver a fascist cuz he won't let her smoke on the bus
& skinny Derrick rolls up in a borrowed Pontiac w/ room
for me, my kicks & Ella on his way to see *The Lost World*
alone & though I think the title could mean something else,
I give him some skin & remember the last time I saw him
I was on the B-ball court after dark w/ a white girl

who'd borrowed my shorts & the only other person out
was Derrick throwing a *Spalding* at the crooked rim
no one usually shoots at while I tried not to look his way
& thought how we used to talk about black women
& desire & how I was betraying him then creeping out
after sundown with a girl in my shorts & white skin
that slept around me the 5 or 6 weeks before she got tired
of late night hoop lessons & hiding out in my crib
there at the top of the hill Derrick drove up still talking,
not about black girls, but dinosaurs which if I was listening
could have been talk about loneliness, but I wasn't,
even when he said, "We should go to the movies sometime,"
& stopped.

Touch

for Y.K. & brothers playing football
in the parks, in the streets, in the dark

We made our own laws.
I want to be a Hawk,
A Dolphin, a Lion, we'd say

In stores where team logos hung
Like animal skins.

Even by moonlight,
We'd chase each other
Around the big field

Beneath branches sagging
As if their leaves were full of blood.

We didn't notice when policemen
Came lighting tree-bark
& our skin with flashlights.

They saw our game
For what it was:

Fingers clutching torso,
Shoulder, wrist—a brawl.
Some of the boys escaped,

Their brown legs cut by thorns
As they ran through the brush.

It's true, we could have been mistaken
For animals in the dark,
But of all possible crimes,
Blackness was the first.
So they tackled me,

And read me my rights without saying:
You Down or Dead Ball.
We had a language

They did not use, a name
For collision. We called it Touch.

Wind in a Box

This ink. This name. This blood. This blunder.
This blood. This loss. This lonesome wind. This canyon.
This / twin / swiftly / paddling / shadow blooming
an inch above the carpet—. This cry. This mud.
This shudder. This is where I stood: by the bed,

by the door, by the window, in the night / in the night.
How deep, how often / must a woman be touched?
How deep, how often have I been touched?
On the bone, on the shoulder, on the brow, on the knuckle:
Touch like a last name, touch like a wet match.
Touch like an empty shoe and an empty shoe, sweet
and incomprehensible. This ink. This name. This blood
and wonder. This box. This body in a box. This blood
in the body. This wind in the blood.

Major Jackson

(1968–)

NARRATIVE WAS ONE of the first modes of writing I consciously sought to master. Mainly because the greatest poets I admire have exhibited remarkable skill at "storying." The illusion of selecting and introducing elements of a tale is that it comes forth from the speaker as if it were memory; this act of "rememorying" is seductive and seems to reach from some subterranean collective reverie. Storytelling, no matter what genre of art is employed, is the one sovereign act of communication which commands so much of our total attention, that makes listening and awareness appear effortless on our behalf, where the present world collapses and another replaces it. That kind of magic has such concentrated pleasure when employed in a poem.

Don Pullen at the Zanzibar Blue Jazz Café

Half past eight Don Pullen just arrived
from Yellow Springs. By his side
is the African-Brazilian Connection.
If it were any later, another space,
say "Up All Night Movie Hour"
on Channel 7, he might have been
a cartel leader snorting little mountains
of cocaine up his mutilated nostrils
from behind his bureau as he buries

a flurry of silver-headed bullets
into the chests of the good guys:
an armlock M-16 in his right hand,
a sawed-off double barrel shotgun
in his left, his dead blond
girlfriend oozing globules of blood
by the jacuzzi. No one could be cooler
balancing all those stimulants. No one.

She said she couldn't trust me,
that her ladybugs were mysteriously
disappearing, that I no longer
sprinkle rose petals in her bath,
that some other woman left a bouquet
of scented lingerie and a burning
candelabra on our doorstep, that she
was leaving, off to France—
the land of authentic lovers. In this club
the dim track lights reflecting off
the mirror where the bottles are lined
like a firing squad studying their targets
makes the ice, stacked on top of ice,
very sexy, surprisingly beautiful & this
is my burden, I see Beauty in everything,
everywhere. How can one cringe upon
hearing of a six-year-old boy snatched
from a mall outside of London, two
beggarly boys luring him to the train
tracks with a bag of popcorn only to beat
his head into a pulp of bad cabbage!
Even now, I can smell them
holding his hand promising
Candyland in all its stripes & chutes.

Nine-fifteen, Don & the African-
Brazilian have lit into Capoeira.
The berimbau string stings my eyes
already blurring cognac, my eyes
trying to half-see if that's my muse
sitting up front, unrecognizable,

a blue specter. Don's wire fingers are
scraping the ivory keys, off-
rhythm. It doesn't matter, the Connection
agrees there's room as they sway
& fall against the ceiling, a band
of white shadows wind-whipped
on a clothesline. Don's raspy hands—
more violent than a fusillade of autumn
leaves pin-wheeling like paper rain
over East River Drive in blazing reds
& yellows—hammers away, shivers in
monstrous anarchy. Don's arms arch like
orange slices squirting on my mouth's roof,
juice everywhere. His body swings up
off his haunches. The audience, surveying each
other's emotions, feel the extensions; their
bodies meld against the walls, leaving
a funeral of fingerprints as they exhale back
to their seats. Ten minutes to twelve,
I'm waving a taxi through holes
in the rain. I will tell her about tonight,
tell her how a guy named Don & his crew
The Connection hacked harmonies,
smashed scales, pulverized piano keys,
all in rhythm as each brutal chord
exploded in a moment's dawning.

Some Kind of Crazy

It doesn't matter if you can't see
Steve's 1985 Corvette: Turquoise-colored,
Plush purple seats, gold-trimmed
Rims that make little stars in your eyes

As if the sun is kneeling, kissing
The edge of sanity. Like a Baptist
Preacher stroking the dark underside
Of God's wet tongue, he can make you

Believe. It's there, his scuffed wing-
Tips—ragged as a mop, shuffling
Concrete—could be ten-inch Firestone
Wheels, his vocal chords fake

An eight-cylinder engine that wags
Like a dog's tail as he shifts gears. Imagine
Steve, moonstruck, cool, turning right
Onto Ridge Avenue, arms forming

Arcs, his hands a set of stiff C's
Overthrowing each other's rule,
His lithe body and head snap back
Pushing a stick shift into fourth

Whizzing past Uncle Sam's Pawn
Shop, past Chung Phat's Stop & Go.
Only he knows his destination,
His limits. Can you see him? Imagine

Steve, moonstruck, cool, parallel,
Parking between a Pacer and a Pinto—
Obviously the most hip—backing up,
Head over right shoulder, one hand

Spinning as if polishing a dream;
And there's Tina, wanting to know
What makes a man tick, wanting
A one-way trip to the stars.

We, the faithful, never call
Him crazy, crackbrained, just a little
Touched. It's all he ever wants:
A car, a girl, a community of believers.

from Urban Renewal

viii. Block Party
[for *The Roots*]

Woofers stacked to pillars made a disco of a city block.
Turn these rhymes down a notch and you can hear
the child in me reverb on that sidewalk where
a microphone mushroomed with a Caliban's cipher.
Those couplets could rock a party from here to Jamaica.
Its code was simple: *Prospero's a sucker-emcee.*
Smoke rising off a grill threatens to cloud all memory;
my only light, the mountainous cones of streetlamps.
Did not that summer crowd bounce in ceremonial fits?
Ah yes! It was the deejay, and his spinning TECHNICS
delicately needled a groove, something from James Brown's
FUNKY PRESIDENT. Then, working the cross-fade
like a light switch, he composed a stream of scratches,
riffs. Song broken down to a dream of song flows
from my pen; the measured freedom coming off this page
was his pillared spell of drums—it kept the peace.
A police car idled indifferently at the other end of the street.
What amount of love can express enough gratitude
for those reformulations, life ruptured then looped back,
def and gaudy like those *phat*, gold chains?
Keep to sampling language, keep it booming
like Caliban yelling, *Somebody! Anybody! Scream!*

xvi.

A squeegee blade along your tongue's length.
Most dances are crimes against the face. Ash is
a mirror, & mornings you'll wake not particularly heroic,
but eager to glisten like the silvering of office panes,
light gilding down between your teeth. Make easy listening.
Sigh & gargle. Freedom? Fierce attention to dirt
one might possess. Remember Sonny Boy Sam,
back-door windows & Flava Flav. Subdue a grin, yet mouth—
Well-mannered, soft, an entrance, a conference room.
Oh! Rossi? That's Italian. But the lady said he was
Puerto Rican. All the stoops and dreams, trileveled
seats of speculation, which foam like portraits of deeds
mist, blur, first as vaporish powder, blue crystals
ground-fine, then spume, rain-bowed bubblings.
Now, you are classical, at least your eyes, marble-white,
tinge and tingle: fresh, newly heard harmonies.

xxi.

That moment in church when I stared at the Reverend's black
kente-paneled robe & sash, his right hand clasping the back
of my neck, the other seizing my forehead, standing
in his *Watch this* pose, a leg behind him ready to spring,
his whole body leaning into the salvation of my wizened soul,
I thought of the Saturday morning wrestlers of my youth who'd hold
their opponents till they collapsed on a canvas in a slumberous
heap, and how it looked more like a favor, a deed, though barbarous,
a graceful tour out of this world, that chthonic departure
back to first waters, and wondered what pains I endured
in Mr. Feltyburger's physics class, worshipping light, density, mass,
preferring to stare long at snowdomes or the carcasses
of flies pooling above in the great fluorescent cover, and how beds
are graves, my mother and father kissing each other's head,

cupping faces, unhurriedly laying the other down,
and how all locked embraces light in my mind from below
in blue-neon like you'd find on the undercarriage of sports cars,
and then what came was the baker stacking her loaves,
one by one, into little coffers, and Desdemona's
last surrender to Othello's piercing glance, and Isaac shown
a militia of clouds over Moriah, and the dying we submerge
in a baptism of pillows, and how we always loiter at this verge,
there, between rising up and falling back, as in now, this tank
of sound I'm frozen in, gripped between the push and yank
of his clutch, caught in that rush of tambourines next to solemn
trays of grape juice and bits of crackers held by deacons when
the Reverend, serious as a pew, whispered, "Fall, my son. Fall."

Honorée Fanonne Jeffers

(1967–)

M Y POETRY IMAGINES and inhabits the history of folk, mostly unknown, unrecorded, and unheralded, folk who relied on a belief in a higher power to move them from a place of *can't* to *can*. . . . To paraphrase a poem by Lucille Clifton, who is the real winner of history? The one who takes or the one who is taken from—yet who still survives and remembers and prays to a god who pays attention?

These are the questions I constantly ask in my creative work, but I like to interrogate the emotional interiority, the minutiae, of blackness along with the political consideration of that identity; I want to move past mere polemic. And in case there is any question about the *how* of my art, my poems try to reconsider black folk through the foregrounding of poetic craft, technique, and nuance.

The Gospel of Barbecue

for Alvester James

Long after it was
necessary, Uncle
Vess ate the leavings
off the hog, doused
them with vinegar sauce.

He ate chewy abominations.
Then came high pressure.
Then came the little pills.
Then came the doctor
who stole Vess's second
sight, the predication
of pig's blood every
fourth Sunday.
Then came the stillness
of barn earth, no more
trembling at his step.
Then came the end
of the rib, but before
his eyes clouded,
Uncle Vess wrote
down the gospel
of barbecue.

Chapter one:
Somebody got to die
with something at some
time or another.

Chapter two:
Don't ever trust
white folk to cook
your meat until
it's done to the bone.

Chapter three:
December is the best
time for hog killing.
The meat won't
spoil as quick.
Screams and blood
freeze over before
they hit the air.

Chapter four, Verse one:
Great Grandma Mandy
used to say food
you was whipped
for tasted the best.

Chapter four, Verse two:
Old Master knew to lock
the ham bacon chops
away quick or the slaves
would rob him blind.
He knew a padlock
to the smokehouse
was best to prevent
stealing, but even the
sorriest of slaves would
risk a beating for a full
belly. So Christmas time
he give his nasty
leftovers to the well
behaved. The head ears
snout tail fatback
chitlins feet ribs balls.
He thought gratitude
made a good seasoning.

Chapter five:
Unclean means dirty
means filthy means
underwear worn too
long in summertime heat.
Perfectly good food
can't be no sin.
Maybe the little
bit of meat on ribs
makes for lean eating.
Maybe the pink flesh
is tasteless until you add
onions garlic black
pepper tomatoes

soured apple cider
but survival ain't never been
no crime against nature
or Maker. See, stay alive
in the meantime, laugh
a little harder. Go on
and gnaw that bone clean.

Fast Skirt Blues

for V.

You Mama's son. You
sister's brother. You
baby's Daddy. You
woman's husband. You

take me someplace.
Help me burn off a midnight crazy.
The tune in this head as hard

to hold as smoke in my clothes.
Tell me what ails me, baby.
I ain't got no shame—that's
what I say to myself.

I want to teach you the pigmeat
story this evening. I'm an angel
stabbed by the point I dance on.

I need the sanctified blues.
I need the hallelujah nasty.
Take me there.
I don't care where we go.

Out past County Line Road
and a dark field shout.
On a cracked backseat.

On my big brass bed.
I don't care.
I'll sing you the gap-legged
words the last man heard,

explain how I got born
with this sorry caul on my face.
You know a bad girl's gone

pay for her sugar one day.
I know it,
God knows it.
Now, the Devil do, too.

Hagar to Sarai

Don't give me nothing in
exchange for a beating
in my belly, sore nipples
way after the sucking is gone.
Don't thank me for my body,
a fine drinking skin
turned inside out for you.
Don't thank me for the back
that don't break from Abram's weight.
I know what you need—a baby's
wail in the morning,
smile on your man's face,
his loins full of much obliged.
I know what you need;

don't give me your grief
to help this thing along.
I know how emptiness feels.
Woman, I know how
to make my own tears.

The Wife of Lot Before the Fire

First time I lay with him
music came from my mouth
I ain't never heard
such strong music

You the one gone save me
You the one gone take me
away from here

Lately a humming
coming from the other
corners of the house
The whispering

His walking in the night hours
His blood on the backs
of our daughters' skirts

Baby please
You the one gone save me
You the one supposed
to take me away from here

Lately a humming
coming from the other
corners of this house

First time I lay with him
who knew I could
reach those notes
Now I done forgot his tune

The man said a thief
done plucked my tongue
right from my singing throat

A. Van Jordan

(1965–)

THE IMAGE IS WHAT comes to mind first. Trying to correlate that image with an emotion is the rest of the process.

You're always trying to find the proper container for the content. If I want something to be more elegant, maybe I'll use a sonnet or a villanelle. For brevity of image and language, maybe an Asian form.

I spend most of my time researching. I like having search and rescue missions, finding erasures from our history and culture. I'm trying to connect historical events to a larger theme of the human condition. It's a way of putting the work in conversation with the world.

You have to think about how language associates within the poem and look for patterns in the images, the metaphors, the setting. You have to think as if you are directing a film—what's the ambient noise? What's the sound track? What's the dialogue? What's the sound level? What props do you put in the scene?

The role of the poet has always been to record the culture and history of a people. The thing that's changed is that there are many more competing ways of recording that. Why put it in a poem? Why not a film or a novel or a blog? For me it has to be because a poem is the highest form of language.

Regina Brown Hears Voices, Kills Son
Week Before Christmas, December 18, 1996

Sylvester, my eight-year-old son, lives in sin.
I tell his grandmother—his father's mother, mind you—
and she asks me what I'm talking about,

like she can't hear me. She says,
"Regina, he's eight years old.
What are you talking about?"

When I told her I'd take care of it,
she, once again, asked,
"Regina, what are you talking about?"

*

I watch Jay Leno on the *Tonight* show,
but I keep the sound on mute: the voices
speak through him. It's getting worse though:

every time he moves his lips,
I can now read what he's saying,
what *they're* saying through him.

And I know they're trying to use Sylvester;
they're going to make him do terrible things,
my baby. I wish they'd take me

and leave him alone. I watch him play
with his Hot Wheels and Nintendo;
I watch him ride his bike;

I watch him play with the older boys,
who got over his lisp because he's so tough;
I watch him sleep in his bunk bed,

the one I bought so his friends could sleep over.
I watch him and wait as he changes before my eyes.
I watch and wait for a way to stop the change.

        *

I'm watching Ted Koppel talk about a war in Lebanon.
He switches to taped coverage of soldiers defending their land,
their women and their children against an enemy

who appears unclear to me. Soldiers shooting guns,
civilians scream and run for cover,
cars burn along the side of the road.

He switches back to his report from the studio,
when, in the middle of his report, he starts
speaking this other language, at first his voice

just sounds slowed down like a record
at the wrong speed, but then he looks right at me,
right at me and says, clearly, "Regina . . ."

        *

I'm at work the next day
at the U.S. Patent and Trademark Office,
early, 7 a.m. I couldn't sleep:

I looked in on Sylvester all night,
Who just slept away
as if nothing were wrong.

I've been doing this job for years,
copying microfilm for the government,
but this day is different. I'm looking

through the eye of the stat camera,
and there's no image; there's no color—
just a white expanse of the world

washed away under an avalanche
of nothingness. And, goddamn it,
voices silence me at home;

I'll be damned if I'm going to let *them*
blind me at work. I don't know how
long I can keep dragging myself in here.

*

Days ahead, I just wish I could talk
to someone and see—in their eyes, I mean—
see them hear me. I woke up yesterday

and put my face in my hands, speaking
right into my palms, I asked
"Where have my friends gone?"

And I could hear the echo
of my voice bounce back
and forth between the lifelines of each hand.

*

When I look at Sylvester, I don't want him to live
like me. I don't want my baby
to know what it's like to feel betrayed

by your own mind. Once you lose confidence
in yourself, who can you trust? Not your own mind,
not your own ears and eyes, not your own hand—

this is when you play tug of war with the future,
yours and the ones you love. Soon, an anniversary
or a birthday or even this Christmas comes up,

you try to dig your heels in, you really try to pull
the future along, but then, just when you think
you feel like you're feeling strong, when you think

your life, your family and friends, all at once,
all pull together and the future begins to fall
over to your side, suddenly,

the rope   snaps in two.

from (⇨) *prep.* 1. Starting at (a particular place or time): As in, John
was *from* Chicago, but he played guitar straight *from* the Delta; he
wore a blue suit *from* Robert Hall's; his hair smelled like coconut;
his breath, like mint and bourbon; his hands felt like they were *from*
slave times when he touched me—hungry, stealthy, trembling. 2. Out
of: He pulled a knot of bills *from* his pocket, paid the man and we
went upstairs. 3. Not near to or in contact with: He smoked the weed,
but, surprisingly, he kept it *from* me. He said it would make me too
self-conscious, and he wanted those feelings as far away *from* us as
possible; he said a good part of my beauty was that I wasn't conscious
of my beauty. Isn't that funny? So we drank Bloody Mothers (Hennessy
and tomato juice), which was hard to keep *from* him—he always did
like to drink. 4. Out of the control or authority of: I was released *from*
my mama's house, *from* dreams of hands holding me down, *from* the
threat of hands not pulling me up, *from* the man that knew me, but of
whom I did not know; released *from* the dimming of twilight, *from* the
brightness of morning; *from* the love I thought had to look like love;
from the love I thought had to taste like love, *from* the love I thought I
had to love like love. 5. Out of the totality of: I came *from* a family full
of women; I came *from* a family full of believers; I came *from* a pack of
witches—I'm just waiting to conjure my powers; I came *from* a legacy
of lovers—I'm just waiting to seduce my seducer; I came *from* a pride
of proud women, and we take good care of our young. 6. As being other
or another than: He couldn't tell me *from* his mother; he couldn't tell
me *from* his sister; he couldn't tell me *from* the last woman he had
before me, and why should he—we're all the same woman. 7. With
(some person, place, or thing) as the instrument, maker, or source:
Here's a note *from* my mother, and you can take it as advice *from* me:
A weak lover is more dangerous than a strong enemy; if you're going
to love someone, make sure you know where they're coming *from*. 8.

Because of: Becoming an alcoholic, learning to walk away, being a good speller, being good in bed, falling in love—they all come *from* practice. 9. Outside or beyond the possibility of: In the room, he kept me *from* leaving by keeping me curious; he kept me *from* drowning by holding my breath in his mouth; yes, he kept me *from* leaving till the next day when he said *Leave*. Then, he couldn't keep me *from* coming back.

The Flash Reverses Time

DC Comics, November 1990, #44
"Never Look Back, Flash
Your Life Might Be Gaining On You"

When I'm running across the city
on the crowded streets
to home, when, in a blur,
the grass turns brown
beneath my feet, the asphalt
steams under every step
and the maple leaves sway
on the branches in my wake,
and the people look,
look in that bewildered way,
in my direction, I imagine
walking slowly into my past
among them at a pace
at which we can look one another in the eye
and begin to make changes in the future
from our memories of the past—
the bottom of a bottomless well,
you may think, but why not dream a little:
our past doesn't contradict our future;
they're swatches of the same fabric
stretching across our minds,

one image sewn into another,
like the relationship between a foot and a boot,
covariant in space and time—
one moves along with the other,
like an actor in a shadow play—
like a streak of scarlet light
across the skyline of your city
sweeping the debris, which is simply confetti,
candy wrappers, a can of soda,
all the experience of a day discarded
and now picked up
even down to the youthful screams of play
that put smiles on the faces of the adults
who hear remnants of their own voices
through a doorway leading back
to a sunrise they faintly remember.

Black Light

Our bodies cast a shadow of one
Body under a black-bulb pulse
In your mother's basement. Light, even

When it's black, moves faster than
Youth or old age; it's the constant in
Our lives. But I remember when

I thought your house—always ready for
A party, even during the week—
Was the fastest element in my life.

Toenails, lint, teeth,
Eyes—everything was holy
Under the glow. I suspect

Even my bones were ultraviolet
When we danced, which was always more
Of a grind than a dance.

Whether the song sung came
From Rick James or Barry White,
We called what we did in the coatroom

Dancing, too: My hands, infrared
Under your dress, but innocent: We
Were only kids, after all,

I was 16 and you were a woman of 18.
Already, we knew how to answer each other
Without asking questions, how to satisfy by seeing

What nearly satisfied looked like
In each other's faces. This all before
I ran out to sneak back into my mother's

House in the middle of the night.
But, now, it's eight years later,
You're walking, it seems, so I offer

You a ride. And you look in and smile.
And when I see you I wonder
What would have happened

If we had stayed in touch. I have to get back
To work the next morning in DC,
A five-hour drive; it's near dark

And I want to get on the road before night
Falls completely, but I stop anyway.
It's been too many years.

And I mistake your gesture.
And then I realize you
Don't really recognize me,

Until you back away and turn
On your heels.
Then a man with a Jheri curl

And a suit that looks like it's woven
From fluorescent thread
Walks up and looks at me

Like I wasn't born in this town,
And for the first time in my life,
I question it myself. He walks up as slow

And sure as any old player should on Sunday night.
While walking away, you two exchange
Words. You don't look back. But

We see each other in our heads—aglow,
Half-naked—under our black-bulb pulse
In your mother's basement. Given a diadem

By the lucid night and the streetlamp's
Torch, the man wearing the fluorescent
Suit casts a broad shadow

Like a spotlight into which you step.
Maybe he's the reason we're here tonight
Beneath these dim stars, casting

A light true enough . . . finally,
For us, after all these years, to see each other.

from Thought Clouds

FADE IN:

INT—Newsreel of D. W. GRIFFITH in his library at home
after the release of his biggest financial success, *Birth of a
Nation*. 1915.

D. W. Griffith

This story surprises even me: *Birth of a Nation* arrives forged
from a love story, and ignites controversy across the country.
Between a man and a woman bred in Southern soil, who could
eclipse its importance with the cloud of race hovering over their
destiny, with the world watching Elsie (Lillian Gish) fall into Ben's
(Henry Walthall's) on-screen kiss? The public—largely in the
North, it seems—sets sanctity aboil. I want the light of the South
to shine across a unified nation, shine to awaken the magnolias
and cypresses in the chests of men who believe in the virtues of
womanhood. This is in defense of the couple with a thousand eyes
beating down upon them: Elsie and Ben, entwined as the South,
under Klieg lights, burning with survival, attempts to end this
feud from beneath flash powder and smoke. Ben wants to protect
his lover without losing his brother in the North. Elsie wants the
world to stop fighting and allow her to marry. They, sepia-toned
and sure-footed, take on a world full of harsh colors. They take
on the mantle of manners representing the country from which
they're bred. Bougainvillea, kudzu and cotton, embroils the
North and the South, distends the bond till it bursts into flame.
Sometimes the link comes so close, sometimes it's so beautiful
in the exchange, neither believes the other deserves the union.
When the passion implodes, we call it Civil War. The soldier on
his journey goes back and forth, advancing and retreating, cover-
ing ground for brother and sister; no one knows who's the enemy
and, after a while, no one cares but the fallen bodies carpeting
the field. All seems found just as all seems lost, till both sides
push their passion to a point of rest. As he falls, he sees her—in a
photograph or a memory or a dream of regret—all while a hint of
sweat, just a touch slides down her breast, gently wiped away by

some devil's finger, pointing north.

CUT TO: EXT—FLASHBACK—Porch of home in Gregory,
SD, of OSCAR MICHEAUX, farmer and Negro novelist. He
contemplates his affection for and relationship with his
Scottish neighbor's daughter, SARAH. 1908.

Mixed Couple, 1908

Oscar to Sarah

Once I glanced at—I admit, a second too long—a hint of sweat,
just a touch on your breast—once I bought the land from your
father, once he named the fairest price offered to me from any-
one in the county, and once it became clear that he respected
me as a man should respect other men—like your reflection in
water, which you admire but prefer not to disturb—I knew the
spirit of your house embraced me like family. I changed. Talk-
ing to you now sends me to think of our night in shadow, first
of many to follow, on which I came 'round back of your house
under your window, hiding from your father's gaze, he doesn't
know—at least I don't think he does, but his eyes—and he would
not mind, really, but . . . rest that thought: I only remember his
eyes. His eyes of Atlantic Ocean and onyx stone, of forgiveness
and regret. His stares assure that folks down the road would
nest not like robins but like buzzards. I see them daily here in
Gregory, SD, in Kansas City, MO, in Greensboro, NC, through the
South and the North: men on every corner to slit our throats,
the two regions are more united than Griffith would lead us to
believe, this journey of us—if lucky: the world builds gallows,
after all—waiting for a world in which we're free enough to hold
each other; but, for now, it's worse for mixed couples, a true test
of the country's union and reconstruction, of our fearful dream.
The true sleep of pain, the true nightmare rises not from sleep
but from glowers across a room, from refusal of service at res-
taurants, from this person we encounter daily who is a dream of
fear, or a nightmare. I live both by day, a riddle: what promises
freedom and then denies me a suit fitting in a haberdashery? To

some, this may sound cavalier for a Negro, even critical of North-
ern freedom, yet, it's a small freedom to ask, but it can play like a
child on my mind and gut as I strain to walk in my country like
a man through it all. This shows how we dare thrive, day-to-day,
person-to-person, through trials won, and verdicts we survive;
we simply hold hands not in public but in the near safety of our
home.

CUT TO: INT—Living room of Oscar Micheaux with his
first motion picture camera. He decides to make a film of
one of his novels, *The Homesteader.* 1918.

Discovering the Camera

Oscar Micheaux
There's a likeness between the eye and the world over which it
peers—the same striking image in dreams as in our daily lives,
the same trials won and verdicts we survive—the same forked
tongues branching into truth and deceit: something truer than
the close up of the girl in the frame, something more false than
her face caught off camera; than the life in which we live: where
makeup becomes beauty, and a hero becomes flawless, and a gun
becomes messiah, and a man against an army of men becomes
myth, and all honest-pay-for-a-day's work and all cards-up-a-
dealer's-sleeve, become a reflection in a single mirror.

Nevertheless, with the camera comes a feral tool: its lens
increases scrutiny, a focus as two-faced as Juno; and, now
intrigued, evolves to the moving picture by way of its roving
eye: finally we find a means to view others without the shame of
gawking; we adore the reflection of light through a lens in a dark
theater.

We view actors with the heart of a secret admirer viewing the
neck of she who he cannot kiss, but breaking and renting fan-
tasies; the pillar of art, yet a shaky pillar; an embrace with an

angel, which on second glance looks more like a match between wrestlers, which brings our blood to the surface, which cuts off our breath, which overshadows with soft shoe and piano, which brings the mob to their feet and their hands to applause.

This isn't about the dutiful wife who makes robes from the white sheets; it isn't about the father worried his daughter might love out of her race; it isn't about the book by Thomas Dixon clutched both in the hands of the illiterate and the teacher; not about the man forcing the woman under the knife; it isn't about finding a rope to adorn the neck; it's not about the murder we could not solve.

This is the one about the dreamer who breaks convention; the one about the electrician who becomes a best boy; the one about the seamstress who makes the costumes; the one about the guy with the razor who edits the film; the one about the Pullman porter who sets the props in the scene; the one about the farmer who, finally, puts down his hoe, picks up the camera, and, after he can't take it anymore, yells *Action!*

Carl Phillips

(1959–)

FROM THE VERY BEGINNING, I've been most concerned in my poems with the tension between how we conduct our bodies and how society says we *should* conduct our bodies, and more generally with the tension between a chosen and an implied notion of morality. Who is to say what is normal, what is acceptable? I think Greek tragedy probably influenced my thinking to a great degree, where personal obligations so frequently conflict with societal ones, just as human concerns conflict with divine ones. But I know that much of my thinking about morality came together around my understanding—and being at last able not only to accept but to embrace—my homosexuality. My poems tend to look at outsiderness in the sexual arena, ideas of risk and transgression, and the possibilities for human relationships that can incorporate both risk and devotion, fidelity and—perhaps incongruously—betrayal.

As for poetics and style, I seem to have chosen syntax as the place where power relations get enacted. The sentence—as I learned from my classical training but also from the sentences of such writers as Henry James, George Eliot, [Marcel] Proust—the sentence has seemingly infinite possibilities when it comes to a system of deferral and delivery that, to my mind, is very sexual, hence my use of the term "an erotics of syntax" to describe at least one aspect of my work. Syntax *can* be erotic, even as the sexual can be divine, a manner of prayer.

Blue

As through marble, or the lining of
certain fish split open and scooped
clean, this is the blue vein
that rides, where the flesh is even
whiter than the rest of her, the splayed
thighs mother forgets, busy struggling
for command over bones: her own,
those of the chaise lounge, all
equally uncooperative, and there's
the wind, too: this is her hair, gone
from white to blue in the air.

This is the black, shot with blue, of my dark
daddy's knuckles, that do not change, ever.
Which is to say they are no more pale
in anger than at rest, or when, as
I imagine them now, they follow
the same two fingers he has always used
to make the rim of every empty blue
glass in the house sing.
Always, the same
blue-to-black sorrow
no black surface can entirely hide.

Under the night, somewhere
between the white that is nothing so much as
blue, and the black that is, finally, nothing,
I am the man neither of you remembers.
Shielding, in the half-dark,
the blue eyes I sometimes forget
I don't have. Pulling my own stoop-
shouldered kind of blues across paper.
Apparently misinformed about the rumored
stuff of dreams: everywhere I inquired,
I was told look for blue.

X

Several hours past that
of knife and fork

laid across one another
to say done, X

is still for the loose
stitch of beginners,

the newlywed
grinding next door

that says no one
but you, the pucker

of lips only, not yet
the wounds those lips

may be drawn to. X,
as in variable,

anyone's body, any set
of conditions, your

body scaling whatever
fence of chain-metal Xs

desire throws up, what
your spreadeagled limbs

suggest, falling, and
now, after. X, not

just for where in my
life you've landed,

but here too, where
your ass begins its

half-shy, half-weary
dividing, where I

sometimes lay my head
like a flower, and

think I mean something
by it. X is all I keep

meaning to cross out.

Leda, After the Swan

Perhaps,
in the exaggerated grace
of his weight
settling,

the wings
raised, held in
strike-or-embrace
position,

I recognized
something more
than swan, I can't say.

There was just
this barely defined
shoulder, whose feathers
came away in my hands,

and the bit of world
left beyond it, coming down

to the heat-crippled field,

ravens the precise color of
sorrow in good light, neither
black nor blue, like fallen
stitches upon it,

and the hour forever,
it seemed, half-stepping
its way elsewhere—

then
everything, I
remember, began
happening more quickly.

As from a Quiver of Arrows

What do we do with the body, do we
burn it, do we set it in dirt or in
stone, do we wrap it in balm, honey,
oil and then gauze and tip it onto
and trust it to a raft and to water?

What will happen to the memory of his
body, if one of us doesn't hurry now
and write it down fast? Will it be
salt or late light that it melts like?
Floss, rubber gloves, a chewed cap

to a pen elsewhere—how are we to
regard his effects, do we throw them
or use them away, do we say they are
relics and so treat them like relics?
Does his soiled linen count? If so,

would we be wrong then, to wash it?
There are no instructions whether it
should go to where are those with no
linen, or whether by night we should
memorially wear it ourselves, by day

reflect upon it folded, shelved, empty.
Here, on the floor behind his bed is
a bent photo—why? Were the two of
them lovers? Does it mean, where we
found it, that he forgot it or lost it

or intended a safekeeping? Should we
attempt to make contact? What if this
other man too is dead? Or alive, but
doesn't want to remember, is human?
Is it okay to be human, and fall away

from oblation and memory, if we forget,
and can't sometimes help it and sometimes
it is all that we want? How long, in
dawns or new cocks, does that take?
What if it is rest and nothing else that

we want? Is it a findable thing, small?
In what hole is it hidden? Is it, maybe,
a country? Will a guide be required who
will say to us how? Do we fly? Do we
swim? What will I do now, with my hands?

Fretwork

        Reports are various—
conflicting also:

many fell,
           a few;

like taken cities. . . .

      *

Whether or not
to any loss there is weight
assignable,

           or a music given

—some play of notes,
slow-trumpeted,

for which to listen
is already to be
too late;

        whether forgetting is
or is not proof of
mercy, henceforth let

others say.

      *

        Is not victory itself
the proof of victory?

      *

Little hammer, chasing—onto
unmarked metal—pattern,
decoration,

a name,

a scar upon the face
of history, what

has no face

                *

                Of briar
and thorn, my bed.

        *

—I stand in clover.

Speak Low

The wind stirred—the water beneath it stirred accordingly . . .
The wind's pattern was its own, and the water's also. The
water in that sense was the wind's reflection. The wind was,
to the water, what the water was to the light that fell there,
or appeared to fall, spilling as if the light were a liquid, or as
if the light and the water it spilled across

                                were now the same.
It is true that the light, like the water, assumed the pattern of
what acted upon it. But the water assumed also the shape
of what contained it, while the light did not. The light seemed
fugitive, a restiveness, the less-than-clear distance between
everything we know we should do, and all the rest—all
the rest that we do. Stirring, as the wind stirred it, the water
was water—was a form of clarity itself, a window we've
no sooner looked through than we've abandoned it for what
lies past that: a view, and then what comes

                                into view, or might,

if we watch patiently enough, steadily—so we believe, wishing
for what, by now, even we can't put a name to, but feel certain
we'll recognize, having done so before. It looked, didn't it,
just like harmlessness. A small wind. Some light on water.

Civilization

There's an art
   to everything. How
the rain means
   April and an ongoing-ness like
   that of song until at last

it ends. A centuries-old
   set of silver handbells that
once an altar boy swung,
   processing . . . *You're the same*
   wilderness you've always

been, slashing through briars,
   the bracken
of your invasive
   self. So he said,
   in a dream. But

the rest of it—all the rest—
   was waking: more often
than not, to the next
   extravagance. Two blackamoor
   statues, each mirroring

the other, each hoisting
   forever upward his burden of
hand-painted, carved-by-hand
   peacock feathers. *Don't*
   you know it, don't you know

I love you, he said. He was
   shaking. He said,
I love you. There's an art
   to everything. What I've
   done with this life,

what I'd meant not to do,
   or would have meant, maybe, had I
understood, though I have
   no regrets. Not the broken but
   still flowering dogwood. Not

the honey locust, either. Not even
   the ghost walnut with its
non-branches whose
   every shadow is memory,
   memory . . . As he said to me

once, *That's all garbage*
   down the river, now. Turning,
but as the utterly lost—
   because addicted—do:
   resigned all over again. It

only looked, it—
   It must only look
like leaving. There's an art
   to everything. Even
   turning away. How

eventually even hunger
   can become a space
to live in. How they made
   out of shamelessness something
   beautiful, for as long as they could.

Reginald Shepherd

(1963–2008)

I HAVE AN AMBIVALENT relationship to literary tradition, to the "canonical" literary language. Every writer is alienated from his own language: language belongs to no one, and writing is always about trying to find or construct a place for yourself in this system based on negation. [Ferdinand de] Saussure points out that language is based on negation, on *bat* not being *cat* and *b* not being *p* (between its elements, he wrote, is only difference), and [Jacques] Lacan points out that the psyche itself is built on negation, on the self being always other and always unattainable, a kind of asymptote toward which one strives. That's what identity is, the attempt toward identity. But just as a straight white male individual can more easily rest in the illusion of a fixed, stable identity, similarly a straight white male writer can have a more settled, though still illusory, sense that the language belongs to him: he can have a sense of security, however false, I never had. I had a sense from a very early age that literature was a world to which I aspired, something preferable to the circumstances in which I grew up. I believed that language would save me from the housing projects and tenements of the Bronx, would save me from myself, even, if only I could get to it. And when I got there, when I arrived at "literature," I realized that a) it was not going to save me and b) there was an ambiguity in my relationship to it in that it was a language that did not acknowledge my existence. There was a paradox in that I looked to this language both to make me exist in the world and at the same time to make me into something else, someone else. It was a language that, insofar as I was a black person, insofar as I was a gay person, didn't speak of me, and that was both an attraction (the world literature proposed wasn't part of the trap in which I was living) and a problem.

Orpheus Plays the Bronx

When I was ten (*no, younger
than that*), my mother tried
to kill herself (*without the facts
there can't be faith*). One death
or another every day, Tanqueray bottles
halo the bed and she won't wake up
all weekend. In the myth book's color
illustration, the poet turns around
inside the mouth of hell to look at her
losing him (*because it's not her fault
they had to meet there*): so he can keep her
somewhere safe, save her place
till she comes back. Some say
she stepped on an asp, a handful of pills
littered the floor with their blues,
their red and yellow music. Al Green
was on the radio. (*You were
at school, who's ever even seen
an asp?*) It bruised her heel
purple and black. So death
could get some color to fill out
his skin, another bony white boy
jealous of all her laugh too loud, her
That's my song when Barry White
comes on. He's just got
to steal it, he can't resist
a bad pun, never never gonna give her
up, or back. The pictures don't prove
anything, but one thing I remember
about the myth's still true:
the man can't live if she does.
She survived to die for good.

How People Disappear

If this world were mine, the stereo
starts, but can't begin
to finish the phrase. I might survive
it, someone could add, but that
someone's not here. She's crowned
with laurel leaves, the place
where laurel leaves would be
if there were leaves, she's not
medieval Florence, not
Blanche of Castile. Late March
keeps marching in old weather,
another slick of snow to trip
and fall into, another bank
of inconvenient fact. The sky
is made of paper and white reigns,
shredded paper pools into her afterlife,
insurance claims and hospital reports,
bills stamped "Deceased," sign here
and here, a blank space where she
would have been. My sister
said *We'll have to find another*
Mommy.
           And this is how
loss looks, my life in black plastic
garbage bags, a blue polyester suit
a size too small. Mud music
as they packed her in
damp ground, it's always raining
somewhere, in New Jersey,
while everyone was thinking about
fried chicken and potato salad,
caramel cake and lemonade.
Isn't that a pretty dress
they put her in? She looks so
lifelike. (Tammi Terrell
collapsed in Marvin Gaye's arms

onstage. For two hundred points,
what was the song?) Trampled
beneath the procession, her music.
Pieces of sleep like pieces of shale
crumble through my four a.m.
(a flutter of gray that could be
rain), unable to read this thing
that calls itself the present.
She's lost among the spaces
inside letters, moth light, moth wind,
a crumpled poem in place of love.

Skin Trade

And then I said, That's what it means
to testify: to sit in the locked dark muttering
when you should be dead to the world. The muse
just shrugged and shaded his blue eyes. So naturally
I followed him down to his father's house
by the river, a converted factory in the old
industrial park: somewhere to sit
on threadbare cushions eating my words
and his promises, safe as milk
that dries the throat. If I had a home,
he'd be that unmade bed. He's my America
twisted in dirty sheets, my inspiration
for a sleepless night. No getting around that
white skin.
                He throws things out the window
he should keep; he collects things
he should feed to the river. He takes me
down. While there, I pick them up.

The river always does this to me:
gulls squawking and the smell of paper mills
upstream, air crowded with effluents
like riding the bus underwater. I'm spending nights
in the polluted current, teaching sunken bodies how
to swim. My feet always stay wet. Sometimes
I leave footprints the shape of blood; sometimes glass
flows through broken veins, and I glitter.
Every other step refers to white men
and their names. The spaces in between
are mine. *Back of the bus with you,*
nigger. They're turning warehouses
into condos, I'm selling everything
at clearance prices: here's a Bronze Star
for suffering quietly like a good
boy.

       River of salt, will I see my love again?
Cold viscous water holds its course even after
it's gone. Throw a face into it and you'll never look
again, throw a voice and you'll hear sobbing
all the way down. Narcissus, that's my flower
forced in January, black-eyed bells echoing
sluggish eddies. Who hit him first?

The muse has covered his face
with his hands. It's just a reflex
of the historical storm that sired him:
something to say, "The sun is beating down
too hard on my pith helmet, the oil slick
on the river's not my fault, when are you going
home?" What he doesn't want to see, he doesn't
see. In the sludge that drowns the river, rats
pick fights with the debris. He calls them all
by their first names, he's looking through his fingers
like a fence. They make good neighbors. His friends
make do with what they can. They drink beer
from sewer-colored bottles in the dry stream
bed, powdered milk of human kindness and evaporated

silt. They stay by the river till past
sunrise, crooning a lullaby
to help it to sleep. The words
of their drinking songs are scrawled on the ceiling,
Mene, mene, tekel, upharsin: a madrigal
for the millennium's end.
I'm counting
down the days in someone else's
unmade bed, let these things break
their hold on me. The world
would like to see me dead, another gone
black man. I'm still awake.

Icarus on Fire Island

Two loves I have, each one
too fair for me to be completed
in his eyes, summer open with Mediterranean blue
where care is left aside, the most
of available light. The Sunday beach with you,
spangled with tan men, their perfect skin
reproach and visible reward (until the sun abandons
them and they withdraw into the inked-in sky
to shine unseen for those who don't concern themselves
with light), I searched the air dazzled with kites
for them, I couldn't want them less. *Since shunning pain
I ease can never find*, I'll score the sky
with string, and there incise my name,
until the gusts decline.
I have dispersed
the clouds with one small wisp of breath,
his hand commands a paper dragon
through an insurgent breeze. The painted silk
is stolen by flight, the line snaps or he

lets go of the line, playing it out
against a sudden updraft. That was my future
life, lost track of all a summer
afternoon: black point in a northeast corner of blue
descending, a mote across an open eye of sky
where light drains away.

Homeric Interim

Distance is money just out of reach,
a kindness like rain-laden clouds
that never drops its coins. Epochs
of fossilized trees crawl rusting hillside
strata: they smell like somewhere else
I've never been, an Anatolia
just outside the mind. Geometries
of travel and desire (from here to want
and back again), the myths of pleasure
reinvent another ancient world: oiled boys
racing naked around the circular walls
of Troy to find out who will wear
the plaited wreath, parade painted circuits
of unburnt parapets waving
to the crowds. See, even night
adores him, dresses him in its moon
and apparition. The sheen of intention
is on him, translates his motions
into marble, alabaster. (Cassandra
wakes and says *There isn't going to be
a Trojan War*. Centuries of fossil speech
fill up the space that comes after
currently, years spent talking
to paper.) Man and moment
become one, his reliquary skin
makes white occur (by now
the sweat has faded from his garish

details). The things his hands become
act out interruption, history
is his story, held at bay. He wears time
on his body (wears it out), chases gods
from mountaintops until the myth-smoke
clears. His old world's blurred
and hard to read, misunderstanding
becomes a place: galley
run aground on shallow skin
the color of no event.

Patricia Smith

(1955–)

IT BEGAN WITH MY FATHER.

Grizzled and slight, flasher of a marquee gold tooth, Otis Douglas Smith was Arkansas grit suddenly sporting city clothes. Part of the Great Migration of blacks from the South to northern cities in the early 1950s, he found himself not in the urban mecca he'd imagined, but in a roach-riddled tenement apartment on Chicago's West Side. There he attempted to craft a life alongside the bag boys, day laborers, housekeepers, and cooks who dreamed the city's wide, unreachable dream.

Many of those urban refugees struggled to fit, but my father never really adopted the no-nonsense-now rhythm of the city. There was too much of the storyteller in him, too much unleashed southern song still waiting for the open air. From the earliest days I can recall, my place was on his lap, touching a hand to his stubbled cheek and listening to his growled narrative, mysterious whispers, and wide-open laughter. He turned people we knew into characters. There was always a new twist to be added to stories we knew by heart. The boundaries of our tiny part of Chicago moved farther and farther apart. Magic abounded. There were tales everywhere, and my own personal griot knew just how to infuse them with life.

Because of him, I grew to think of the world in terms of the stories it could tell. From my father's moonlit tales of steaming Delta magic to the sweet slow songs of Smokey Robinson, I became addicted to unfolding drama, winding narrative threads, the lyricism of simple words. I believed that we all lived in the midst of an ongoing adventure that begged for voice. In my quest for that voice, I found poetry.

Poetry is the undercurrent of every story I hear and read. I can think of no better way to communicate, stripping away pretense, leaving only what is beautiful and vital. Or in the case of "Blood Dazzler," my work about Hurricane Katrina, leaving what is terrible and necessary.

Prologue—And Then She Owns You

This is not morning. There is a nastiness
slowing your shoes, something you shouldn't step in.
It's shattered beads, stomped flowers, vomit—
such stupid beauty,

beauty you can stick a manicured finger
into and through, beauty that doesn't rely
on any sentence the sun chants, it's whiskey
swelter blown scarlet.

Call this something else. Last night it had a name,
a name wedged between an organ's teeth, a name
pumping a virgin unawares, a curse word.
Wail it, regardless.

Weak light, bleakly triumphant, will unveil scabs,
snippets of filth music, cars on collapsed veins.
The whole of gray doubt slithers on solemn skin.
Call her New Orleans.

Each day she wavers, not knowing how long she
can stomach the introduction of needles,
the brash, boozed warbling of bums with neon crowns,
necklaces raining.

She tries on her voice, which sounds like cigarettes,
pubic sweat, brown spittle lining a sax bell,
the broken heel on a drag queen's scarlet slings.
Your kind of singing.

Weirdly in love, you rhumba her edges, drink
fuming concoctions, lick your lukewarm breakfast
directly from her crust. Go on, admit it.
You are addicted

to her brick hips, the thick swerve she elicits,
the way she kisses you, her lies wide open.
She prefers alleys, crevices, basement floors.
Hell, let her woo you.

This kind of romance dims the worth of soldiers,
bends and breaks the back, sips manna from muscle,
tells you *Leave your life*. Pack your little suitcase,
flee what is rigid

and duly prescribed. Let her touch that raw space
between cock and calm, the place that scripts such jazz.
Let her pen letters addressed to your asking.
You s-s-stutter

New Orleans, p-please. Don't. Blue is the color
stunning your tongue. At least the city pretends
to remember to be listening.
She grins with glint tooth,

wiping your mind blind of the wife, the children,
the numb ritual of job and garden plot.
Gently, she leads you out into the darkness
and makes you drink rain.

She Sees What It Sees

> *The eye of Hurricane Katrina passes over New Orleans.*

And the levees crackled,
and baptism rushed through the ward,
blasting the boasts from storefronts,
sweeping away the rooted, the untethered,
bending doors, withering the strength of stoops.
Damn! Like a mantra, drummed and constant comment
on the rising drink. *Shit!* Skirts shamelessly hefted,
pants legs ripped away, babies balanced in the air.
But still, acceptance, flurries of *Ha ha I'll be damned,*
because breakage has always been backdrop
and water—well, water sears through us,
drenches our white garb and reveals the savior's face.
It has provided hard passage,
sparkled its trickery
and shepherded us to death before.

Up on the Roof

Up on the roof, stumbling slickstep, you wave all your sheets and
    your blouses,
towels, bandanas, and denims, and etch what you ask on the
    morning:

When are they coming to save us? 'cause sinking is all that you're
    feeling.
Blades spin so close to your breathing. Their noise, crazy roar, eats
    invective,

blotting out words as you scream them. They turn your beseeching to
    vapor.
Water the dark hue of anger now laps at the feet you can't stand on.

Cameras obsess with your chaos. Now think how America sees you:
Gold in your molars and earlobes. Your naps knotted, craving a
    brushing.

You clutch your babies regardless, keep roaring your spite to where
    God is.
Breast pushes hard past your buttons. Then mud cracks its script on
    your forearm,

each word a misspelled agenda. But here come the flyboys to save
    you,
baskets to cram your new life in, the drama of fetching and swinging.

Some people think that you're crazy. As you descend from the
    heavens,
you choose to head for the questions. The earth and its water. The
    swallow.

Don't Drink the Water

A dog's sudden slickness slices such raw terror
through the surface, its collar biting into bloat,
jaunty bone-shaped tag a dollop of odd on black.

Sluggish miracle silvers of oil clutch Tuesday's
stupid brazen light and wink gorgeous while belching
sudden scattered flames. And over there, a window—

its dusty shadowed pane spidered into hundreds
of crusted pins in search of bared skin or dwelling.
Skimming leviathan vermin, their teeth bared, snort

the sugar of such leaving. Gleeful, they survive
on odor, exploded food, the gooey glued spine
of—wait—that looks like *How Stella Got Her Groove Back*.

Some mama's body, gaseous, a dimming star splayed
and so gently spinning, threatens its own soft seams,
collides sloppily with mattresses, power lines,

shards of four-doors. And trees, of course, are the monsters
we always knew they were. With lengthy gnarled arms raw
and lightning-slashed, they fist through the dark rushing depths

to etch hungered talons against blue. On the soft
bark of an oak, *H-E-L-p*, knifed in fever.
The water's black teeth reach for the helpless vowel.

Networks deftly edit and craft this sexy glint
of sudden ocean, wait for mama's bobbing bulk
to sweetly swirl into view, framed—*now!*—by the word.

Beneath this wet, at deeper wet, soulless shit reigns,
a sludge of skitters and screams, everything that drains
from the dying curdles, folds into hellish soup.

Winn-Dixie checkers, baby daddies, vague Baptists,
scared cops slog through, the slow wilting jazz of their legs
razored by the murk. What claws at their stride is piss,

lies about wind. What slows their forward is fetid,
fervently lapping, E. coli, fuel, old meat.
Nudges toward hellfire hiss against forearm and knee.

It's almost laughable, this wading through the thick
toward other rain. That mama whirls such splayed grace
on drenched sky. Better to rest, succumb to float, shine.

Sharan Strange

(1959–)

POETRY IS THE QUEST for freedom, born of silence and stutter and song (shackled tongue, but hopeful tongue), watchful remembering, the will to unearth the obscurities and contradictions of our rich and plundered histories, motherlore/lode of wit, compassion, ancient knowing... past turned inside out as present-future possibilities. And, more particularly, there is my native South of hamstrung promise and wrenched fulfillment... flight to discovery... footsore, weary legacy, angst and anger, midwifery of ancestored dreams, reclamations, and, mostly, questions....

Toi Derricotte has said, "Twenty-first-century poetry is African American poetry." Which is to say, perhaps, that the spirit of this century, its characteristic forms and modes—hybrid, fluid, dynamic, diasporan, global—resonate most vibrantly in African American experience and expression. Or, that the flowering of poetry that our great griot Gwendolyn Brooks invoked and evoked achieves its fullness in this century.

Childhood

Summer brought fireflies in swarms.
They lit our evenings like dreams
we thought we couldn't have.
We caught them in jars, punched
holes, carried them around for days.

Luminous abdomens that when charged
with air turned bright. Imagine!
mere insects carrying such cargo,
magical caravans flickering beneath
low July skies. We chased them, amazed.

The idea! Those tiny bodies
pulsing phosphorescence.
They made reckless traffic,
signaling, neon flashes forever
into the deepening dusk.

They gave us new faith
in the nasty tonics of childhood,
pungent, murky liquids promising
shining eyes, strong teeth, glowing skin,
and we silently vowed to swallow ever after.

What was the secret of light?
We wanted their brilliance:
small fires hovering,
each tiny explosion
the birth of a new world.

Froggy's Class
South Carolina, 1969

She was an old maid, Froggy was,
and she was mean, with bulging eyes
that strained more when she got cross,
and a lumpy sack of gland-swollen throat.
We thought her some crazy crone who
took delight in chastising the innocent.
Her classroom seemed our punishment,
as we were dubbed the smart ones.
But among our bunch the usual stunts

were devised, and her madness was
the antidote to our attempts at anarchy.

I mostly don't remember her abuses—
except the shrill, cracking voice
that harangued us daily, or the hard-rapped
satisfaction of a ruler across knuckles—
but in them she was democratic.
She also favored the word *nigra*,
which made Tina Fogle snicker
and eye me triumphantly. One day reciting
vocabulary, Stuart Williams, brilliant-haired,
the class sweetheart—whose liberal parents
no doubt had drilled its pronunciation—
corrected her, loudly enunciating *nee-gro*,
amid a chorus of half-hearted mimics.
Froggy bristled, glared at his cheerful
nerviness. I loved him for it.

Then after the year-end spelling test, which
I alone aced, she railed against my all-white
peers, summoned me to stand before
the *knuckleheads* she said (or warned)
might someday fall victim to my supervision.

On the last day, silently driving me home,
she pushed a dusty bound notebook
into my hands, and I—out of discomfort
at being alone with her, and shame at
my squalid, small house—scrambled out
of the car, barely caught *will make something
of yourself* and *college* and *proud*.

Last Supper

I've seen hogs herded for slaughter.
Penned on the truck, they whine like saws
biting into stubborn trees. Exiting,
their final exercise is a wild dance
skirting madness, a graceless capitulation.

I witnessed Herman,
who learned his name, ate from my hand,
and his holy-eyed terror said more to me
than any apostle's text. Poor swine,
surrogate Christ, you got no redemption,
though you left this world your blood and body.

Cows fare no better, though in India
millions would die in their place—
neither for sacrifice nor grace.
"You don't eat meat? No wonder you're so thin!"
But will gauntness save me, make me
thin enough to slip the knife, noose,
shackles, or the needle's eye?
Could any of us escape the legacy
of Christ's body offered up to save us,
the legacy of bloodshed that continues
in the name of God and State?

Elsewhere this is not an issue.
A *Village Voice* reporter tallies
"Final Meals Requested by Inmates
Executed in Texas: Steak was the entrée
most frequently asked for . . . seven T-bones
and one smothered. Hamburgers and
cheeseburgers were next at six."

Yes, on death row, flesh is the redeemer,
a final consolation. The industry
of slaughter feeding dead men—reluctant

sacrificial calves, marked, their fate
decided nearly from birth. With T-bones
they get the cross, though it's beheaded.
They get the apportioned body,
a sanctioned measure of salvation.

Natasha Trethewey

(1966–)

WHEN I READ James Baldwin's words, "This is the only real concern of the artist: to recreate out of the disorder of life that order which is art," I felt he was speaking directly to me. I began writing, then, because I had some things to make sense of—experiences from my past, as well as a collective past, that I needed to grapple with in order to understand. So memory exists for me, like the burden of history, as a necessary part of my work informing the way I understand things that are happening around me now. I am especially drawn to those things that suggest absence, and I am constantly attempting to investigate the reality beneath all things I've seen or known such as what's not said or written down yet or what's occurred outside the frame of a photograph. I write to discover what else is there, to uncover secrets.

Flounder

Here, she said, *put this on your head.*
She handed me a hat.
You 'bout as white as your dad,
and you gone stay like that.

Aunt Sugar rolled her nylons down
around each bony ankle,
and I rolled down my white knee socks
letting my thin legs dangle,

circling them just above water
and silver backs of minnows
flitting here then there between
the sun spots and the shadows.

This is how you hold the pole
to cast the line out straight.
Now put that worm on your hook,
throw it out and wait.

She sat spitting tobacco juice
into a coffee cup.
Hunkered down when she felt the bite,
jerked the pole straight up

reeling and tugging hard at the fish
that wriggled and tried to fight back.
A flounder, she said, *and you can tell*
'cause one of its sides is black.

The other side is white, she said.
It landed with a thump.
I stood there watching that fish flip-flop,
switch sides with every jump.

Limen

All day I've listened to the industry
of a single woodpecker, worrying the catalpa tree
just outside my window. Hard at his task,

his body is a hinge, a door knocker
to the cluttered house of memory in which
I can almost see my mother's face.

She is there, again, beyond the tree,
its slender pods and heart-shaped leaves,
hanging wet sheets on the line—each one

a thin white screen between us. So insistent
is this woodpecker, I'm sure he must be
looking for something else—not simply

the beetles and grubs inside, but some other gift
the tree might hold. All day he's been at work,
tireless, making the green hearts flutter.

Bellocq's Ophelia

from a photograph, circa 1912

In Millais's painting, Ophelia dies faceup,
eyes and mouth open as if caught in the gasp
of her last word or breath, flowers and reeds
growing out of the pond, floating on the surface
around her. The young woman who posed
lay in a bath for hours, shivering,

catching cold, perhaps imagining fish
tangling in her hair or nibbling a dark mole
raised upon her white skin. Ophelia's final gaze
aims skyward, her palms curling open
as if she's just said, *Take me.*

I think of her when I see Bellocq's photograph—
a woman posed on a wicker divan, her hair
spilling over. Around her, flowers—
on a pillow, on a thick carpet. Even
the ravages of this old photograph
bloom like water lilies across her thigh.
How long did she hold there, this other
Ophelia, nameless inmate in Storyville,
naked, her nipples offered up hard with cold?

The small mound of her belly, the pale hair
of her pubis—these things—her body
there for the taking. But in her face, a dare.
Staring into the camera, she seems to pull
all movement from her slender limbs
and hold it in her heavy-lidded eyes.
Her body limp as dead Ophelia's,
her lips poised to open, to speak.

Letter Home

New Orleans, November 1910

Four weeks have passed since I left, and still
I must write to you of no work. I've worn down
the soles and walked through the tightness
of my new shoes, calling upon the merchants,
their offices bustling. All the while I kept thinking
my plain English and good writing would secure
for me some modest position. Though I dress each day

in my best, hands covered with the lace gloves
you crocheted—no one needs a *girl*. How flat
the word sounds, and heavy. My purse thins.
I spend foolishly to make an appearance of quiet
industry, to mask the desperation that tightens
my throat. I sit watching—

though I pretend not to notice—the dark maids
ambling by with their white charges. Do I deceive
anyone? Were they to see my hands, brown
as your dear face, they'd know I'm not quite
what I pretend to be. I walk these streets
a white woman, or so I think, until I catch the eyes
of some stranger upon me, and I must lower mine,
a *negress* again. There are enough things here
to remind me who I am. Mules lumbering through
the crowded streets send me into reverie, their footfall
the sound of a pointer and chalk hitting the blackboard
at school, only louder. Then there are women, clicking
their tongues in conversation, carrying their loads
on their heads. Their husky voices, the wash pots
and irons of the laundresses call to me. Here,

I thought not to do the work I once did, back-bending
and domestic; my schooling a gift—even those half days
at picking time, listening to Miss J—. How
I'd come to know words, the recitations I practiced
to sound like her, lilting, my sentences curling up
or trailing off at the ends. I read my books until
I nearly broke their spines, and in the cotton field,
I repeated whole sections I'd learned by heart,
spelling each word in my head to make a picture
I could see, as well as a weight I could feel
in my mouth. So now, even as I write this
and think of you at home, *Good-bye*

is the waving map of your palm, is
a stone on my tongue.

Elegy for the Native Guards

> Now that the salt of their blood
> Stiffens the saltier oblivion of the sea . . .
> —ALLEN TATE

We leave Gulfport at noon; gulls overhead
trailing the boat—streamers, noisy fanfare—
all the way to Ship Island. What we see
first is the fort, its roof of grass, a lee—
half reminder of the men who served there—
a weathered monument to some of the dead.

Inside we follow the ranger, hurried
though we are to get to the beach. He tells
of graves lost in the Gulf, the island split
in half when Hurricane Camille hit,
shows us casemates, cannons, the store that sells
souvenirs, tokens of history long buried.

The Daughters of the Confederacy
has placed a plaque here, at the fort's entrance—
each Confederate soldier's name raised hard
in bronze; no names carved for the Native Guards—
2nd Regiment, Union men, black phalanx.
What is monument to their legacy?

All the grave markers, all the crude headstones—
water-lost. Now fish dart among their bones,
and we listen for what the waves intone.
Only the fort remains, near forty feet high,
round, unfinished, half open to the sky,
the elements—wind, rain—God's deliberate eye.

Pastoral

In the dream, I am with the Fugitive
Poets. We're gathered for a photograph.
Behind us, the skyline of Atlanta
hidden by the photographer's backdrop—
a lush pasture, green, full of soft-eyed cows
lowing, a chant that sounds like *no, no. Yes,*
I say to the glass of bourbon I'm offered.
We're lining up now—Robert Penn Warren,
his voice just audible above the drone
of bulldozers, telling us where to stand.
Say "race," the photographer croons. I'm in
blackface again when the flash freezes us.
My father's white, I tell them, *and rural.*
You don't hate the South? they ask. *You don't hate it?*

Incident

We tell the story every year—
how we peered from the windows, shades drawn—
though nothing really happened,
the charred grass now green again.

We peered from the windows, shades drawn,
at the cross trussed like a Christmas tree,
the charred grass still green. Then
we darkened our rooms, lit the hurricane lamps.

At the cross trussed like a Christmas tree,
a few men gathered, white as angels in their gowns.
We darkened our rooms and lit hurricane lamps,
the wicks trembling in their fonts of oil.

It seemed the angels had gathered, white men in their gowns.
When they were done, they left quietly. No one came.
The wicks trembled all night in their fonts of oil;
by morning the flames had all dimmed.

When they were done, the men left quietly. No one came.
Nothing really happened.
By morning all the flames had dimmed.
We tell the story every year.

Myth

I was asleep while you were dying.
It's as if you slipped through some rift, a hollow
I make between my slumber and my waking,

the Erebus I keep you in, still trying
not to let go. You'll be dead again tomorrow,
but in dreams you live. So I try taking

you back into morning. Sleep-heavy, turning,
my eyes open, I find you do not follow.
Again and again, this constant forsaking.

*

Again and again, this constant forsaking:
my eyes open, I find you do not follow.
You back into morning, sleep-heavy, turning.

But in dreams you live. So I try taking,
not to let go. You'll be dead again tomorrow.
The Erebus I keep you in — still, trying —

I make between my slumber and my waking.
It's as if you slipped through some rift, a hollow.
I was asleep while you were dying.

Kevin Young

(1970–)

WRITE NOT LIKE something endangered—not like a spotted owl—or reintroduced into the wild, but dead already. (The poetry of "they're coming to get us," the poetry of the horror movie I've seen too much of, the poetry of lament, of victimization, or worse, of declaring the various and nefarious threats to freedom, equality, blackness, or justice seems to take too much pleasure in watching the killer even as it shouts out warnings in the theater. This poetry is over, but unfortunately not yet dead.) Write not like a coming extinction, but like the extinction already. That said, do not write like a dodo, something rare and flightless—but like the passenger pigeon, a poetry once plentiful and ever-present and so therefore killed off.

Do not write a poetry of rarity, or of rarification, but of *never again*.

Do not even write this poetry but find it, come across it, and step over it. The helpless ant that in the end can lift more than ten times its weight: that is a poetry.

Letters from the North Star

Dear you: the lights here ask
nothing, the white falling
around my letters silent,
unstoppable. I am writing this
from the empty stomach of sleep

where nothing but the cold
wonders where you're headed;
nobody here peels heads sour
and cheap as lemon, and only
the car sings AM the whole

night through. In the city,
I have seen children half-
bitten by wind. Even trains
arrive without a soul
to greet them; things do

not need me here, this world
dances on its own. Only bridges
beg for me to make them
famous, to learn what I had
almost forgotten of flying,

of soaring free, south,
down. So long. Xs, Os.

Eddie Priest's Barbershop & Notary
Closed Mondays

is music   is men
off early from work   is waiting
for the chance at the chair
while the eagle claws holes
in your pockets   keeping
time   by the turning
of rusty fans   steel flowers with
cold breezes   is having nothing
better to do   than guess at the years
of hair   matted beneath the soiled caps
of drunks   the pain of running
a fisted comb through stubborn

knots   is the dark dirty low
down blues   the tender heads
of sons fresh from cornrows   all
wonder at losing   half their height
is a mother gathering hair   for good
luck   for a soft wig   is the round
difficulty of ears   the peach
faced boys asking Eddie
to cut in parts and arrows
wanting to have their names read
for just a few days   and among thin
jazz   is the quick brush of a done
head   the black flood around
your feet   grandfathers
stopping their games of ivory
dominoes   just before they reach the bone
yard   is winking widowers announcing
cut it clean off   I'm through courting
and hair only gets in the way   is the final
spin of the chair   a reflection of
a reflection   that sting of wintergreen
tonic   on the neck of a sleeping snow
haired man   when you realize it is
your turn   you are next

The Game

Here the ashtrays smoke
by themselves, wind

kicking up enough
thick grey to choke

even the dead awake.
I sit with my back

to the wall, face
the glassless door.

This place. Trust
only those you don't

know. When Johnny
Two-Tone waltzes by

silently pat your
packed side. Heat.

Saturday night
special. 38. The small

door in the back,
a judas eye, hides

rooms where hands pray
to dice lopsided

as my walk. Flush. Three
ladies. Two ace.

While Abyssinia Ned
cashes in

& Walter Walleye
wins again—a straight—

while Cootie Le Curfew
curses his fate & Delilah

Redbone charms the place,
let's you & me wash

down the day—a toast—
To my enemies' enemies!

Let's try to spirit away
her beautiful, half-lit face

raising dirty mason jars
of soured grapes.

For the Confederate Dead

I go with the team also.
　　　—WHITMAN

These are the last days
my television says. Tornadoes, more
rain, overcast, a chance

of sun but I do not
trust weathermen,
never have. In my fridge only

The milk makes sense—
expires. No one, much less
my parents, can tell me why

my middle name is Lowell,
and from my table
across from the Confederate

Monument to the dead (that pale
finger bone) a plaque
declares war—not Civil,

or Between
the States, but for Southern
Independence. In this café, below sea-

and eye-level a mural runs
the wall, flaking, a plantation
scene most do not see—

it's too much
around the knees, height
of a child. In its fields Negroes bend

to pick the endless white.
In livery a few drive carriages
like slaves, whipping the horses, faces

blank and peeling. The old hotel
lobby this once was no longer
welcomes guests—maroon ledger,

bellboys gone but
for this. Like an inheritance
the owner found it

stripping hundred years
(at least) of paint
and plaster. More leaves each day.

In my movie there are no
horses, no heroes,
only draftees fleeing

into the pines, some few
who survive, gravely
wounded, lying

burrowed beneath the dead—
silent until the enemy
bayonets what is believed

to be the last
of the breathing. It is getting later.
We prepare

for wars no longer
there. The weather
inevitable, unusual—

more this time of year
than anyone ever seed. The earth
shudders, the air—

if I did not know
better, I would think
we were living all along

a fault. How late
it has gotten . . .
Forget the weatherman

whose maps move, blink,
but stay crossed
with lines none has seen. Race

instead against the almost
rain, digging besides the monument
(that giant anchor)

til we strike
water, sweat
fighting the sleepwalking air.

Crowning

Now that knowing means nothing,
now that you are more born
than being, more awake
than awaited, since I've seen
your hair deep inside mother,
a glimpse, grass in late

winter, early spring, watching
your mother's pursed, throbbing,
purpled power, her pushing
you for one whole hour, two,
almost three, almost out,
maybe never, animal smell
and peat, breath and sweat
and mulch-matter, and at once
you descend, or drive, are driven
by mother's body, by her will
and brilliance, by bowel,
by wanting and your hair
peering as if it could see, and I saw
you storming forth,
taproot, your cap of hair half
in, half out, and wait, hold
it there, the doctors say, and
she squeezing my hand, her face
full of fire, then groaning your face
out like a flower, blood-bloom,
crocussed into air, shoulders
and the long cord still rooting
you to each other, to the other
world, into this afterlife
among us living, the cord
I cut like an iris, pulsing,
then you wet against mother's chest
still purple, not blue, not yet
red, no cry,
warming now, now opening
your eyes midnight
blue in the blue-black dawn.

THIRD WAVE, POST-1960s

Jericho Brown

(1976–)

I THINK OF WRITING, first, as a process of listening to some series of sounds that enter my mind and, second, as a process of embodying those sounds. I try and leave as much as I can to instinct, intuition, and reflex—even in the final stages of revision. Because I'm so interested in both music and voice, I find myself trying to figure the personality of the sounds as I am composing. At some point in the writing of a first draft, I start to take on the characteristics of the voice that is asking to be channeled through words that convey what I think of as a necessary mixture of the sacred and the profane, the ironic and the ecstatic. An example of this might be something as simple as punching the computer if the voice is pissed to the point of violence.

I hardly feel that I have any control or power over the "story" that begins to emerge from a poem while composing it. I do my best writing when I am most vulnerable to the writing, when I allow for the construction of images and lines that, in the midst of composing, frighten me.

Track 1: Lush Life

The woman with the microphone sings to hurt you,
To see you shake your head. The mic may as well
Be a leather belt. You drive to the center of town
To be whipped by a woman's voice. You can't tell
The difference between a leather belt and a lover's

Tongue. A lover's tongue might call you *bitch*,
A term of endearment where you come from, a kind
Of compliment preceded by the word *sing*
In certain nightclubs. A lush little tongue
You have: you can yell, *Sing bitch*, and, *I love you*,
With a shot of Patrón at the end of each phrase
From the same barstool every Saturday night, but you can't
Remember your father's leather belt without shaking
Your head. That's what satisfies her, the woman
With the microphone. She does not mean to entertain
You, and neither do I. Speak to me in a lover's tongue—
Call me your bitch, and I'll sing the whole night long.

Prayer of the Backhanded

Not the palm, not the pear tree
Switch, not the broomstick,
Nor the closest extension
Cord, not his braided belt, but God,
Bless the back of my daddy's hand
Which, holding nothing tightly
Against me and not wrapped
In leather, eliminated the air
Between itself and my cheek.
Make full this dimpled cheek
Unworthy of its unfisted print
And forgive my forgetting
The love of a hand
Hungry for reflex, a hand that took
No thought of its target
Like hail from a blind sky,
Involuntary, fast, but brutal
In its bruising. Father, I bear the bridge
Of what might have been
A broken nose. I lift to you
What was a busted lip. Bless

The boy who believes
His best beatings lack
Intention, the mark of the beast.
Bring back to life the son
Who glories in the sin
Of immediacy, calling it love.
God, save the man whose arm
Like an angel's invisible wing
May fly backward in fury
Whether or not his son stands near.
Help me hold in place my blazing jaw
As I think to say, *excuse me.*

Track 4: Reflections
as performed by Diana Ross

I wanted to reflect the sun.

I wore what glitters, smiled,
Left my eyes open, and,

On the ceiling of my mouth,

Balanced a note as long as God allowed,
My head tilted backwards, my arms stretched

Out and up, I kept praying,

If the red sun rising makes a sound,
Let my voice be that sound.

I could hear the sun sing in 1968.

I learned the word *assassin*
And watched cities burn.

Got another #1 and somebody

Set Detroit on fire. That was power—
White folks looking at me

Directly and going blind

So they wouldn't have to see
What in the world was burning black.

Track 5: Summertime
as performed by Janis Joplin

God's got his eye on me, but I ain't a sparrow.
I'm more like a lawn mower . . . no, a chainsaw,
Anything that might mangle each manicured lawn
In Port Arthur, a place I wouldn't return to
If the mayor offered me every ounce of oil
My daddy cans at the refinery. My voice, I mean,
Ain't sweet. Nothing nice about it. It won't fly
Even with Jesus watching. I don't believe in Jesus.
The Baxter boys climbed a tree just to throw
Persimmons at me. The good and perfect gifts
From above hit like lightning, leave bruises.
So I lied—I believe, but I don't think God
Likes me. The girls in the locker room slapped
Dirty pads across my face. They called me
Bitch, but I never bit back. I ain't a dog.
Chainsaw, I say. My voice hacks at you. I bet
I tear my throat. I try so hard to sound jagged.
I get high and say one thing so many times
Like Willie Baker who worked across the street—
I saw some kids whip him with a belt while he
Repeated, *Please*. School out, summertime
And the living lashed, Mama said I should be
Thankful, that the town's worse to coloreds

Than they are to me, that I'd grow out of my acne.
God must love Willie Baker—all that leather and still
A please that sounds like music. See.
I wouldn't know a sparrow from a mockingbird.
The band plays. I just belt out, *Please*. This tune
Ain't half the blues. I should be thankful.
I get high and moan like a lawn mower
So nobody notices I'm such an ugly girl.
I'm such an ugly girl. I try to sing like a man
Boys call *boy*. I turn my face to God. I pray. I wish
I could pour oil on everything green in Port Arthur.

Michael Sibble Collins

(1959–)

P OEMS ARE PROMISES. "So long as men can breathe or eyes can see / so long lives this [poem]," Shakespeare insists, "and this gives life to thee." Or, "At the end of this line, there is an opening door / that gives on a blue balcony where a gull will settle," Derek Walcott promises.

To borrow from the language of the dollar, poems aspire to be "legal tender for all debts [that is to say, all promises], public and private": legal tender for debts we incur in promising to be good as our word, to love "till death do us part" (for the marriage vow is itself a little poem), to sprout up under the reader's boot soles, like Walt Whitman, or to look long into the Medusa face of reality, so that the reader will not turn to stone. (Prayers and psalms are these sorts of poems.)

The fact that poems are promises gives the poet (at least at my level) something in common with the Ponzi schemer: For, like a Ponzi scheme, a poem is a lie whose worth is based entirely on what people invest in it. But, unlike a Ponzi scheme, a poem is a lie that becomes truer the more people invest in it, the more they allow it to structure their imaginations: Who would think of "Homer," who may or may not have existed—may or may not have been made out of "a mouthful of air," as Yeats said one of his poems was—if the *Iliad* had not made the fires of war and the wills of gods and nations grow out of Helen's red hair?

Six Sketches: When a Soul Breaks

1. The spy

Years later, the house paid for, the church his rock, he was caught
      selling
his nation's secrets. The sudden silences, the sudden executions
      overseas
now had their explanation. A woman whose husband's cover
he'd blown tried to shoot him, failed, shot herself. Interviewed
in jail, he pleaded frustration, money problems, office politics:
"It got so bad I thought, 'The enemy can't be worse . . .'"

> *When a soul breaks*
> *There's no outward sign at first.*

2. The hooker

Deborah, gorgeous, sixteen, could not decide which one was worse:
going home to mom and school and giving up Larry John, or selling
herself to buy a place as his woman. Arguments shook her, as politics
shake a statehouse. But a touch from him drove them into the seas.
After the knife fight with Mary Jack the Bear, Deborah, interviewed
about her rival's death, said: "I was freezing. Her blood was warm
      cover."

> *When a soul breaks, they say,*
> *The devil is its lover.*

3. The poet

The poet, plotting suicide, planned to be found once more, to recover.
She'd written of her resurrection, and expected nothing worse
than a triumphant convalescence, Cerberus left whimpering, herself
      interviewed
anew by some severe psychiatrist. How could she have foreseen the
      selling
of her death, the secrets cracked like eggs, the word war across seas,
the perverse success of her plan to rout defeat, and mold the muse's
      politics?

> *When a soul breaks*
> *Triumph and folly are in the mix.*

4. The musician

The guitarist builds a city of air. With sidewinding feedback, pitch
    politics,
he drives democracy past the speed of sound. His blues riffs uncover
the will of the people: his overtones guide it arklike over seas . . . .
And born of doubt, that ark carries all: swindles, acid hits, power
    trips, worse-
than-flimsy philosophies—but also what the heavens are selling:
infinity in a gracenote, fulfillment rising up, the Mystery
    interviewed.

> *When a soul breaks all hail*
> *the voodoo tune that is debuted.*

5. The philosopher

His reason rode the centuries, probing beyond good and evil. It
    interviewed
the universe, plunged past creditor and debtor and mere politics.
But syphilis rode along, a monstrous link back to buying and selling,
to shyness and pride that left only a pain-drunk prostitute to cover
his hurt. As the books spilled out and idols trembled, the disease
    grew worse,
devoured his mind, plunged him in madness deep as the seas.

> *When a soul breaks,*
> *Accidents crush philosophies.*

6. Manias

Greed and skill can make a tulip worth more than the seven seas
or bring a storied bank crashing down, or topple a much-interviewed
CEO, leaving him rich with his word worth nothing. But worse,
some say, is purity, bright in the strongman's heart as the moon,
    shining politics
in place of gold, and sending thinker, poet and singer running for
    cover—
purity that leaves spy and pimp trading favors where selling

is banned: Purity of the moon-bright man of politics, interviewed,
selling again his old guerilla triumphs, and saying, "Tighten belts! It's
    worse to cover
our battles with foreign credit, or throw bridges across protecting
    seas."

> *When a people's soul breaks, they say,*
> *the ruler raises his fees.*

> *And when a soul breaks,*
> *the devil is its lover.*
> *And triumph and folly are in the mix*
> *when a soul breaks.*
> *But there's no outward sign at first—*
> *until a voodoo tune gets debuted,*
> *and the ruler raises his fees,*
> *and accidents crush philosophies,*
> *and souls break.*

Poetry

If Ezra Pound couldn't make it cohere
who am I, small-voiced, half-blind, to interfere
with what people like to do to each other?

Why try to make sense of lunatic aggressions,
knives in the sweetest backs, corkscrew passions
in Götterdämmerung's cork, and poetry that no matter

How many knots in feeling it loosens, teaches nothing
but part-time transcendence, or godlike phrases any worldling
can mouth? Ezra famously fell for Mussolini

despite discipleship to Dante and Sextus Propertius
and others who are sacred to love.
Was Plato right, saying poetry leads us

into unguardianlike, dime-a-dozen passions that can
grind Achilles in the dust? But Plato, some say, was a bit
of a fascist himself, eager to make mankind fit

procrustean forms. That woman on the street
in her high heeled slippers, a tattooed dragon
curled round her ankle, a lotus pattern blossoming on

her shimmering dress, the top like a rhyme against her breasts,
her large eyes fixed far off on some complex concern—
all the men she passes feel their leaping minds caught,

pulled out of time, stopped like clocks: She could set
them to any hour she chooses with a single word.
That's what poetry can do: give its passing impetus to the herd.

Bryan, Texas Procession

Having nothing else to do
The dead march in procession
In Bryan up Texas Avenue
Past the courthouse and police station.

One comes from his execution
In law-guzzling Gatesville, having lost
His last appeal. "To think," he says,
"a low-down D.A.'s career move cost

me my life—and now he's up there ruling on
the federal bench. There's just no justice
in this life. All my life I heard about it
but it never once showed me its face—

hey!—you righteous citizens who can quote
the Bible from Ezekiel to Revelations, listen:
God has never heard of you and wouldn't
Care to." This bitter new-minted shade

Had punched a hole through nature, and others
Followed. Like air from an untied balloon, they hissed
into the sunlight, into time, talking and talking
lest their heart knowledge go to waste.

But no one paid them any mind. Only lunatics
Talk to the dead, and as you see, I've set
This down in stanzas of drunken verse
To absolve my senses of all and any

Responsibility. Still, to tell the truth,
I was lost, desperate for any sort
Of wisdom just then; I couldn't say no
To all those talky spirits holding court.

2.

I stood transfixed by one who'd seen a lynching
As a boy. He said he'd spent his death
Searching death's kingdom for the one
He'd seen die. "It's really the truth,"

He kept repeating "My father took me there.
And I suffered from nightmares for years. But I never
Wanted to watch that murder. And now
I can't find the lynched man. I've been everywhere

The dead go—but he is nowhere to be
Found—unless I've ended up in hell
And he's above the sun somewhere. Jesus—
I only want to say I'm sorry. If you see

him, tell him that." And he staggered
off, a bit of burnt rope gripped in one
hand, and I wondered if he really was
the son, or the father wishing he were, being alone

with his lynching for all eternity
and unable to take it. Can the dead
go mad? Was I, an utter lunatic
for listening, a piggy bank for self-delusion?

But then one I could only see as sane
Came up; he was powerful but politic,
A wizard of sorts, though dressed
Like a banker—a man of the party line,

Unwilling to shout or throw his weight
Around, but so assured as to be magnetic.
"Dead or alive," he said, "people are intemperate,
insatiable, drunk on their own transience.

"I, though, thought in terms of generations,
not of years. If I hoarded power
it was not for my use alone. I knew
I was the one who could best gather

The coins of might in the still war-broken
land—gather them and pile them up
Like a Pisgah for my people to stand on.
For since the powerless are always crushed,

The crushed must have some power. Remember:
In me the industrialist and the ex-
Slave holder grow out of the backbone
Of the slave. The bullet-riddled land began to fix

Itself, to knit torn parts together
In the channels of my brain.
In my weighed words the future where you live unfurled."
"Farinata!" I said, but he left me without a word.

Kyle Dargan

(1980–)

BELIEVE THAT if one is a "formally trained" poet, it is necessary to go through a phase of unlearning where he or she rediscovers the word and the concept of the poem not as familiar means to familiar ends, but as alien changelings that morph with your mood, state of mind, and even understanding of self.

When I began writing poetry, I wrote as if my blackness was an actual condition. I wrote against its degradation and in praise of its strength and dynamism. Since then, I've been able to internalize the truth of this American crutch we call race—that being, as James Baldwin suggested, it is a political reality and nothing more. And for us (a "we" inclusive of our "white," "yellow," "brown," etc., countrymen and countrywomen) to continue to play this *sport bête* known as racial identification/loathing/ supremacy is to limit our creativity and inhibit the potential cathartic strangeness that can rise from the art of poetry.

So I was, and remain, a "black" poet ("African American," if we must be technically imprecise). It is just that now I've turned the "blackness" in my person and my work into a bottomless pool protected only by a HUMANS ONLY sign on the gate.

Search for Robert Hayden

The garage has not been allowed to breathe
for months now. The smell of moving,
uprooting, cures in the arid Texas heat—
scents not to be romanticized but handled
carefully so that no boxes topple.
We are looking for "The Middle Passage,"
first we must clear a walking path.
Books yelp like kennel pups through holes in their crates,
books that are no longer books
but subheads in chimeras of collected poems.
Next, Copacetic, Victims of the Latest Dance Craze—
all originals bearing signatures
like birth certificates. Clifton, no gray.
Komunyakaa, w/ beard. Eady,
looking young as the lost member of New Edition.
Most out of print, and born before I was pressed
in flesh. The past presented, Hayden is still hiding somewhere.
Putting an ear to the walls doesn't help, this year-old house
barely knows its own nooks and stashes.
Hell, round them all up—in minutes
we'll be standing knee deep in
the unselected poems of black literature.
This is how we will find him:
on our hands and knees,
combing over flailed books—seashells
beneath a forgotten tide.
Occasionally we'll wrench something up,
not what we are looking for, and read it anyway.

Microphone Fiend

The child freestyles in the shower,
battling yellow tiles
with a steam-heavy tongue.

Siblings can wait
while s/he rhymes the hot water to an end.

Braggadocio and bubblegum toothpaste
blend, beatless. S/he spits and spits
and spits until words harden
like lime crust on the spray head.

Have to get the neck into it—flexing
inward then out, recoiled

from the force of breath. *Did I
say I'm number one? Um, sorry
I lied. I'm number one-two-three-four
-and-five.*

And the crowd goes . . .

water applauding
against the basin. Momma goes
"If you don't get your narrow behind
out that bathroom with all that nonsense!"

The water stops,
the shower curtain makes way.

S/he wipes the condensation from the cabinet mirror,
barely eye-level with reflection. On tiptoes,

s/he anticipates emceedom like a growth spurt.

Palinode, Once Removed
Bloomington, Indiana

> *The Negro is America's metaphor.*
> —RICHARD WRIGHT

The girl from Martinsville sets her eyes on me
like they are elbows—intently boring
at my cheeks. This sentiment bleeds
throughout my class. Slouched, heads
tilted, they wait for the day I come in,
pull out a handkerchief, a vial of alcohol,
and wipe this vexing complexion from my skin.

Before I left home, Uncle called—said,
"You're going to teach *them* people, huh?
Well, teach 'em."

The day we pursue metaphor, I will
teach them about the brain—how there is a center
to catch discrepancy between the expected
and the perceived. Stimulate the mechanism,
you are working in metaphor.

Though surprising
I am not a metaphor. This is: I am a period,
small and dark. If you read me correctly,
you are to stop. Pause. Breathe.

Man of the Family

Your sister calls from college to say, "There's an asshole in my bed." Usually, it was *under* and *a monster*. You realize a flashlight and the can of air freshener that doubled as goblin-repellent won't help this situation. Think like a doctor, the asshole a condition: "When did you first notice the asshole? How long has he been in your bed?" But such histories no older brother desires to jot down. She begs you treat her symptom with fists, lots of them. So, you drive to your friends' homes with a burlap sack, filling her prescription one rung doorbell at a time, wishing your father's giant hands were still a mere phone call away.

Camille T. Dungy

(1972–)

A S I WROTE my first two books, it was crucial that the poems were viable, tangible, that they dealt with their subjects in a way that would ring true for people who didn't know the eras under consideration as well as for people who knew them very well. To manage this I did plenty of research, but I also made sure to render my subjects in ways that were full of life. This often meant the poems incorporated resistance to expectations and norms. *What to Eat, What to Drink, What to Leave for Poison* is a collection of rogue sonnets. Though I began *Suck on the Marrow* partly as an effort to move as far from the sonnet as possible, I knew the collection was complete when I drafted three new sonnets for that book. I love the sonnet's compactness. I love the little argument each sonnet contains, its turn. I love how little space there is and how the heavy tradition of the form requires that much be said and said succinctly. As much as I love and respect the sonnet, I do not believe it is an inalterable form. Many of my sonnets play fast and loose with rules. I've written about folks who take the restrictions and traditions that have been handed to them and do what they can to make beautiful things with their lives. They can't act just like Spenser or Shakespeare or Shelley. They do things their way, and so the fact that the sonnets follow some rules and flout others is a direct reflection of their subjects. The impetus for these poems is both resistance and revelation.

Form and subject, form and content, form and intent: these are codetermined entities in my writing. For me the *how* and the *what* are never very far apart. They discover each other, they push back against each other, and through these explorations I find my poems.

What to Eat, and What to Drink, and What to Leave for Poison

1.

Only now, in spring, can the place be named:
tulip poplar, daffodil, crab apple,
dogwood, budding pink-green, white-green, yellow
on my knowing. All winter I was lost.
Fall, I found myself here, with no texture
my fingers know. Then, worse, the white longing
that downed us deep three months. No flower heat.
That was winter. But now, in spring, the buds
flock our trees. Ten million exquisite buds,
tiny and loud, flaring their petalled wings,
bellowing from ashen branches vibrant
keys, the chords of spring's triumph: fisted heart,
dogwood; grail, poplar; wine spray, crab apple.
The song is drink, is color. Come. Now. Taste.

2.

The song is drink, is color.   Come now, taste
what the world has to offer.   When you eat
you will know that music comes in guises—
bold of crepe myrtle, sweet of daffodil—
beyond sound, guises they never told you
could be true.   And they aren't.   Except they are
so real now, this spring, you know them, taste them.
Green as kale, the songs of spring, bright as wine,
the music.   Faces of this season grin
with clobbering wantonness—see the smiles
open on each branch?—until you, too, smile.
Wide carnival of color, carnival
of scent.   We're all lurching down streets, drunk now
from the poplar's grail.   Wine spray: crab apple.

3.

From the poplar's grail, wine spray.   Crab apple
brightens jealously to compete.   But by

the crab apple's deep stain, the tulip tree
learns modesty.   Only blush, poplar learns,
lightly.   Never burn such a dark-hued fire
to the core.   Tulip poplar wants herself
light under leaf, never, like crab apple,
heavy under tart fruit.   Never laden.
So the poplar pours just a hint of wine
in her cup, while the crab apple, wild one,
acts as if her body were a fountain.
She would pour wine onto you, just let her.
Shameless, she plants herself, and delivers,
down anyone's street, bright invitations.

4.

Down anyone's street-bright invitations.
Suck 'em.   Swallow 'em.   Eat them whole.   That's right,
be greedy about it.   The brightness calls
and you follow because you want to taste,
because you want to be welcomed inside
the code of that color: red for thirst; green
for hunger; pink, a kiss; and white, stain me
now.   Soil me with touching.   Is that right?
No?   That's not, you say, what you meant.   Not what
you meant at all?   Pardon.   Excuse me, please.
Your hand was reaching, tugging at this shirt
of flowers and I thought, I guess I thought
you were hungry for something beautiful.
Come now.   The brightness here might fill you up.

5.

Come.   Now the brightness here might fill you up,
but tomorrow?   Who can know what the next
day will bring.   It is like that, here, in spring.
Four days ago, the dogwood was a fist
in protest.   Now look.   Even she unfurls
to the pleasure of the season.   Don't be
ashamed of yourself.   Don't be.   This happens
to us all.   We have thrown back the blanket.
We're naked and we've grown to love ourselves.
I tell you, do not be ashamed.   Who is

more wanton than the dancing crepe myrtle?
Is she ashamed?   Why, even the dogwood,
that righteous tree of God's, is full of lust
exploding into brightness every spring.

6.

Exploding into brightness every spring,
I draw you close.   I wonder, do you know
how long I've wanted to be here?   Each year
you grasp me, lift me, carry me inside.
Glee is the body of the daffodil
reaching tubed fingers through the day, feeling
her own trumpeted passion choiring air
with hot, colored song.   This is a texture
I love.   This is life.   And, too, you love me,
inhale my whole being every spring.   Gone
winter, heavy clod whose icy body
fell into my bed.   I must leave you, but
I'll wait through heat, fall, freeze to hear you cry:
Daffodils are up.   My God, what beauty!

7.

Daffodils are up, my God!   What beauty
concerted down on us last night.   And if
I sleep again, I'll wake to a louder
blossoming, the symphony smashing down
hothouse walls, and into the world: music.
Something like the birds' return, each morning's
crescendo rising toward its brightest pitch,
colors unfurling, petals alluring.
The song, the color, the rising ecstasy
of spring.   My God.   This beauty.   This, this
is what I've hoped for.   All my life is here
in the unnamed core—dogwood, daffodil,
tulip poplar, crab apple, crepe myrtle—
only now, in spring, can the place be named.

Cleaning

I learned regret at Mother's sink,
jarred tomatoes, river-mud brown,
a generation old, lumping
down the drain. Hating wasted space,
I had discarded what I could
not understand. I hadn't known
a woman to fight drought or frost
for the promise of winter meals,
hadn't known my great-grandmother,
or what it was to have then lose
the company of that woman
who, upon seeing her namesake,
child of her child, grown and gliding
into marriage, gifted the fruit
of her garden, a hard-won strike
against want. Opening the jar,
I knew nothing of the rotting
effect, the twisting grip of years
spent packing, of years spent moving,
further each time, from known comforts:
a grandmother's garden, her rows
always neat, the harvest: bright wealth
mother hoarded. I understood
only the danger of a date
so old. Understanding clearly
what is fatal to the body,
I only understood too late
what can be fatal to the heart.

To Put Things Right

What I saw first was an elephant rising,
and though the sight was glorious, it was not
half so decadent as other feasts offered up
that day—women robed in flame wishing
through air toward men in hats as tall as I
on legs as tall as father who held hoops
through which the women sped before arrowing,
violent and graceful as phoenix, into a pool
and streaming out, one, two, three, four, five
spangled flyers from one, two, three, four,
even five corners of the cornerless pool,
into our thick applause—so that I let go
her rising and fed my eyes to gluttony.

But it is that first sight I would sip up

had I to choose just one of my lives
to live again. The first crunch of sawdust
beneath my feet, her knees. Popcorn stalled
between my hand and mouth. There was meal enough
in the sight of her rising. First, just her
on her knees, skin char-gray under those glares—
even her naked hairs showing—and then her rising;
the earth shifted forward under the press of her knees,
and I tilted with it, we all tilted forward, so she could rise
ever so slowly (we heard trust in her heaves of breath),
and we were not breathing; an elephant stumbled,
we understood, as anyone might, we swallowed;
and then her rising, and the world put right,
and women, robed in flame, wishing through air.

Vievee Francis

(1963–)

M OST OF MY WORK has focused on the persona poem because that was the way in for me. I read Robert Browning at fifteen years old, then Ai at nineteen. Here were two poets from different eras, of differing backgrounds using an approach that at its best demands a difficult empathy. I found that considering another's perspective, exploring another's interior landscape, helped me to discover, develop, and value my own. Imagining the world through this panoply of eyes suggested the world was far vaster than my experience, and paradoxically instructed me in the relational value of all of our experiences in its insistence upon a universalizing humanization. These imagined interiors gave me the strength to eventually turn my gaze inward and confront my personal story. I write against any externally imposed or culturally self-imposed otherization. As with Detroiter Robert Hayden, I find the idea of an American canon sans a wealth of African American authors as reductive as the idea of a narrowly constructed monolingual "black" voice. In this era, freed of mandates, I add my own poetic, bringing to bear the full measure of my *personal take* to the broad swath of voices rising from the *variegation* of African American experiences. This is the art of it: to let the artist do what the artist must without any directive other than that indefatigable internal one that compels all artists. And in this, communities *as well as* artists are enriched.

Amarillo
(1971)

Inland where no seagulls circled,
       no sea, but storms of dust and dust,
the heartland, mouthless heart
       of thistles, and waves of sun, of salt,
and meals of fish in their cans of oil,
       every surface boiled to rust.

Dusk brought howls, the trickster gods,
       whom cowboys shot and then impaled.
A scruff of scarecrows lined the fence-posts,
       coyotes with their lolling miens,
their smiles now fixed as any man's.

Sons, so much like fathers, strung and roped
       their own small finds: frogs, rats and prairie dogs.
From that panhandle the years rose
       like a dust of gulls.
O water-eyed calf lowing from the maze,

how yellow the world?
How the bluebonnets mock the sea.

Horse in the Dark

Brown as a mule, I stomped
through the flocking geese
who thought themselves swans—

but a mule knows its opposite
and so did I. They were no swans.
A horse can be broken by such

beauty. A horse may follow it
down a slope that will slice its hooves.
Beauty, like a restless man in a tall hat,

a wandering boy with teeth
white as if he had never known meat,
the score of water over stones—

I leapt up for the rain-cloud
shaped like a darker horse,
jumped a too-tall fence believing

a horse could be loved more
and ridden less, until we fell apart,
the horse I was and I.

We who had prayed for a heaven
of toothless grass and barley. How
did we untwine? When

did my long face pull itself back
into this form? How
did words replace neigh?

Two legs took my trot.
And I, freed of my horse-self
who lay dead to the world,

ran through the clover. On two legs

                ran and ran . . .

Smoke Under the Bale

My story—hieroglyphics of scuff and blister.
How can you know me? Tin and bridle,
neigh and crocker sack. My gandy-song—
this blue-buzz of flies.
Sugar from your palm? No.
Give me your fingers. Under this hairshirt
steams the vocabulary of the flesh,
crosshatched and scarred into meaning.

Still Life with Summer Sausage, a Blade, and No Blood
(East Texas, 198_)

I remember, we walked (we didn't walk)
from the farmhouse to the store in Palestine,
(we drove the truck, got out, went in) Texas.
The storefronts hadn't changed since
my father was a child. He grabbed saltines from the bin
(he bought a box) and he bought some sausage.
We walked (yes, then we walked) around town
as we ate (he shared). He gave me some summer
sausage, cut with his pocket knife. I pulled the pieces
from the point of the blade. I knew (knew)
nothing would happen (though he was silent)
to alter this memory. We were together
in Texas and we ate and walked in silence
and it felt like smiling, like skipping, like saying
"Daddy" and him not minding, not minding at all.

Alena Hairston

(1974–)

I AM CONCERNED with paying attention, truth, complexity. What terrifies. What soothes. What needs to be validated, justified. What needs to be known. Ignored, beautiful things. Intricacy. Madness. Sorrow. Atonement. Love.

[The tyranny of pig boys]

THE TYRANNY OF PIG boys: brotherhood of menchildren whose hands
    split coal
and faces that sweat more than smile, like their own.
But they do not own these sweating faces that shout and pray, like
    their own.
And they are not home and, thus, they are not welcome. Nor
    welcoming.
Homelessness makes home for the despot: even the caress of clover
    or phlox
does not sway cruelty when cruelty knows its own.

Yet there are those who plow for other water, dare love through any
    loam.
Exogamists, willing history and death, but more, smiling lives
    beyond their own.

Children born in a land of mines to daughters and sons of tunnel-
    walkers, estranged,
must smile, for their first picture of the world is a tiny window of
    mulberry
and faces fighting surprise. They smile because they are born
from a dare men who eat their own flesh must abide.

[The fathers worked their hands to meat]

THE FATHERS WORKED THEIR hands to meat, side by side, tarry mat-
    ter lining throats.
This one, an early man, alabastered, avowed, helmed by immigrant
    arrogance,
a willful ignorance. And sometimes not. It was work and he needed
    Sicily
in his small garden behind the three family company house.
The other, brailed believer, mafic and refined by the quiet of boot-
    strap mobility,
this, too, a willful ignorance, a necessary erasure of plantation
    prologues,
bred long and deep in Alabaman fields.

The sweat of days on homemade collars, britches crackling tar and
    sulfur ash.
Down there, in tunnel after blackening tunnel, away and anaerobic,
    danger
was a walking shadow camouflaged in coal. The early man did not
    see it,
panicked, threw his shovel into its belly and was enveloped, the gil-
    sonite now on tongue,

in ears, legs broken under rock after rock, dark now and darker.
The brailed believer crawled, clawed, hollered, heaved through silt
    and lime, ash pressed
close and heavy as skin. Found him. Pulled him out. Wiped his black
    face
so that he might breathe, the two of them black together on blacker
    rock, pressed
against the shadows of the hole. It was work yet they were brothers.
    Only then.

Outside the caves, in the daylight of public, there remained and grew
    continental drift.
A saved life could not steer the course.

[Edges in the rhododendron]

EDGES IN THE RHODODENDRON. There is not always enough cloud or
    fog.

When the Mingo knew only themselves, the sky was not a frontier.

Though coal was sacred, it was made for use.

Before any table, there was prayer about this "curious" land.

What they knew.

And then the taking and the losing.
The taking and the losing.

The devil at a table. What is seen is not territory.   Is home.

[Their greatgreatgranddaddies]

THEIR GREATGREATGRANDDADDIES were paid in scrip yet thrived a
   wrong geography.
inherited legacy intermittent but carrouselling generations and
   cokeyard dreams.
grandmommas lemonade porches and gospel skins. wifely witness.
birthdeathbirthdeathbirthdeathbirthdeathbirthdeathbirthdeath-
   birthdeathbirth.
mommas merogony: two browngirls whose flowers stay untrained.
they make poems with their lips, holding hands at the Table, three
   boulders gorged
in a canopy of free air. a mango sun behind them. a morning gloried
   affair.
their greatgreatgranddaddies were paid in scrip yet thrived a wrong
   geography.
good daughters on a fourwheeler listening to sky: the rites of girls:
a laughing flight.

[Daughters of four generations]

DAUGHTERS OF FOUR GENERATIONS of undines
honey and maple bodies of branches anticipating warmer weather
in a world not wanting them
because boys have souls already and promise more dollars
the rites of browngirls can go unpublished (remember their flowers
   untrained)
but they swim the fish and seawater between them
because boys are a cold place
and when one says "i feel you passing through me"
the choice to stay or leave is one
either is flight

[Because we love wrong]

BECAUSE WE LOVE WRONG we are no one's daughter. We cannot go
    home.
Even though we got coal between our teeth and shovels for legs.
Not all motherly struggles are our own and boys not our priority.
We live a small place and so our discovery large, even behind
    mountain.

They surround us, they, grand and fatherly, boys we love and don't.

And we know how to speak, our mouths always lined in summers,
    kisses of faith
between us. In front of them. We cannot go home. They know this.
    And push.

Though we ride hard and nightly; though we know there should be a
    place of lemonade
and careful hands and passed on passing on wood for us; though we
    know granddaddy's shovel
and the bees in his head; though we can count the layers of caked on
    coal, lime, shale
on britches thrown out or cut up; though we find the thrown out
    ones and mend the cut-up ones;
though we wash them all in vinegar all day long; though daily we
    nightly watch granddaddy
counting his stickers and coins to our fathers and brothers like a
    deacon
at benediction.   Silent we, proud in our removal, proud
    in our pain.

Love is a careful line they don't want us to read or speak.

We ride hard.

Janice N. Harrington

(1956–)

I STRIVE TO WRITE a lyrical poetry that plays with the musicality of language. It's a poetry characterized by the deep breath of long lines and rhythmic repetitions, and often by narrative. It tests the bonds between past and present, between multiple and simultaneous worlds, searching for the transformative events in daily life. Can a living daughter speak with her dead father? Can a woman bear the child of a goat god? Can the life of an obscure African American folk artist of the 1930s speak to later audiences? My answer is always yes.

I try to weave language, narrative, cultural history, memory, and personal mythology together in ways that encourage readers to invest in acts of transformation. I want to widen what readers believe possible. I enjoy storytelling, but some topics don't call for narrative's straight line. I try to write poetry that invites readers to make imaginative leaps across dissociative images. The aggregation of images and emotions sparks unexpected connections and understandings.

My poems explore the particular. They reach for the lyrical. But I also use indirection to bear witness, challenge boundaries, question truisms, and show, quietly, that a whisper can sound as forceful as a shout. The whisper draws the ear closer.

The Warning Comes Down

1

A colored woman stands beside a red dirt road
watching these strangers, these gypsies.
And hadn't her eye twitched just that morning,
nerve-whipping like a wire. This sign:
a jumping eye and company coming.

They offer to augur the future, to repair
the broken. They ask for well water,
but she gives them nothing, runs them off.
Not like Webster, who would have given
them anything, even the heart out of his chest.
With her, family would always come first.

But later she'll discover her missing trove:
all that she saved, tied in a handkerchief
and hidden in a steamer trunk, gone.
She will blame the gypsies for her grief,
the warning will come down.

An object lesson, you see how people do?
You learn that trust cannot be given,
never tied tight enough, or its loss shriven.
How two eyes in the back of your head
are too few. And people will steal the hinges
from the gates of hell, if you let them.

2

When my father came home, on leave,
he brought us a mason jar filled
with francs, centimes, and sous
and taught me to say *s'il vous plaît, bonjour,
parlez-vous français*, and hold a cup
with my pinky up as gentle ladies do.

A mason jar of French coins, that is absence.
Loss is the sound of it shaking, how we
were marooned, mother and daughter,
without him, to red dirt, to cleaning
other people's houses, poke salad,
and knowing we were poor but clean.

And now the chanson of centimes and sous
lies buried beneath red soil, resounding
in a colored child's coppered skin
and the whisper of spilling sand.

France is where daddies go,
overseas, in silver-bellied planes, and maybe
they'll come home again, tomorrow, tomorrow.

But now the days, minutes, months are all AWOL,
flat as francs, *un, deux, trois, quatre, cinq.*

3
And maybe this is 1960,
and I'm a colored serviceman
waving goodbye to a wife and child.

Or maybe I'm the daughter,
copper-eyed, searching desperately
for shoes, on bare feet calling, *Bye! bye!*
Bye, bye, Daddy!

Maybe I am a mason jar.

No, I am the father, a colored
man in khaki, leaving
in a yellow station wagon
and a hem of red dust,

going back to France or Germany,
to an Air Force base, to the other
who will lean his body into mine,

his longing a ripe persimmon,
sweet, swollen, and my mouth made
round swallows the black seed,
the orange flesh, and centimes

fall from my mouth, and red sand,
red, sperm-sand spills everywhere.

4
And the past, the handkerchief
of a colored woman, unties itself.

And in its cotton corners
all the missing, all we've tried to save.

And memory is a mendicant
shaking its palms, auguring these lives
and their absolution.

Beneath the Eiffel Tower
a Romany child pinches the moon between two fingers,
its tambourine light ringing against a hard world,

and the darkness swirls like a gypsy's skirt.

5
What is the half-life of a copper coin?

What grows from a buried jar of centimes and sous?

From the economy of our losses?

In Vernon, at the Old Negro Cemetery
amid scrub grass and red sand
this grave, the sky-blue tombstone

of a colored woman who went to Nebraska
and Kansas, once, but never to Paris,

beneath the pine-splintered shadows, the graves of many,
each a buried coin, under the turpentine heat
and the wind's green needles, whispering,
s'il vous plaît, s'il vous plaît.

Falling

With lengths of string and canted chairs, my father
struggles to raise the wide wings and bright belly,
every attempt unraveling, breaking, or crashing.
On crooked knee he tries again, but it never flies.
In the ancient story, another father watches
as his beloved plunges into the sea, leaving
only these signs: wax and twine and the quills of gulls.
But what father ever binds the cords tight enough?
Shy from that scalding sea! Shy from that searing
light! Aspire less and take the midmost course,
the one your father chose. Lift yourself on wings
he made for you, and when you fall into the devouring
sea whisper *Daddy, Daddy, oh,* but loud enough
for him to hear, loud enough to soften wax or sever

a gull's extended wing. In a backyard, in Vernon,
a colored man attempts to teach his daughter *flight*
and *boundlessness,* their shadows stretching
wingtip to wingtip, while between them
an airplane teeters on a cotton string but never
flies. And black Icarus plummets into a Tuskegee
airfield, a black bird from a clear sky,
a crow's field holler when you are the only one
to hear it. Dark Icarus riven against
red sand, black Icarus swinging, swinging
from a yella pine. The black feather that falls
upon your shoulder weighs more than grief.

No, the plane never flew. But we forgive
our fathers their broken flights: sometimes.
Aileron, airfoil, wing root, wingtip, we lift
ourselves through perilous moments unaware,
beneath pinions of mercy. How are wings
made? Wax, twine, and the quills of gulls?
And in the ancient story, a fisherman,
a plowman, and a tenant farmer from Sulligent
look up in amazement, seeing father and daughter

walking across the clouds. It is evening now,
and the heart has done its barrel-rolls
and loop-the-loops, and whatever we've written
on this pale page turns to vapor and rains
down into the sea. There is only this last act: rising,
full throttle into a breathless fall.

Fire

In his knapsack, he tucked a notebook of sketches
limned in hurried slashes and pencil strokes:
the 369th Infantry, France during the spring
and summer of the war, lovely names—
St. Nazaire, Bois d'Hauzy, Maffrecourt,
and unlovely—Champagne-Marne, Aisne-Marne,
Meuse-Argonne. Battles and blasts delicately
drawn, delicately shaded by the colored sketches
of a Negro Doughboy, leaves of witness that—
for security's sake—he burned. Nothing whispered:

*Don't. They will want to know. Your memory
will be trophy and ossuary and record.* Nothing
stayed his hand or shouted: *Stop!*

A Negro soldier burns the pages of his notebook
beside the door of a dugout, undisturbed. The pages,
like paper fists, open and curl to grasp each flame's
finger. The blackened leaves rise as smoke rises.

And in the trenches, black men pass around
the last smoke before the wire, the stub passed
from mouth to mouth, sweet with spit, sweet
because it is the last, drawing the smoke deep
into their lungs, letting it rise, knowing they must follow.

Tyehimba Jess

(1965–)

MY AESTHETIC SEEMS to be grounded in the themes of history, musicality, and the art of the image. When I write, I do so with a desire to tell stories or project images that have been buried, obfuscated, distorted, deracinated, crushed into near oblivion by the workhorses of mass media and public miseducation. When I write, I am trying to inform myself of how far language can go in search of these lost stories, and I pray for fellow passengers who will follow the path alongside me, and the closest, bestest thing I come to prayer is a truckful of blues lines that lay themselves down on the crossroads of a twentieth-/twenty-first-century timeline. If I write, I want to claim the tradition of Fred MacDowell and Jimi Hendrix. I want John Lee Hooker on my front porch and Blind Boone in the parlor and something that tastes like Dinah Washington's voice in my glass.

blind lemon taught me

i remember a useless eyed street busker, twin holes shriveled small behind smoked spectacles. the parables he taught in the troubled space between each note. sometimes, i would close my eyes, run my fingers through landscape where he'd placed his hands to solve the riddle of my features, his fingertips supple winged blackbirds. fluttering from brow to eyelash to cheek to chin, he found my true face, stretched those knuckle jointed roots from ebony trunk of wrist and ashen palm to grow as one with the wood of his twelve string. there, he told how a man can trade pieces of himself for a song. an eye here, an ankle there, a ball if he's not careful, and the fret board's friction that turns silken skin to callus. i remember how he bottlenecked blues caught between the teeth of each tin pan alley tune, nailed it in a patent leather stomp, moved street-corner crowds down another mile of his train tracked voice with every beat. i remember how every song stitched together my story, how he took something away when he discovered my face beneath his palms, gave it back on layaway plan of bent notes, bloodied moons.

leadbelly sings to his #1 crew

Gonna jump

gotta jump up to go down in the bottom land, a brown bird of sweat strapped to a sack of feathered stone. gotta tumble down to the basement of

down,

hell after i done lifted up to heaven and the steel toed angels kicked me back under the sun's bright red sickle drippin' with dawn spinnin' in a sky so

spin

so dizzy with heat 'til it spills its weight on my back and wraps its blistered arms around my neck pulls down 'til i pick 500 pounds of dirty

around,

cloud from prisoned-up farm i mean 1 ton a week i mean 52 tons a year i mean bale after bale cause it ain't no bail i mean what could i make if i had

pick

bail and all the bales i ever picked? *10,000 handkerchiefs to dry my mama's tears. 20 years of double breasted suits to glide home in every day. a new*

a bale

tie for every time i strut through a feelgood woman's smile. a fresh tablecloth for every homemade meal

of cotton,

I missed, and if i took a scrap from every denim and linen and dyed piece of cloth that got spun from them bales, could i patchwork a shroud wide enough, heavy enough, bright enough, dark enough, mended and torn and mended enough to lay this place to rest? and what if i set that shroud on fire?

Gonna jump

down,

spin

around,

pick

a bale a day.

gonna? got to. can't say no. can't walk away. got to jump in. jump for the sun. jump against sky. jump across pain. jump up when i'm beat down by the riverside, where my sword and shield is my song and my word and my breath and my mama spun me around and slapped me down when i lied and stole and if only i'da listened to my mama i wouldn't be in the shape i'm in hangin' round the whiskey still and drunk on gin is what i picked is what got me here pickin' my way through this handtostalk to bolltobag to handtostalk to bolltobag to reachtotwist to plucktostuff to reachtotwist to plucktostuff a blizzard of casket-sized bales heavy enough to outweigh me and all i've ever owned, big enough to coffin up the boy i was before a pistol flash made me man, that schoolboy smotherin' in the soft strangle of cotton that i heave up from soil every day

Oh Lawdy,

pick a bale of cotton,

Oh Lawdy,

pick a bale,

a day . . .

oh lawdy jesus god did you ever carry a cotton sack i mean did you ever feel the bud in the palm of your hand i mean did you ever lift a bale like you lifted that cross jesus and did it weigh as much as a cotton field and when you show me the holes in your hands and feet can i show you the blisters in my hands and feet and can we size up the lashes on our backs and when you fell in the sun in the dust in the thorns did they wipe your face and did they look at the cloth and see my face scorched in the cotton of their cloth and was my mouth wide open my eyes squinted up from singing this song every every every every every every . . .

martha promise receives leadbelly, 1935

when your man comes home from prison,
when he comes back like the wound
and you are the stitch,
when he comes back with pennies in his pocket
and prayer fresh on his lips,
you got to wash him down first.

you got to have the wildweed and treebark boiled
and calmed, waiting for his skin like a shining baptism
back into what he was before gun barrels and bars
chewed their claim in his hide and spit him
stumbling backwards into screaming sunlight.

you got to scrub loose the jailtime fingersmears
from ashy skin, lather down the cuffmarks
from ankle and wrist, rinse solitary's stench loose
from his hair, scrape curse and confession
from the welted and the smooth,
the hard and the soft,
the furrowed and the lax.

you got to hold tight that shadrach's face
between your palms, take crease and lid
and lip and brow and rinse slow with river water,
and when he opens his eyes
you tell him calm and sure
how a woman birthed him
back whole again.

mistress stella speaks

you think i'm his property
'cause he paid cash
to grab me by the neck,
swing me 'cross his knee
and stroke the living song from my hips.

you think he is master of all
my twelve tongues, spreading notes
thick as a starless night, strangling spine
till my voice is a jungle of chords.

the truth is that i owned him
since the word *love* first blessed his lips
since *hurt* and *flight* and *free*
carved their way into the cotton
fused bones of his fretting hand,
since he learned how pleading men hunt
for my face in the well of their throats
till their tongues are soaked with want.

yes, each day he comes back
home from the fields,
from chain gang fury,
from the smell of sometime women
who borrow his body. he bends
his weight around me
like a wilting weed,
drinking in my kiss
of fretboard across fingertip
'til he can stand up straight again,
aching from what he left behind,
rising sure as dawn.

Ruth Ellen Kocher

(1965–)

L ET'S SAY I WORK SOMEWHERE within that liminal space between what many call lyric and what many call innovation. I can often use very formal elements to do so, as in the "gigans." The "gigans," a group of poems dedicated to a sixteen-line form I've developed from a fragmentation and synthesis of other traditional prosodies, came about because I wanted to understand how to write with significant limitation, to understand how a very formal construct can tell us something about poetic impulse, and yet also allow me to make formal prosody "new," which translates into something strangely and contrarily freeing. Those poems in particular also convey the way rocks and grass and all things earth often inhabit my writing. But regardless of how I play with both formal performance and the disruption of that performance, or the landscape of the image, the sonic element is without doubt the most important and foundational aspect of my writing. I want my poems to be sonic indulgence, pure song. I want my poems to ask the reader, "what of you?" I—to connect with them in that way. I want to ask my reader to come back for more.

Meditation on Breathing

> When we love words, words catch fire.
> —ÉDOUARD GLISSANT

—for A.M.

I.

I have finally learned to speak to God
through my hunger for air, asthmatic
searching: a dog paddling in deep sea,
wave carries his churning home
somewhere between the lungs' pink folds.

II.

Call God. Remember the gift of music.
How a flute gives breath a body,
undulates the chord between A and C,
or a horn wets its wings on a lake
invisible behind the tree's night shadow.
Hear staccato fill an evening while friends
gather around, their audible laughing, God
expelling breath from the body's instrument.

III.

Incense on the back of the throat
does not taste like God. Lilac does not
taste like God. Breathe in the failing
season, the rotting blossoms of an overgrown
tree, or a rabbit's severed leg
left to rot on a garden wall.
You will not exhale the taste of God.

IV.

God is not home. God skirts the refrain
of a hymn. God jogs from here to Atlanta,
and here is an everywhere place. God pants
souring saguaro scent through the desert and stops
to fill the chests of gecko with scorched
morning air. Even the kingfishers woodwind
their wishes to God's absence.

V.

The same pulse, long and short, pull
and push. Pause to exhale fully. Inhale,
pause. Breathe into the deep
cavity of your summer, the hollowed cask
of wordlessness as you cross the street,
the quick draw in as your knees bend
into each stairwell step. Shudder the sound
you make in the world. Breathe. Breathe hard,
as though someone might hear you.

The Window Cleaner Writes to the Astronaut's Husband

Now that she has not come back
I will tell you.

It is not that her face disappeared among
the constellations

or that you wake space-tumbled from sleep,
the last digital glimpse of dark skin, her tied-back hair

leaving you. You expect this way of mourning
as you expect an open door to lead to a room

which leads to another room, a corridor of blank walls
that contain your passage. You are shaken

by gravity. Each morning your feet touch the floor.
You stand. You walk. The sink twists the light above

into reflection as you brush your teeth. Understand
it is pull that failed her, fails you—

our insistent, magnetic planet,
a wanting back what it dared release

to a rocket's surge. Understand the physics
of greed, the orbit of earth as a circle of want,

the way we are each held beyond our will
and that never, never, could it have left her free.

gigan 63

if you killed me now my legs would walk to another country
happy for their journey away from the hips' locked carriage

my eyes would roll into glass reflect first all we have ever
forgotten about the creeping westward blue that hovers above
and slowly then roll from my skull into the distant green horizon

tired of all they've seen at the moment of my death my body would
cascade into four thousand ripples as though remembering the water

from which it came remembering your hand the vortices'
swirl of each imprint you made on me waterfall and white foam

come together again belly heave and fraction of each touch
if you killed me now my face would become your face brother

soldier shopkeeper nurse and at this moment of my death this
    moment
crisp with the smell of smoke that circles autumn know this the blue
scarf tied around the head of the old woman at the bus stop is me her
    square

hands her clenched jaw me and within her an animal outline deltoid
    curve
soft sagging flesh an animal fanged within all me in her skin's perfect
    folds

Dawn Lundy Martin

(1968–)

A POETICS OF APPROXIMATION, looking sidewise, and failure. The leaning toward, the striving, the reach, the misstep, the fall over into, tumble despite restraint. We ask here about the strain toward utterance—the impossibility wired into any approach. When there are the particularities of the poetic concern or that which might compel the poem into being (a brute force, perhaps, or a discursive subjugation) we face other impossibilities: that language falls apart in the face of the thing, that it folds the tongue up, makes it stammer, splinter, that

> **Who is the speaker at the center of the work?**

the throat closes in verbal suffocation. Circle around to the beginning. A moving target. A representa- tional resistance. The work is adamantly *not* interested in representation. It wants to innovate around representa- tion, to point at or prod, to tease or run away from—a kind of fugitive in the midst of seem- ing coherence. I'm a nonbeliever, you see, faithless among the faithful. The poem is compelled into existence by the very thing that prohibits its speech. Here the body is bent over awkwardly. There is a critical alliance with alienation; a what it means to say, "I am" or "I will be" or simply "I"; all this around the loathed body (its markers of "race," its methods of entry)—its piecemeal effects, its attendant gestures and speech; the will and persistence of things in the face of linguistic atheism. Effort (again) in speaking. What does it mean to speak into persistent noise? Or, conversely, what does it mean to speak into flattened registers, regulated speech, into that which is condoned and thus distributed massly? These are questions that fuel how the poem slips into being.

Negrotizing in Five or How to Write a Black Poem

One: Formlessness.

One enters an unforgiving, inchoate world. No mold to make, fossilizing. Here is the secret: I cannot tell you because it is not known. My fingers obtund with effort. One asks about stuff, considers what comes next, is maddened by possibility. Some castigating black marks condition the body, soften the skin, open into sepulcher. But the body will not be buried there. It will put down a thing, someplace on a page, emancipated [nearly] by the imagination.

Two: Mutilation.

Hands are scarred, almost dead. You bleed from the knees, ruddy. Feebly scratch out signs including "as if." You are on the floor. You plead. You make filth. What to bare out? What to pitchfork? You want to be rid of the black. And you want to embrace the black. You write "grandmother" and cross it out. You peel. You acknowledge the pain of peeling. You are hollowing in, coarse carving a sound to resemble that which must be said. You drag your canvas over and finally write with whatever fluid has spilled.

Three: Sing a song that cannot be sung.

A maw. A silence. It wanted to say, I am, but said instead, it was. Noted the skin's purple hue, fell into longing, thought of what was made and what was done. Went to speak and said, sith sith, and then, mmmoss. Finger pointed at the body and then at the sun, realized nothing and fell again taciturn. There was, too, a craving: a stale remembrance that came a jolting. A hard feeling, a swallowed rock. Wanted to wrench a cavity and pull, expose the stone, as if I could, but could not.

Four: I/M/A/G/E.

Tell me—I am telling you—the scent of your coming down, breathe already at my belly button, easing. Or, the black room of terror that you half-recall, half-invent. Tell me of the exact moment you slashed through your surprisingly tough skin with a pocket knife and how it felt like rain. I want to tell you about the splitting, of a female body— how I squeezed into it—fitting barely, of the texture of melancholy, of a sycophantic love, draw a flicker for you, let you enter as if entering me.

Five: Completion cleaved.

All that has been spoken. All that threatens the legitimacy of that which is attempting to be said. Phonemic struggle—I'll call it a precursor to blathering. Scintilla. Something dragged in the sand. An ocean of debris. In the instants before arrivals some things happened. What is perpetually almost, spilling off its imagined page, signaling an infinite number of openings, leakages, stuck tongues. Blath, said by mistake, and begun again. Bath, said clearly. But, in the end, blath returned, more persistently [unofficially]. Because it was dirty.

The Undress

They say, erased.

Someone once said, once sung, a lament for the destruction of the beautiful. Emblem brandished upon entrance into tribe. He spoke
   two
words I did not understand. I think he said it's hateful or it happened.

That the body—trespassed—troped—made haven—made him
  awful—
deeply recognized. He unraveled—epithelium peeled—pelted first,
then simply removed. He was what we might call—would
most likely call—an ugly, black man.

To dance, he thought, in the cover of night, finally unseen.

He wore robes.

He untied his robes.

Let them fall gracefully to the floor.

Some kind of spiral, he thought,
some kind of mirror for my lakes of grief.

They say, betrayal.

He had undone it, reversed time, made no allowances, poured it all
into a stinking black bowl.

                              [What human form sleeves out of]

                              [An imagining outside itself]

                              [A grasping of the garrote]

                              [A phylum called unsatisfactory]

The meat is work.

Porous skin finally gone, gouged. He no longer sings gospel but hums
silently in his head, *What I have done, what I have done.*

                              [One can hear it falling]

[Pecked out of order]

[Racing in a circumference]

[To be not forgotten]

Upon driving on an absent road, the body shivers. Resonates itself. Dittos for a moment. Incision cut [niggardly] [whimsical] and let go, pleads, Let me go. Struggles with wretchedness, attempts to scream, curls back into, settles [settles as butterfly would].

I am unpractical, wanting desire.

Not to be fragrant. To be raw. A bone.

Not to bend. To slumber.

They say, love your body, love yourself.

Have seen the blur of it. Have endured cosmology. As a crack on a wall endures flawlessness.

When the basement sweats, a mental note: the body is not indestructible. Click. One can create erosion. O, my tin cup is too full—it smothers—I stumble, stammer, the word, *strings*.

Had a body with blood in it. Blood that stinks, comes in tumors, drops as pennies drop.

Had turned monstrosity, from fledging thing, weak, to vague resemblance of human tissues. (To burn, to blast, to shell, to cut.) To blaze, to deep entirety, his leaves gone back black, gangs that leapt gnashing into the surface of what could be human form.

Genus: speculation.

When the wax dries, finally, alongside the glass,
what rises when the dead are buried?

I happened. Someone happened. We might call it a happening—
breathing, living beings gathered—
brought together as if drunk—as if unbroken,
as if able to speak against fraught with—washed over.

Somewhere, a dog stands alone on a street at night.

In the war, a woman soldier is taken hostage and no one
will say what happened.

There are empty hands pissing. A matter of folding clothes,
of waiting.

When we are lost and mute. When we are sold into strangeness.

[Hole dug in] [Strong desire to speak] [Categories of silence]
[Asphyxiation] [Bloating from here] [Asphalt] [Mouth full of bees] [The
body castrate] [A bright, white day] [If only a signal, a breaking—does it
splinter? In reverence?

                    In increments, a seeping—that multiple hands will
attempt to cover.]

There are mothers who are already buried.

There are mothers who never sung.

The Symbolic Nature of Chaos

There were robberies and thieves, deft cutting into and savaging,
portents like a yelling and a tree. What would come now
that the drifting had begun? Now that the swinging, inconsistent
with landscapes [what cyclones left] in the darkness of this bereft body.
A thing ungroomed.

> Hears the butcher. Bends into
> supplication. The meat of the body.
> Series of punctures, microscopic
> holes. Pungent. Perpendicular.
> Constructed as likeness.
>
> Fabrication. It emits. It gags.
> Streams into lips, slightly,
> unconsciously parted. Putrid
> breath escapes, unbeknownst.

Amid this fury, she wrote me a love letter. She said, "If you were
here I wouldn't miss you this much." She said, "There is cauliflower
growing amongst what has been planted."

> The body bends down so the wrists
are at the ankles. Exposed. Buckling.

> [a matter of gathering
>
> [the stray, unremarkable—
>
> the reason of wings, you'll notice.

Amid some beauty, one wall, for example, paved in patterned red
paper. Of please, please, I'm waiting. To cut. [This is a cutting.] And run.
Skin is felt, is raised, surfaced. Pulling down into haggard drown.
The stench of one's own desire. They call and call from dark channels,
by hoards, knowing this—her viscera.

Her blue mound, a sapling. One remembers the gesture of a deep
footstep, the legs only, extending as if in awe. One remembers
the gutted r's and o's, the white haw, like my devil,
like the devil I keep.

[I said to her "maybe" and "if it comes," "interesting" and
"possibility." I said, "I want, I want" and "what if."] [She wanted to
know about lying. I said no. She wanted to know about trust. I said
trust is relative. She wanted me to love her. I said I did but did only
in the way that all things are palatable.]

       One is bowed. Cranked. One ciphers. ˙
You can hear it over the trees at night. Things are forgotten.
Become unknown. Absent as in synapsed void. Someone is
debased. A strict figure designed for fucking. Deciduous.

There could be divisions. Latent fallacies, facial twitches, when the
I spoke, when it said, *I am the yearner.* It set out, through decades,
brushed by stray bristles, poked at and prodded. *I am the yearner,*
it repeated. Graceless figure, unexuberant claws.

They say there are no dolls. It is night. I wander. The body
wants. Is choked by lust. Occupied fully, mechanically. Greased up
and will-less: a drone.

(Ambling toward tall green
and black desert of trees.
In the wind, leaves clack
too rapidly. Are they hovering?)

The say lust is a sin, *concupiscence of the flesh*. Flesh of
formidable volume. Listens attentively. Near gleeful. Exhumes.
Must smell of it. Where reek inhabits particularity. A glass of red wine
on the breath. Tell me what happens. What happens in a dark park
on the edge of this debilitating desire?

solemnity of fish
there were no dancers
understand this
do not weep
do not weep
from the belly
from the bowels
what is anger?
where does the deep end?
there were walls here
housed like fruit in skin
it ripped
hum of traffic
lull of striptease
what happened three decades ago?
there is an end to this story?
(wrap it up)
say grace and everything
padlock the door
when leaves fall from trees
when birds can be heard a mile away
here, like a dove in hand
(mystery obscured)
so white
so white with filth

what I will say to you will not be heard
it will be unnatural
it will be like something opening up
a row of corpses
proportionless
I want to tell you of my perennial
gracelessness, of an epithet hunger
of a joy that is neither sadness nor joy
a joy that is a rung of teeth
say something

from Discipline

On CNN a girl's fingers slack, empty of weapons. Behind her, shrapnel
fires. My mother says, O, holy, O, O, and then presses her lips together
like a snake. Our purposeful living spaces made from taciturn
rooms. Entire houses of trapped utterances—mouths saturated with
them. Bodies can be easily carried across borders. Tangy fissures cre-
ated from single breaths. Wooden slights bribe doctors to say *This is
a whole body. It's complete and useable.* We all believe that anyway. A
useable body must demonstrate its use.

How do we encounter the many hours past twilight? We understand
that the light is something other, that it catapults us toward a desire
or two if we're lucky. But, lately, daylight eats itself, and is percussive
in its chewing, a carnival of curses and thumps. Nothing is wrong. In
the hours after the whinny of the long train passing, we continue to
think, how special we are, how born and cosmic, how just plain indi-
vidual, but it is not enough. Nothing out there. Everything out there.
What does it matter then, if the body climbs into a plastic car, drives
into a deserted driveway and becomes another self? Elsewhere: One
body found. One policeman shot. One 4-year-old girl shot. Teeter,
tweeter, la, la, la, la, la. I am the I watching the I lift. Roads are short
with darkness. I think, this is what they mean when they say, Savage.

Every night the body winds through the unlit corridors of the house. It tries to be quiet but there is nothing more quiet than the quiet itself. At the first glimpse of sun rising, panic. We are separated from the city. If this is a room in the country then there are other rooms like this one. A boy smells of hemp and bug spray. Cool cats, you know, float up, a mystery. Domesticity lingers.

> *Women in dresses, men in shirts.*
> *Just an approach—*
> *—a waiting or*
> *since there is time, some tea*
> *and wallpaper.*

The body-carts are of a particular shape and size so everyone doesn't have one. We are assured that there were errors. Sleep, little bodies, sleep.

People are fond of saying, "Everything happens for a reason," which is complete bullshit. Required reading dots the bookshelf. There's Fanon breathing holes into us. And my brother reading in the halty sidesteps of a grade schooler. I know what my brother smells like when he's sick, angling for air, his body deep in the sweat of acquiescence. I want him to be someone else. My father liked to blame any crime in our neighborhood on "American blacks." When he mumbled under his breath, I think he was saying "Goddamned niggers," but I can't be sure.

Constance Merritt

(1966–)

T HIS IS WHERE IT STARTS for me, not only poetry but any hope of a
reasonable and humane adult existence and of our continuance, as
a species, on this planet: in the acknowledgment of the hard facts that
condition any life and their acute magnification through the singular gift
of human consciousness. To acknowledge pain as pain, let alone the pov-
erty of life, let alone that this poverty—that anything—is irremediable
is a powerful antidote to our much-cherished doctrines of the imminent
perfectibility of our species and our world, doctrines we continue to cling
to despite their destructiveness having been proven again and again.
While politics of whatever stripe pursues remedies for real and perceived
ills through shifts in the balance of power, poetry eschews power, culti-
vates vulnerability instead, traces social problems back to psychic roots,
does not so much seek to heal divisions inherent in the human heart as
to effect provisional re-integrations, peaceable coexistence, and peace-
ful conflicts. "The mind is the most terrible force in the world," [Wallace]
Stevens writes, "principally in this that it is the only force that can defend
us against itself. The modern world is based on this pensée." And then
one day, if we are lucky, acknowledgment takes a subtle turn, becomes
acceptance, becomes celebration: *a present perfecting, a satisfaction in the
irremediable poverty of life.* In one reading, poetry is a little island adrift
in the ocean of life's irremediable poverty, but in another, life, its irreme-
diable poverty notwithstanding, becomes the source of one's satisfaction,
as the world is subtly altered by our imagination and our words. To teach
men how to love their lives—this life, this world, the only one there is—
and passionately, this, this seems to me the most radical end of poetry.

Lying

awake at 4 A.M.
whatever the space beside you holds
you are   yourself   alone

and whatever there is of truth
turning in crevices light can't touch
it must be that which wakes you

*

in a quiet room a woman works
arranging words, a world
where she might live

it changes little day to day
but the mind is changed
as light changes, as the leaves turn

and whatever holds that space inside her
it is so much harder, vaster, colder
than this near mortal, however breathing, however loved.

The Mute Swan

White silence on the water pulls me in and under. And I know it is a lady.

The impossibility of naming her desire has kept her white and beautiful, while she has kept our secrets. She holds them deep within the throat of her graceful neck, and it is hard to say whether, when she bows her head, she is praying to take voice or to go on giving silence.

It is also hard to say whether hers is the silence of before speaking or after. Almost as hard as saying nothing.

Woman of Color

The splendid coat that wrapped the favored son
In fevered dreams of adulation
And turned his brothers' hearts from jealousy
To rage (*Behold, this dreamer comes.*)—though long
Since rent and soaked in blood, dried and decomposed—
Arrives through the long centuries over
Sea and land, the unexpected birthright
Of this particular girl. Its separate
Magic beads and threads spill onto the floor
Indistinguishable from alphabet
Blocks, the many pieces of her country,
And its citizens loud and teeming from
Their cramped Crayola crayon box. Each state,
Each letter has a color, a shape, its own,
Soft curves and sharp angles, compassionate
Contours promising something not hers to keep,
An abundance utterly unasked for and
Nearly impossible to give. *What is*
This dream that thou hast dreamed? Shall I and thy
Mother and thy brethren indeed come
To bow down ourselves to thee to the earth?

It is loneliness that bows her head, that breaks
Her free from silence's sweet spell, spilling
Her voice onto the brittle air, breathless
In its rush: green of sea, pine, forest, spring;
Blue of midnight, cerulean, cornflower;
Sky, navy, cadet, and royal blue; blue
Violet, turquoise, aquamarine; teal blue,
Blue green, periwinkle; burnt and raw
Sienna, bittersweet, brick and in-
Dian red, goldenrod and thistle, white.
And exile enters here, the lull and pull
Of distance between the voice's deepest source
And its unmappable destinations.
And they sat down to eat bread and they lifted

Up their eyes and looked, and, behold, a company
Of Ishmaelites came from Gilead with
Their camels bearing spicery and balm
And myrrh going to carry it down to
Egypt. And Judah said, what profit is it
If we slay our brother and conceal his blood?
Let us sell him for he is our brother and our flesh.

For her there is no Egypt to seduce
With strange, mad song, no famished countrymen
Falling to their knees and near enough
To make her tremble afraid she will be tender
Instead of stern. Instead there is only
This brilliant coat, a gift of love, that leaves
Her vulnerable to cold and knowing eyes
Until it seems she has no skin at all
Except for silence, except the weave of words:
Hound's-tooth, gingham, tulle, eyelet, chambray;
Broad-cloth, denim, paisley, linen, wool.
Her dreams grow full of birdsong; each bird says
Its name: Cardinalis Cardinalis,
Anas Carolinensis, Cyanthus
Latirostris, Mimus Polyglottos,
Cyanocitta Stelleri, Agelaius
Phoenecius—over and over,
Until, finally, sure it's meant for her,
She gently stirs the waters' smooth bright skin,
And bursting from the deep into the world,
Its fear, its hurt, its roar; she tries her tongue.

Self-Portrait: Lilith, Eve

The austere angels dozing at their posts,
The flaming sword floats between us like
A bridal veil stirred by breath or wind,
Utterly transparent and vulnerable

To tears at slightest touch. So how explain
This chronic failure of eyes, of hands, to meet?
Those who come after will say it was
He who hulked between us like a wall
Of rock dividing countries, estranging
Sea from land. Will say that I abandoned
You to a life I would not stand. Or, I
Supplanted you in the garden with the man.

Not in the slightest do we grudge them
The comfort of such myths, neither can we
Forget what we have known:
An orange presence in a circle of stones.
How it seemed to leap inside us as we stroked
The length of his unfurled body over
And over with our tongue. How live things seemed
To clench and ripple just beneath his skin.
How his body was a flask full of brightness
Spilt with little provocation.
How easily stopped his breath; how fragile his bone.
How we could not tell his heartbeat from our own.

Some mornings the ground was strewn with flowers torn
From their stalks by wind; the world was quiet then.
No, too ablaze with sound. What happened then?
Nothing. And after that? Nothing. There is
No story here. Bending above his body,
Tending its delicate milkweed flower,
We trembled with pleasure to hold such power
Over him. For me there was no pleasure,
And I was still and very much afraid.
Little by little you began to leave
The garden? Yes, as more and more you stayed.
Nothing clean or simple about that split.

And it's still ongoing. Too soon to sort it out.
One good eye, one breast, two hands, a single tongue
Between us—how we wrestle over words,
Strain to wring some blessing from the silence,
Deliverance from violence, its fear, its lure,

The tyranny of names: night day,
Sable and alabaster, flint shale,
Steel and lace. Who among us can afford
To speak the language—any language—rightly?
As if it weren't enough to bear one heart
Eternally divided in its chambers.

We stand close enough to touch. We do
Not touch. Between us burns a sword of fire,
A rusted turnstile glinting in the sun.

Fred Moten

(1962–)

T HERE IS A KIND of pressure that music and poverty (constraint) put
on the sentence; the remainder (escape) is poetry. Over the course of
history the demands of truthful expression (as either or both correspon-
dence and discovery) become more and more severe, but at the same time
"the plain sense of things" becomes more plain and the striated polyvo-
cality of the vessel, the medium, the conductor strives for directness. I
think poetry is what happens or is conveyed on the outskirts of sense,
on the outskirts of normative meaning. I'm trying precisely to work on
that edge, and I assume that the content that is conveyed on that edge,
on that fault line, is richer, deeper, and fuller than those things that are
given in writing that passes for direct. That's definitely a kind of preju-
dice of mine—and I could be wrong. The art that always threatens the
boundaries of sense has been the art that has been the most beautiful for
me. What I love about Schoenberg or Olson is not the same thing as what
I love about my cousin Reverend L. T. Marks's sermons, but it's nothing
other than that either. I want my poems to carry that weight, and part
of what I do to accomplish this is maintaining a wide range of reference.

gayl jones

my daddy drank red soda pop.
once he wanted a fleetwood
then he wanted a navigator,

so he could navigate, check out
his radio towers, deliver flowers,
drive back to give me long kisses,

watch mama burn her books. said nancy
wilson can't sing but she can style—
hold back the force of random operators/
return to the line refuse to punctuate. a moon—
but his actual drive was watching clay circle,
tight-breath'd gesture tight shoulder. sweet

nancy wilson was just cold analytics:
the difference between a new coat and the
one with ink on the pocket, calculate
like a fat young minister, strokin like
clarence carter, increase like creflo
dollar. mama and me stayed up over

the club, cried sometimes in the same
broke off the same piece, left each other
the last piece, practiced the same piece,
got warm on the same. however
I'm so full this morning I have
to try and make you understand

johnny cash

first diesel came through cuba
long possible hard stream to memphis
gravel on the edge of that black water
white flowers till that river black motel

like making groceries at drake's on saturday
but no new lectronics of the sun. gotta get home to

that light by box car, slip through cotton plant
at night between the track and the river,

short sleeves but mo'nin' like a man with

a movie camera, but he took that hat off mystery

dead slate brought back with friction. the sound
of the horn makes the flat ones skim
till the edge and sharpen it
then red then green then dyad then severed

politically man
dwells down here
in cubie

that same train from dave cash

the central valley. wood water asphalt steel pine

tremor flint michigan. fresh desert (cleared wood), out
from the center wheel but deep
in that high social cotton, social ground, I don't know when,
whistle smoke drive on

this diesel came thu kingsland then dyess on severn

trumpeters thought about gabriel
maybe they heard it like sunshine
honey bee heard it like sunshine
baby b mine like sunshine

rosetta tharp

ΜΕΤΟΙΚΕ

She one of them impossible
domestics shirtwaisted walking
out together dark mornings in the

evening come home pan-toting.

Her hand blew up inside blew up
the house inside where she work
to blow it up and somehow love

them while she be cleaning up

and scheming. Sewing seeds from

reading laying out with reeds her
hand blew up inside. In her air
she have a migrant curve her hand
blew up inside. She harass the
sheets she fold by singing
hellhounds in the crease. This
was her air and hand.

        The excluded
middle passion with a right to

philosophy sing hellhounds while
folding and grace to that boy's
winding sheet.

        She the source of air that
rip where she did not come from.
She blur the air precisely through

a comb or string her hand blew up
inside and blurred prose. She bend
sheets and notes by folding and

rub strings with bottles. Sunday
morning in the corner juke and
brush the air her hand blew up
inside. She always be escaping
coming home at night with things
again and walking out again with
them real early. Her air black city

in her hand blew up inside. She
always be talking about Cedric
Robinson.

elizabeth cotten

she put a statue of a surprise on the windowsill. it was the size of a
chess piece. it smelled like a chess pie, rose up from itself in a dream
as festival music, for leftovers and late planning, till new years day's

excision curled exhaust, cut out, cut back, outlet, second, unthreaded,

a dusty veer on the avenue bus for the new survival of carolina statues.
she stayed at van gelder's, whose central fact was space, for seven years.
the material of poetry is so vast, she said, and we make delightful
instructions. we make them up by digging and chip away until we fall

in love with buried, made up things and understand that as a ghostly

matter. we fall in love with making plain confection, the taffy seriality

and braid to dig and dig and dig, then kept alive in phrasing for the
submarine, the beautiful way we go downstairs impossibly, and dig and
dig a hole in the open basement, happy with the feedback uncontrolled.
she had the snappy cereality of a little diving bird, and dig a hole for
gapped obstruction, sounding new black rice as a kind of candy, a public
fragment of a private strain, some scratched dirt on the off edge and dig.

her chorographic history of tuning upside down is uncanny and surreal,
the culinary marvelous wrapped up tight in brightleaf lace to breathe

for andrew cyrille, for kiril lakota, for evangeline's burnt cyrillic chord,
for uncalled for, unheard of in what they call for, out of breath in the

workmen's circle, the little books get cut and sewn that way to move
from warehouse to warehouse in reserve. little critical books with lines

to savor, microdances in held bodies in the warehouse, that turn out to

revive the warehouse, enthusiasm in the warehouse city, the little sewn

books of the low country, thrown in the air as little books of movement
of stone passage as liquid, arrangements on fire with the informal form
of the workmen's broken circle, flown out of looking ahead, walking for
the incidents, passage involved in our steps, in dressage, fallen like our
mothers, the fallen dance of mama and her commonness on fire, didn't
she send me any word, ain't she ready for the world? you see the ones

who know what it is to be prayed for. when they fasten up their little

transportation, the thing is how they all stay here. The complex word

of never to return makes them optimistic and pastoral. they give what
they do not possess—O, miracle of my life. we plan the commune as
epic instruments; we held in reverse for study and movement in safety;

we gathered all our little alls in four blocks of black notes. they were
hiding behind the counter at the corner store. in exorbitant small
bundles, the whole idea of the burst is a brand new start. for the ones
who can't start over, once again left with leaving as a kind of little all,

who raise a school up as the corner store, fill the shelf up with groove

habitation, the shrift and tide of black study in a cube or mass, in a

course of blown flare, a fanfare, Jacques Corsair, having flown, to begin

our studies of the little all, all held in counter, the under in
    Middleton's
black book, her new black mass and thrift habilitation, saving, sewing

music in the air, sown air in clothes and jewels for sacramental running, for the soulfeast, for shift and stonefruit, her unknown constitution in a highway that a ship stole, racked up in occult practice, to prayers in the name of tabla and tamla, all and all's uncounted pulse to trade, gone in a

mellow dance, everybody long and sugar on the floor, soft coils in tore up social density, turning in a violent chapel, a drive sound under a pier for stepping out on quiet foil, edenton sung through hamlet in resolve,

the new general strike is jumpin! this is the flavor of our region, she said. the regulators are breaking loose together and they still want us still, but every amazing crush in us is that we got something prodigal, left out fold

and flight. running lines on the intercom, otolithic spirit photograph still broken for the balance of our line to make it go right. we fold the line in our own head and surge and stumble in the shadow. in slug's our

folded head bows down. we mime and trade in the everyday line, for the accident to hold down unreal chances, to stop running and staying away inside, once and for all, 'cause it's all right to have a good time. we were

thinking on the open lines and found a word we hid to start this new system of lines for you. will you and yours come see how much is hid in us? then you have to follow me away from you, come to yourself for

following the thing that's deep in you that comes up as a gesture for the

reindeer on your turquoise fleece, the little deictic pleasures of the

babies, the small textures of your cooking and the way you make me

copies of the new thing you keep listening to sometimes, how good of you to underrepresent. this is the music of my own head and you can hear it in the way I sound when I come away from that for you, twisted away in being folded up when I move away from that to turn my lines out for the other line inside. but let me stop beginning to let you come to this openness I hope for. hopefully it's forming itself from behind against just about every other folding you could think of just for you.

I want you to have this running away from you so you'll remember me

sometimes and love the way you let me get to you so I'm gon' really try

to make it good. will you be surprised again at who you are? I hope so 'cause it always makes me feel brand new to see you back to your old self, curling around in that extra way. maybe this will be open again as a great tightness that we drape around the world. yes, I do believe in the world, the edge, the stage is a complement and we are held together, saved, my love. that's all I've been wanting to show you along these lines.

nahum chandler

frank ramsay

What can't be said, can't be said, and it can't be whistled either. It can't be whispered. The burden can be muted. No wave and the barren sequence rise on our account, triple soft but lashed, like in the first instance, which can be sung. The right to love refusal is black music. The song about desire always wants to disappear. In the second instance, she released in public chastity, flirting at the club and wound. Damaged from repeating, can you stay? Be my ontograph and discompose. If only you do not try to utter what is unutterable then *nothing* gets lost. But the unutterable will be—unutterably—*enjoyed* in what has been enjoyed.

nancy wilson

John Murillo

(1971–)

I N MY WORK, I try to capture, or at least approach, what theologian Cornel West refers to as the "tragicomic hope" of African Americans, the "blues sensibility" that sustains marginalized people through difficult, often overwhelming, experiences. Perhaps this spirit of resilience is best expressed in song lyrics by the group Parliament-Funkadelic: "With the rhythm it takes to dance to / what we got to live through / you can dance underwater and not get wet." Such impossible grace is born of struggle. It is both the struggle ("what we got to live through") and the grace (the dancing underwater) I hope to speak to in my poems. In these poems, people fight. They sing blues and breakdance. They carry guns, smoke weed, go to prison. They inflict and suffer great pain. This is due, in part, to who I read during my early stages as a poet—Etheridge Knight, Miguel Piñero, Gwendolyn Brooks, among others—but mostly, it has to do with neighborhoods in which I grew up, the people who have shared their lives and deaths with me—in short, the worlds I've known. One of the reasons I started writing in the first place was to give voice to those rendered voiceless, *those people* who live on the margins and undersides of acceptable discourse. It is my firm belief that these folks need their poets as much as anyone else.

Sherman Ave. Love Poem

A street sweeper rounds
    the corner, headlights
stretching a man's silhouette
    across the cool brick
of a brownstone. A window
    rattles, creaks, lifts open
from his rib, and a woman
    steps through, pushes

off the ledge. Doesn't flail,
    doesn't scream, or scratch
at passing brick. Mid-flight,
she lies flat, spreads her
    swollen shadow onto
a fire hydrant. She is sure

as gravity. The man
    crossing the street, all rib
and open eye, clutches
    his Koran. Read in prison
    how pregnant women
would dive from slave ships.
    Thought then, and believes
now more than ever: this is
    the one true act.

Enter the Dragon
Los Angeles, California, 1976

For me, the movie starts with a black man
leaping into an orbit of badges, tiny moons

catching the sheen of his perfect black afro.
Arc kicks, karate chops, and thirty cops

on their backs. It starts with the swagger,
the cool lean into the leather front seat

of the black and white he takes off in.
Deep hallelujahs of moviegoers drown

out the *wah wah* guitar. Salt & butter
high-fives, *Right on, brother!* and Daddy

glowing so bright he can light the screen
all by himself. This is how it goes down.

Friday night and my father drives us
home from the late show, two heroes

Cadillacking across King Boulevard.
In the car's dark cab, we jab and clutch,

Jim Kelly and Bruce Lee with popcorn
breath, and almost miss the lights flashing

in the cracked side mirror. I know what's
under the seat, but when the uniforms

approach from the rear quarter panel,
when the fat one leans so far into my father's

window I can smell his long day's work,
when my father—this John Henry of a man—

hides his hammer, doesn't buck, tucks away
his baritone, license and registration shaking as if

showing a bathroom pass to a grade school
principal, I learn the difference between cinema

and city, between the moviehouse cheers
of old men and the silence that gets us home.

Practicing Fade-Aways

after Larry Levis

On a deserted playground in late day sun,
My palms dusted black, dribbling
A worn, leather ball behind my back, this loneliness
Echoes from the handball courts nearby.
Nearly all the markings—free throw lane, sideline,
Center circle—all rubbed to nothing.
A crack in the earth cuts across the schoolyard
Jagged as a scar on a choir boy's cheek.

Twenty years ago,
I ran this very court with nine other
Wannabe ballers. We'd steal
Through peeled chain links, or hop
The gate, to get here: Our blacktop Eden.
One boy, who had a funny pigeon-toed set shot
And a voice full of church bells, sang spirituals
Every time he made a basket,
The other boys humming along, laughing,
High-fives flying down the court.

And a boy we called "the Sandman"
For how he put you to sleep with his shoulder fake or drop step,
Over six feet tall in the tenth grade,
Smooth talker with an itch for older guy's girlfriends.
One Sunday morning, they found him stabbed to death
Outside the Motel 6, pockets untouched,
Bills folded neatly against his beautiful cooling thigh.
And "Downtown" Ricky Brown,
Whose family headed west when he was two,
But still called himself a New Yorker,
Who never pulled from less than thirty feet out,
And could bank shots blindfolded.
He went to Grambling, drove himself
Crazy with conspiracy theories and liquor,

Was last seen roaming the French Quarter, shoeless, babbling
About the Illuminati's six hundred sixty-six ways
To enslave the populace.

At sixteen, I discovered
Venice Beach, with its thousand bodybuilders,
Roller skates, and red thong bikinis.
I would stand on the sidelines and watch
The local ballplayers, leaping and hollering
Quicksilver giants, run and gun,
Already grown into their man bodies,
Funkadelic rising from a boombox in the sand.
Now, all I hear are chain nets chiming as I sink
One fade-away after another,
The backboard, the pole, throwing a long shadow
Across the cracked black asphault.

What the nets want must be this caress,
This stillness stretching
Along every avenue, over high school
Gymnasiums and deserted playgrounds,
And the ambulance drivers drifting into naps
Back at the station house.
What the boys who ran these courts wanted was
A lob pass high enough
To pull them into the sky,
Something they could catch in both hands
And hang from,
Long enough for someone to snap
A photograph, to hold them there,
Skybound. Risen.

Gregory Pardlo

(1968–)

I HOPE TO INVESTIGATE the meaning of representation—what it means to shoulder the weight of cultural, racial, and literary expectations, and its costs. My obsession is the impossibility of fully capturing the image, and the larger question of the role of the New World writer and his relationship to history, marginalization, and the politics of representation.

I supported myself as an undergraduate by managing the jazz club my grandfather owned. A jazz piano player, my grandfather spent much of his retirement performing with his house band in weekly jam sessions featuring some of the Philadelphia area's most renowned musicians. This period served as a dual apprenticeship for me. While not studying the diverse literature I shelved beneath the bar of the jazz club, I was mentored by the community of musicians who recognized a kindred creative spirit developing in me. How does one defy the tradition that he loves? My hope is to expand it, to take my cues from jazz musicians, those incorrigible reinventors and reshapers of meaning and expectation.

Double Dutch

The girls turning double-dutch
bob & weave like boxers pulling
punches, shadowing each other,
sparring across the slack cord
casting parabolas in the air. They

whip quick as an infant's pulse
and the jumper, before she
enters the winking, nods in time
as if she has a notion to share,
waiting her chance to speak. But she's
anticipating the upbeat
like a bandleader counting off
the tune they are about to swing into.
The jumper stair-steps into mid-air
as if she's jumping rope in low-gravity,
training for a lunar mission. Airborne a moment
long enough to fit a second thought in,
she looks caught in the mouth bones of a fish
as she flutter-floats into motion
like a figure in a stack of time-lapse photos
thumbed alive. Once inside,
the bells tied to her shoestrings rouse the gods
who've lain in the dust since the Dutch
acquired Manhattan. How she dances
patterns like a dust-heavy bee retracing
its travels in scale before the hive. How
the whole stunning contraption of girl and rope
slaps and scoops like a paddle boat.
Her misted skin arranges the light
with each adjustment and flex. Now heather-
hued, now sheen, light listing on the fulcrum
of a wrist and the bare jutted joints of elbow
and knee, and the faceted surfaces of muscle,
surfaces fracturing and reforming
like a sun-tickled sleeve of running water.
She makes jewelry of herself and garlands
the ground with shadows.

Copyright

Paul Green
Of course I know the story of the scorpion
and the frog. I've known Biggers all my life.
I've cast down my buckets where I've
stood with them, shoulder to shoulder, our bodies
bent like double helices in the fields. And
when the mob came for Dick didn't I sit anyways
outside his quarters all night like a jailhouse lawyer,
him ignorant of the nature of his custody?
It was me who kept the townsmen at bay after he
provoked them. My cousin among them
had watched him grin and wheedle,
consort with white people carelessly, our naïve
and guileless women, at the civil gathering where
he was my ward. And later, because of me,
his offense went unanswered, un-atoned.
I know the hearts of men are governed
by the endowments of nature. Some children
are faithful. Some are made to obey.

Charles Leavell
First I had to capture the boy
in a thicket of print.
He tried to make my happy darky
dangerous, make my darky
an idea that I couldn't bear to swallow. So
I made him a hothouse flower, writing, *His hunched
shoulders and long, sinewy arms that dangle
almost to his knees*, but warned
readers that Nixon, the "Brick
Slayer," as I christened him,
*had none of the charm of speech
or manner that is characteristic of so many
Southern darkies.* I am a gentle man.
He is very black—almost pure Negro. Withal,
I had to cleave that slate with first words, in order

to get at him, get the nature right, and I
could almost hear the stone sing
like the brick
he used to beat the white woman
who discovered him, that June day in '38,
bagging her Philco radio—as if it were
me doing the slaying.

Richard Wright
One quarter argument two
quarters confession. I engender
my experience in the characters
and they thrive; for the balance
I tracked Robert Nixon, so-called
"Brick Slayer," through rows
and columns, finding him breathing
in the margins of the *Chicago Tribune*.
I loved that boy like redemption
loves a sinner and saw in him
the mute pronouncements of the proletariat,
mutiny on the *Potemkin*. No wonder I
was reluctant to ditch the script I wrote
with Paul Green, that playwright
accused of being a lover of the down-
trodden. Much as I wished to avoid
controversy, when Welles demanded
a Bigger without dream sequences, without
singing, for the Broadway production,
I sighed relief. I knew I had to protect
my creation from the caustic
ministrations of Southern sensibility.
By North Star or candlelight, by necessity,
I had to spirit him away.

Robert Nixon
More crucial than surveillance in the round
house of corrections called a panopticon is the being
watched the prisoner faces raising hairs on the ears.
Like the sun's warmth on the back recognized as light,
recognized as presence. White noise.

The confinement of plain sight. The vertiginous spin
siphoning off the will to question, to doubt,
g-forces pinning back the cheeks, prisoners
reduced to images affixed by the weight of the guard's
transparent eyeball the unreasoning stump of muscle
itself imprisoned like the figures stenciled on an urn.

Shades of Green: Envy and Enmity in the American Cultural Imaginary

Images of the stud and the buck have an amorously crafted reso-
nance burnished by cultural anxieties, an addict's logic toward the
habit they place in the mind and the mysteries we lay at their feet.
This course will begin by focusing on models represented in the 1994
Charles Russell film *The Mask,* and Ang Lee's 2003 *The Hulk.* The
mojo and the genetic regression, the hyper-sexuality and the rage:
these qualities are thrust and airbrushed onto the bacchic body of
the Other, as we fantasize our repression of them in ourselves, the
unquiet threat of psychosomatic greening; a silk garrote, an onan-
istic envy of the Other's capacity for release; a monumental iconog-
raphy of the hermetical black box of the brain. While we might be
tempted to reduce these types to the pat dichotomy of comedy and
tragedy, this course will examine the ways in which there is but one
mask, a Janus-faced cleavage of thou art and thus am I, our goat-
sung desires adrift in the wilderness, our tell-tale passions pulsing
beneath the gladiolas in a mildewed hatbox, trembling the bulb on
its stem; the act of masking triumphal and deadly.

Four Improvisations on Ursa Corregidora

after Gayl Jones

My husband Mutt backhanded me down the fire
escape out back a blues bar called *Happy's*. Nothing
holds a family together like irony and a grudge.
Depends on what you call family. What's left now
of the generation I hadn't known I made is just a scar
squoze shut like a mouth that won't eat, a score
where doctors had to retrieve the fetus, its tub
and my plumbing altogether. Now I'm soundproof,
and now I'm forever hollow as a plaster statue.
Just as I can't go back to where my mothers cast
me out to flatter their memories chiming, echoing,
braiding the wind with their eccentric melody, Mutt
can't come back to me no more. I can picture him though
harassing the shadows of my voice, drunk as a judge.

My husband Mutt handled the hose that doused the fire,
the reason I can't make babies. I've claimed the blues
is a current like electricity, but mine was a combustion
engine cutting shapes out of noise. Lying at the bottom
of those stairs I could already feel my machine slipping
into pictures of still water. I began swallowing water-
melon seeds by the handful hoping something take root:
a vine, a silence. I was reborn at the crime scene;
I survived the rent in time to look back on it squeezing
shut like a fist. A refrain: echolalia: bad penny: menses.
Evidence of a pattern we are determined to reveal
when we find ourselves standing before the judge.
Evidence of the devil we're determined to reveal
when we're testifying for the jury and the judge.

My husband Mutt stared back down the barrel of his years,
came up loaded and hapless. I was determined
to take him in spite of my history, to refrain from adding
to the pattern emerging from the rueful chorus: my mothers
cast me as amanuensis to record their versions

of the crime. Once upon a time means once and for always
and for wherever you are and now I'm singing blues
in a bar revealing as much skin as you should
be willing to reveal when you pouring your seed
into the electric element. We are given two names:
one to work like witness protection, and one to carry
mechanically to the grave. I never took my husband's name.
I imagine that would be as useful as a newspaper covering
my head in the rain. Useful as letting my eyes be the judge.

My husband Mutt handed me back all the love he felt
I had failed to give him. That's saying something close
to nothing. "Do nothing 'til you hear from me," he said,
and smiled. Whoever owns these blues is a matter
of some debate. The story of my people unfolds
each day like a newspaper detailing the catechism
that connects me to history: *Are you hurt?* Yes, I am
the hurt, the silent mouth is the barter. *What's a husband
good for?* Seed money. Generations working the fields. *Why
do we make dreams?* A little ritual. A little lining for the purse.
Each song is a number of the seven veils: each number is
a revelation of skin measuring degrees of distance from
the crime and from the guilt of the crime. Corregidora:
as much kin as we're willing to reveal lest we be judged.

Written by Himself

I was born in minutes in a roadside kitchen a skillet
whispering my name. I was born to rainwater and lye;
I was born across the river where I
was borrowed with clothespins, a harrow tooth,
broadsides sewn in my shoes. I returned, though
it please you, through no fault of my own,
pockets filled with coffee grounds and eggshells.
I was born still and superstitious; I bore an unexpected burden.
I gave birth, I gave blessing, I gave rise to suspicion.

I was born abandoned outdoors in the heat-shaped air,
air drifting like spirits and old windows.
I was born a fraction and a cipher and a ledger entry;
I was an index of first lines when I was born.
I was born waist-deep stubborn in the water crying
                  ain't I a woman and a brother I was born
to this hall of mirrors, this horror movie I was
born with a prologue of references, pursued
by mosquitoes and thieves, I was born passing
off the problem of the twentieth century: I was born.
I read minds before I could read fishes and loaves;
I walked a piece of the way alone before I was born.

giovanni singleton

(1969–)

Uncaged: A Poetics of Transcendence
Things are not as they seem, nor are they otherwise.
—THE LANKAVATARA SUTRA

FROM AN EARLY AGE, I have worn heavily prescribed eyeglasses. I was often teased by other kids. I eventually tired of their taunting. I needed to say something, to respond. A single sentence pushed its way out of my mouth. "Because I wear glasses, I can see things that you can't." I think they believed me. Curiosity trumped meanness. And in that moment I discovered the power of language and the pen became my lens.

My poetry has a spare quality to it that I attribute to my reading of the Objectivists, Asian literature, Buddhist texts, and meditation. Additional influences include gospel music, spiritual narratives of nineteenth-century African American women, abstract expressionism, and avant-garde jazz. Additionally, editing and teaching are integral to my writing practice.

For the past few years, I have been working on a project that investigates the visual aspects, possibilities, and implications of hiddenness in plain sight as it relates to race, gender, the sacred, and the profane. I view writing as an act of paying attention. My aspiration is to transcend appearances in order to see clearly the essence of things.

el corazón
—*toward an ars poetica*

dear grandma
la luna
the moon

dear grandad
el sol
the sun

eagle above   *el cielo*
tortoise below   *la tierra*

       crayon in hand
       lapis de cera

a child *inocencia*
tries to get her
eyes back

from ascension

Day 33

the water by
itself at first.

{seawork}

a black pomfret washed
ashore. its scaled flesh
flapping against the rocks.

a door off its hinges.

why she often kept
the red kettle brewing.

Day 36

we are busy and wanting
to push through light

the bowl i drink from
says we humans keep

cutting back the trees
so that we alone can live

and i realize too just how
much i don't want to be lost

Day 41

in a place beyond
sleep i was on the
ground in

the center of a
circle formed by
half-naked people

their faces covered
with brightly
painted masks

horns curved out
from the tops
of their heads

cowbells hung
from collars
around their necks

and cowbells too
where their hands
should've been.

Day 48

elders on their bench upright
and knowing. such and so.

for what would they trade
the solid whites of their eyes?

a right turn. patience nests
in the mind.

salvationers, dark pupils
point themselves into angels.

Tracy K. Smith

(1972–)

OR ME, THE SUCCESS of a poem is almost always based upon the
degree to which the process itself has managed to teach me some-
thing I didn't think I knew, or reveal to me a new way of considering the
material with which I started. Sometimes that lesson is based in lan-
guage, and at other times it has more to do with events or ways of per-
ceiving events. During composition, I am less concerned with a potential
reader's stake in the poem than I am with my own sense of completing the
movement from vague curiosity to palpable discovery. The reader, and my
wish to communicate clearly and honestly with him or her, arrives much
later in the process.

Drought

1.

The hydrangea begins as a small, bright world.
Mother buries rusty nails, and the flowers
Weep blue and pink. I am alone in the garden,
And like all else that is living, I lean into the sun.

Each bouquet will cringe and die in time
While the dry earth watches. It is ugly,
And the earth is ugly to allow it. Still, the petals
Curl and drop. Mother calls it an exquisite waste,

But there is no choice. I learn how:
Before letting go, open yourself completely.
Wait. When the heavens fail to answer,
Curse the heavens. Wither and bend.

2.
We go to the lake. I am the middle son
And most beautiful, my face and chest,
All of me, brown with sun. I ride to the lake
With my brothers and sister, and the smells
Of asphalt and dirt fill me with happy rage.
I am twelve, and the voices I carry know how to obey.
When the blades of grass catch my spokes,
There is a quick *twit* when the blades snap.

The others giggle near shore but I am swimming
Toward the island in the center, a vacant country.
The black water bids me farther.
Out past the people speckling the lake
To the cold, cold center and that island's empty shore.
The syllables of my name skip across like smooth stone,
And when they reach me, my lungs shrink to fists.
I flail upright and the waves lash out in my wake.

3.
Not the flame, but what it promised.
Surrender. To be quenched of danger.
I torched toothpicks to watch them
Curl around themselves like living things,
Panicked and aglow. I would wake,
Sheets wrinkled and damp, and rise
From that print of myself,
That sleep-slack dummy self.
Make me light.

No one missed my shadow
Moving behind the house, so I led it
To the dry creek-bed and laid it down
Among thistledown, nettle,
Things that hate water as I hate

That weak, ash-dark self.
I stood above it,
A silent wicked thing that would not beg.
I crouched, and it curled before me.
I rose, and it stretched itself, toying.

And the brambles whispered.
And my hands in their mischief.

A spasm, a spark, a sweet murmuring flame
That swallowed the creek-bed and spread,
Mimicking water. A gorgeous traffic
Flickering with light, as God is light.
I led my shadow there and laid it down.
And my shadow rose and entered me.
And on the third day, it began to speak,
Naming me.

Self-Portrait As the Letter Y

1.

I waved a gun last night
In a city like some ancient Los Angeles.
It was dusk. There were two girls
I wanted to make apologize,
But the gun was useless.
They looked sideways at each other
And tried to flatter me. I was angry.
I wanted to cry. I wanted to bury the pistol,
But I would've had to walk miles.
I would've had to learn to run.

2.

I have finally become that girl
In the photo you keep among your things,
Steadying myself at the prow of a small boat.
It is always summer here, and I am
Always staring into the lens of your camera,
Which has not yet been stolen. Always
With this same expression. Meaning
I see your eye behind the camera's eye.
Meaning that in the time it takes
For the tiny guillotine
To open and fall shut, I will have decided
I am just about ready to love you.

3.

Sun cuts sharp angles
Across the airshaft adjacent.

They kiss. They kiss again.
Faint clouds pass, disband.

Someone left a mirror
At the foot of the fire escape.

They look down. They kiss.

She will never be free
Because she is afraid. He

Will never be free
Because he has always

Been free.

4.

Was kind of a rebel then.
Took two cars. Took
Bad advice. Watched people's
Asses. Sniffed their heads.

Just left, so it looked
Like those half-sad cookouts,
Meats never meant to be
Flayed, meant nothing.

Made promises. Kept going.
Prayed for signs. Stooped
For coins. Needed them.
Had two definitions of family.

Had two families. Snooped.
Forgot easily. Well, didn't
Forget, but knew when it was safe
To remember. Woke some nights

Against a wet pillow, other nights
With the lights on, whispering
The truest things
Into the receiver.

5.

A dog scuttles past, like a wig
Drawn by an invisible cord. It is spring.
The pirates out selling fakes are finally
Able to draw a crowd. College girls
Show bare skin in good faith. They crouch
Over heaps of bright purses, smiling,
Willing to pay. Their arms
Swing forward as they walk away, balancing
That new weight on naked shoulders.
The pirates smile, too, watching
Pair after pair of thighs carved in shadow
As girl after girl glides into the sun.

6.

You are pure appetite. I am pure
Appetite. You are a phantom
In that far-off city where daylight
Climbs cathedral walls, stone by stolen stone.
I am invisible here, like I like it.
The language you taught me rolls
From your mouth into mine
The way kids will pass smoke
Between them. You feed it to me
Until my heart grows fat. I feed you
Tiny black eggs. I feed you
My very own soft truth. We believe.
We stay up talking all kinds of shit.

Theft

In 1963 John Dall, a Ho-Chunk Indian, was taken from his mother's home as part of a federal project to reduce poverty in Native American communities. He moved from foster home to foster home, haunted by recurring dreams and unsure of his own history. Years later, he was located by members of his tribe.

The word Ho-Chunk means "people of the big voice."
—FROM THE *CHICAGO READER*

The world shatters
Through Mother's black hair.
I breathe smoke,
Tincture of sudden berries.
Mother covers my eyes,
But this heat is inside.
It trickles out, a map

Of hot tears across my face.
And rivers, my own rivers,
Pushing out from the desert
Between my legs.

Frantic birds lift off
And their flight takes me.
I float above dark thickets,
Thick air. Above voices
That rush and rise. A mad cloak.
Sirens in my mother's mouth.
Sirens in the far corners
Of the flat black globe.
I wake again and again,
Ears ringing, eyes dry.

                * * *

One night when our bellies groan,
I quiet myself watching bare branches
Scratch against the moon. If night
Has a voice, it is surely this wind
In these trees. Is surely Mother's
Heavy shoes climbing the steps,
Trampling leaves. I am the only one
Who knows what that voice means
To say. It is trying to tell us
To hurry. But it does not say
For what.
            One brother twirls
A pencil over a notebook. Answers
He's erased hover like stalled ghosts.
He shakes his head. All wrong.
Another laughs at the TV. We are many,
Each in his own Now. I have never
Thought to cross from mine to theirs,
But I've held my hand inches
From my brother's back and felt
His heat.
            A knock at the door,

The walls cough. Again.
And mother doesn't ignore it.
I feel what the moon must feel
For the branches night after night.
This can't go on. Come in.
Then I watch our house come undone
And Mother get smaller,
And the road ahead like a serpent
Racing into pitch.
                    In the station,
We get blankets and a civics lesson.
We get split up. All night
The drunks and devils
Sing, rattle.

                    * * *

I live:
        In the house behind the chain link fence
        With smoke stenciling the sky above the roof
        In a room with three boys
        And a window that wheezes winter

I wear my hair shorn

The mother here leans
Against the kitchen counter
Scrubbing forks and bowls
Staring into steam
If you interrupt her
She'll surprise you with an elbow
The back of her hand
Her fist squeaks in yellow gloves

        I live in Chicago
        In America

We have rules:
        Don't flush
        Unless necessary
        And only four squares

Of tissue a day—
Two in the morning
Two at night or
All at once
But just four
And someone
Is counting

When you brush
Turn the water on once
Then off
Then on again
Say *sir* and *ma'am*
But only when necessary
Otherwise don't talk
And don't stare
What are you stupid
And what kind of Indian
Are you   What kind
If you don't know
You must not be

This is my eighth home
I am seven

* * *

When I skip school, I get on the El
And scour the city from inside,
From above. I listen to

The iron percussion, track
Soldered to track. A story
That turns and returns,

Refuses to end. I ride it,
Write it down: I'm in my seat
In the first car. A hologram

In the window, in the battered doors.
A stick figure in the chrome poles.
I reach for myself. Grab me by the neck.

What do I hear? Time.
What does it say? I can't tell.
What does it sound like? It sounds

Angry. Why angry? Because we keep it
Waiting. When it's not waiting,
It is always begging us to go.

I get off the train. Walk backwards
Over bridges. Watch perspective
Diminish. Watch my breath,

My ideas hover and drift
In perfect clouds. They'll
Drop eventually, mingle

With a river or lake. Might
Even one day make it back to me.
As rain, maybe, or a tall glass

I drink quickly, blind
With thirst. I shout my name
Into the traffic, and if my voice

Is big enough, someone will hear it.
It will land where it needs to land,
And someone will catch it

And come looking.

When Zappa Crashes My Family Reunion

My eight aunts titter. *Look at all that hair.* He takes a plate
And a seat near Mary, whose Newport burns in a saucer
At her feet. When Zappa speaks, his magnificent nose
Reverberates like a canyon where the bear has just yawned.

Great googely moogely! Mary ashes her skirt. Gert,
On my father's side, smoothes her blouse, electric with static.
Zappa slides a long foot toward the amp, sweeps guitar to hip,
Rakes the strings like an epileptic till the goblets topple and burst.

My aunts keep their knees clasped tight, as if a piece of ice,
Or a marble that burns, might shake loose between their thighs.
Speakers fart and chirp. Somewhere in the vast Los Angeles
Of his mind, a thimbleful of plasticized dust bursts

Into purple flame. This is earnest. The bwap and waddle
Catches Uncle Richmond under the collar. He sweats, grins.
The synclavier giggles. Mary's cigarette snuffs out at the filter
And her left shoe dangles like a tipped wig. She smiles

Way back to the sides of her mouth. *This fool is crazy!*
Somewhere else in the city of New Orleans, a woman watches
The panes in her windows rattle hard against wood. Then she listens:
Val-a-rie. Val-a-rie. Don't you want me? Don't you need me?

It sounds like a heartfelt kazoo. She puts her palm to the glass,
Then laughs. In the morning, she'll go out front still in her gown
And knock the little jockeys off the rich people's lawns. A house down,
A man slides his empty plate towards his wife. What he really means is:

There's something gliding slowly up our block and it sounds
Like amusement park music. Like a houseboat full of marionettes.
Makes me want to put on my gaiters and go. So—goodbye—he goes.
Which is just another way of saying: *Ain't this boogey a mess?*

Back at our semi-annual family reunion, Zappa winds all the cables
Up tight, lays his guitar like a dummy back in the casket. Nobody says,
Come again next time, Frank. We'll meet you in Cleveland. All the dumb dogs
Go right on braying at planes they think are stars. Aunt Neet fingers

The ring his glass has left on the table. No coaster. What she means is:
I want the kind of life people get dragged from early.

The Nobodies

> *Los nadies, los hijos de nadie, los dueños de nada.*
> *Los nadies, los ningunos.*
>
> —EDUARDO GALEANO

1.
They rise from the dawn and dress.

They raise the bundles to their heads
And their shadows broaden—
Dark ghosts grounded to nothing.

They grin and grip their skirts.

They finger the gold and purple beads
Circling their necks, lift them
Absently to their teeth. They speak

A language of kicked stones.

And it's not the future their eyes see,
But history. It stretches
Like a dry road uphill before them.

They climb it.

2.
With small hands
They pat wet earth
Into brick.

And we wonder
What they eat
And why they believe

In their gods
With faces
Like frightening toys.

We pay what they ask,
Minus something
For our trouble,

Wondering why they don't
Pack up from the foot
Of the volcano,

Why they ruin their hands,
Their teeth, why they swallow
What they are given

Without a smile,
Or the hint of anger.

3.

A goat watches with eyes the inverse of danger,
Knowing there will always be some wafer of meaning
To savor on the tongue. Its munching
Is belief in the body and in the long dry grass.
What it finds, it takes into its mouth as proof
that necessity is the same as plenty.

The child who tends the goat
Sits on his knees in the shade of a low tree.
He considers what he knows. He lies down
On his side, takes the teat into his mouth
And drinks. What he does not know
Flickers in the breeze, brushes past his cheek,

The tip of his ear, and is quickly behind him.

4.

If it is true that the earth respires,
That it speaks only to those
Who command nothing—

If it is true that the first man
Was fashioned of corn.
Of divine shit. Of dust—

If a bale of cotton—

If color is trance,
And trance is to ride the back
Of the first great bird
In first flight—

If the world has ended twelve times—

If the atom is cognizant, coy;
If light is both pow-wow
And tango—

If, at the final trumpet,
Oil magnates will kiss the ankles
Of earth-caked girls who traipse
Along the highway's edge,
Hugging the mountain
When trucks barrel past—

If Satchmo. If Leadbelly—

If wind on the horizon,
Thundering the trees,
Making all of our houses small—

Duende

1.
The earth is dry and they live wanting.
Each with a small reservoir
Of furious music heavy in the throat.
They drag it out and with nails in their feet
Coax the night into being. Brief believing.
A skirt shimmering with sequins and lies.
And in this night that is not night,
Each word is a wish, each phrase
A shape their bodies ache to fill—

> *I'm going to braid my hair*
> *Braid many colors into my hair*
> *I'll put a long braid in my hair*
> *And write your name there*

They defy gravity to feel tugged back.
The clatter, the mad slap of landing.

2.

And not just them. Not just
The ramshackle family, the *tíos,*
Primitos, not just the *bailaor*
Whose heels have notched
And hammered time
So the hours flow in place
Like a tin river, marking
Only what once was.
Not just the voices scraping
Against the river, nor the hands
Nudging them farther, fingers
Like blind birds, palms empty,
Echoing. Not just the women
With sober faces and flowers
In their hair, the ones who dance
As though they're burying
Memory—one last time—
Beneath them.
                    And I hate to do it here.
To set myself heavily beside them.
Not now that they've proven
The body a myth, parable
For what not even language
Moves quickly enough to name.
If I call it pain, and try to touch it
With my hands, my own life,
It lies still and the music thins,
A pulse felt for through garments.
If I lean into the desire it starts from—
If I lean unbuttoned into the blow
Of loss after loss, love tossed
Into the ecstatic void—
It carries me with it farther,
To chords that stretch and bend
Like light through colored glass.

But it races on, toward shadows
Where the world I know
And the world I fear
Threaten to meet.

3.
There is always a road,
The sea, dark hair, *dolor.*

Always a question
Bigger than itself—

> *They say you're leaving Monday*
> *Why can't you leave on Tuesday?*

Amber Flora Thomas

(1972–)

To MY DISMAY, I find that much of my poetry is shaped through disassembly. First of all, I have a spotty memory. I don't remember whole narratives from my childhood, but rather single images that contain clues, but no real solid evidence of what happened. Yet I live with this sense that a terrible thing has happened to me, and still continues to happen to my body on a psychic level every day. As a woman poet, I can't help my continual return to the body politic. My poems often draw on the voices of biblical characters like Eve, Mary, and Magdalene to understand what it means to contain an obligation to the world that rests so fully on being in a woman's body. I suppose I see the poem as a bowl in which all of my experiences are poured; however, I must pick and choose only a few to leave in at a time; leave in too much and the poem will not make sense. Sometimes I see an infinite number of connections between all of my experiences and I want these connections to be understandable in a poem, but the reader can't be expected to follow such huge leaps, so I continue to shrink and shape my poems until they contain a single thread of feeling or thought. Sometimes a single image or action is enough to support an entire poem; however, I find the solitary images do amount to longer narratives the more I write.

Chore

> The serpent beguiled me,
> and I did eat.
> —GENESIS 3:13

Blue jays balance on the chicken wire fence
while she falls from sleep into the substantial landscape.
The compost heap's reliquary of household

meats ferments under lawn clippings.
The dog chained to a redwood in the yard
learns all morning to untangle itself.

Beauty comes by accident over each scene
and ends: unbroken silver as ice poses release
on the clothesline, the subtle disappearance

of black beetles into heads of lettuce, the radish
whose bright surface breaks a pale interior.
Like cold water hitting her wrist, suddenly every pore

knows itself and flinches. Life that makes restless
even the rug she shakes, tail whipping
dust and animal hair like clover into the day.

She expects the bone vexing want. Its redundancy.
Its tide of touch. A guttural nonsense. When he asks
what she's thinking: an arrow, a lip, the low brow

where porch eaves hang loose, the irises
blooming despite her. Say work. Say danger.
Dare she open her mouth if not to take his tongue,

his breath as he sinks back into sleep. Every morning
she senses the impossible balance: haphazard
in its well-defined plot to leave her numb.

The refrigerator chokes in the shadows
of the kitchen. The ladder rusting on the porch
will one day be left at the dump. So many chores

she didn't expect. Always, some creature needs
its back stroked. Heads bow to eat as she pours
food into bucket and trough. All those mouths

opening around her. Iridescent bubbles
bursting their sour smell. The bleat of pink
tongues, snapping along the edge of her hand.

From a blessed sleep, those curses crowd
to be named, to drag from her the suspicion
that this was always the plan: wet and muddy work.

An admission that won't leave her
without waking him & the whole damn world.

She snaps the long neck of the garden hose
and waters her tomatoes.

Dress

I turn the dress loose—its hand-sewn collar,
its seven bodice buttons, the hem's frayed edge.
I follow each stitch as it slips
from its hold. I'll reconcile with time later
this habit of proceeding toward the smallest task
unhurried. My arms draw back and fan
the massive skirt. I lay the sleeve pieces
to one side, unfold the waist ties and stretch them
flat. I cut out the fringes of buttonholes
and lose hook & eye in my lap.
I'm pulling open this mystery,

knotted flaws where a seamstress hurried
over her error, threaded paths ending
in the hidden cusp of the waist, lint sewn
into a pocket's seam. I take it from intricacy,
from fragility, from a tenement of irreproachable
lightness. No dress for a shoulder to ease against,
a thigh burn on, none to take account
of the crescent curve an arm makes.
No angles coming to life on a hanger.
Just this current of bygones exhausting its hold.
A neck hole that gapes for form, for the body it fitted,
for sweats and perfumes, the hairs
caught willy-nilly in a fold, for the order
begetting size and season. No memory unhooks
down the breastbone's swell
and excuses me from today.

Swarm

A honeybee queen lays the nettle
and the weather in a black cloud that falls
on two white men lifting a rotten tree
toward their truck on the fire road. It's just luck

come up from hiding, a nether world
she sends into the August groan. The men hack
and flail pale limber arms at the air, their clothing,
and their ears. They jig around the truck
in this unexpected season.

I stand alone across the gulley and kill
the helpful girl trying to rise up
in me. If they had found me alone
on my afternoon walk in the forest?

Their baseball caps shucked, the red rising
on their arms and faces. The bees go up
and come down, a dizzy swarm. The men
throw themselves in the cab of the truck,

the haze ascending on their dust, until
nothing they could have done was done to me.

The Killed Rabbit

In its eye a convex universe:
the white sea of a cutting board,
the gray muffled fringe of a foot,
and the whiskered spikes converging

in there, intruding equally on one another;
a knowing endless with the moment
of the room. No longer able to look away,
or gaze past, or see into, yet obligated

by depth and light. Fixed with all
that is far-gone. Distilled to believe
all at once in geographies.

Electric with repeating the truth,
not blinking away from the ceiling fan's
blades, churning the steamy kitchen air.

Renewed in the execution of being seen.
Then you chop the head off, overcome by
the need for disregard, to remember
the necessity of flesh and the crude jarrings

of meat being stripped down to a stasis of red.
The eye assumes a transfixed nature while gazing
at black plastic lining a bucket. Displaced

in all that is held there, vision
is in fact a reckless understanding.

Lyrae Van Clief-Stefanon

(1971–)

N "THE GOOD CITY" Tim Seibles writes:

> I am weighed down by what I
> didn't say to you. I
> am like some fat man dragging the moon on a rope.

As a graduate student I spent hours reading poems from *Hurdy-Gurdy* aloud in the bathtub to the steam rising off my skin, poems that made me feel present—in my body, in my life. "Maybe we can speak more irresistibly," he suggests in his open letter, "more often and to more people." And I say yes. It is possible. To introduce Rilke to a classroom of high school readers as neo-soul. And I wonder. Is it possible? To entice an academic to YouTube Van Hunt's video and take one look at that little observation chamber and think: sonnet. You feel me?

Garden

I too have turned
to the yard

turning the yard
into

frustration of flowers
I have felt for

a knot in the soil
coaxing pulling at

bindweed roots
pulling gently so

they give
half inch by half inch

the vines wound
silently violent

round the necks
of black-eyed

Susans
Name each

flower and the yard
loses

ground becomes
brunnera

bleeding heart bearded
iris

peony purple coneflower
lupine lily

I enter the garden
I enter hackles raised

one finger then two three
sliding into the earth

It falls away from itself
like cake crumbs

If I lower my mouth to it
I can catch the grains

of dirt on my lips
sweep them

away with my tongue

A man who wanted
to tie me to a tree

once licked raw sugar
from my open hand

a policeman he wanted me
to behave

like an animal
From yard to garden

misprision a prisoning
measure   of space

I hold up my hand
and drizzle strikes

at every target
but my palm

I cannot be touched
by anything above me

Lost

The river, unrolled bolt of silk, gives
evening the smell of fish, wet leaves,
loosening matter. We glide through
its blue-plum tint toward night, the leftover
tang of red wine in our mouths. Upstream
an idea waits for us: if we were lost
how much more would we love each other.
We four move toward this losing with
the steady creak and drip of our rowing.
We cannot in lowering darkness tell direction,
whether the frog's croak came from behind
or before us. Our bellies full, the swamp beckons us
behind its green drapery. Whatever hides
in the tangle—the surprise of cypress knees;
the fierce, sharp-edged palms welting our forearms as
we walk blind through mottled night's
sulfur rot and sucking mud; what flies
into our mouths, impossible to see;
mosquitoes lighting in our ears, their constant
whine high-pitched and crazy-making;
the silent patience of gators and our
wary estimation of their hunger—
we will keep, we are certain, as we lose
ourselves for hours, when we find ourselves again
bank-side, and two must choose to swim because
we're not where we began. The river moves
despite our stillness, our breath
breathing itself into the wet heat, whether
they disappear for good, the two who
splash away, their heavy kicking swallowed by
this evening. I am of the two who wait,
waist high in water, eyes stretched wide to see
nothing but night, washing itself, black
over black in muggy layers inches from

my face, not my hands, skin of water, curve
of meniscus, my breasts where I displace it,
my undissolved legs immersed, merged
with water, losing above, in, out of, but for
these hands sliding over me, another's
hands to keep me from becoming
current tongue, lisp of leaf tips touching
water, but for we, two, touching, agreeing
this is my body. Agreeing, I still belong in it.

Bop: The North Star
—Auburn, NY

Polaris sits still in the sky and if I knew
which one it was I could follow it all the way
to Auburn. Oh, Harriet, who did not need the poise
of freedom knocked into your head like sense, who found it more
than possible to sleep, pistol shoved deep into your pocket
along this route, I cannot tell a dipper from Orion.

Yes, the springtime needed you. Many a star was waiting
for your eyes only.

The university twinkles on the hill above my house.
The fat moon rises and a girl holds out her arms. She twirls
in a blue Polly Flinders dress. Mama's precious
cameo—a white woman's silhouette on black satin ribbon
choker tied around her neck. Poise begins here:
in cinders, in rhyme, in splintering beauty into this
and this—: the image at my throat: the summer's pitching
constellations: the ten o'clock scholar's midnight lesson.

Yes, the springtime needed you. Many a star was waiting
for your eyes only.

At the prison at Auburn I cross the yard. Inmates whet tongues against
my body: cement—sculpted—: poised for hate—: pitch
compliments like coins:—(*wade*)—their silver slickening—(*in the water*)—:
uncollected change. A guard asks, *Think they're beautiful? Just wait til they're out here stabbing each other.* Oh, Harriet, the stars
throw down shanks—: teach the sonnet's a cell—: now try to escape—

Yes, the springtime needed you. Many a star was waiting
for your eyes only.

Crystal Williams

(1970–)

M Y SENSE OF WHAT literature should be doing has translated into a
desire to write poems which are of service to readers who like me
turn to literature for some sort of truth-telling. My poems argue for what
I want to see more of in the world—sentiment, love, empathy, forgiveness,
and acceptance. That means that sometimes what I am telling is a mirror
to our/my most base behaviors. More simply, my poems are reflections of
my attempts to be a better human being. That is what my work argues for,
fundamentally and principally: I, we, should and can be better. Of course,
as I contemplate writing a *Poetics*, there are other elements to the poems
which, while significant, are less important and to my thinking less inter-
esting, but which are worth mentioning as elements important to me as
I write: language and metaphor, sound, accessibility, subject matter, and
giving voice to folks who look like me. But I understand those elements
to be in service to the primary purpose of my art-making. Which is all to
say: In this work, the poem is an extension of the heart, which is an exten-
sion of the soul that connects me to you in ways that are immeasurable,
and rightly so.

This Parable, This Body
—*after Adrienne Rich*

I tell you,
    this sack,
        this sock, thew & vein,

has been
      a chronic
            problem, a condition,
an other
      around which
            I work. I am a super duper
navigator,
      have been
            jacques cousteauing
for years,
      & I'm telling you, this
            has been a chronic problem
this body
      against which
            the world, upon which
the world,
      & the me of it
            inside, as if a bean or a bead,
a kernel
      of something, maybe
            a glimmer, maybe a chunk of ore,
hard & steadfast
      & improbably mashed.
            I tell you, this is a problem
of too little
      language, a lie—this body,
            conundrum, this other me, me
this body, this,
      this, I tell you, this
            is not me, I tell you. Not me.

Extinction

—after Robert Hass

All the new thinking is about loss. Like a diseased lung,
the city is shutting down & the parks are first to go.
The grass is long-toothed & wicked, not grass at all,
mostly weeds, their tough tongues covered with trash.
& the trash is all magic: it mysteriously appears & disappears.

Beside it today, lovers lie. & beneath the goldfinch on its branch
lovers sit on the park bench. & another pair, oddly entwined,
roll down the street, she on his lap, her head resting on his shoulder,
he sitting straight in an electric blue motorized wheelchair,
a bony arm cradling her back.

Oliver cocks his head because they are odd. His glistening snout
pokes the air as if to taste what sort of love this is,
this homeless love, this dirty in the grass love,
this broke-down park bench, middle-of-the-empty-street love
which is all about holding onto something, I think, stroking his
     sweet head,
which is nothing more than a long, slow song about loss. This
     neighborhood.
Love. Detroit. The purple martin overhead. The dog with his cancer.
These paramours amid their abandonment. Something is always
     dying.

Brush Park is so much like the city it is nothing more than the city:
mansions burnt or shackled by time or remade into monuments
to fortitude & foresight. & amid the ruins, people
insistent & loving. This panorama is what life looks like
in my city where loss & cliché wear the same tight dress,
where the music is exquisite & slow & nothing more than a moan
on most days & then too, on most nights.

But these crazy lovers, in the weeded grass, high on something,
eyes full of magic, some wispy memory, the life before this life,
the possibility of a perfect & round orange,
make me happy with their surprise & stubborn headedness.

& as the wind rustles the weeds' spiky fingers, bustles
a plastic bag across the street, fluffs Oliver's poodle ears,
another sound begins its haunt: Something lonely,
something that approximates the sound of extinction, proof
of an exact & impending death: an echo perhaps,
a trill of the last Heath Hen, small avian spine
gone from the earth seventy years ago,
his throat coarse & quivering with need.
There were people beneath him that last day too,
listening to his bleak beak bleating & bleating for a mate.
How odd that these lovers in the thickets
almost fool me into believing something more than the facts,
that ambering history, that bleak branch.

Enlightenment

—Detroit, Michigan

She is merging onto the Edsel Ford Freeway in a car no longer
made,

in a city that no longer makes it, talking on her cellular phone,
slouched to the left,

fingernails purple & red & caging the wheel, head cocked & foot
heavy.

In pursuit of a race car, she has bought a roll of black duct tape,
has rolled three racing stripes down the sedan's hood

as if she has been whispering with Buddha & he said, *Sister,*
relinquish your resistance, your discomfort, forsake

your ego. Which she has done, which is what it means to want but
not have

in a city stacked with desire, to know that desire is our most
ruinous trait,

is the moment in the morning when you decide to be unsatisfied
and unhappy.

Our want is just one of many in a line of wants & the line of wants
is ancillary to the line of needs.

People close to you are hungry & you have ignored it. People
close to you have lost their jobs.

Today somebody's mother has died. Today somebody's child has
been murdered. Today some body lost sight.

& your Lumina runs.
Your Lumina runs well; Luminosity,

woman: No one is coming to save you. There is nothing from
which to be saved.

Ronaldo Wilson

(1970–)

I N THIS WORLD—the extenuation of consciousness/unconsciousness through objects, the space between *dream* and *awake*—is a poetics of slowing down perception enough to hold the shrill of crows that *caw caw caw caw* outside my window, or the voices that fade from a party dying down the distant hall of a house in which I chose to retreat. Perhaps I am after what Laura Riding followed into "the journey to truth—to the plane of utterance on which human speaking spoke the language of being with full, universal explicitness of sense."

I want to trace a set of aesthetic instances where my body touches language, where desire delineates in form, from sleepy stupor to drawn subject. What enacts when I let go is what releases when my body reacts, giving up as I linger in the screen, nest, down the hall, or on the gym shower floor, my senses open to the poem that comes.

Brad Pitt, Kevin Bacon, and the Brown Boy's Mother

When he wakes up out of sleep, the brown boy remembers two things: his white man calls and breaks the groans of Kevin Bacon, naked and writhing in pain on a hard and wet black street. Bacon has been beaten with broken bottles and has had his chest smashed in with a large flaming couch section. A mob of whites poured gaso-

line all over his chiseled stomach and then lit him afire. Brad Pitt
lay next to him, his stomach prone, breathless and glistening in the
flame's light.

The brown boy knows this is somewhere between movie and
dream, staring at each stomach; but more importantly, he knows
that despite the fire, the bodies did not burn. They did not char or
turn black. They simply shined in sweat.

The brown boy will commit to his memory, most, Brad Pitt's
dying, and how he eventually turned over on his stomach, his penis
turned down and scrape-fucking the street—Brad Pitt ejaculating
and on fire, the liquid shooting out of him as he looked up, staggered
to his feet to let out something between groaning and laughter out to
the black sky. Though Pitt had been beaten with bottles and wood, it
was not clear where he was hurt, only that he was a screaming sur-
face, dripping with lit gasoline and semen.

As the brown boy ponders this surface, the white man has chosen
to phone his brown boy. Their first conversation of the day is bound
by this scene—and dutifully, for the white man, he wants to start
from the beginning:

*Brad Pitt and Kevin Bacon are in a boxing ring in the middle of a
football field. They are both wearing white boxer shorts, no gloves, and
about to perform a dance routine. I am standing next to them, looking
at Brad Pitt's hair flop down over his face. He smiles at me before the
music starts. From everywhere, broken glass bottles hurl at their bod-
ies, and they are splashed with gasoline. We are also in a dark alley lit
by fire. The two are still standing, looking over at me, though I can't tell
who is smiling. I only know Brad Pitt winks at me while Kevin Bacon
is on the street, writhing as a large white flaming couch section is
smashed onto his chest.*

*My mother was dead in the dream. I was looking through a dense
stash of clothes in a cabinet. All of them were soiled, and none of the
clothes were hers. I remember holding a pair of purple and green
Speedos that were woven to a pair of matching polyester tennis
shorts. These shorts were my father's. I remember my mother mak-*

ing all of his tennis shorts. I also remember pulling out a pair of long sweatpants that were much too large for my mother and holding them up as crumbs fell from the legs. I tried to smell them, wanting to think of her alive.

What the brown boy doesn't say is that he wondered, in the dream, how his father was getting through this—living alone with only her smell left behind. Or how he pulled the sweatpants up to his nose and mouth, absorbing the whole of her scent through his body. Without revealing his father's grief or his own, the brown boy breathes in the smell of Giorgio mixed with eleven years of shifts at the convalescent home, and gives the white man what he thought he wanted. He quickly shot to the end, where Brad Pitt grinds his fat cock in the pavement, the curve of it pushing down bent and spewing semen into the street.

Kevin Bacon stands up and groans, laughing as his bowels leak from his stomach. I was thinking about that before you called.

The brown boy knows the white man wants to hear the brown boy rise from sleep, hear the spill from his head in the morning without saying a word. Though this morning, to this dream, the white man has two responses: He calls the dream *bizarre* and says nothing about the brown boy's mother, only *I feel sorry for Brad Pitt.*

Serena Williams, Whiteness, and the Act of Writing

The brown boy is afraid, because he can't tell, exactly, what his work is. He identifies with Serena Williams, the gorgeous, black tennis star who was booed at Indian Wells. The rumor is that her father, Richard, fixed an earlier match in the tournament where she was to play her sister, Venus, who pulled out with tendinitis in her knees seconds before they were about to begin. The theory is that he rigged this meeting, just as he did their first All-Williams Wimbledon Semifinal, where Serena is rumored to have thrown the contest.

In his apartment in Brooklyn, the brown boy has dozens of photos of both sisters that plaster the walls above his computer. In the one where they are standing next to one another at Wimbledon, Serena is crying. Venus's consoling arm is around her sister's shoulder. This photo is next to cut-up shots of two old men with fat cocks, a collage he made and covered with a sheet of paper that reads: *travelogue*. Behind this cover, one man is bald and his eyes are glazed shut, the other is all crotch, grainy black and white hands, fat fingers and thigh.

When he thinks of the connection between his sad sisters and his turned-on old men strangers caught sucking and being sucked, and covered, he feels that his mind is one confused object that pulses about unknowing, wound up, a note toward itself with no answers but the need to cut, suspend, look. Paste, cover, and tape.

Each piece locks up to the next, making sense only in his own mind. Somehow, he thinks, if he could bring these shots together, things would start to make sense, the whole of them becoming more like a finished puzzle.

What would it have been like? If when the brown boy was small playing tennis with his mother at Cabrillo Park, he could have imagined being Serena instead of Tracy Austin?

He liked Tracy because of her size, the small pink purse of her mouth, her tough little ponytails, Pony tennis shoes, and short, triangular, one-piece dresses. He loved what the announcers called her *moon balling,* the way she hit the ball high over the net, back and forth, looping it deep against an opponent like Andrea Jaeger or Chris Evert. Though the brown boy's father taught him a one-handed backhand for better reach and cleaner volleys, the brown boy switched to two because of the power he felt he could have striking the ball, double-fisted. It was as though he had no choice but to hit with two hands, to forget what his father taught him and to rear back and try to stroke the ball with the whole of Amelia Island, Tracy's crowd, behind him.

What would have happened to his small, dreaming brown frame of a body if it had not pudged out into the impossible desire to be white, small, and a girl like Tracy Austin? What if he could have seen Serena then, imagined invading her body, becoming her muscled frame, pounding the ball back into oblivion? What if he could have seen her powerful torque, unleashing and winning against all that booing at Indian Wells?

Still, he finds himself, while swimming, shaking his head forward and to the left, his fingers brushing aside an imagined blonde slick of chlorine waterlogged hair, stuck then freed from in front of his eyes.

But he also remembers when he was six that his hair was straight; and even when dry, it lay flat on his head. There is a photo of him, his face covered by the gaping bottom of an RC paper cup stuck around his mouth. His hair, then, is straight and light brown, bleached by the sun, flat and just lying there. The quiet of this picture and the smoothed down curls that he palms down to his grown up head remind him, again, of who he is, and who he is not.

On the C Train the Black Object Ponders Amuzati's Family Eaten in the Congo

Cut the adults. Huck-um dun the chest,
the deceased lumps.

In the story of edible blacks, hacked and splayed on lattice,
how am I to finish the dishes

with all this dining
in the fields of my instance?

Unremit by browned lung, blister are blisters, dry by sun,
bucks into bits.

Lattice, works: business is business after all,
but did the Black-Back-Fat deserve its end like the tic I popped?

Sure, if the tic could, it would visa out of grip.
But, sorry, the sweet, sweet spleens!

In the Magazine, NYT, a teeny pink baby
teeters on the crease of a big palm, cream and light:

Daddy! I am so hungry for some Pyg.

Such hunger, subwayed, the crust on the bittle lack's head
skin, where hair, a spiral spurns beneath flesh.

Ring worm, rung'un, crunk of nap. Mother to baby: *Shut up!*
Don't touch me. Suckcandysuckit. *C'mon now chile.*

Biographical Notes

Ai (**1947–2010**), Professor of English at Oklahoma State University, is author of seven volumes of poems, *Cruelty* (Houghton Mifflin, 1973), *Killing Floor* (Houghton Mifflin, 1979), *Sin* (Houghton Mifflin, 1986; winner of the American Book Award from the Before Columbus Foundation), *Fate* (Houghton Mifflin, 1991), *Greed* (Norton, 1993), *Vice: New and Selected Poems* (Norton, 1999), and *Dread: Poems* (Norton, 2004). She was given the 1978 Lamont Poetry Award of the Academy of American Poets for *Killing Floor,* and the 1999 National Book Award for Poetry for *Vice.* She also received a fellowship from the Guggenheim Foundation (1975), as well as the 2000 Henry Blakely Award, and two fellowships from the National Endowment for the Arts (1978 and 1985). She received a number of other awards and fellowships from such agencies as the Bunting Fellowship Program at Radcliffe College and the Guggenheim Foundation. The late Ben Hazard, the Basement Workshop in New York City, and the Royal Scottish Academy of Dramatic Art have performed her work. Ai received a BA in Japanese from the University of Arizona and an MFA in creative writing from the University of California (Irvine). Born Florence Anthony in Albany, Texas, to a Japanese father and a mother who was black, Native American, and Irish, she legally changed her name to Ai, the Japanese word for "love."

Elizabeth Alexander (**1962–**), Professor and Chair of the Department of African American Studies at Yale University, is author of five books of poems, *The Venus Hottentot* (University Press of Virginia, 1990), *Body of Life* (Tia Chucha, 1996), *Antebellum Dream Book* (Graywolf Press, 2001), *American Sublime* (Graywolf Press, 2005), and *American Blue: Selected Poems* (Bloodaxe Books, 2006). She is also author of two books of prose, *The Black Interior: Essays* (Graywolf Press, 2004) and *Power and Possibility: Essay, Reviews, Interviews* (University of Michigan Press, 2007), and with Marilyn Nelson and Lyrae Van Clief-Stefanon, respectively, two other books, *Miss Crandall's School for Young Ladies and Little Misses of Color* (Front Street Press, 2007) and *Poems in Conversations and a Conversation* (Slapering Hol Press, 2008). For her poetry, Elizabeth Alexander has been given a number of fellowships, awards, and prizes, including the John Simon Guggenheim Fellowship (2002) and the Jackson Poetry Prize (2007). A graduate of Yale University (1984) with an MA degree in creative writing from Boston University (1987), she received a PhD degree in English from the University of Pennsylvania (1992). She has also taught at Haverford College, Northwestern University, the University of Chicago, and other institutions.

Amiri Baraka (1934–; Everett LeRoi Jones), with more than forty books of poetry, fiction, drama, and cultural criticism to his name, is the most prolific of African American authors. He served in the US Air Force in 1954, and studied at Howard, Rutgers, and Columbia Universities. In 1958, he founded Totem Press and, until 1963, served as co-editor with Hettie Cohen Jones of *Yugen* magazine, both literary outlets which published a number of the Beat writers, including Jack Kerouac and Allen Ginsberg. During the early 1960s he published three of his most important books: *Preface to a Twenty Volume Suicide Note* (Totem Press/Corinth Books, 1961); *Blues People: Negro Music in White America* (William Morrow, 1963); and *Dutchman: A Play,* which premiered off Broadway in 1964 and won the Obie Award. He also co-edited (with Larry Neal) *Black Fire: An Anthology of Afro-American Writing* (William Morrow, 1968), the first text to define the Black Arts Movement. Since the publication of his first three books, Baraka has written numerous volumes, including *The System of Dante's Hell* (Grove, 1965; fiction), *Home: Social Essays* (William Morrow, 1965), *The Dead Lecturer* (Grove, 1964; poetry), *Tales* (Grove, 1967; fiction), *Black Magic: Collected Poetry 1961–1967* (Bobbs Merrill, 1969), *Selected Poetry of Amiri Baraka/LeRoi Jones* (William Morrow, 1979), *Poetry for the Advanced* (1979), *The Autobiography of LeRoi Jones/Amiri Baraka* (Freundlich, 1984), *The LeRoi Jones/Amiri Baraka Reader* (Thunder's Mouth Press, 1991), *Transbluesency: The Selected Poems of Amiri Baraka/LeRoi Jones* (Marsilio Publishers, 1995), *Wise Why's Y's: The Griot's Tale* (Third World Press, 1994), *Conversations with Amiri Baraka,* edited by Charlie Reilly et al. (1994), *Funk Lore: New Poems* (1996), *Somebody Blew Up America* (Philipsburg, St. Martin: House of Nehesi Publishers, 2003), *The Essence of Reparations* (Philipsburg, St. Martin: House of Nehesi Publishers, 2003), and *The Book of Monk* (2005). An American Academy of Arts and Letters Award, the Langston Hughes Award from the City College of New York, the James Weldon Johnson Medal, the PEN/Faulkner Award, and grants from the Rockefeller Foundation, the Guggenheim Foundation, and the National Endowment for the Arts are some of the honors he has received for his work as a writer. This Poet Laureate of New Jersey is Professor Emeritus at the State University of New York at Stony Brook. He lives in Newark, New Jersey, where he was born.

Gerald Barrax (1933–) was born in Attala, Alabama, as Gerald William Barrax, and in 1944 moved with his parents to Pittsburgh, where he received his education, a BA degree from Duquesne University (1963) and an MA degree from the University of Pittsburgh (1969). In 1969, he became a faculty member of the Department of English at North Carolina State University in Raleigh, from which he retired in 1997. He is author of five books of poetry: *Another Kind of Rain* (University of Pittsburgh Press, 1970), *An Audience of One* (University of Georgia Press, 1980), *The Deaths of Animals and Lesser Gods* (Callaloo Poetry Series, 1984), *Leaning Against the Sun* (University of Arkansas Press, 1992), and *From a Person Sitting in Darkness: New and Selected Poems* (Louisiana State University Press, 1998). His honors include the 1973 Gold Medal from the Catholic Poetry Society of America, the 1983 Callaloo Creative Writing Award for Nonfiction Prose, the 1991 Sam Regan Award (for his contributions to the arts in North Carolina), and the 1993 Raleigh Medal of Arts for "Extraordinary Achievement in the Arts." He lives in West Chester, Pennsylvania.

Gwendolyn Brooks (1917–2000), the first African American to win the Pulitzer Prize for poetry (1950), was Poet Laureate of Illinois (1968–2000) and Poetry Consultant to the Library of Congress (1985–1986). She wrote numerous books of poems, including *A Street in Bronzeville* (Harper, 1945), *Annie Allen* (Harper, 1949), *The Bean Eaters* (Harper, 1960), *Selected Poems* (Harper, 1963), *In the Mecca* (Harper, 1968), *Riot* (Broadside Press, 1969), *Blacks* (David Co., 1987), and *In Montgomery, and Other Poems* (Third World Press, 2003). She is also author of a novel, *Maud Martha* (Harper, 1953); two autobiographical texts, *Report from Part One* (Broadside Press, 1972) and *Report from Part Two* (Third World Press, 1996); and books for young readers, *Bronzeville Boys and Girls* (Harper, 1956; poems for children) and *The Tiger Who Wore White Gloves* (Third World Press, 1974, 1987). She also edited two anthologies, *A Broadside Treasury* (Broadside Press, 1971) and *Jump Bad: A New Chicago Anthology* (Broadside Press, 1971). Her other awards, prizes, and honors include the American Academy of Arts and Letters Award (1946), the Frost Medal (National Endowment for the Arts, 1989), the Shelley Memorial Award (1976), the Black Academy of Arts and Letters Award (1971), and the Jefferson Award (National Endowment for the Humanities, 1994). In 1999, she was elected Fellow of the Academy of American Poets. She was born in Topeka, Kansas, and spent most of her life in Chicago, where she encouraged writing, and supported and promoted new writers.

Jericho Brown (1976–) is Assistant Professor of English at the University of San Diego and author of *Please* (New Issue, 2008), his first collection of poems. He has also published poetry in *jubilat, New England Review, The Iowa Review, Oxford American, Callaloo,* and a number of other journals. He has held two travel fellowships to the Kraków Poetry Seminar in Poland and a Bunting Fellowship from the Radcliffe Institute at Harvard University. A native of Shreveport, Louisiana, he graduated from Dillard University and received an MFA in creative writing from the University of New Orleans, and a PhD degree in literature and creative writing from the University of Houston, where he was the poetry editor of *Gulf Coast*.

Cyrus Cassells (1957–) is Professor of English at Texas State University (San Marcos) and author of *More Than Peace and Cypresses* (Copper Canyon Press, 2004), a Lannan Literary Selection; *Beautiful Signor* (Copper Canyon Press, 1997), the Lambda Literary Award winner; *Soul Make a Path Through Shouting* (Copper Canyon Press, 1994), winner of the William Carlos Williams Award; and *The Mud Actor* (Holt, 1982; republished by Carnegie Mellon University Press, 2000), which won the 1982 National Poetry Series award. His poetry has also garnered for him other honors, including a 1993 Lannan Literary Award, a Pushcart Prize, a 1992 Peter Lvan Younger Poet Award, and grants from the National Endowment for the Arts, as well as residencies at the Rockefeller Foundation Center in Bellagio, Italy (1993 and 2006), Yaddo, the Mallay Colony, and the Helene Wurlitzer Foundation in Taos. In 2006, the Ramon Llull Institute (Institut Ramon Llull) awarded him a grant and residency in Barcelona, Spain, to work on translations of Catalan poetry. He has also written books of poems for children—e.g., *The Crossed-Out Swastika* and *Down from the Houses of Magic*. He received his education at Stanford University and Centro Fiorenza Italian Language Institute (Florence). Born in Dover, Delaware, he lives in Austin, Texas.

Lucille Clifton (1936–2010), Poet Laureate of Maryland (1979–1985), was born in Depew, New York. When Random House published her first book of poems, *Good Times*, in 1969, *The New York Times* listed it among the ten best books of that year. Random House published her next two collections, *Good News About the Earth* (1972) and *An Ordinary Woman* (1974). She is author of ten other books of poems, *Two-Headed Woman* (University of Massachusetts Press, 1980), *Good Woman: Poems and a Memoir: 1969–1980* (BOA Editions, 1987), *Next: New Poems* (BOA Editions, 1987), *Ten Oxherding Pictures* (Moving Parts Press, 1988), *Quilting: Poems 1987–1990* (BOA Editions, 1991), *The Book of Light* (Copper Canyon Press, 1993), *The Terrible Stories* (BOA Editions, 1996), *Blessing the Boats: New and Collected Poems 1988–2000* (BOA Editions, 2000), *Mercy* (BOA Editions, 2004), and *Voices* (BOA Editions, 2008). She is also author of *Generations: A Memoir* (Random House, 1976) and several books for children, including *Dear Creator: A Week of Poems for Young People and Their Teachers* (Doubleday, 1997), *The Lucky Stone* (Delacorte, 1979), *All Us Come Cross the Water* (Holt, 1973), and the eight books in the award-winning Everett Anderson series, beginning with *Some of the Days of Everett Anderson* (Holt, 1970) and ending with *One of the Problems of Everett Anderson* (Holt, 2001). In 2000, she received the National Book Award for *Blessing the Boats: New and Selected Poems, 1988–2000* and numerous honors for her work as a writer—e.g., the Lenore Marshall Poetry Prize in 1997, the *Los Angeles Times* Poetry Award in 1997, the Lila Wallace-Reader's Digest Award in 1999, the Lannan Literary Award for poetry in 1997, and honorary doctorate degrees from such institutions as Colby College, George Washington University, Trinity College, and the University of Maryland. In addition to serving as Distinguished Professor of Literature and Distinguished Professor of Humanities at St. Mary's College, Maryland (1989–1991), she also taught at Fisk University, the University of California (Santa Cruz), Duke University, Columbia University, and a number of other institutions. From 1999 to 2005, she was Chancellor of the Academy of American Poets.

Wanda Coleman (1946–) was, at birth, named Wanda Evans, and grew up in Watts in Los Angeles. Without graduating from either institution, she attended Valley Junior College in Van Nuys (California) and California State University at Los Angeles. She is author of fourteen books of poems and fiction, which include *Mad Dog Black Lady* (Black Sparrow Press, 1979), *African Sleeping Sickness: Stories & Poems* (Black Sparrow Press, 1990), *American Sonnets* (Woodland Pattern Book Center, 1994), *Bath Water Wine* (Black Sparrow Press, 1998; winner of the 1989 Lenore Marshall Prize and nominated for the National Book Award), *Mambo Hips and Make Believe: A Novel* (Black Sparrow Press, 1999), *Mercurochrome* (Black Sparrow Press, 2001; National Book Award finalist), *The Riot Inside Me: More Trials & Tremors* (David R. Godine, 2005), and *Jazz and Twelve O'Clock Tales* (David R. Godine/Black Sparrow Press, 2008). In 1976, she won an Emmy for her writing in Daytime Drama. She has received fellowships from the California Arts Council (for poetry and fiction), the National Endowment for the Arts, and the Guggenheim Foundation. Her 2002 review of Maya Angelou's *A Song Flung Up to Heaven* caused a major stir across the country. Wanda Coleman lives in Los Angeles.

Michael Sibble Collins (1959–) is Associate Professor of English at Texas A&M University in College Station. He has published poems, critical articles, reviews, and interviews in *The Best American Poetry 2003, Michigan Quarterly Review, Parnassus: Poetry in Review, The World & I, The Norton Anthology of African American Literature, Salamander, The Encyclopedia of Ethnic American Literature, The Oxford Companion to African American Literature, Modern Philology, PMLA, Callaloo,* and in other periodicals and books. He has also guest edited two special issues of *Callaloo,* one on politics and the other on the poet Yusef Komunyakaa. He received his BA from Wesleyan University (Middletown, Connecticut), an MA from the University of Chicago, and a PhD from Columbia University.

Jayne Cortez (1936–), born in Fort Huachuca, Arizona, is a founder and co-founder of numerous cultural and political organizations, including the Watts Repertory Theater, Bola Press, and the Organization of Women Writers of Africa.

Her ten volumes of poetry include *Jazz Fan Looks Back* (Hanging Loose Press, 2002), *Somewhere in Advance of Nowhere* (Serpent's Tail, 1997), *Poetic Magnetic* (Bola Press, 1991), and *Coagulations: New and Selected Poems* (Thunder's Mouth Press, 1984). In addition to being known as a poet, this New York resident is also an actor, film director, and educator. Her work has been translated into over twenty languages, and her recordings with the Firespitters, her band, are also widely known.

Kyle Dargan (1980–) is author of two collections of poems, *Bouquet of Hungers* (University of Georgia Press, 2007) and *The Listening* (University of Georgia Press, 2004), winner of the Cave Canem Prize. His poems have also appeared in *Ploughshares, Shenandoah, Denver Quarterly, Poet Lore, Callaloo,* and other journals. He is Assistant Professor of literature at American University and editor of *Post No Ills Magazine* (online), which he founded in 2008. In 2008, he won the Hurston-Wright Legacy Award for Poetry, and he was selected as the 2007 Drew Darrow Memorial Reader at Bucknell University. The University of Virginia, Indiana University, and American University are the institutions where he received his undergraduate and graduate education. He was born in Newark, New Jersey.

Toi Derricotte (1941–), a graduate of Wayne State University, received an MA degree in English literature and creative writing at New York University. She is Professor of English at the University of Pittsburgh and author of one book of prose, *The Black Notebooks* (Norton, 1997), and four books of poetry, *Tender* (University of Pittsburgh Press, 1997), *Captivity* (University of Pittsburgh Press, 1989), *Natural Birth* (Crossing Press, 1983; republished by Firebrand Books 2000), and *The Empress of the Death House* (Lotus Press, 1978). She is co-editor (with Ellen Smith) of Antonia Baquet's *Bread on the Water: Recollections of a "Li'l Half-White, Stuck-up Nigga Girl"* (2007) and co-editor (with Cornelius Eady and Camille T. Dungy) of *Gathering Ground: A Reader Celebrating Cave Canem's First Decade* (University of Michigan Press, 2006). Her poems have appeared in numerous anthologies and journals, including *The Garden Thrives: Twentieth-Century African-American Poetry, Parnassus: Poetry in Review, The American Poetry Review, Callaloo, The Iowa Review, Ploughshares,* and *The Kenyon Review.* She has received a number of awards, fellowships, and other honors, including the 1998 Anisfield-Wolf Book Award for Nonfiction, the 2008 Distinguished Alumni/ Alumnae Award (New York University Graduate School of Arts and Science), and the Paterson Poetry Prize. In 1996, she (and Cornelius Eady) co-founded the Cave Canem Foundation.

Melvin Dixon (1950–1992), a native of Stamford, Connecticut, was a poet, fiction writer, translator, and an educator. *Change of Territory* (Callaloo Poetry Series, 1983) and *Love's Instruments* (Tia Chucha Press, 1995; posthumous) are his two books of poems, and *Ride Out the Wilderness: Geography and Identity in Afro-American Literature* (University of Illinois Press, 1987) is his book of literary criticism. He also authored two novels, *Vanishing Rooms* (Cleis Press, 1991; reprint, 2001) and *Trouble the Water* (Fiction Collective, 1989), which won the Charles H. and N. Mildred Nilon Award for Excellence in Minority Fiction. The University Press of Mississippi published *A Melvin Dixon Critical Reader* (edited by Justin A. Joyce and Dwight A. McBride) in 2006. In 1991, the University Press of Virginia published Dixon's translation of Léopold Senghor's poetry under the title of *Léopold Sédar Senghor: The Collected Poetry* in its CARAF (Caribbean and African Literature) Series. The following year Dixon died of AIDS at the age of forty-two, while he was Professor of English at Queens College of the City University of New York.

Rita Dove (1952–) is Commonwealth Professor of English at the University of Virginia, Charlottesville, where she teaches courses in creative writing. In 1987, she received the Pulitzer Prize for poetry for *Thomas and Beulah* (Carnegie Mellon University Press, 1986), and in 1993 she was appointed Poet Laureate of the United States, a position she held until 1995. This Akron, Ohio, native is author of eight other books of poems, *Sonata Mulattica* (Norton, 2009), *American Smooth* (Norton, 2004), *On the Bus with Rosa Parks* (Norton, 1999), *Mother Love* (Norton, 1995), *Selected Poems* (Pantheon/Vintage, 1993), *Grace Notes* (Norton, 1989), *Museum* (Carnegie Mellon University Press, 1983), and *The Yellow House on the Corner* (Carnegie Mellon University Press, 1980); two books of fiction, *Through the Ivory Gate* (Pantheon, 1992; a novel) and *Fifth Sunday* (Callaloo Fiction Series, 1985; short stories); one play, *The Darker Face of the Earth: A Verse Play in Fourteen Scenes* (Story Line Press, 1994); and a book of nonfiction prose, *The Poet's World* (Washington, DC: Library of Congress, 1995). Dove has a long history with music, musical performances, and dance: in her youth she learned to play the cello; after college she played the viola da gamba; and more recently she performed as a vocalist in an opera, and she collaborated with John Williams on his composition "Seven for Luck," a song cycle, which was first performed in 1998 by the Boston Symphony in Tanglewood. She and her husband, Fred Viebahn, are avid ballroom dancers. As a poet, Dove has received numerous honors—for example, a Fulbright Fellowship (1974–1975), a Mellon Fellowship at the National Humanities Center in North Carolina (1988–1989), presenting the Harvard University Phi Beta Kappa poetry lecture (1993), the 1993 NAACP Great American Artist Award, the 1996 National Humanities Medal, the 1996 Heinz Award in the Arts and Humanities, the Poet Laureate of Virginia (2004–2006), the 2006 Common Wealth Award of Distinguished Service in Literature (PNC Bank), the Chubb Fellowship at Yale University (2007), the 2008 Library of Virginia Lifetime Achievement Award, the 2009 Premio Capri (Italy), and the 2009 Fulbright Lifetime Achievement Medal. She has been awarded more than twenty honorary doctorates from such institutions as Miami University

(1988), Washington University in St. Louis (1994), Boston College (1995), University of Pennsylvania (1996), and University of North Carolina (1997). She graduated summa cum laude from Miami University of Ohio (1973), studied at Tübingen University in West Germany (1974–1975), and received an MFA degree from the University of Iowa in 1977. Dove was president of AWP (Associated Writing Programs) in 1986–1987, served as senator of Phi Beta Kappa from 1994 to 2000, and is currently serving as Chancellor of the Academy of American Poets from 2006 to 2012.

Camille T. Dungy (1972–), who was born in Colorado and raised in California and Iowa City, is Associate Professor in the Department of Creative Writing at San Francisco State University. She is author of *What to Eat, What to Leave for Poison* (Red Hen Press, 2006) and *Suck on the Marrow* (Red Hen Press, 2010); assistant editor (with Toi Derricotte and Cornelius Eady) of *Gathering Ground: A Reader Celebrating Cave Canem's First Decade* (University of Michigan Press, 2006); co-editor (with Jeffrey Thomson and Matt O'Donnell) of *From the Fishouse: An Anthology of Poems that Sing, Rhyme, Resound, Syncopate, Alliterate, and Just Plain Sound Great* (Persea Books, 2009), and editor of *Black Nature: Four Centuries of African American Nature Poetry* (University of Georgia Press, 2009). Her poems have appeared in a number of periodicals, including *The Southern Review, Poetry Daily, Crab Orchard Review, The Missouri Review,* and *The American Poetry Review.* She has received awards and fellowships from such agencies as the American Antiquarian Society, the Bread Loaf Writers' Conference, the Virginia Center for the Creative Arts, Yaddo, the Sewanee Writers' Conference, the Ragdale Foundation, and the National Endowment for the Arts. She received her BA degree from Stanford University and an MFA from the University of North Carolina in Greensboro.

Cornelius Eady (1954–) was born in Rochester, New York, where he received his undergraduate education from Monroe Community College (1975–1976) and Empire State College (1976–1978). He published his first book of poems, *Kartunes,* in 1980, and the year he received an MFA in creative writing from Warren Wilson College in Swannanoa Valley, North Carolina, he published his second book of poems, *Victims of the Latest Dance Craze* (Ommation Press, 1986), which was reprinted by Carnegie Mellon's Classic Contemporary Series in 1997. His other volumes of poems are *Boom, Boom, Boom* (State Street, 1988), *The Gathering of My Name* (Carnegie Mellon University Press, 1992), *You Don't Miss Your Water* (Holt, 1995), *The Autobiography of a Jukebox* (Carnegie Mellon University Press, 1997), *Brutal Imagination* (Marian Wood/Putnam, 2001), and *Hardheaded Weather: New and Selected Poems* (Marian Wood/Putnam, 2001). He has also published poems in many different periodicals, including *Gulf Coast, Ploughshares, Callaloo, AGNI, TriQuarterly, The American Scholar, Harper's Magazine,* and *The New Yorker.* Some of the many honors he has received for his poetry are fellowships from the National Endowment for the Arts, the New York Foundation for the Arts, the Rockefeller Foundation, the Lila Wallace-Reader's Digest Fund, and the Guggenheim Foundation; and awards and prizes from the Academy of American Poets (Lamont Prize, 1985), *Prairie Schooner* (Strousse Award, 1994), and Poets House (Elizabeth Kray Award for Service, 2008). With poet Toi Derricotte, he co-founded the Cave Canem Workshop in 1996. He lives in South Bend, Indiana, where he teaches and directs the Creative Writing Program at Notre Dame University.

Thomas Sayers Ellis (1963–) graduated from Paul Laurence Dunbar High School (Washington, DC) and received an MFA from Brown University. Before he graduated from Brown in 1995, he studied at Harvard University in Cambridge, where he co-founded the Dark Room Collective in 1988. A contributing editor to *Callaloo* and *Poets & Writers,* he is author of *The Maverick Room* (Graywolf, 2005), winner of the 2006 John C. Zacharis First Book Award; *The Genuine Negro Hero* (Kent State University Press, 2001), a chapbook; *Song On* (WinteRed Press, 2005), a chaplet; and *The Good Junk [Take Three #1]* (Graywolf, 1996). *Skin, Inc.: Identity Repair Poems*, his second full-length book, was published by Graywolf Press. His poetry has also appeared in such journals and anthologies as *Poetry, Ploughshares, AGNI, Grand Street, Tin House, The Nation, The Best American Poetry* (1997, 2001 and 2010), and *Making Callaloo* (St. Martin's, 2002). For his work he has also received fellowships, grants, awards, and recognition from such institutions and arts agencies as Yaddo, the Fine Arts Work Center, and the Ohio Arts Council. Before joining the creative writing faculty at Sarah Lawrence College and the Lesley University Low-Residency MFA program (Cambridge, Massachusetts), he taught at Case Western Reserve University in Ohio. This Washington, DC, native lives in New York City.

Mari Evans (1923–) was born in Toledo, Ohio, attended the University of Toledo, and currently lives in Indianapolis, Indiana. She is author of five books of poetry, *Where Is All the Music?* (P. Breman, 1968), *I Am a Black Woman* (William Morrow, 1970), *Night Star 1973–1978* (Writers & Readers, 1981), *A Dark and Splendid Mass* (Harlem River Press, 1992), and *Continuum: New and Selected Poems* (Black Classic Press, 2007); a collection of essays, *Clarity as Concept: A Poet's Perspective* (Third World Press, 2006); five books for children, *JD* (Doubleday, 1973); *Rap Stories* (Third World Press, 1974); *Singing Black: Alternative Nursery Rhymes for Children* (Reed Visuals, 1976); *Jim Flying High* (Doubleday, 1979); *Dear Corinne, Tell Somebody! Love, Annie: A Book About Secrets* (Just Us Books, 1999); and two plays, *Eyes* (1979) and *River of My Song* (1977). She is editor of *Black Women Writers (1950–1980): A Critical Evaluation* (Doubleday, 1984). In 2002, she was nominated as author of the liner notes for *The Long Road Back to Freedom: An Anthology of Black Music.* The National Endowment for the Arts, the MacDowell Colony, Yaddo, the Woodrow Wilson Foundation, and the John Hay Whitney Foundation are other agencies that have honored her for her writing. She has taught at such institutions as Indiana University, Purdue University, Spelman College (Atlanta), and Cornell University.

Vievee Francis (1963–) received her BA in English from Fisk University (1990) and an MFA in creative writing from the University of Michigan at Ann Arbor (2010), where she later served as the poet-in-residence for the Alice Lloyd Hall Scholars Program. She is the author of *Blue-Tail Fly* (Wayne State, 2006). She has also published poems in such literary magazines as *Rattle, Gargoyle, Black Renaissance, Concho River Review, Crab Orchard Review,* and *Callaloo,* and in the anthology *Best American Poetry 2010.* This San Angelo, Texas, native received the Rona Jaffe Foundation Writers' Award in 2009. A Cave Canem Fellow, she has lived for years in metropolitan Detroit, where she conducts independent poetry workshops, teaches for Springfed Arts, and advocates for the InsideOut Literary Arts Project.

Christopher Gilbert (1949–2007), poet and psychologist, graduated from the University of Michigan (Ann Arbor) and received MA and PhD degrees from Clark University (Worchester, Massachusetts). He is author of *Across the Mutual Landscape* (Graywolf, 1984), a collection of poems, which won the Academy of American Poets' Walt Whitman Award in 1983. He also won the Robert Frost Award (1986) and received fellowships from the Massachusetts Artists Foundation (1981) and the National Endowment for the Arts (1986). His poems also appeared in such periodicals and books as *Inventions in Farewell, The Virginia Quarterly Review, Indiana Review, The Massachusetts Review, Crab Orchard Review, City River of Voices, Ploughshares, The Practice of Poetry,* and *Callaloo.* He was born in Birmingham, Alabama, and grew up in Lansing, Michigan.

Nikki Giovanni (1943–), University Distinguished Professor of English at Virginia Tech in Blacksburg, is not only a poet but also an essayist and an educator, who was born in Knoxville, Tennessee, and reared in Cincinnati, Ohio. A graduate of Fisk University, she also attended Columbia University and the University of Pennsylvania. *Black Feeling, Black Talk* and *Black Judgement,* her first two collections of poems, were published during the same year by Dudley Randall's Broadside Press in Detroit, which also published her third book of poems, *Black Feeling, Black Talk/Black Judgement,* in 1970. William Morrow has remained the publisher of her numerous other volumes of poems, which include *Bicycles: Love Poems* (2009), *Acolytes* (2007), and *The Collected Poetry of Nikki Giovanni: 1968–1998* (2003). Her prose texts are collected in *The Prosaic Soul of Nikki Giovanni* (HarperCollins, 2003). She has written a number of books for young readers— e.g., *The Girls in the Circle (Just for You!)* (2004), *Lincoln and Douglass: An American Friendship* (2008), and *Hip Hop Speaks to Children: A Celebration of Poetry with a Beat* (2008). Her conversations with Baldwin, *A Dialogue with James Bald-*

win (Lippincott, 1973) and with Walker, *A Poetic Equation: Conversations Between Nikki Giovanni and Margaret Walker* (Howard University Press, 1983) are also important texts. Smith College, Indiana University, Fisk University, and the University of Maryland are some of the many that have bestowed upon her honorary doctorate degrees. In addition to such women's magazines as *Essence, Mademoiselle,* and *Ladies' Home Journal,* a number of city and state governments have also honored her for her work. She was a major voice in the building of the Black Aesthetic of the Black Arts Movement.

C. S. Giscombe (1950–), who was born in Dayton, Ohio, graduated with a BA in English from the State University of New York and received an MFA in English from Cornell University. He is author of *Into and Out of Dislocation* (North Point Press, 2000), which has been described as a memoir and travelogue, and six volumes of poetry, *Prairie Style* (Dalkey Archive Press, 2008), *Inland* (LeRoy Books, 2001), *Two Sections from Practical Geography* (Diaresis Chapbooks, 1999), *Giscombe Road* (Dalkey Archive Press, 1998), *Two Sections from Giscombe Road* (Leave Books, 1995), and *Here* (Dalkey Archive Press, 1994). His work has afforded him several honors and awards—e.g., a Fulbright Research Award (to Canada, 1994–1995), the Carl Sandburg Award for Poetry (1998), a Canadian Embassy Faculty Research Grant (2005), and the American Book Award (2008) for *Prairie Style.* He is Professor of English at the University of California (Berkeley), and has taught at Brown University, the University of British Columbia (Vancouver), and a number of other institutions.

Jewelle Gomez (1948–) is a poet, fiction writer, playwright, and activist living in San Francisco. She is author of three collections of poems, *Oral Tradition: Selected Poems Old & New* (1995), *Flamingoes & Bears* (1986), and *The Lipstick Papers* (1980); a collection of essays, *Forty-Three Septembers* (Firebrand Books, 1993); and two books of fiction, *Don't Explain: Short Fiction* (Firebrand Books, 1997) and *The Gilda Stories: A Novel* (Firebrand Books, 1991). She co-edited (with Eric Garber) *Swords of the Rainbow* (Alyson Publications, 1996), an anthology of fantasy fiction; and she selected the stories for *Best Lesbian Erotica 1997* (Cleis Press, 1996; an annual edited by Tristan Taormino). She has also published in various periodicals, including *Essence, The Village Voice,* the *San Francisco Chronicle, Ms.,* and *The New York Times.* The National Endowment for the Arts, the San Francisco Arts Commission, and the California Arts Council have supported her as an artist with fellowships. She received two Lambda Awards for her novel *The Gilda Stories,* which she adapted for the stage as *Bones & Ash: A Gilda Story* (Paperback Book Club, 1999). The Urban Bush Women performed it in cities across the United States.

Alena Hairston (1974–), a poet and fiction writer, graduated with honors from Guilford College (Greensboro, North Carolina) and received an MFA in English and creative writing from Brown University. *The Logan Topographies,* her first book of poetry, was published in 2007 by Persea Books. In 2008, *The Logan Topographies,* which won Persea's inaugural Lexi Rudnitsky Poetry Prize (2006), was also a finalist for the Rona Jaffe Foundation Writers' Award, the Weatherford Award for Best Nonfiction Writing on Appalachia, and the Poetry Society of America's Norma Farber First Book Award. Hairston has lived in various states and countries as the child of an Air Force sergeant (father) and Eritrean nurse (mother). She lived some of her formative years in Logan County, West Virginia, and now lives in Oakland, California. She is currently a PhD candidate in psychology at Saybrook University, where she is studying humanistic and transpersonal psychology with an emphasis on creativity, consciousness, and spirituality studies. She also teaches English at Solano College.

Forrest Hamer (1956–) is a poet and psychoanalyst, whose poems have appeared in over thirty literary journals, including *The American Poetry Review, The Antioch Review, Callaloo, The Kenyon Review, The Massachusetts Review, Ploughshares,* and *TriQuarterly.* He is author of three volumes of poems, *Rift* (Four Way Books, 2007), *Middle Ear* (Roundhouse Press, 2000), winner of the Northern California Book Award, and *Call & Response* (Alice James Books, 1995), winner of the Beatrice Hawley Award. He has also received other honors for his poetry, among them a Bread Loaf Writers' Conference Fellowship (1999) and a California Arts Council Fellowship (2002). He has taught poetry writing at the Callaloo Creative Writing Workshops. A former lecturer at the University of California (Berkeley), this North Carolina native has received degrees from Yale University and the University of California. He lives in Emeryville, California.

Bobb Hamilton (1928–1998), sculptor and poet, was also East Coast editor of *Soulbook* and resided in New York City.

Kendra Hamilton (1958–) is a poet, essayist, journalist, and a student of the literature and culture of the American South. She received her BA degree from Duke University and an MFA from Louisiana State University, and she is completing a PhD in English at the University of Virginia. A native of Charleston, South Carolina, she is author of *The Goddess of Gumbo* (Word Press, 2006) and editor of *The Essence of a People II: African Americans Who Made Their World Anew in Loudoun County, Virginia, and Beyond* (2002). She has also published in *The Southern Review, Obsidian III, River Styx, Shenandoah,* and *Callaloo,* as well as such anthologies as *Bum Rush the Page: A Def Poetry Jam, Letters to the World: Poems from Wom-Po,* and *The Ringing Ear: Black Poets Lean South.* She has held fellowships from the Woodrow Wilson and the Rockefeller Foundations, the latter of which supported her residency at the Bellagio Center in Italy. As a resident of Charlottesville, Virginia, she has served as the city's vice mayor (2006–2007).

Myronn Hardy (1972–) graduated from the University of Michigan with a major in English literature, and received an MFA in creative writing from Columbia University. He is author of two collections of poems, *Approaching the Center* (New Issues, 2001) and *The Headless Saints* (New Issues, 2008). He has also published his poems in numerous periodicals, including *The Swarthmore Literary Review, The Virginia Quarterly Review, Gargoyle, Ploughshares,* and *Callaloo*. For his work, he has received a number of awards and fellowships from different institutions and foundations, such as Bread Loaf (2009), the Fundación Valparaíso in Mojácar, Spain (2005), the Annenberg Foundation (2004), and PEN Oakland (2002). His interest in a variety of international subjects has taken him to Johannesburg, South Africa (apartheid), Salvador, Brazil (slavery), and Grenada, Spain (the Moorish occupation).

Michael S. Harper (1938–), who was born in Brooklyn but grew up in Los Angeles, has been, from his position as Professor of Literature and Creative Writing at Brown University and from other venues, a major force in the education of American writers. He studied at the Writers' Workshop at the University of Iowa, where he received an MFA. He also received an MA degree from Los Angeles State University, from which he received a BA in 1960. In 1970, the University of Pittsburgh Press published his first collection of poems, *Dear John, Dear Coltrane* (nominated for the National Book Award), and nine other volumes have followed: *History Is Our Heartbeat* (University of Illinois Press, 1971; winner of the 1972 Black Academy of Arts and Letters award), *Song: I Want a Witness* (University of Pittsburgh Press, 1972), *Debridement* (Doubleday, 1973), *Nightmare Begins Responsibility* (University of Illinois Press, 1975), *Images of Kin* (University of Illinois Press, 1977; winner of the Poetry Society of America's Melville Cane Award and a 1978 National Book Award nomination), *Healing Song for the Inner Ear* (University of Illinois Press, 1985), *Honorable Amendments* (University of Illinois Press, 1995), *Songlines in Michaeltree* (University of Illinois Press, 2000), and *Use Trouble* (University of Illinois Press, 2009). In 1996, he edited *The Collected Poems of Sterling A. Brown* for TriQuarterly Books, and in 2000 he edited *The Vintage Book of African American Poetry*. He has co-edited (with Robert B. Stepto) *Chant of Saints: A Gathering of Afro-American Literature, Art, and Scholarship* (University of Illinois Press, 1979) and (with Anthony Walton) *Every Shut Eye Ain't Asleep: An Anthology of Poetry by African Americans Since 1945* (Back Bay Books, 1994). He has received fellowships from the National Endowment for the Arts and the Guggenheim Foundation. From 1988 to 1993, Harper served as Poet Laureate of the State of Rhode Island.

Janice N. Harrington (1956–), born in Vernon, Alabama, is author of two books of poems, *Even the Hollow My Body Made Is Gone* (BOA Editions, 2007) and *Going North* (for children; 2004) as well as three books of prose for children, *The Chicken-Chasing Queen of Lamar County* (2007), *Roberto Walks Home* (2008), and

Mama Nsoso Builds a New House (2010). Her poems have also appeared in *The Southern Review, Prairie Schooner, Indiana Review, Harvard Review, New Letters, Callaloo,* and numerous other periodicals. She graduated from the University of Nebraska in 1978, and, in 1981, received an MA degree in library science from the University of Iowa. She teaches creative writing in the Department of English at the University of Illinois in Urbana-Champaign.

Robert Hayden (1913–1980), a member of the Bahá'í Faith, was born in Detroit and attended Detroit City College (Wayne State University) and the University of Michigan, from which he received an MA degree in 1944. The year before he enrolled at the University of Michigan he published his first collection of poems, *Heart-Shape in the Dust* (1940), which was followed by (with Myron O'Higgins) *The Lion and the Archer* (Hemphill Press, 1955). Hayden is also author of *Figure of Time* (Hemphill Press, 1955), *A Ballad of Remembrance* (P. Breman, 1962), *Words in Mourning Time* (October House, 1970), *The Night-Blooming Cereus* (P. Breman, 1972), *Angle of Ascent: New and Selected Poems* (Liveright, 1975), *American Journal* (Effendi Press, 1978), and *Robert Hayden: Collected Poems* (Liveright, 1985). His nonfiction prose has been collected and published as *Collected Prose: Robert Hayden* (University of Michigan Press, 1984). He edited such anthologies as *Afro-American Literature: An Introduction* (1971) and *Kaleidoscope: Poems by American Negro Poets* (Harcourt, Brace & World, 1967). He taught at Fisk University from 1946 to 1969, when he joined the faculty at the University of Michigan. Hayden was Poet Laureate of the United States from 1976 to 1978. He received a Rosenwald Fellowship, a Ford Foundation Fellowship, and the Grand Prix de la Poésie at the First World Festival of Negro Arts in Dakar, Senegal, in 1966, the year he was appointed Poet Laureate of Senegal. In 1975, he was made a Fellow of the American Academy of Poets.

Terrance Hayes (1971–), a native of Columbia, South Carolina, is Professor of Creative Writing at Carnegie Mellon University. He graduated from Coker College (Hartsville, South Carolina) and received an MFA from the University of Pittsburgh. *Muscular Music* (Tia Chucha Press, 1999), his first book of poetry, won the Kate Tufts Discovery Award. He is also author of three other collections of poetry, *Lighthead* (Penguin, 2010), *Wind in a Box* (Penguin, 2006), which was named one of the best books of 2006 by *Publishers Weekly,* and *Hip Logic* (Penguin, 2002), winner of the National Poetry Series, runner-up for the James Laughlin Award from the Academy of American Poets, and finalist for the *Los Angeles Times* Book Award. His poems have appeared in such journals as *Poetry, Callaloo, The Kenyon Review, Harvard Review, Ploughshares, The American Poetry Review, Fence, jubilat,* and *The New Yorker.* He has also received a number of prizes, awards, fellowships, and other honors, such as four selections for the *Best American Poetry* anthology, a National Endowment for the Arts Fellowship, the Whiting Writers' Award, and a Guggenheim Fellowship. He lives in Pittsburgh.

David Henderson (1942–), born in Harlem, is a co-founder of *Umbra*, the organ of the Society of Umbra, a New York-based literary organization with a magazine that supported the early careers of a number of writers—Alice Walker, Nikki Giovanni, and Ishmael Reed among them. Henderson's poetry books are *Felix of the Silent Forest* (Poets Press, 1967), *De Mayor of Harlem* (Dutton, 1970; North Atlantic Books, 1985), *The Low East* (North Atlantic Books, 1980), and *Neo-California* (North Atlantic Books, 1998). He is editor of two anthologies, *Umbra Anthology 1967–1968* (Society of Umbra, 1968) and *Umbra/Latin Soul 1974–1975* (Society of Umbra, 1975). He is also author of *Jimi Hendrix: Voodoo Child of the Aquarian Age* (Doubleday, 1978; one of the editions of this book is entitled *'Scuse Me While I Kiss the Sky—Jimi Hendrix: Voodoo Child*, published in 2006). His work has been widely published in a number of periodicals and anthologies, including *The Paris Review, The Black Scholar, Evergreen Review, The New York Times, Saturday Review, Essence,* and *The Def Jam Poetry Reader.*

Calvin C. Hernton (1932–2001) is author of three collections of poems, *The Coming of Chronos to the House of Nightsong: An Epical Narrative of the South* (Interim Books, 1964), *Medicine Man* (Reed, Cannon & Johnson, 1976), and *The Red Crab Gang and Black River Poems* (with Carla Bank; Reed, Cannon & Johnson, 1999); a novel, *Scarecrow* (Doubleday, 1974); and five books of nonfiction prose, *Sex and Racism in America* (Doubleday, 1965), *White Papers for White Americans* (Doubleday, 1966), *Coming Together: Black Power, White Hatred, and Sexual Hang-ups* (Random House, 1971), *The Cannabis Experience: An Interpretative Study of the Effects of Marijuana and Hashish* (with Joseph Berke; Quartet Books, 1977), and *The Sexual Mountain and Black Women Writers: Adventures in Sex, Literature, and Real Life* (1987). He also wrote three plays, *Glad to Be Dead* (1958), *Flame* (1958), and *The Place* (1972). This native of Chattanooga, Tennessee, graduated from Talladega College (Alabama), and received an MA degree from Fisk University (Nashville). During the early 1960s, when Calvin Hernton was employed as a social worker in New York City, he became one of the founders and editors of *Umbra*, a very important literary magazine which published such writers as Tom Dent, David Henderson, Ishmael Reed, and Lorenzo Thomas. In the second half of the 1960s, he studied under the aegis of R. D. Laing, the renowned Scottish psychiatrist, at the Institute of Phenomenological Studies in London. Hernton taught at a number of American colleges and universities, the last being Oberlin College (Ohio), where, from 1970 until his death in 2001, he served as a Professor of creative writing and black studies.

Angela Jackson (1951–) received her formal education at Northwestern University and the University of Chicago. She is author of *Solo in the Boxcar Third Floor E* (Oba House, 1985; winner of an American Book Award), *Dark Legs and Silk Kisses: The Beatitudes of the Spinners* (TriQuarterly Books, 1993; winner of the Chicago Sun-Times/Friends of Literature Book of the Year Award and the

Carl Sandburg Award), and *All These Roads Be Luminous: Poems Selected and New* (TriQuarterly Books, 1998; nominated for the National Book Award). She is also author of *Voodoo/Love Magic* (1974), *The Greenville Club in Four Black Poets* (1978), and *The Man with the White Liver* (Contact II Publications, 1987). Her plays *Shango Diaspora: An African-American Myth of Womanhood and Love* (1993) and *Comfort Stew* (1997; originally *When the Wind Blows,* 1985) have been performed in theaters in the United States and the Caribbean. For her short fiction as well as her poetry, she has won other awards and honors, including the Daniel Curley Award for Recent Illinois Short Fiction (1979, 1980, 1986, 1988, and 1997), a National Endowment for the Arts Fellowship for Fiction (1980), and the Illinois Arts Council Literary Award for Poetry (1986). Stephens College, Columbia College of Chicago, and Howard University are some of the institutions where she has taught. This native of Greenville, Mississippi, was a twenty-year member (and, after Hoyt Fuller, the chair) of the Organization of Black American Culture (OBAC) Writers' Workshop of Chicago, where she was reared in its South Side community. She lives in Chicago.

Major Jackson (1968–) is an Associate Professor of English at the University of Vermont (Burlington), where he teaches courses in creative writing and literature. He has also taught at Columbia University, New York University, Princeton University, Queens University of Charlotte, and the University of Oregon. Currently, he serves as the Sidney Harman Writer-in-Residence at Baruch College, and as a core faculty member of the Writing Seminars at Bennington College. He is the poetry editor of *Harvard Review.* To date he has authored three volumes of poetry, *Leaving Saturn* (University of Georgia Press, 2002); *Hoops* (Norton, 2006); and *Holding Company* (Norton, 2010). His poems and essays have also appeared in numerous periodicals, including *Poetry, Grand Street, The American Poetry Review, The Paris Review, The New Yorker,* and *Callaloo.* His poetry has garnered recognition from the NAACP 38th Annual Image Award for Outstanding Literary Work (poetry finalist, 2007), the Pushcart Prize (2004), the Whiting Writers' Award (2003), a Witter Bynner Fellowship (2003), the National Book Critics Circle Award (poetry finalist, 2003), and the Pew Fellowship in the Arts (1995). Born in Philadelphia, he graduated from Temple University and received an MFA in creative writing from the University of Oregon.

Honorée Fanonne Jeffers (1967–) graduated from Talladega College (1989) and received an MFA degree in creative writing from the University of Alabama (1996). This Georgia native is author of *Red Clay Suite* (Southern Illinois University Press, 2007), *Outlandish Blues* (Wesleyan University Press, 2003), and *The Gospel of Barbecue* (Kent State University Press, 2000), three volumes of poems for which she has received a number of honors, awards, and fellowships, including the Rona Jaffe Foundation Award for Women Writers (1997), the Julia Peterkin Award for Poetry (Converse College, 2002), an Alan Collins Fellowship in Poetry (Bread Loaf Writers' Conference, 2003), the Paterson Award for Excellence (2008), and the Robert and Charlotte Baron Foundation Fellowship (American Antiquarian Society, 2009). *The Kenyon Review, Iowa Review, Gettysburg Review, Ploughshares, American Poetry Review, Callaloo, Brilliant Corners: A Journal of Jazz and Literature, Crab Orchard Review,* and *Poet Lore* are only a few of the periodicals where her poetry has been published. She is currently an Associate Professor of English at the University of Oklahoma in Norman. She has also taught at Cleveland State University, Knox College, the University of Pittsburgh, and other institutions.

Tyehimba Jess (1965–) is author of *Leadbelly* (Wave Books, 2005), which won the 2004 National Poetry Series, and *African American Pride: Celebrating Our Achievements, Contributions, and Legacy* (Citadel Press, 2004; nonfiction prose). He has also published poetry and fiction in such anthologies and periodicals as *Soulfires: Young Black Men on Love and Violence* (Penguin, 1996), *Obsidian III, Slam: The Competitive Art of Performance Poetry* (Manic D Press, 2000), *Bum Rush the Page: A Def Poetry Jam* (Three Rivers Press, 2001), *Role Call: A Generational Anthology of Social & Political Black Literature & Art* (Third World Press, 2002), and *Dark Matter 2: Reading the Bones* (Aspect Press, 2004). A former member of the Illinois Arts Council roster, he has received fellowships from the National Endowment for the Arts and the Illinois Arts Council, the 2001 Gwendolyn Brooks Open Mic Poetry Award, and First Prize in the *Chicago Sun-Times* Poetry Award. In 2000, he was a Duncan YMCA Writer's Voice Fellow; in 2001–2002, a Ragdale Fellow; and in 2004–2005, a Winter Writing Fellow at the Provincetown Fine Arts Work Center. He won a 2006 Whiting Writers' Award for his work in *Leadbelly*. He was born in Detroit and received his BA at the University of Chicago and an MFA from New York University. He has taught at the Juilliard School and the University of Illinois (Urbana-Champaign). He is currently Assistant Professor of English at the College of Staten Island.

Gayl Jones (1949–) is probably better known for her fiction than her poetry. She is, however, author of three books of poetry, *Song for Anninho* (Lotus Press, 1981), *The Hermit-Woman* (Lotus Press, 1983), and *Xarque and Other Poems* (Lotus Press, 1985); one play, *Chile Woman* (1974); and one book of literary criticism, *Liberating Voices: Oral Tradition in African American Literature* (Harvard University Press, 1991). Her books of fiction are *Corregidora* (Random House, 1975), *Eva's Man* (Random House, 1976), *White Rat* (Random House, 1977; short stories), *The Healing* (Beacon Press, 1998; finalist for the National Book Award), and *Mosquito* (Beacon Press, 1999). While she and her husband were in exile during the 1980s, she published *Die Vogelfängerin (The Birdwatcher)* in Germany. A graduate of Connecticut College, she received MA and Doctor of Arts degrees from Brown University. She has taught at Wellesley College and the University of Michigan (Ann Arbor). She currently lives in her native Lexington, Kentucky.

Patricia Spears Jones (1951–), a native of Arkansas, is author of two books of poems, *Femme du Monde* (Tia Chucha Press, 2006) and *The Weather That Kills* (Coffee House Press, 1995); and two chapbooks, *Mythologizing Always* (Telephone Books, 1981) and *Respuestas!* (Belladonna Books, 2007). "Ghosts" was selected by Rita Dove for *The Best American Poetry 2000*. Her plays *"Mother"* (1994) and *Song for New York: What Women Do When Men Sit Knitting* (2007) were commissioned and produced by Mabou Mines in New York City. She is also co-editor of *Ordinary Women: Poems of New York City Women*, and editor and contributor to *Think: Poems for Aretha Franklin's Inauguration Day Hat*. She was a program coordinator for the Poetry Project at St. Mark's Church in New York. She has been honored for her work by the Foundation for Contemporary Arts, the Goethe Institute, the New York Foundation for the Arts, the National Endowment for the Arts, and with fellowships to Yaddo, the Virginia Center for Creative Arts, Bread Loaf, and the Squaw Valley Community of Writers.

A. Van Jordan (1965–) is author of *Rise* (Tia Chucha Press, 2001), winner of the PEN/Oakland Josephine Miles Award and a Book-of-the-Month Club selection (from the Academy of American Poets); *M-A-C-N-O-L-I-A* (Norton, 2004), winner of an Anisfield-Wolf Award and one of *TLS*'s Best Books of 2005 (*The London Times*); *Que Sera Sera: Special Limited Edition* (Aureole Press, 2005); and *Quantum Lyrics* (Norton, 2007). He has also published poems in numerous periodicals, including *The Georgia Review, Seneca Review, Callaloo, New England Review, Gulf Coast, Crab Orchard Review,* and *Ploughshares.* He received a Whiting Writers' Award in 2005, a Pushcart Prize in 2006, a John Simon Guggenheim Fellowship in 2007, and in 2008 a United States Artist Williams Fellowship. This Akron, Ohio, native is Professor of English at the University of Michigan (Ann Arbor).

June Jordan (1936–2002) was born in Harlem to West Indian parents. *Soldier: A Poet's Childhood* (Basic Civitas Books, 2001) is her memoir, which recounts her youthful relationship with her father. She was a political activist whose ideology permeates her many volumes of poems—e.g., *Things That I Do in the Dark: Selected Poems, 1954–1977* (Random House, 1977), *Passion: New Poems 1977–1980* (Beacon Press, 1980), *Naming Our Destiny: New and Selected Poems* (Thunder's Mouth Press, 1989), *Kissing God Goodbye: Poems 1991–1997* (Anchor, 1997), and *Directed by Desire: The Collected Poems of June Jordan* (Copper Canyon Press, 2007; posthumous). Her books of prose include *Some of Us Did Not Die: New and Selected Essays* (Basic Civitas Books, 2003), *Civil Wars* (Touchstone, 1995), and *Technical Difficulties: African-American Notes on the State of the Union* (Vintage, 1994). *Who Look At Me* (1969), her first book, is a collection of poems for children. She also wrote other books for young readers, *Fannie Lou Hamer* (Crowell, 1972) and *His Own Where* (Crowell, 1971), which was nominated for the National Book Award (1971). *The New York Times* cited *His Own Where* as one of the Most

Outstanding Books, and the American Library Association listed it among the Best Books of 1971. Jordan taught at Yale, Sarah Lawrence, the University of California (Berkeley), and other institutions. She died of breast cancer in Berkeley, California.

Bob Kaufman (1925–1986) was born the tenth of thirteen children in New Orleans, and in 1958 he moved to San Francisco. He co-founded and published *Beatitude,* a literary magazine, in 1965, and authored the following volumes of poetry: *Solitudes Crowded with Loneliness* (New Directions, 1965), *Golden Sardine* (City Lights Books, 1967), *Watch My Tracks* (Knopf, 1971), *The Ancient Rain: Poems, 1956–78* (New Directions, 1981), and *Cranial Guitar: Selected Poems by Bob Kaufman,* edited by Gerald Nicosian (Coffee House Press, 1996; posthumous). His poem "Bagel Shop Jazz" received a nomination for England's Guinness Poetry Award (1960), an honor bestowed on T. S. Eliot instead. *Golden Sardine,* which was translated, garnered for him a large readership in Europe and South America. A merchant marine during the 1940s and 1950s, he published *The Ancient Rain* after he ended his vow of silence, which he began after the assassination of President John F. Kennedy and ended with the conclusion of the war in Vietnam. Hoping to be forgotten as a writer and person, he returned to silence during the early 1980s, and in 1986 he died of emphysema and cirrhosis.

Etheridge Knight (1931–1991) published his first book of poems, *Poems from Prison* (Broadside Press), in 1968, the year he married Sonia Sanchez. Earlier that same year he was released from the Indiana State Prison, where he had been confined since 1960, and where he began to write poetry. He wrote about his prison experience not only in his first collection of poems, but also in the anthology *Black Voices from Prison* (Pathfinder Press, 1970; translated and published in Italian as *Voce negre dal carcere* [Laterza, Italy]). He is author of three other volumes of poems, *A Poem for Brother/Man (after His Recovery from an O.D.)* (Broadside Press, 1972), *Belly Song and Other Poems* (Broadside Press, 1973), and *Born of a Woman: New and Selected Poems* (Houghton Mifflin, 1980). In 1986, the University of Pittsburgh Press published *The Essentials of Etheridge Knight,* which won the American Book Award. The Guggenheim Foundation, the National Endowment for the Arts, and the Poetry Society of America are three of the many institutions that have honored him for his work as a poet. Knight was born into a poor family of eight children in Corinth, Mississippi. He only finished the ninth grade in school, after which he entered the US Army and served in the Korean War as a medical technician.

Ruth Ellen Kocher (1965–), Associate Professor of English at the University of Colorado-Boulder, is author of three collections of poems, *Desdemona's Fire* (Lotus Press, 1999), *When the Moon Knows You're Wandering* (New Issues Press, 2002), and *One Girl Babylon* (New Issues Press, 2003). She has published poems in numerous periodicals, including *The Missouri Review, The Gettysburg Review, Prairie Schooner, Crab Orchard Review,* and *Callaloo.* The Green Rose Prize (from New Issues Press, 2001), the Naomi Long Madgett Poetry Award (Lotus Press, 1998), and the Tom McAfee Discovery Feature (*The Missouri Review,* 1994) are some of the honors she has earned for her poetry. A graduate of Pennsylvania State University, she received MFA and PhD degrees from Arizona State University (Tempe). She was born and raised in Wilkes-Barre, Pennsylvania.

Yusef Komunyakaa (1947–), a Vietnam veteran with a Bronze Star, was born in Bogalusa, Louisiana, where he received his early formal education. In the military he served as an editor and a correspondent for the newspaper *The Southern Cross.* It is that Vietnam experience he used to create *Dien Cai Dau* (Wesleyan University Press, 1988), his sixth book of poems. After his tour of duty in the military, he enrolled in the University of Colorado, where he decided that he would seriously make writing his career. He later received an MA degree from Colorado State University and an MFA from the University of California at Irvine. *Dedications and Other Darkhorses* (R.M.C.A.J. Books, 1977), *Lost in the Bonewheel Factory* (Lynx House Press, 1979), *Copacetic* (Wesleyan University Press, 1984), *Toys in a Field* (Black River Press, 1986), *I Apologize for the Eyes in My Head* (Wesleyan University Press, 1986), *Dien Cai Dau* (Wesleyan University Press, 1988), and *February in Sydney* (Matchbooks, 1989), his first seven books, had represented him as an extraordinary poet, but it was not until he published the next two—*Magic City* (Wesleyan University Press, 1992) and *Neon Vernacular* (Wesleyan University Press, 1993)—that he became known as a significant voice of North American poetry. *Neon Vernacular* won him the 1994 Pulitzer Prize for poetry and the 1994 Kinsley Tufts Prize for poetry. *Thieves of Paradise* (Wesleyan University Press, 1998), *Pleasure Dome* (Wesleyan University Press, 2001), *Talking Dirty to the Gods* (Farrar, Straus and Giroux, 2001), *Taboo* (Farrar, Straus and Giroux, 2004), *Gilgamesh* (Wesleyan University Press, 2006), and *Warhorses* (Farrar, Straus and Giroux, 2008), the volumes that followed, have increased his reputation as a major poet. His *Conversations with Yusef Komunyakaa,* edited by Shirley A. James Hanshaw (University Press of Mississippi, 2010), and *The Eye of the Poet: Six Views of the Art and Craft of Poetry,* with David Citino, Billy Collins, and other poets (Oxford University Press, 2001) are important texts for understanding the poetry of Komunyakaa. He has received other honors, fellowships, grants, and awards for his work as a poet—the Ruth Lily Poetry Prize (2001), the 2007 Louisiana Writer Award, membership in the Fellowship of Southern Writers (2007), the Levinson Prize from *Poetry* magazine (1997), the Hanes Poetry Prize (1997), the William Faulkner Prize from the University of Rennes in France (1994), the San Francisco Poetry Center Award (1986), the Kenyon Review Award for Literary Excellence (1991), National Endowment for the Arts fellowships, and many others. Komunyakaa is a Professor of creative writing at New York University and was Chancellor of the Academy of American Poetry (1999–2005).

Audre Lorde (1934–1992), a native New Yorker who often referred to herself as "a warrior poet," graduated from Hunter College and later received an MA degree in library science from Columbia University. In 1968, Poets Press published *The First Cities,* Lorde's first collection of poems, which was followed by three of her collections that Dudley Randall's Broadside Press would publish: *Cables to Rage* (1970), *From a Land Where Other People Live* (1973; nominated for the National Book Award), and *New York Head Shop and Museum* (1974). She wrote five more published volumes of poems: *Coal* (Norton, 1976), *Between Our Selves* (Eidolon Editions, 1976), *The Black Unicorn* (Norton, 1978), *Chosen Poems Old and New* (Norton, 1982), *Our Dead Behind Us* (Norton, 1986), and *The Collected Poems of Audre Lorde* (Norton, 1997; posthumous). She also wrote very important nonfiction, *The Cancer Journals* (Spinsters Ink, 1980), *Sister Outsider* (Crossing Press, 1984), and *A Burst of Light* (Firebrand Books, 1988; winner of the 1989 American Book Award); and one volume of fiction, *Zami: A New Spelling of My Name* (Crossing Press, 1982). With Barbara Smith and Cherríe Moraga, Lorde co-founded Kitchen Table: Women of Color Press, the first of its kind in the United States. She was also an editor of *Chrysalis,* a lesbian journal. The State of New York elected her its Poet Laureate for 1991–1992. She taught at Tougaloo College (Mississippi), Hunter College, and John Jay College of Criminal Justice in New York. She died of breast cancer in the US Virgin Islands, where she spent the last ten years of her life.

Nathaniel Mackey (1947–), a native of Miami, is an editor, literary critic, and novelist, as well as a poet. His books of poems are *Eroding Witness* (University of Illinois Press, 1985), *School of Udhra* (City Lights Books, 1993), *Whatsaid Serif* (City Lights Books, 1998), and *Splay Anthem* (New Directions, 2006), winner of the 2006 National Book Award for poetry. He is also author of five chapbooks of poems, *Four for Trane* (Golemics, 1978), *Septet for the End of Time* (Boneset, 1983), *Outlantish* (Chax Press, 1992), *Song of the Andoumboulou: 18–20* (1994); and *Four for Glenn* (Chax Press, 2002). In 1995, Spoken Engine Company published his *Strick: Song of the Andoumboulou 16–25,* a compact disc recording of poems (with music by Royal Hartigan and Hafez Modirzadeh). In 2001, he was elected to the Board of Chancellors of the Academy of American Poets. Mackey is also the editor of *Hambone,* a literary journal, and, with Art Lange, co-editor of *Moment's Notice: Jazz in Poetry and Prose* (Coffee House Press, 1993). His books of literary criticism and interviews are *Discrepant Engagement: Dissonance, Cross-Culturalty, and Experimental Writing* (Cambridge University Press, 1993), and *Paracritical Hinge: Essays, Talks, Notes, Interviews* (University of Wisconsin Press, 2005). He is a Professor in the Department of Literature at the University of California, Santa Cruz.

Haki Madhubuti (1942–; Don L. Lee) is a poet, educator, editor, and publisher who was instrumental in promoting and developing the ideas of the Black Arts Movement. This Little Rock, Arkansas, native grew up in Detroit and attended Roosevelt University, the University of Illinois, and the University of Iowa, where he received an MFA in 1984. In 1967, he became the editor and publisher of Third World Press, which has published many black writers. Beginning in 1967, Dudley Randall's Broadside Press, however, published Madhubuti's books of poems under the name of Don L. Lee: *Think Black* (1967), *Cry, Scream* (1969), *We Walk the Way of the New World* (1970), *Directionscore: Selected and New Poems* (1971), and *Book of Live* (1973; as Haki R. Madhubuti). His other volumes of poetry include *Earthquakes and Sunrise Missions: Poetry and Essays of Black Renewal, 1973–1983* (Third World Press, 1978), *Killing Memory, Seeking Ancestors* (Lotus Press, 1987), *Ground Work: Selected Poems of Haki R. Madhubuti* (Third World Press, 1996), *HeartLove: Wedding and Love Poems* (Third World Press, 1998), and *Liberation Narratives: Collected and New Poems (1966–2009)* (Third World Press, 2009). He also published *YellowBlack: The First Twenty-One Years of a Poet's Life* (Third World Press, 2006; an autobiographical novel), *Black Men: Obsolete, Single, Dangerous?: The African American Family in Transition* (Third World Press, 1991), and *Tough Notes: A Healing Call for Creating Exceptional Black Men* (Third World Press, 2002).

Clarence Major (1936–), Professor of English at the University of California at Davis, is a prolific poet, fiction writer, essayist, and painter, who has also been engaged as an editor, lexicographer, anthologist, critical reader, and literary judge in the contemporary literary and cultural scenes of the United States. He is author of eleven books of poems and ten books of fiction, as well as such nonfiction volumes as *Juba to Jive: A Dictionary of African-American Slang* (Viking, 1994), *Necessary Distance: Essays and Criticism* (Coffee House Press, 2000), and *Come by Here: My Mother's Life* (John Wiley & Sons, 2002). *Swallow the Lake* (Wesleyan University Press, 1970), *The Cotton Club* (Broadside Press, 1972), *The Syncopated Cakewalk* (Barlenmir House, 1974), *Surfaces and Masks* (Coffee House Press, 1988), *Configurations: New and Selected Poems 1958–1998* (Copper Canyon Press, 1999), and *Waiting for Sweet Betty* (Copper Canyon Press, 1999) are some of his books of poems, and *All-Night Visitors* (Olympia Press, 1970), *Reflex and Bone Structure* (Fiction Collective, 1975), *My Amputations* (Fiction Collective, 1986), *Painted Turtle: Woman with Guitar* (Sun & Moon Press, 1988), and *One Flesh* (Kensington Books, 2003) are some of his most popular novels. He is the editor of two widely used anthologies, *The Garden Thrives: Twentieth-Century African-American Poetry* (HarperCollins, 1996) and *Calling the Wind: Twentieth-Century African-American Short Stories* (HarperCollins, 1993). He was born in Atlanta, and when his parents divorced, he moved with his mother to Chicago, the city in which he began his study of the practices and production of modern visual artists. From 1991 to 1993, he served as director of the creative writing program at the University of California at Davis, where he has taught since 1989.

Dawn Lundy Martin (1968–), born in Hartford, Connecticut, received her PhD in English literature at the University of Massachusetts (Amherst). She is author of *A Gathering of Matter/A Matter of Gathering* (University of Georgia Press), winner of the 2006 Cave Canem Poetry Prize, and *Discipline,* chosen by Fanny Howe as winner of the 2009 Nightboat Books Poetry Prize (Nightboat Books, 2011). She is also author of *The Morning Hour,* a chapbook that garnered for her the 2003 Poetry Society of America's National Chapbook Fellowship. Her second chapbook, *The Undress: Poems,* was published by Belladonna Books, 2006. With Vivien Labaton, she co-edited the anthology of essays *The Fire This Time: Young Feminists, Activism, and the Global City* (Anchor, 2004), and this indefatigable activist-academic-poet co-founded the Black Took Collective and the Third Wave Foundation. Her poems have also been published in a number of periodicals, including *Hambone, Tuesday Journal, nocturnes (re)view of the literary arts,* and *Callaloo.* For her work she has received such prizes, fellowships, and awards as the Ragdale Foundation Fellowship, a Massachusetts Cultural Council Artist Grant for Poetry, and the American Academy of Arts & Sciences May Sarton Prize for Poetry. Currently, she is an Assistant Professor of English in the writing program at the University of Pittsburgh.

Colleen J. McElroy (1935–), born in St. Louis, received her BS and MS degrees from Kansas State University and a PhD from the University of Washington (Seattle), where she is Professor Emeritus of English and creative writing. From 1995 to 2006, she served as editor-in-chief of *The Seattle Review.* She is a poet, folklorist, and short story writer, whose collections of poems include *Sleeping with the Moon* (University of Illinois Press, 2007; winner of the 2008 PEN/Oakland National Literary Award), *Travelling Music* (Story Line, 1998), *What Madness Brought Me Here: New and Selected Poems* (Wesleyan University Press, 1990), *Bone Flames* (Wesleyan University Press, 1987), *Queen of the Ebony Isles* (Wesleyan University Press, 1984; winner of the Before Columbus American Book Award for poetry and a Pushcart Prize), *Lie and Say You Love Me* (Circinatum Press, 1981), *Winters Without Snow* (Reed, Cannon & Johnson, 1980), and *Music from Home* (Southern Illinois University Press, 1976). In 1987 and 1990, Creative Arts Book Company published, respectively, her two books of fiction, *Jesus and Fat Tuesday* and *Driving Under the Cardboard Pines.* Her publications include two nonfiction collections, *Page to Page: Retrospectives from Writers of The Seattle Review* (University of Washington Press, 2006), and *Over the Lip of the World: Among the Storytellers of Madagascar* (University of Washington Press, 2001), a finalist for the PEN Award for Creative Nonfiction (research-based). Her other nonfiction volumes are *Speech and Language Development of the Preschool Child* (Charles C. Thomas, 1972) and *A Long Way from St. Louie* (Coffee House Press, 1997). A Fulbright Creative Writing Fellowship to Yugoslavia, a Fulbright Research Fellowship to Madagascar, two National Endowment for the Arts fellowships (poetry and fiction), and a Rockefeller Foundation Fellowship to the Bellagio Center in Italy are some of the fellowships she has received.

Constance Merritt (1966–) was born in Pine Bluff, Arkansas. She is author of three books of poetry, *Two Rooms* (Louisiana State University Press, 2009), *Blessings and Inclemencies* (Louisiana State University Press, 2007), and *A Protocol for Touch* (University of North Texas Press, 2000). In her youth, she attended the Arkansas School for the Blind in Little Rock, and later received her BA and MA degrees in English from the University of Utah, a PhD from the University of Nebraska in Lincoln, and an MFA from Warren Wilson College. A finalist for the William Carlos Williams Book Award, she was awarded the Academy of American Poets College Prize and the Vassar Miller Prize for poetry. She has also received grants and fellowships from the Radcliffe Institute for Advanced Study at Harvard and the Rona Jaffe Foundation.

Thylias Moss (1954–) was born in Cleveland, attended Syracuse University for two years, and later graduated with a BA in creative writing from Oberlin College in 1981. In 1983, she completed an MA degree in English at the University of New Hampshire, and from 1984 to 1991 she taught English at Phillips Andover Academy in Massachusetts. Since 1993, she has been Professor of English, and since 2009, Professor in the School of Art and Design at the University of Michigan in Ann Arbor. In 1983, the Cleveland State University Poetry Center published her first book of poems, *Hosiery Seams on a Bowlegged Woman*. She is author of eight other volumes of poems, *Pyramid of Bone* (Callaloo Poetry Series, 1989; first runner-up for the 1989 National Book Critics Circle Award), *At Redbones* (Cleveland State University Poetry Series, 1990), *Rainbow Remnants in Rock Bottom Ghetto Sky* (Persea Books, 1991; National Poetry Series), *Small Segregations* (Ecco, 1993), *Small Congregations: New and Selected Poems* (Ecco, 1999), *Chance for Tarzan Holler* (Persea Books, 1999), *Slave Moth: A Narrative in Verse* (Persea Books, 2006), and *Tokyo Butter* (Persea Books, 2006). She has written two books for children, *I Want To Be* (Puffin, 1998) and *Tale of a Blue-Sky Dress* (Harper Perennial, 1999); and two plays, *The Dolls in the Basement* (1984) and *Talking to Myself* (1984). For her work she has received numerous grants, prizes, awards, and fellowships from the Kenan Charitable Trust (1984–1987), the Artists' Foundation of Massachusetts, the National Endowment for the Arts (1989), Pushcart (1990), the Witter Bynner Foundation (1991), the Mrs. Giles Whiting Foundation (1991), the Guggenheim Foundation (1995), and the MacArthur Foundation (1996). In 1991, she received a Dewar's Profiles Performance Artist Award.

Fred Moten (1962–), Associate Professor of English at Duke University, is author of five books of poems, *Arkansas* (Pressed Wafer Books, 2000), *Poems* (with Jim Behrle; Pressed Wafer Books, 2003), *I ran from it and was still in it* (with collages by Theodore Harris; Cusp Books, 2007), *Hughson's Tavern* (Leon

Works, 2008), and *B Jenkins* (Duke University Press, 2010). He is also author of *In the Break: The Aesthetics of the Black Radical Tradition* (University of Minnesota Press, 2003) and *Open Secret/Stolen Life: The Aesthetics of the Black Radical Tradition* (University of Minnesota Press, 2010). He has also taught at the University of Iowa, the University of California (Irvine), and the University of Southern California. Born in Las Vegas, he graduated from Harvard University in 1985, and received a PhD in English from the University of California (Berkeley) in 1994.

Harryette Mullen (1953–), poet and educator, is author of *Tree Tall Woman* (Energy Earth Communications, 1981), *Trimmings* (Tender Buttons, 1991), *S*PeRM**K*T* (Singing Horse Press, 1992), *Muse & Drudge* (Singing Horse Press, 1995), *Blues Baby: Early Poems* (Bucknell University Press, 2002), *Sleeping with the Dictionary* (University of California Press, 2002; finalist for the *Los Angeles Times* Book Award, National Book Critics Circle Award, and National Book Award), and *Recyclopedia: Trimmings, S*PeRM**K*T, and Muse & Drudge* (Graywolf Press, 2006; winner of a PEN Beyond Margins Award). *MELUS, American Book Review, The Antioch Review, Diacritics*, and *Callaloo* are some of the periodicals in which her poetry and literary criticism have appeared. A native of Florence, Alabama, she received her PhD degree in English from the University of California in Santa Cruz, and is currently serving as Professor of English at the University of California (Los Angeles). In 2009, she was made a Fellow of the Academy of American Poets.

John Murillo (1971–), a graduate of Howard University, received his MFA degree in creative writing from New York University. This native of Upland, California, is a two-time winner of the Larry Neal Writers' Award and the 2008–2009 Elma B. Stuckey Visiting Emerging Poet-in-Residence at Columbia College in Chicago. He has also received fellowships from *The New York Times,* Cave Canem, the Fine Arts Work Center in Provincetown, Massachusetts, and the Wisconsin Institute for Creative Writing. His first full-length collection, *Up Jump the Boogie,* was published by Cypher Books in 2010.

Larry Neal (1937–1981), who was born in Atlanta, wrote poetry, literary criticism, and plays. He was author of two books of poems, *Black Boogaloo: Notes on Black Liberation* (Journal of Black Poetry Press, 1969) and *Hoodoo Hollerin' Bebop Ghosts* (Howard University Press, 1971); and three plays, *Moving On Up* (screenplay, 1973), *In an Upstate Motel: A Morality Play* (1980), and *The Glorious Monster in the Bell of the Horn* (1979). Michael Schwartz has edited Neal's essays under the title *Visions of a Liberated Future: Black Arts Movement Writings* (Thunder's Mouth Press, 1989), texts which represent him as one of the architects of the Black Arts Movement. Neal also co-edited two books with Amiri Baraka, *Black Fire: An Anthology of Afro-American Writing* (William Morrow, 1968) and *Trip-*

pin': A Need for Change (1969; also with A. B. Spellman). This graduate of Lincoln University and the University of Pennsylvania taught at the City College of New York, Wesleyan University, and Yale University.

Marilyn Nelson (1946–), Poet Laureate of Connecticut (2001–2006), studied at the University of California (Davis), the University of Pennsylvania, and the University of Minnesota, from which she received a PhD degree in 1979. This University of Connecticut Emeritus Professor of English is founder and director of Soul Mountain Retreat (East Haddam, Connecticut). Her third collection of poems, *The Homeplace* (Louisiana State University Press, 1991), won the 1992 Annisfield-Wolf Award and was a finalist for the 1991 National Book Award. *The Fields of Praise: New and Selected Poems* (Louisiana State University Press, 1997), her fifth collection, won the 1998 Poets' Prize and was a finalist for the 1997 National Book Award, the Lenore Marshall Prize, and the PEN Winship Award. She is also author of other volumes of poems, *For the Body* (Louisiana State University Press, 1978), *Mama's Promises* (Louisiana State University Press, 1985), *Magnificat* (Louisiana State University Press, 1994), and *The Cachoeira Tales and Other Poems* (Louisiana State University Press, 2005). *A Wreath for Emmett Till* (Houghton Mifflin, 2005), *Fortune's Bones: The Manumission Requiem* (Front Street, 2004; Coretta Scott King Honor Book), *Carver: A Life in Poems* (Front Street, 2001; winner of the Newberry Honor Award, the Coretta Scott King Award, the American Library Association's Best Book of the Year Award, and others), *Beautiful Ballerina* (Scholastic Press, 2009), and *The Cat Walked Through the Casserole* (Carolrhoda Books, 1984) are some of the books she has written for younger readers. She has translated a number of texts and has written books in collaboration with other writers. Her other honors and awards include the 1990 Connecticut Arts Award and fellowships from the National Endowment for the Arts and the Guggenheim Foundation. She was born in Cleveland.

Gregory Pardlo (1968–), an associate editor of *Callaloo*, graduated from Rutgers University (1999) and received a MFA in poetry from New York University in 2001. He is author of *Totem* (*American Poetry Review*/Copper Canyon Press, 2007), winner of the *American Poetry Review*/Honickman First Book Prize; and translator of *Pencil of Rays and Spiked Mace: Selected Poems of Niels Lyngsø* (Toronto: BookThug, 2005). He is an Assistant Professor of creative writing at George Washington University in Washington, DC.

Carl Phillips (1959–) is Professor of English at Washington University in St. Louis, where he has also served, from 1996 to 1998 and 2000 to 2002, as director of its creative writing program. He is author of two books of nonfiction prose, *Coin of the Realm: Essays on the Art and Life of Poetry* (Graywolf, 2004) and a translation of Sophocles' *Philoctetes* (Oxford University Press, 2003); and ten volumes of poems, *Speak Low* (Farrar, Straus and Giroux, 2009; finalist for the National Book Award), *Quiver of Arrows: Selected Poems 1986–2006* (Farrar, Straus and Giroux, 2007; finalist for the NAACP Image Award), *Riding Westward* (Farrar, Straus and Giroux, 2006), *The Rest of Love* (Farrar, Straus and Giroux, 2004; winner of the Theodore Roethke Memorial Foundation Poetry Prize and the Thom Gunn Award for Gay Male Poetry, and finalist for the National Book Award); *Rock Harbor* (Farrar, Straus and Giroux, 2002), *The Tether* (Farrar, Straus and Giroux, 2001; winner of the Kingsley Tufts Prize and the Society of Midland Authors Award in Poetry), *Pastoral* (Graywolf Press, 2000; winner of the Lambda Literary Award in Poetry); *From the Devotions* (Graywolf Press, 1998; National Book Award finalist); *Cortège* (Graywolf Press, 1995; finalist for the National Book Critics Circle Award and the Lambda Literary Award in Poetry); and *In the Blood* (Northeastern University Press, 1992; winner of the Samuel French Morse Poetry Prize). Born in Everett, Washington, to a British mother and an African American father, Carl Phillips spent his early teen years in Zweibrücken, Germany, with his career military parents, and in 1981 he graduated magna cum laude with a BA degree in Greek and Latin from Harvard University. In 1983 he received an MTA from the University of Massachusetts in Latin and classical humanities, and an MA in creative writing from Boston University in 1993. In 2006, he was elected a Fellow of the Academy of American Poets, and he is currently a Chancellor of the Academy.

Ishmael Reed (1938–), born in Chattanooga, Tennessee, is known mainly as a novelist, but he has also written a number of volumes of poems, *Catechism of D Neoamerican Hoodoo Church* (Broadside Press, 1971), *Conjure: Selected Poems, 1963–1970* (University of Massachusetts Press, 1972; nominated for a Pulitzer Prize), *Chattanooga: Poems* (Random House, 1973), *A Secretary to the Spirits* (NOK Publishers, 1978), *New and Collected Poetry* (NOK Publishers, 1988), and *New and Collected Poems 1964–2007* (Da Capo Press, 2007; awarded the California Gold Medal in Poetry by the Commonwealth Club). His books of fiction and nonfiction prose include *The Freelance Pallbearers* (Doubleday, 1967), *Yellow Back Radio Broke-Down* (Doubleday, 1969), *Mumbo Jumbo* (Doubleday, 1972), *The Last Days of Louisiana Red* (Random House, 1974), *Flight to Canada* (Random House, 1976), *Airing Dirty Laundry* (Basic Books, 1993), *Writin' Is Fightin': Thirty-Seven Years of Boxing on Paper* (Atheneum, 1988), *God Made Alaska for the Indians: Selected Essays* (Garland Publishing, 1982), and *Barack Obama and the Jim Crow Media: The Return of the Nigger Breakers* (Baraka Books, 2010). He grew up in Buffalo, New York, and from 1956 to 1959 was enrolled at the University of Buffalo, which awarded him an honorary doctorate in humane letters in 1995. After he moved to New York City in 1962, he became a member of the Umbra workshop and worked with Lorenzo Thomas, David Henderson, Calvin Hernton, and others who helped to set in motion the Black Arts Movement. In 1965, he co-founded a newspaper called *East Village Other*. In fact, wherever he has lived he has been very active in creating venues to serve the productions of marginalized people:

he founded the Before Columbus Foundation, the Oakland chapter of PEN, and There City Cinema, an organization that furthers the distribution and discussion of films from throughout the world. He has further supported writers by founding and operating two book publishing outlets, I. Reed Books and Reed, Cannon & Johnson; and four periodical publications, *Konch, Yardbird Reader, Quilt,* and *Y'Bird.* In 1978, the Studio Museum of Harlem honored him with the Lewis H. Michaux Literary Prize, in 1998 he received a John D. and Catherine T. MacArthur Foundation Fellowship award, and twice he has been selected as a finalist for the National Book Award. In 1998 he received an honorary doctorate of letters from Johnson C. Smith University at Charlotte, North Carolina. For over thirty years, he taught creative writing courses in the English Department at the University of California at Berkeley, and he was a Visiting Artist/Scholar at San Jose State University, holding the Lurie Chair in Creative Writing. He has also taught at Harvard, Yale, Dartmouth, and the University of California at Berkeley.

Ed Roberson (1939–) was born in Pittsburgh, where, as a youngster, he studied art on Saturday mornings at the Carnegie Institute. He is author of eight books of poetry, *The New Wing of the Labyrinth* (Singing Horse Press, 2009), *City Eclogue* (Atelos, 2006), *Atmosphere Conditions* (Sun & Moon Press, 2000; winner of the 2000 National Poetry Award), *Just In: Word of Navigational Challenges: New and Selected Work* (Talisman House, 1998), *Voices Cast Out to Talk Us In* (University of Iowa Press, 1995; winner of the 1994 Iowa Poetry Prize), *Lucid Interval as Integral Music* (University of Iowa Press, 1995; winner of the Iowa Poetry Prize), *Etai-eken* (University of Pittsburgh Press, 1975), and *When Thy King Is a Boy* (University of Pittsburgh Press, 1970). In 2008, he received the Shelley Memorial Award from the Poetry Society of America, and in 2010 was featured as the focus of an issue of *Callaloo.* He has traveled to and studied the natural world in Afognak Island, Bermuda, Alaska, Peru, and Ecuador. From 1990 to 2003, he worked in the Office of Special Programs at Rutgers University, and from 2004 to 2006, he taught at Columbia College in Chicago. Currently, he is the Distinguished Artist-in-Residence at Northwestern University in Evanston, Illinois.

Carolyn Rodgers (1940–2010), a native of Chicago, is author of *Paper Soul* (1968), *Songs of a Blackbird* (Third World Press, 1969), *how i got ovah* (Anchor, 1975), *The Heart As Ever Green* (Anchor/Doubleday, 1978), *Eden and Other Poems* (Eden Press, 1983), *A Little Lower Than Angels* (Eden Press, 1984), *Echoes from a Circle Called Earth* (Eden Press, 1984), *Finite Forms* (Eden Press, 1985), *Morning Glory: Poems* (Eden Press, 1989), and *We Are Only Human* (Eden Press, 1994). In 1968, she received the first Conrad Kent Rivers Memorial Fund Award, in 1970 the Poet Laureate Award from the Society of Midland Authors, and a fellowship from the National Endowment for the Arts. She studied at Roosevelt University, the University of Illinois, and the University of Chicago, from which she received an MA degree in English. She was a member of Chicago's Organization of Black American Culture (OBAC) from 1967 to 1971. She taught at Indiana University, the University of Washington, and other institutions.

Sonia Sanchez (1934–; Wilsonia Benita Driver) was born in Birmingham, Alabama, where she lived until her family moved to New York City in the early 1940s. In addition to writing poems, she has written six plays and two books for children, *It's a New Day* (Broadside Press, 1971) and *A Sound Investment* (Third World Press, 1980); and edited two anthologies, *We Be Word Sorcerers* (Bantam Books, 1974) and *360° of Blackness Coming at Ya!* (5X Publishing, 1971). Her national presence as a poet began with the Broadside Press publication of her first two collections, *Homecoming* (Broadside Press, 1969) and *We a BaddDDD People* (Broadside Press, 1970). Her subsequent collections include *A Blues Book for a Blue Black Magic Woman* (Broadside Press, 1974), *Homegirls and Handgrenades* (Thunder's Mouth Press, 1984; winner of the American Book Award), *I've Been a Woman: New and Selected Poems* (Third World Press, 1985), *Wounded in the House of a Friend* (Beacon Press, 1997), *Does Your House Have Lions?* (Beacon Press, 1997; finalist for the National Book Critics Circle Award and recipient of the Poetry Society of America's 2001 Robert Frost Medal), *Like the Singing Coming off the Drums* (Beacon Press, 1998), and *Shake Loose My Skin* (Beacon Press, 1999). In 2007, the University Press of Mississippi published *Conversations with Sonia Sanchez*, edited by Joyce Ann Joyce. Sanchez received her BA degree in political science, and later studied poetry under Louise Bogan at New York University. In 1969, she received the PEN Writing Award, the Langston Hughes Award in 1999, and numerous other honors, including the National Education Association Award, a National Endowment for the Arts Fellowship, the Governor's Award for Excellence in the Humanities, the Lucretia Mott Award, and the Community Service Award from the National Black Caucus of State Legislators. She was one of the architects of the Black Arts Movement. Until her retirement in 1999, Sanchez held the Laura Carnell Chair in English at Temple University, where she began her tenure as a professor in 1977. She is now Poet-in-Residence at Temple University in Philadelphia, where she lives.

Ntozake Shange (1948–; Paulette L. Williams) is author of *for colored girls who have considered suicide / when the rainbow is enuf* (1974), a choreopoem, which received nominations for an Emmy Award, a Tony Award, and a Grammy Award. She is also author of numerous other books of poetry, fiction, plays, and essays, including *Nappy Edges* (St. Martin's, 1978; poems), *Spell #7: a theater piece in two acts* (Samuel French, 1981), *Sassafrass, Cypress & Indigo: A Novel* (St. Martin's, 1982), *A Daughter's Geography* (St. Martin's, 1983; poems), *From Okra to Greens: A Different Kinda Love Story: A Play with Music & Dance* (Samuel French, 1983), *See No Evil: Prefaces, Essays & Accounts, 1976–1983* (Momo's Press, 1984), *Betsey Brown* (St. Martin's, 1985; a novel), *Daddy Says* (1989; drama), and

The Sweet Breath of Life: A Poetic Narrative of the African-American Family (Atria Books, 2004). She also writes books for children—e.g., *Coretta Scott* (Harper-Collins, 2009), *Ellington Was Not a Street* (Simon & Schuster, 2003), and *White-wash* (Walker, 1997). She has received numerous awards for her work, including the Obie Award, the Outer Critics Circle Award, the Audelco Award, the Mademoiselle Award, the Frank Silvera Writers' Workshop Award, the Black Theatre Network Winona Fletcher Award, a Columbia University Medal of Excellence, and a Guggenheim Fellowship. She studied at Barnard College (New York) and the University of Southern California, from which she received an MA degree. She was born in Trenton, New Jersey, to upper-middle-class parents.

Reginald Shepherd (1963–2008), born in New York City, is author of two collections of essays, *Orpheus in the Bronx: Essays on Identity, Politics, and the Freedom of Poetry* (University of Michigan Press, 2008) and *A Martian Muse: Further Readings on Identity, Politics, and the Freedom of Poetry* (University of Michigan Press, 2010; posthumous), as well as five books of poems, *Some Are Drowning* (University of Pittsburgh Press, 1994; Associated Writing Programs' Award in Poetry, 1993), *Angel, Interrupted* (University of Pittsburgh Press, 1996), *Wrong* (University of Pittsburgh Press, 1999), *Otherhood* (University of Pittsburgh Press, 2003; 2004 Lenore Marshall Poetry Prize finalist), and *Fata Morgana* (University of Pittsburgh Press, 2007; awarded the Silver Medal of the 2007 Florida Book Awards). Some of his work also appeared in journals and anthologies, including *The Best American Poetry* (1995, 1996, 2000, and 2002), *jubilat, Shade, Open House, The Beacon Best of 1999,* and *Callaloo*. He also edited *The Iowa Anthology of New American Poetries* (University of Iowa Press, 2004) and *Lyric Postmodernisms: An Anthology of Contemporary Innovative Poetries* (Counterpath Press, 2008). For his work, he received a number of other awards and honors, including fellowships from the Guggenheim Foundation and the National Endowment for the Arts, and grants from the Illinois Arts Council and the Florida Arts Council. He studied at Bennington College, Brown University, and the University of Iowa, and taught at Cornell University. He grew up in the Bronx and died of cancer in Pensacola, Florida.

giovanni singleton (1969–) is the founder and editor of *nocturnes (re)view of the literary arts* (1999–present), which has been described as a "journal dedicated to the work of artists and writers of the African Diaspora and other contested spaces." This Richmond, Virginia, native received an MFA in creative writing and poetics from the New College of California, and has taught poetry at Saint Mary's College (Moraga, California), the Oakland Museum, the De Young Museum, and for California Poets in the Schools (CPITS) in Marin County. Her poetry has appeared in a number of periodicals and anthologies, including *Chain, Fence, Five Fingers Review, Callaloo, The Breast: An Anthology* (Global City

Press, 1994), and *Beyond the Frontier: African-American Poetry for the 21st Century* (Black Classic Press, 2002). Her work has garnered awards and commendations from a number of institutions, including the New Langton Bay Area Literature Award, the Squaw Valley Community of Writers Poetry Workshop, and the Hurston/Wright Writers' Week Poetry Workshop. She has lived in the United Kingdom and has traveled to Tunisia, St. Lucia, Barbados, Mexico, and France. She has also made solo pilgrimages to Nepal, India, Sikkim, and Vietnam.

Patricia Smith (1955–), born in Chicago, is both a spoken-word performance poet and a literary poet, whose *Blood Dazzler* (Coffee House Press) was a 2008 National Book Award Finalist. She is also author of *Life According to Motown* (Tia Chucha Press, 1991), *Big Towns, Big Talk* (Zoland Books, 1992), *Close to Death* (Zoland Books, 1993), and *Teahouse of the Almighty* (Coffee House Press, 2006), winner of the 2007 Paterson Poetry Prize, the National Poetry Series, and a 2007 Hurston/Wright Legacy Award. She is also a playwright, a journalist, and author of other forms of prose, such *Janna and the Kings* (Lee & Low, 2003), a book for children that won the New Voices Award, and *Fixed on a Furious Star* (Crown, 2009), a story of the life of Harriet Tubman. Her other awards and honors for her writing include a National Poetry Series award, a Pushcart Prize, and the Carl Sandburg Literary Award. This graduate of the Stonecoast MFA program (Maine) has also published in major literary journals—*TriQuarterly, Poetry,* and *The Paris Review* among them—and has taught at a number of workshops and institutions, including Cave Canem and Georgia Tech University, where she held the Bruce McEver Chair in Writing. As a performance poet, she was four times selected as champion of the National Poetry Slam and was a featured poet on HBO's *Def Poetry Jam.*

Tracy K. Smith (1972–) is an Assistant Professor in the creative writing program at Princeton University. This native of Northern California is author of three books of poems, *Duende* (Graywolf Press, 2007), which won the 2006 James Laughlin Award of the Academy of American Poets; *The Body's Question* (Graywolf Press, 2003), winner of the 2002 Cave Canem Poetry Prize; and *Life on Mars* (Graywolf Press, 2011). She has also published poems in a number of periodicals, including *Callaloo, The Harvard Advocate, Ploughshares, The Ontario Review,* and *The New Yorker.* An Artist's Residency at Fundación Valparaíso in Almería, Spain (2003), the Rona Jaffe Foundation Writers' Award (2004), the Mrs. Giles Whiting Foundation Writers' Award (2005), an *Essence* Magazine Literary Award (2007), a Bicentennial Preceptorship from Princeton University (2009)—these are some of the awards and honors she has received in recognition of her work as a poet. She graduated from Harvard College, received an MFA from Columbia University, and studied as a Wallace Stegner Fellow at Stanford University. She lives in New York City.

.. Spellman (1935–), poet and cultural critic, studied political science and law at Howard University in Washington, DC. Born in Elizabeth City, North Carolina, he is author of *The Beautiful Days* (Poets Press, 1965; poems), *Things I Must Have Known* (Coffee House Press, 2008; poems), *Four Lives in the Bee-Bop Business* (Pantheon, 1966; nonfiction; other editions under the title of *Four Jazz Lives*, University of Michigan Press), and *Art Tatum: A Critical Biography* (a chapbook). He has taught at a number of institutions, including Rutgers University, Morehouse College, and Harvard University. His non-literary career has centered on over three decades of work for the National Endowment for the Arts, where he has served in various positions such as director of the Arts in Education Study Project and the Arts Endowment Expansion Program, and deputy chairman for the Office of Guidelines, Panel and Council Operations, among other appointments.

Edward S. Spriggs (1934–) is one of the architects of the Black Arts Movement and was a member of the boards of *Journal of Black Poetry* and *Black Dialogue Magazine*, two major forums for African American authors during the height of the Movement. He is the founder of the Hammonds House Museum in Atlanta, where he served as director and curator for fifteen years. He also served in numerous other national and international arts positions, including executive director of the Studio Museum of Harlem and different positions supporting the World Black and African Festival of Arts and Culture (FESTAC) and the National Endowment for the Arts. Recently, he founded Acts of Art Appraisals, a fine art appraisal service in Atlanta, where he lives. This poet and essayist gives lectures on visual art.

Primus St. John (1939–) is Professor of English at Portland State University, where he has taught literature and creative writing since 1973. He has also taught at Whitman College, Pitzer College, Lewis & Clark College, Reed College, and the University of Utah. He is author of four books of poetry, *Communion: New and Selected Poems* (Copper Canyon Press, 1999), *Dreamer* (Carnegie Mellon University Press, 1990), *Love Is Not a Consolation: It Is a Light* (Carnegie Mellon University Press, 1982), and *Skins on the Earth* (Copper Canyon Press, 1976). *Communion* won the 2000 Western States Book Award for poetry, and in 1990 *Dreamer* won the Hazel Hall Award for Poetry. He is the editor of *From Here We Speak* (Oregon State University Press, 1994) and *Zero Makes Me Hungry* (Scott Foresman, 1976). His poems have also appeared in such journals as *The Iowa Review, Northwest Review, The Southern Poetry Review, The American Poetry Review,* and *Callaloo,* and in various anthologies. He was born in New York City to parents of West Indian heritage.

Sharan Strange (1959–), a native of Orangeburg, South Carolina, graduated from Harvard College and received her MFA from Sarah Lawrence College. She is co-founder of the Dark Room Collective, a gathering of African American writers who met in Cambridge, Massachusetts, when most of them were students at Harvard. She is author of *Ash* (Beacon Press, 2001), a collection of poems. Her work has been published in *Callaloo, The Best American Poetry 1994, AGNI, In Search of Color Everywhere, The American Poetry Review, The Garden Thrives: Twentieth-Century African-American Poetry,* and in other periodicals and books. She has served as Poet-in-Residence at Fisk University, California Institute of the Arts, Spelman College, and the University of California at Davis. She lives in Washington, DC.

Amber Flora Thomas (1972–) received her MFA in poetry writing from Washington University in St. Louis in 1998. In 2005, the University of Pittsburgh Press published her first book of poems, *Eye of Water,* which won the 2004 Cave Canem Poetry Prize. *Eye of Water* was also a finalist for the PEN USA 2005 Literary Awards and for the Lambda Literary Awards. Her poems have appeared in various periodicals, including *American Literary Review, Crab Orchard Review, The Southern Poetry Review, Gulf Coast, Callaloo, Rattle,* and *The Carolina Quarterly.* She is currently an Assistant Professor of creative writing (poetry) at the University of Alaska in Fairbanks.

Lorenzo Thomas (1944–2005) is author of three collections of poems, *Dancing on Main Street* (Coffee House Press, 2004), *Bathers* (Reed International Books, 1981), and *Chances Are Few* (Blue Wind Press, 1979); and three books of literary and cultural criticism, *Extraordinary Measures: Afrocentric Modernism and 20th-Century American Poetry* (University of Alabama Press, 2000; *Choice* magazine's selection for Outstanding Academic Book for 2001), *Sing the Sun Up: Creative Writing Ideas from African American Literature* (Teachers & Writers Collaborative, 1998), and *Don't Deny My Name: Words and Music and the Black Intellectual Tradition* (University of Michigan Press, 2008; a posthumous text, edited by Aldon Lynn Nielsen). The Lucille Medwick Prize, two grants from the Poetry Foundation, a Houston Festival Foundation Arts Award (1984), and a National Endowment for the Arts Fellowship (1983) are other honors and awards he received for his work. He published numerous essays and poems in such periodicals as *Living Blues, Ploughshares,* the *Houston Chronicle, Popular Music and Society, Blues Unlimited* (England), and *Callaloo.* During the early 1960s, he was a member of the Umbra workshop, a Lower East Side group of New York–based writers, such as David Henderson, Ishmael Reed, Calvin Hernton, and others, whose social, political, and literary ideas are some of the roots of the Black Arts Movements. In 1973, Thomas, a Vietnam veteran, moved to Houston and began teaching as Writer-in-Residence at Texas Southern University, where he also conducted creative writing workshops in the Black Arts Center and edited *Roots.* In 1984, he joined the faculty of the University of Houston-Downtown. Thomas was born in the Republic of Panama, reared in the Bronx and Queens in New York, and spent the last two decades of his life in Houston.

Melvin B. Tolson (1898–1966) was not only a poet; he was also a politician, an educator, and a columnist. Born in Moberly, Missouri, he authored *Rendezvous with America* (Dodd, Mead, 1944), *Libretto for the Republic of Liberia* (Twayne

Publishers, 1953), *Harlem Gallery: Book I, The Curator* (Twayne Publishers, 1965), and *Gallery of Harlem Portraits* (published posthumously; University of Missouri Press, 1979). He was elected Poet Laureate of the Republic of Liberia in 1947, and wrote *Libretto for the Republic of Liberia* to celebrate the West African nation's 1956 centennial. In 1982, the University of Missouri Press published *Caviar and Cabbage: Selected Columns by Melvin B. Tolson,* the columns he wrote between 1937 and 1944 for the *Washington Tribune.* He attended Fisk University for a brief period, and later transferred to Lincoln University of Pennsylvania, from which he graduated with honors in 1924. After completing his course work and a thesis entitled "The Harlem Group of Negro Writers," he was awarded an MA degree from Columbia University in 1940. He taught at historically black institutions in Oklahoma, Texas, and Alabama. While he taught at Wiley College (1924–1947) in Marshall, Texas, he developed a debate team that defeated the team from the University of Southern California, the basis for Denzel Washington's film *The Great Debaters.* In 1965, he received the District of Columbia's Citation and Award for Cultural Achievement in the Fine Arts, a second honorary doctorate of letters from Lincoln University, a grant from the National Institute, a poetry award from the American Academy of Arts and Letters, and a two-year appointment as Avalon Poet at Tuskegee Institute. He died of cancer in 1966, the same year he received a Rockefeller Foundation Award.

Natasha Trethewey (1966–) holds the Phillis Wheatley Distinguished Chair in Poetry at Emory University, where she has taught in the English Department since 2001. From 2005 to 2006, she was Lehman Brady Visiting Joint Chair Professor in Documentary Studies and American Studies at Duke University and the University of North Carolina at Chapel Hill. She is author of three books of poetry, *Native Guard* (Houghton Mifflin, 2006), *Bellocq's Ophelia* (Graywolf Press, 2002), and *Domestic Work* (Graywolf Press, 2000). In 2007, she was awarded the Pulitzer Prize in Poetry for *Native Guard.* Her *Beyond Katrina: A Meditation on the Mississippi Gulf Coast* was published in 2010 by the University of Georgia Press. She has received numerous awards and honors for her work, including a James Weldon Johnson Fellowship (Beinecke Library, Yale University), a Bunting Fellowship (Radcliffe Institute for Advanced Study at Harvard University), a National Endowment for the Arts Fellowship, the Richard Wright Literary Excellence Award, Georgia Woman of the Year, the Mississippi Institute of Arts and Letters Poetry Prize, a Bellagio Fellowship from the Rockefeller Foundation, and a Guggenheim Fellowship. She graduated from the University of Georgia, received an MA in English and creative writing from Hollins University (Virginia), and an MFA in poetry from the University of Massachusetts at Amherst. She was born in Gulfport, Mississippi.

Lyrae Van Clief-Stefanon (1971–) is author of *Open Interval* (University of Pittsburgh Press, 2009; nominated for the National Book Award, 2009) and

Black Swan (University of Pittsburgh Press, 2002; winner of the 2001 Cave Canem Poetry Prize). She is co-author (with Elizabeth Alexander) of *Poems in Conversation: and a Conversation. Callaloo, Crab Orchard Review, African American Review,* and *Shenandoah* are some of the journals where she has published her poetry. She is an Assistant Professor of English at Cornell University, where she teaches courses in the creative writing program.

Alice Walker (1944–) was born in Eatonton, Georgia. Although she enjoys a very large audience for her work as a novelist and an essayist, she is also a poet. Her eight books of poems include *Once* (Harcourt Brace, 1968), *Revolutionary Petunias & Other Poems* (Harcourt Brace Jovanovich, 1973; nominated for the National Book Award and the Lillian Smith Award), *Good Night, Willie Lee, I'll See You in the Morning* (Dial, 1979), *Horses Make a Landscape Look More Beautiful* (Harcourt Brace Jovanovich, 1979), *Her Blue Body Everything We Know: Earthling Poems* (Harcourt Brace Jovanovich, 1991), *Absolute Trust in the Goodness of the Earth* (Random House, 2003), *A Poem Traveled Down My Arm: Poems and Drawings* (Random House, 2003), and *Collected Poems* (Phoenix, 2005). *The Third Life of Grange Copeland* (Harcourt Brace, 1970), *In Love and Trouble: Stories of Black Women* (Harcourt Brace Jovanovich, 1973; the Richard and Hinda Rosenthal Foundation Award, American Academy and Institute of Arts and Letters), *Meridian* (Harcourt Brace Jovanovich, 1985), *You Can't Keep a Good Woman Down* (Harcourt Brace Jovanovich, 1981), *The Color Purple* (Harcourt Brace Jovanovich, 1982), *The Temple of My Familiar* (Harcourt Brace Jovanovich, 1989), *In Search of Our Mothers' Gardens: Womanist Prose* (Harcourt Brace, 1983), *Living by the Word: Selected Writings, 1973–1987* (Harcourt Brace Jovanovich, 1988), *Warrior Marks* (Harcourt Brace, 1993), *Anything We Love Can Be Saved: A Writer's Activism* (Random House, 1997), and *We Are the Ones We Have Been Waiting For* (New Press, 2006) are some of her most widely known fiction and nonfiction books. Her novel *The Color Purple*, which won the Pulitzer Prize for fiction and the American Book Award, was later adapted to film by Steven Spielberg. She has received other honors, awards, prizes, and fellowships, including a Guggenheim Foundation fellowship, a DHL degree from the University of Massachusetts, the California Governor's Arts Award, the National Endowment for the Arts, the Langston Hughes Award from the City College of New York, and the Rosenthal Foundation Award from the American Academy and Institute of Arts and Letters, among others. At the beginning of the 1960s, she attended Atlanta's Spelman College, where she began working in the Civil Rights Movement, and in 1964 she transferred to Sarah Lawrence College, from which she graduated in 1965.

Crystal Williams (1970–) graduated cum laude from New York University in 1997, and received an MFA degree in creative writing (poetry) from Cornell University in 2000. She is author of three books of poetry, *Troubled Tongues* (Lotus Press, 2009), *Lunatic* (Michigan State University Press, 2002), and *Kin* (Michigan

State University Press, 2000). Many of her poems have also been published in periodicals and anthologies, including *Efforts and Affections* (University of Iowa Press, 2008), *Callaloo, American Poetry: The Next Generation* (Carnegie Mellon University Press, 2000), *Indiana Review, The American Poetry Review,* and *Short Fuse: The Global Anthology of New Fusion Poetry* (Rattapallax Press, 2002). She is an Associate Professor of creative writing at Reed College.

Sherley Anne Williams (1944–1999) is author of two books of poetry, *The Peacock Poems* (Wesleyan University Press, 1975; nominated for a Pulitzer Prize and a National Book Award) and *Someone Sweet Angel Chile* (William Morrow, 1982). In 1991, her poetic *Letters from a New England Negro,* a one-woman performance, was mounted at the National Black Theater Festival and, in 1992, at the Chicago International Theater Festival. She was probably best known for her novel *Dessa Rose* (Little, Brown, 1986). She also wrote books for children, *Working Cotton* (Harcourt Brace Jovanovich, 1992; winner of an American Library Association Caldecott Award and Coretta Scott King Award) and *Girls Together* (Harcourt Brace, 1999). She studied at the University of California, Howard University, and Brown University. *Give Birth to Brightness: A Thematic Study in Neo-Black Literature* (1972), along with her essays on Zora Neale Hurston, Richard Wright, and Mark Twain, represents her work as an academic. She was a Professor of literature and, from 1977 to 1980, chair of the Department of Literature at the University of California at San Diego. She was born the daughter of migrant workers in Bakersfield, California.

Ronaldo Wilson (1970–) is author of *Narrative of the Life of the Brown Boy and the White Man* (University of Pittsburgh Press, 2008), winner of the 2007 Cave Canem Poetry Prize, and *Poems of the Black Object* (Futurepoem, 2009). He has also published poems in a number of anthologies and periodicals, including *Harvard Review, Black Renaissance Noire, Beyond the Frontier: African-American Poetry for the 21st Century, Fence, Blithe House Quarterly, Gulf Coast, nocturnes (re)view of the literary arts, The Encyclopedia Project, Interim,* and *Callaloo*. A Provincetown Fine Arts Work Center Poetry Fellowship (1999–2000), a Cave Canem Fellowship (1998–2000), a Vermont Studio Center Scholarship (2003), and a Yaddo Residency (2005) are some forms of support he has received for his writing as an artist. A graduate of the University of California at Berkeley, he received an MA from New York University and a PhD from the Graduate Center of the City University of New York. He is a co-founder of the Black Took Collective and teaches at Mount Holyoke College.

Al Young (1939–), Poet Laureate of California (2005–2008), is author of seven volumes of poems, *Dancing* (Corinth Books, 1969), *The Song Turning Back into Itself* (Holt, Rinehart and Winston, 1971), *Geography of the Near Past* (Holt, Rinehart and Winston, 1976), *The Blues Don't Change* (Louisiana State University Press, 1982), *Heaven: Collected Poems 1956–1990* (Creative Arts Books, 1992), *The*

Sound of Dreams Remembered: Poems 1990–2000 (Creative Arts Books, 2006), and *Something About the Blues* (Sourcebooks, 2007). He is also widely known for his novels and books of nonfiction prose on music, including *Sitting Pretty* (Holt, Rinehart and Winston, 1975), *Seduction by Light* (Delacorte, 1988), *Bodies & Soul* (Creative Arts Books, 1981; music memoirs), *Kinds of Blue* (Creative Arts Books, 1984; music memoirs), and *Drowning in the Sea of Love* (Ecco, 1995; music memoirs). *African American Literature: A Brief Introduction and Anthology* (Harper-Collins, 1996), *The Literature of California,* volumes I and II, with Jack Hicks, James D. Houston, and M. H. Kingston (University of California Press, 2000 and 2002), and *Yardbird Lives!,* with Ishmael Reed (Grove, 1972) are three of the anthologies Young has edited. His screenplays and scripts include *Nigger* (1972), *Sparkle* (1972), and *Bustin' Loose* (1979). Young has received numerous awards and honors, including a Wallace Stegner Writing Fellowship (1966), a Guggenheim Fellowship (1974), a Fulbright Fellowship to Yugoslavia (1984), the PEN/ Library of Congress Award for Short Fiction (1991), the Richard Wright Award for Excellence in Literature (2007), and an Honorary Doctorate of Humane Letters degree from Whittier College (2009). Born in Ocean Springs, Mississippi, Young grew up in Detroit and attended the University of Michigan from 1957 to 1960, before moving to California, where he graduated from the University of California in Berkeley with a BA degree in Spanish in 1969.

Kevin Young (1970–), a native of Lincoln, Nebraska, raised on the East Coast and in the Midwest, graduated from Harvard University in 1992 and received an MFA in creative writing from Brown University in 1996. From 1992 to 1994, he was a Stegner Fellow at Stanford University. One of the original members of the Dark Room Collective, Young is author of six books of poems, *Dear Darkness* (Knopf, 2008), *For the Confederate Dead* (Knopf, 2007; winner of the Quill Award in Poetry and the Paterson Poetry Prize for Sustained Literary Achievement), *Black Maria* (Knopf, 2005), *Jelly Roll: A Blues* (Knopf, 2003; winner of the Paterson Poetry Prize, and a finalist for the National Book Award and for the Los Angeles Times Book Prize), *To Repel Ghosts* (Zoland Books, 2001; finalist for the James Laughlin Award), and *Most Way Home* (William Morrow, 1995; a selection for the National Poetry Series and winner of the Zacharis First Book Award). A Guggenheim Fellowship, USA James Baldwin Fellowship, and a MacDowell Colony Fellowship are other acknowledgments of his achievements as a poet. He has also edited five volumes, *Giant Steps: The New Generation of African American Writers* (HarperCollins, 2000), *Blues Poems* (Everyman's Library, 2003), *John Berryman: Selected Poems* (Library of America, 2004), *Jazz Poems* (Everyman's Library, 2006), and *The Art of Losing: Poems of Grief and Healing* (Bloomsbury, 2010). He has also published in such periodicals as *The New Yorker, The Kenyon Review, The New York Times Book Review, Callaloo,* and *Ploughshares.* Young is Atticus Haygood Professor of English and Creative Writing at Emory University, where he is also curator of Literary Collections and the Raymond Danowski Poetry Library.

Permission Credits

Ai: "The Curious Journey of Ulysses Paradeece After a Hurricane," from *Callaloo* 32, no. 1 (2009): 93–96. © 2009 Charles H. Rowell. "Conversation," from *Vice: New and Selected Poems*, by Ai, copyright © 1999 by Ai. Used by permission of W. W. Norton & Company, Inc. "Hoover, Edgar J.," from *Greed* by Ai. Copyright © 1993 by Ai. Used by permission of W. W. Norton & Company, Inc. *Poetics Statement*: Statement for Ai, by Vievee Francis. Copyright © 2011. Used by permission of the author.

Alexander, Elizabeth: "The Venus Hottentot (1825)," "The Blue Whale" and "Boston Year" are copyright in the name of Elizabeth Alexander in 2004, 2005, and 2004, respectively. The material is reprinted with permission of Elizabeth Alexander. *Poetics Statement*: copyright © Elizabeth Alexander. Reprinted by permission of the author.

Baraka, Amiri: "In Memory of Radio," "*An Agony. As Now*," "A Poem for Black Hearts," "Black Art," and "AM/TRAK" reprinted by permission of SLL / Sterling Lord Literistic, Inc. Copyright by Amiri Baraka. *Poetics Statement*: Kimberly W. Benston and Amiri Baraka, "Amiri Baraka: An Interview," in *boundary 2*, 6, no. 2: 303–318. Copyright 1978 Duke University Press. All rights reserved. Reprinted by permission of the publisher.

Barrax, Gerald: "Eagle. Tiger. Whale," from *Leaning Against the Sun* by Gerald Barrax. Copyright © 1992 by Gerald Barrax. Reprinted by permission of the author. "King: April 4, 1968," from *From a Person Sitting in Darkness* by Gerald Barrax. Copyright © 1998 by Gerald Barrax. Reprinted by permission of the author. *Poetics Statement*: Joyce Pettis, "An Interview with Gerald Barrax," *Callaloo* 20, no. 2 (1997): 312–26. © 1997 Charles H. Rowell. Reprinted with permission of the Johns Hopkins University Press.

Brooks, Gwendolyn: "Boy Breaking Glass," reprinted by consent of Brooks Permissions. "An Interview with Gwendolyn Brooks," conducted by Steve Cape, from *Artful Dodge* 1, no. 2 (June 1979). "The Sundays of Satin-Legs Smith," reprinted by consent of Brooks Permissions. "Riot," reprinted by consent of Brooks Permissions. *Poetics Statement*: George Stavros, "Interview with Gwendolyn Brooks." Originally published in *Contemporary Literature* 11, no. 1 (1970): 1–20. © 1970 by the Board of Regents of the University of Wisconsin system. Reproduced by permission of the University of Wisconsin Press.

Brown, Jericho: "Track 1: Lush Life," "Prayer of the Backhanded," "Track 4: Reflection," and "Track 5: Summertime," from *Please* by Jericho Brown. Copyright © 2008. Reprinted with permission from *New Issues Poetry & Prose. Poetics Statement*: by Jericho Brown, unpublished. Copyright © 2010. Printed by permission of the author.

Cassells, Cyrus: "Sally Hemmings to Thomas Jefferson,"*Callaloo* 24, no. 3 (2001): 707–10, copyright © 2001 by Cyrus Cassells. Used by permission of Cyrus Cassells. "The White Iris Beautifies Me,"*Callaloo* 32, no. 1 (2009): 13–14. © 2009 Charles H. Rowell. Reprinted with permission of the Johns Hopkins University Press. "Wild Indigo, Because,"*Callaloo* 32, no. 1 (2009): 12. © 2009 Charles H. Rowell. Reprinted with permission of the Johns Hopkins University Press. *Poetics Statement*: Used by permission of Cyrus Cassells.

Clifton, Lucille: "far memory,"from *The Book of Light*. Copyright © 1993 by Lucille Clifton. Reprinted with the permission of Copper Canyon Press, www.coppercanyonpress.org. "leda 1," "leda 2," and "leda 3," from *The Book of Light*. Copyright © 1993 by Lucille Clifton. Reprinted with the permission of Copper Canyon Press, www.coppercanyonpress.org. "lazarus (first day)," "lazarus (second day)," and "lazarus (third day),"from *Blessing the Boats: New and Selected Poems 1988–2000*. Copyright © 2000 by Lucille Clifton. Reprinted with the permission of BOA Editions, Ltd., www.boaeditions.org. *Poetics Statement*: Charles Rowell, "An Interview with Lucille Clifton," *Callaloo* 22, no. 1 (1999): 56–72. © 1999 Charles H. Rowell. Reprinted with permission of the Johns Hopkins University Press.

Coleman, Wanda: "Bedtime Story" was published by Black Sparrow Press, copyright © 1993 for Wanda Coleman. This poem previously appeared in *The Norton Anthology of African American Literature* (Gates & McKay, eds., 1997) and is reprinted here with permission of the author. "Ars Poetica" was published in *African Sleeping Sickness: Stories and Poems*, Black Sparrow Press, copyright © 1990 for Wanda Coleman. "American Sonnet (17)" was published in *American Sonnets*, Light and Dust Books in cooperation with Woodland Pattern Book Center, copyright © 1994 for Wanda Coleman. This poem previously appeared in *The PIP Anthology of World Poetry of the 20th Century*, Vol. 5: *Intersections*. "American Sonnet (54)" was published in *Bathwater Wine*, Black Sparrow Press, copyright © 1998 for Wanda Coleman. This poem previously appeared in *Callaloo* 19, no. 3 (Summer 1996). *Poetics Statement*: Wanda Coleman.

Collins, Michael Sibble: "Six Sketches: When a Soul Breaks" and "Poetry," from *Callaloo* 25, no. 3, copyright Summer 2003. Reprinted by permission of the author. "Bryan, Texas Procession," from *Callaloo* 27, no. 3, copyright Summer 2004. Reprinted by permission of the author. *Poetics Statement*: Copyright © 2009 by Michael S. Collins. Reprinted by permission of the author.

Cortez, Jayne: "In the Morning" and "Solo Finger Solo" copyright © 2009 by Jayne Cortez. *Poetics Statement*: Copyright © 2010 by Jayne Cortez.

Dargan, Kyle: "Microphone Fiend," from *Ploughshares*, Spring 2006. Copyright © 2006 by Kyle Dargan. Reprinted by permission of the author. "Man of the Family" copyright © Kyle Dargan. Reprinted by permission of the author. "Search for Robert Hayden," from *The Listening*, by Kyle Dargan. Reprinted by permission of the University of Georgia Press. "Palinode, Once Removed," from *Bouquet of Hungers: Poems*, by Kyle Dargan. Reprinted by permission of the University of Georgia Press. *Poetics Statement*: Copyright © Kyle Dargan. Reprinted by permission of the author.

Derricotte, Toi: "Invisible Dreams," from *Tender*, by Toi Derricotte, © 1997. Reprinted by permission of the author and the University of Pittsburgh Press. "The Weakness" and "The Minks," from *Captivity*, by Toi Derricotte, © 1989. Reprinted by permission of the author and the University of Pittsburgh Press. "Holy Cross Hospital," from *Natural Birth*, by Toi Derricotte © 1983. Reprinted with permission of the author. *Poetics Statement*: Reprinted by permission of the author.

Dixon, Melvin: "Paring Potatoes," "Heartbeats," and "Turning Forty in the 90's" appeared first in *Love's Instruments*, © 1995 by the Estate of Melvin Dixon. "Climbing Montmarte" appeared in *Change of Territory* © 1983 by Melvin Dixon. The material is reprinted here, with permission. *Poetics Statement*: Jerome de Romanet and Melvin Dixon, "A Conversation with Melvin Dixon," *Callaloo* 23, no. 1 (2000): 84–109. © 2000 Charles H. Rowell. Reprinted with permission of the Johns Hopkins University Press.

Dove, Rita: "Nestor's Bathtub" and "The Fish in the Stone," from *Museum*, Carnegie Mellon University Press, © 1983 by Rita Dove. "Daystar," from *Thomas and Beulah*, Carnegie Mellon University Press, © 1986 by Rita Dove. "The Bridgetower," from *Sonata Mulattica*, W. W. Norton & Co., © 2009 by Rita Dove. "American Smooth" and "Hattie McDaniel Arrives at the Coconut Grove" from *American Smooth*, W. W. Norton & Co., © 2004 by Rita Dove. "Heroes" and "History," from *Mother Love* by Rita Dove. Copyright © 1995 by Rita Dove. Used by permission of W. W. Norton & Company, Inc. *Poetics Statement*: Charles Rowell, "Interview with Rita Dove," *Callaloo* 31, no. 3 (2008): 695–726. © 2008 Charles H. Rowell. Reprinted with permission of the Johns Hopkins University Press.

Dungy, Camille T.: "What to Eat, and What to Drink, and What to Leave for Poison," "Cleaning," and "To Put Things Right," from *What to Eat, and What to Drink, and What to Leave for Poison,* by Camille Dungy. Copyright © 2006 by Camille Dungy. Reprinted by permission of the author and Red Hen Press. *Poetics Statement*: Copyright © Camille Dungy. Reprinted with permission of the author.

Eady, Cornelius: "Photo of Miles Davis at Lennies-on-the-Turnpike, 1968," from *Autobiography of a Jukebox*, by Cornelius Eady, copyright © 1997 by Cornelius Eady. "Crows in a Strong Wind," from *Victims of the Latest Dance Craze*, by Cornelius Eady, copyright © 1997 by Cornelius Eady. *Poetics Statement*: From "Interview with Cornelius Eady," by Samantha Storey, February 2002, *Organization Newsletter for Seattle Arts and Lectures*. Copyright © 2002.

Ellis, Thomas Sayers: "Mr. Dynamite Splits," reprinted with permission from the April 29, 2007, issue of *The Nation*. "Godzilla's Avocado" and "First Grade, All Over Again" reprinted by permission of the author. "View-Master" by Thomas Sayers Ellis, from *Boston Review*. Copyright © 1995. "Sticks," "Bright Moments," and "All Their Stanzas Look Alike," by Thomas Sayers Ellis, from *The Maverick Room*. Copyright © 2004. Reprinted by permission of the author. Thomas Sayers Ellis, 2010. *Poetics Statement*: Charles Rowell, "A Mixed Congregation: An Interview with Thomas Sayers Ellis," *Callaloo* 27, no. 4 (2004): 884–96. © 2004 Charles H. Rowell. Reprinted with permission of the Johns Hopkins University Press.

Evans, Mari: "I am a Black Woman," by Mari Evans, from *I Am a Black Woman*, published by William Morrow & Co., 1970, by permission of the author. *Poetics Statement*: Excerpt from "My Father's Passage" by Mari Evans from *Black Women Writers (1950–1980): A Critical Evaluation*, edited by Mari Evans. Copyright © 1983 by Mari Evans. Used by permission of Doubleday, a division of Random House, Inc.

Francis, Vievee: "Amarillo," *Callaloo* 32, no. 1 (2008): 114. © 2009 Charles H. Rowell. Reprinted with permission of the Johns Hopkins University Press. "Horse in the Dark," *Callaloo* 32, no. 1 (2008): 111–12. © 2009 Charles H. Rowell. Reprinted with permission of the Johns Hopkins University Press. "Smoke Under the Bale," *Callaloo* 32, no. 1 (2008): 110. © 2009 Charles H. Rowell. Reprinted with permission of the Johns Hopkins University Press. "Still Life with Summer Sausage, a Blade, and No Blood" *Callaloo* 32, no. 1 (2008): 114. © 2009 Charles H. Rowell. *Poetics Statement*: Copyright © Vievee Francis. Reprinted by permission of the author.

Gilbert, Christopher: "Absentee Landlord," from *Ploughshares* 16, no. 1 (Spring), copyright © 1990. "She" and "Touching" from *Across the Mutual Landscape*. Copyright © 1984 by Christopher Gilbert. Reprinted with the permission of Graywolf Press, Minneapolis, Minnesota, www.graywolfpress.org. *Poetics Statement*: from James Zeigler, "An Interview with Christopher Gilbert," *Worcester Review* 17, no. 1 and 2. Copyright © Spring 1996.

Giovanni, Nikki: "Nikki Rosa," from *Black Feeling, Black Talk, Black Judgement*, by Nikki Giovanni. Copyright © 1968, 1970 by Nikki Giovanni. Reprinted by permission of HarperCollins Publishers (William Morrow). "Ego Tripping (there may be a reason why)," from *Ego-Tripping and Other Poems for Young People*, © 1973, 1993 by Nikki Giovanni. Used with permission of Lawrence Hill Books. *Poetics Statement*: By permission of authors. Virginia C. Fowler and Nikki Giovanni, © 1992.

Giscombe, C. S.: "The Northernmost Road," from *Giscome Road* by C. S. Giscombe, copyright © 1998. Reprinted by permission of Dalkey Archive Press. "The 1200N Road, Going East," from *Prairie Style* by C. S. Giscombe, copyright © 2008. Reprinted by permission of Dalkey Archive Press. *Poetics Statement*: Copyright © 2010 by C. S. Giscombe.

Gomez, Jewelle: "My Chakabuku Mama: a comic tale," *Callaloo* 23, no. 1 (2000): 214–15. © 2000 Charles H. Rowell. Reprinted with permission of the Johns Hopkins University Press. "El Beso," *Callaloo* 23, no. 1 (2000): 212–13. © 2000 Charles H. Rowell.

Reprinted with permission of the Johns Hopkins University Press. *Poetics Statement*: Copyright © Jewelle Gomez.

Hairston, Alena: "[The tyranny of pig boys]," "[The fathers worked their hands to meat]," "[Edges in the rhododendron]," "[Their greatgreatgranddaddies]," "[Daughters of four generations]," and "[Because we love wrong]," from *The Logan Topographies* by Alena Hairston. Copyright © 2007 by Alena Hairston. Reprinted by permission of Persea Books, Inc., New York. *Poetics Statement*: Copyright © Alena Hairston. Reprinted by permission of the author.

Hamer, Forrest: *from* Goldsboro narrative, #4, #7, #28, from *Callaloo* 22, no. 1, copyright 1999 © Forrest Hamer. Reprinted by permission of the author. "In the Middle," *Callaloo* 27, no. 4, copyright 2004. © Forrest Hamer. Reprinted by permission of the author. "Lesson," from *Call & Response*, copyright © 1995 by Forrest Hamer. Reprinted by permission of the author. *Poetics Statement*: © Forrest Hamer. Reprinted by permission of the author.

Hamilton, Bobb: "Poem to a Nigger Cop," by Bobb Hamilton, from *Black Fire*. Copyright © 1968 by Bobb Hamilton. Reprinted by permission of the author. *Poetics Statement*: Excerpt from *For Malcolm: Poems on the Life and the Death of Malcolm X* (Broadside Press, 1967). Reprinted by permission of Broadside Press.

Hamilton, Kendra: "The Science of Wearing a Dress," from *The Goddess of Gumbo*, copyright © 2006. "Belle's Promenade: Nassau Street, Princeton" Copyright © by Kendra Hamilton. Unpublished. Used by permission of the author. *Poetics Statement*: Copyright © by Kendra Hamilton. Unpublished. Used by permission of the author.

Hardy, Myronn: "Undertones" by Myronn Hardy from *Ploughshares*, Spring 2005. Copyright © 2005 by Myronn Hardy. Reprinted by permission of the author. "On a Beach: My Life" and "The Headless Saints" from *The Headless Saints*, copyright © 2008 by Myronn Hardy. Reprinted by permission of the author. "Making Stars with Jacob Lawrence," by Myronn Hardy, from *FIELD: Contemporary Poetry and Poetics*, no. 79 (Fall 2008). Oberlin College Press, Oberlin, OH. Copyright © 2008 by Myronn Hardy. Reprinted by permission of the author. *Poetics Statement*: Copyright © Myronn Hardy. Reprinted by permission of the author.

Harper, Michael S.: "The Yellow Dishes," "Coliseum Pool, 1960 (Dream)," and "Don't Explain: A Ballad Played by Dexter Gordon" copyright © 2009 by Michael Harper, used by permission of the author. "Yaddo, Mrs. Ames & Black Men" from *Use Trouble*. Copyright 2009 by Michael S. Harper. Used with permission of the poet and the University of Illinois Press. *Poetics Statement*: from *Songlines in Michaeltree: New and Collected Poems*. Copyright 2000 by Michael S. Harper. Used with permission of the University of Illinois Press.

Harrington, Janice N.: "The Warning Comes Down" and "Falling" from *Even the Hollow My Body Made Is Gone*. Copyright © 2007 by Janice N. Harrington. Reprinted with the permission of BOA Editions Ltd., www.boaeditions.org. "Fire" copyright

© 2010 by Janice Harrington. Used by permission of the author. *Poetics Statement*: Copyright © Janice Harrington. Reprinted by permission of the author.

Hayden, Robert: "For a Young Artist" copyright © 1975 by Robert Hayden, "Elegies for Paradise Valley" copyright © 1978 by Robert Hayden, "A Letter from Phillis Wheatley" copyright © 1978 by Robert Hayden, from *Collected Poems of Robert Hayden* by Robert Hayden, edited by Frederick Glaysher. Used by permission of Liveright Publishing Corporation. *Poetics Statement*: from *Interviews with Black Writers*, by John O'Brien, editor. Copyright © 1973 by Liveright Publishing Corporation. Used by permission of Liveright Publishing Corporation.

Hayes, Terrance: "Touch," from *Hip Logic* by Terrance Hayes, edited by Cornelius Eady, copyright © 2002 by Terrance Hayes. Used by permission of Penguin, a division of Penguin Group (USA) Inc. "Wind in a Box," from *Wind in a Box* by Terrance Hayes, copyright © 2006 by Terrance Hayes. Used by permission of Penguin, a division of Penguin Group (USA) Inc. "What I Am," "At Pegasus," and "Derrick Poem (The Lost World)" from *Muscular Music* by Terrance Hayes, published by Tia Chucha Press. Copyright © 1999 by Terrance Hayes. All rights reserved. Reprinted by permission of the author. *Poetics Statement*: Charles Rowell, " 'The Poet in the Enchanted Shoe Factory': An Interview with Terrance Hayes," *Callaloo* 27, no. 4 (2004): 1068–81. © 2004 Charles H. Rowell. Reprinted with permission of the Johns Hopkins University Press.

Henderson, David: "Downtown-Boy Uptown," by David Henderson, from *Felix of the Silent Forest*, copyright © 1967 by David Henderson. All rights reserved. Reprinted by permission of the author. *Poetics Statement*: © 2010 David Henderson. All rights reserved.

Hernton, Calvin C.: "The Distant Drum," excerpted from *Medicine Man* by Calvin Hernton. Copyright © 1976 by Reed, Cannon and Johnson Publications. Permission granted by Lowenstein Associates, Inc. *Poetics Statement*: Excerpt from *Medicine Man* (Reed, Cannon & Johnson, 1976). Copyright © 1976 by Calvin C. Hernton. Reprinted by permission of Ishmael Reed.

Jackson, Angela: "Two Trains," *from* Suite: Ida. *Callaloo* 31, no. 4 (2008), 1206–8. © 2008 Charles H. Rowell. Reprinted with permission of the Johns Hopkins University Press. "Ida Rewrites," *Callaloo* 31, no. 4. Copyright © Fall 2008. "The Love of Travellers (Doris, Sandra and Sheryl)," *Callaloo* 35 (1988): 211. © 1988 The Johns Hopkins University Press. Reprinted with permission of the Johns Hopkins University Press. *Poetics Statement*: Copyright © Angela Jackson. "Why I Must Make Language," from *And All These Roads Be Luminous* by Angela Jackson. © 1998 Northwestern University Press.

Jackson, Major: "Some Kind of Crazy" and "Don Pullen at the Zanzibar Blue Jazz Café," from *Leaving Saturn*, by Major Jackson. Reprinted by permission of the University of Georgia Press. "viii: Block Party," from *Leaving Saturn* by Major Jackson. Reprinted by permission of the University of Georgia Press. "Urban Renewal xvi.," from *Hoops* by Major Jackson. Copyright © 2006 by Major Jackson. Used by permission of W. W. Norton & Company, Inc. *Poetics Statement*: Excerpt from Jason Olsen, "Interview with Major Jackson," *Third Coast Nineteen* (University of Michigan Press, Fall 2004). Copyright © 2004 by Jason Olsen. Reprinted by permission of Jason Olsen.

Jeffers, Honorée Fanonne: "Fast Skirt Blues," "Hagar to Sarai," and "The Wife of Lot Before the Fire" from *Outlandish Blues* © 2003 by Honorée Fanonne Jeffers and reprinted by permission of Wesleyan University Press. "The Gospel of Barbecue," by Honorée Fanonne Jeffers, from *The Gospel of Barbecue* © 2000. Reprinted with permission of the Kent State University Press. *Poetics Statement*: by Honorée Fanonne Jeffers. Copyright © 2010.

Jess, Tyehimba: "blind lemon taught me," "leadbelly sings to his #1 crew," "martha promise receives leadbelly, 1935," and "mistress stella speaks," from *leadbelly*, copyright © 2005 by Tyhimba Jess. Published by Verse Press. Reprinted with permission of Wave Books and the author. *Poetics Statement*: Copyright © Tyehimba Jess. Reprinted by permission of the author.

Jones, Gayl: "Deep Song," from *The Vintage Book of African American Poetry*, copyright © 2000. Reprinted by permission of the author. "Foxes," *Callaloo*, no. 20, copyright © 1984. Reprinted by permission of the author. "Composition with Guitar and Apples," *Callaloo*, no. 16, copyright © 1982. Reprinted by permission of the author. *Poetics Statement*: Charles H. Rowell, "An Interview with Gayl Jones," *Callaloo* 16 (1982): 32–35. ©1982 The Johns Hoplins University Press. Reprinted with permission of the Johns Hopkins University Press.

Jones, Patricia Spears: "Thanksgiving," published in *Femme du Monde* by Tia Chucha Press, Sylmar, CA. Copyright © 2006 by Patricia Spears Jones. Reprinted by permission of the author. "Wearing My Red Silk Chinese Jacket," from *Callaloo* 11, no 13 (1981). *Poetics Statement*: Copyright © July 2009 by Patricia Spears Jones. Reprinted by permission of the author.

Jordan, A. Van: "Regina Brown Hears Voices, Kills Son Week Before Christmas, December 18, 1996," from *Callaloo* 27, no 4 (2004). Reprinted by permission of A. Van Jordan. "from," from *M-A-C-N-O-L-I-A: Poems*, by A. Van Jordan. Copyright © 2004 by A. Van Jordan. Used by permission of W. W. Norton & Company, Inc. "The Flash Reverses Time" and "Black Light," from *Quantum Lyrics*, by A. Van Jordan. Copyright © 2007 by A. Van Jordan. Used by permission of W. W. Norton & Company, Inc. *from* Thought Clouds by A. Van Jordan. Copyright © A. Van Jordan. Printed with permission. *Poetics Statement*: Jake Silverstein. "Writing a Poem: An Interview with A. Van Jordan," excerpt from *Texas Monthly* (June 2008). Reprinted with permission from the June 2008 issue of *Texas Monthly*.

Jordan, June: "What Would I Do White?," "Current Events," "Adrienne's Poem: On the Dialectics of the Diatonic Scale," from *Directed by Desire: The Collected Poems of June Jordan*. Copyright © 2005 June Jordan Literary Estate trust; reprinted by permission of the June M. Jordan Literary Estate Trust, and Copper Canyon Press. www.june jordan.com. Copyright © 2005 June Jordan Literary Estate Trust. *Poetics Statement*: Julie Quiroz-Martinez, "Poetry Is a Political Act." Originally published in *ColorLines* (1998). © 1998. Reprinted with permission of *ColorLines*.

Kaufman, Bob: "African Dream," "Battle Report," "I Have Folded My Sorrows," "Jail Poems," and "Walking Parker Home," from *Solitudes Crowded with Loneliness*, copyright © 1965 by Bob Kaufman. Reprinted by permission of New Directions Publish-

ing Corp. *Poetics Statement*: Robert Kaufman, from *The Ancient Rain*, copyright ©
1981 by Bob Kaufman. Reprinted by permission of New Directions Publishing Corp.

Knight, Etheridge: "The Violent Space (or when your sister sleeps around for
money)," "The Idea of Ancestry," "Hard Rock Returns to Prison from the Hospital for
the Criminal Insane," and "Belly Song" from *The Essential Etheridge Knight*, by Ether-
idge Knight, © 1986. Reprinted by permission of the University of Pittsburgh. *Poet-
ics Statement*: Charles Rowell, "An Interview with Etheridge Knight," *Callaloo* 19, no.
4 (1998): 967–80. © 1998 Charles H. Rowell. Reprinted with permission of the Johns
Hopkins University Press.

Kocher, Ruth Ellen: "Meditation on Breathing" from *One Girl Babylon* by Ruth Ellen
Kocher. © 2003 Reprinted by permission of *New Issues Poetry & Prose*. "The Window
Cleaner Writes to the Astronaut's Husband," *Callaloo* 27, no. 4 (2004): 947. © 2004
Charles H. Rowell. Reprinted with permission of the Johns Hopkins University
Press. "gigan 63" from the manuscript "55 gigans and 5 notes" by Ruth Ellen Kocher.
Reprinted by permission of the author. *Poetics Statement*: Ruth Ellen Kocher. Copy-
right © 2010 by Ruth Ellen Kocher. Used by permission of Ruth Ellen Kocher.

Komunyakaa, Yusef: "Venus's-flytraps" and "My Father's Love Letters" from *Magic
City*, " 'You and I are Disappearing' " and "Facing It" from *Neon Vernacular*, and "Poet-
ics," and "Blue Light Lounge Sutra for the Performance Poets at Harold Park Hotel,"
from *Pleasure Dome* © 1992, 1993, and 2004 by Yusef Komunyakaa and reprinted
by permission of Wesleyan University Press. "Requiem," *Callaloo* 31, no. 2 (2008):
484–85. © 2008 Charles H. Rowell. Reprinted with permission of the Johns Hopkins
University Press. "Lingo" from *Taboo: The Wishbone Trilogy, Part One*, by Yusef Komu-
nyakaa. Copyright © 2004 by Yusef Komunyakaa. "[The jawbone of an ass. A shank]"
and "The Devil Comes on Horseback" from *Warhorses* by Yusef Komunyakaa. Copy-
right © 2008 by Yusef Komunyakaa. *Poetics Statement*: Copyright © Yusef Komun-
yakaa. Reprinted by permission of the author.

Lorde, Audre: "Fishing the White Water" copyright © 1986 by Audre Lorde. Copy-
right © 1997 by The Audre Lorde Estate. "To My Daughter The Junkie On A Train"
copyright © 1974 by Audre Lorde. Copyright © 1997 by the Estate of Audre Lorde.
"Coal" copyright © 1968, 1970, 1973 by Audre Lorde. Copyright © 1997 by The Audre
Lorde Estate. From *The Collected Poems of Audre Lorde* by Audre Lorde. Used by
permission of W. W. Norton & Company, Inc. *Poetics Statement*: Charles H. Rowell,
"Above the Wind: An Interview with Audre Lorde," *Callaloo* 23, no. 1 (2000): 52–63. ©
2000 Charles H. Rowell. Reprinted with permission of the Johns Hopkins University
Press.

Mackey, Nathaniel: "Glenn on Monk's Mountain," from *Splay Anthem*, copyright ©
2002, 2006 by Nathaniel Mackey. Reprinted by permission of New Directions Pub-
lishing Corp. "Song of the Andoumboulou: 16" © 1998 by Nathaniel Mackey, reprinted
by permission of City Lights Books. "Sound and Severance," *Callaloo* 31, no. 3 (2008):
876–79. © 2008 Charles H. Rowell. Reprinted with permission of the Johns Hopkins
University Press. *Poetics Statement*: Charles Rowell, "An Interview with Nathaniel
Mackey," *Callaloo* 23, no. 2 (2000): 703–15. © 2000 Charles H. Rowell. Reprinted with
permission of the Johns Hopkins University Press.

Madhubuti, Haki: "But He Was Cool, or: he even stopped for green lights," from *Don't Cry, Scream*, copyright 1969, by Haki R. Madhubuti, reprinted by permission of Third World Press, Inc., Chicago, Illinois. *Poetics Statement*: From *The Art of Work*, copyright © 2007, by Haki R. Madhubuti, reprinted by permission of Third World Press, Inc., Chicago, Illinois.

Major, Clarence: "The Great Horned Owl" and "Clay Bison in a Cave" from *Configurations: New and Selected Poems 1958–1998*. Copyright © 1998 by Clarence Major. Reprinted with the permission of Coffee House Press, www.coffeehousepress.com. "On Watching a Caterpillar Become a Butterfly," and "Territorial Claims" copyright © 1994 by Clarence Major, copyright © 1996 by Clarence Major. *Poetics Statement*: Charles Rowell, "An Interview with Clarence Major," *Callaloo* 20, no. 3 (1998): 667–78. © 1998 Charles H. Rowell. Reprinted with permission of the Johns Hopkins University Press.

Martin, Dawn Lundy: Excerpts from "Discipline" copyright © 2010 Dawn Lundy Martin. Reprinted by permission of the author. "The Symbolic Nature of Chaos," "Negrotizing in Five or How to Write a Black Poem," and "The Undress," from *A Gathering of Matter / A Matter of Gathering* by Dawn Lundy Martin, copyright © 2007 Dawn Lundy Martin. Reprinted by permission of the University of Georgia Press. *Poetics Statement*: Copyright © 2010 Dawn Lundy Martin. Reprinted by permission of the author.

McElroy, Colleen J.: "Paris Subway Tango," from *Ploughshares*, Spring 1993, copyright © 1993. Reprinted by permission of the author. "Crossing the Rubicon at Seventy," from *Ploughshares*, Winter 2007–08, copyright © 2008. Reprinted by permission of the author. *Poetics Statement*: Reprinted by permission of the author.

Merritt, Constance: "The Mute Swan," "Woman of Color," and "Self-Portrait: Lilith, Eve" from *A Protocol for Touch*, University of North Texas Press, 2000. © 1999 Constance Merritt. "Lying," from *Two Rooms*, Louisiana State University Press, 2009. Copyright © 2009 by Constance Merritt. Reprinted by permission of Louisiana State University Press. *Poetics Statement*: Constance Merritt, *A Protocol for Touch*, University of North Texas Press, 2000. © 1999 Constance Merritt.

Moss, Thylias: "The Culture of Near Miss," from *Tokyo Butter*, by Thylias Moss. Copyright © 2006 by Thylias Moss. Reprinted by permission of Persea Books, Inc., New York. "Me and Bubble went to Memphis.," copyright © Thylias Moss. "The Day Before Kindergarten: Taluca, Alabama, 1959," "*Timex* Remembered," and "One for All Newborns" from *Small Congregations: New and Selected Poems* by Thylias Moss. Copyright © 1983, 1990, 1991, 1993 by Thylias Moss. Reprinted by permission of HarperCollins Publishers. *Poetics Statement*: Copyright © Thylias Moss.

Moten, Fred: "metoika" from *Hughson's Tavern*, published by Leon Works, 2008. "gayl jones," "johnny cash / rosetta tharp," "elizabeth cotten / nahum chandler," and "frank ramsay / nancy wilson" from *B Jenkins*, by Fred Moten. Copyright, 2010 Duke University Press. All rights reserved. Used by permission of the publisher. *Poetics Statement*: Charles Rowell, " 'Words Don't Go There': An Interview with Fred Moten," *Callaloo* 27, no. 4 (2004): 954–66. © 2004 Charles H. Rowell. Reprinted with permission of the Johns Hopkins University Press.

Mullen, Harryette: "All She Wrote" and "Black Nikes," from *Sleeping with the Dictionary*, by Harryette Mullen, © 2002 by the Regents of the University of California. Published by the University of California Press. Reprinted by permission of the University of California Press. "Unspoken," *Callaloo* 27 (1986): 345–46. © 1986 The Johns Hopkins University Press. Reprinted with permission of the Johns Hopkins University Press. "[if your complexion is a mess]" and "[Of a girl, in white]," excerpts from *Recyclopedia: Trimmings, S*PeRM**T, and Muse & Drudge*. Copyright © 1991, 1995, 2006 by Harryette Mullen. Reprinted with the permission of Graywolf Press, Minneapolis, Minnesota, www.graywolfpress.org. *Poetics Statement*: Calvin Bedient, "The Solo Mysterioso Blues: An Interview with Harryette Mullen," *Callaloo* 19, no. 3 (1996): 651–69. © 1996 The Johns Hopkins University Press. Reprinted with permission of the Johns Hopkins University Press.

Murillo, John: "Sherman Ave. Love Poem," "Enter the Dragon," and "Practicing Fade-Aways" from *Up Jump the Boogie*, Cypher Books, 2010. *Poetics Statement*: Copyright © John Murillo. Reprinted by permission of the author.

Neal, Larry: "Malcolm X—An Autobiography," from *Black Fire*, copyright 1968, by Larry Neal, reprinted by permission of Evelyn Neal. *Poetics Statement*: Joyce Pettis, "An Interview with Larry Neal," *Callaloo* 23 (1985): 11–35. © 1985 Charles H. Rowell. Reprinted with permission of the Johns Hopkins University Press. Larry Neal, "The Black Arts Movement," *The Drama Review*, 12, no. 4 (T40-Summer 1968): 29–39. © 1968 by *The Drama Review*.

Nelson, Marilyn: "Mama's Promise," from *Mama's Promises*. "Daughters, 1990," from *The Home Place*. Copyright © Louisiana State University Press. *Poetics Statement*: Excerpt from Leslie McGrath, "Like Water Remembering Light: An Interview with Marilyn Nelson," *Writers Chronicle* (September 2009). Reprinted by permission of Leslie McGrath.

Pardlo, Gregory: "Double Dutch," from *Totem*, by Gregory Pardlo, copyright © 2007 by Gregory Pardlo. Reprinted by permission of the author. "Copyright," "Shades of Green: Envy and Enmity in the American Cultural Imaginary," "Four Improvisations on Ursa Corregidora," and "Written by Himself" copyright © Gregory Pardlo. Reprinted by permission of the author. *Poetics Statement*: Copyright © Gregory Pardlo. Reprinted by permission of the author.

Phillips, Carl: "X," from *In the Blood*, by Carl Phillips. © University Press of New England, Lebanon, NH. Reprinted with permission. "Leda, After the Swan," from *In the Blood*, by Carl Phillips. © University Press of New England, Lebanon, NH. Reprinted with permission. "Civilization," from *The New Yorker*, March 23, 2009. Copyright © 2009 by Carl Phillips. Reprinted by permission of the author. "Blue," by permission of author. "Fretwork," from *Rock Harbor*, by Carl Phillips. Copyright © 2002 by Carl Phillips. "Speak Low," from *Speak Low*, by Carl Phillips. Copyright © 2009 by Carl Phillips. "As from a Quiver of Arrows," from *Quiver of Arrows: Selected Poems 1986–2006*, by Carl Phillips. Copyright © 2007 by Carl Phillips. *Poetics Statement*: First appeared in *Pleiades: A Journal of New Writing*. Reprinted by permission of Pleiades Press.

Reed, Ishmael: "I Am a Cowboy in the Boat of Ra," excerpted from *New and Collected Poems*, copyright © 1988 Ishmael Reed. Permission granted by Lowenstein Associates, Inc. "The Pope Replies to the Ayatollah Khomeini," excerpted from *New and Collected Poems*, copyright © 1988 Ishmael Reed. Permission granted by Lowenstein Associates, Inc. *Poetics Statement*: From *Interviews with Black Writers*, by John O'Brien, editor. Copyright © 1973 by Liveright Publishing Corporation. Used by permission of Liveright Publishing Corporation.

Roberson, Ed: "Sit In What City We're In," from *City Eclogue*, copyright © 2006. Reprinted by permission of the author. "Ecologue," from *City Eclogue*, copyright © 2006. Reprinted by permission of the author. *Poetics Statement*: From an interview, www.chicagopostmodernpoetry.com, "Poetic Profile: Ed Roberson." Reprinted by permission of the author.

Rodgers, Carolyn: "how i got ovah," from *How I Got Ovah*, copyright © 1968, 1969, 1970, 1971, 1972, 1973, 1975, by Carolyn M. Rodgers. Used by permission of the author and Doubleday, a division of Random House, Inc. "Breakthrough," from *Songs of a Blackbird*, copyright 1969 by Carolyn Rodgers, reprinted by permission of the author. *Poetics Statement*: *Black Women Writers (1950–1980): A Critical Evaluation*, edited by Mari Evans. Copyright © 1983 by Mari Evans. Used by permission of Doubleday, a division of Random House, Inc.

Sanchez, Sonia: "Towhomitmayconcern," from *Under a Soprano Sky*, with the permission of Africa World Press. "Poem No. 3," from *Shake Loose My Skin: New and Selected Poems*. Copyright © 1999 by Sonia Sanchez. Reprinted by permission of Beacon Press, Boston. "Homecoming," "Malcolm," "blk / rhetoric," and "A Poem for My Father." By permission of Broadside Press. *Poetics Statement*: Excerpt from Sonia Sanchez, "Ruminations/Reflections," from *Black Women Writers (1950–1980): A Critical Evaluation*, edited by Mari Evans. Copyright © 1983 by Mari Evans. Used by permission of Doubleday, a division of Random House, Inc.

Shange, Ntozake: "My Father is a Retired Magician," from *Nappy Edges* (St. Martin's Press, 1983). Reprinted by the permission of Russell & Volkening as agents for the author and St. Martin's Press. Copyright © 1983 by Ntozake Shange "nappy edges (a cross country sojourn)" from *Nappy Edges* (St. Martin's Press, 1983). Reprinted by the permission of Russell & Volkening as agents for the author and St. Martin's Press. Copyright © 1983 by Ntozake Shange. *Poetics Statement*: From Henry Blackwell, "An Interview with Ntozake Shange," *Black American Literature Forum* 13, no. 4: 134–38. Copyright © Winter 1979.

Shepherd, Reginald: "Skin Trade," from *Angel, Interrupted*, by Reginald Shepherd, © 1996. Reprinted by permission of the University of Pittsburgh Press. "Icarus on Fire Island," from *Wrong*, by Reginald Shepherd, © 1999. Reprinted by permission of the University of Pittsburgh Press. "Orpheus Plays the Bronx," "How People Disappear," and "Homeric Interim" from *Fata Morgana*, by Reginald Shepherd, © 2007. Reprinted by permission of the University of Pittsburgh Press. *Poetics Statement*: Charles H. Rowell, "An Interview with Reginald Shepherd," *Callaloo* 21, no. 2 (1998): 290–307. © 1998 Charles H. Rowell. Reprinted with permission of the Johns Hopkins University Press.

singleton, giovanni: "Day 33," "Day 36," "Day 41," and "Day 48," from *ascension*, copyright © giovanni singleton. "el corazón—toward an ars poetica," from *Alehouse*, 1999. Reprinted by permission of giovanni singleton. Reprinted by permission of the author. *Poetics Statement*: Copyright © 2009 giovanni singleton. Reprinted by permission of the author.

Smith, Patricia: "Prologue—And Then She Owns You," "She Sees What It Sees," "Up on the Roof," and "Don't Drink the Water," from *Blood Dazzler*. Copyright © 2008 by Patricia Smith. Reprinted with the permission of Coffee House Press, www.coffee housepress.com. *Poetics Statement*: Unpublished. © 2010 by Patricia Smith. Used by permission of the author.

Smith, Tracy K.: "Drought" and "Self-Portrait As the Letter Y" from *The Body's Question*. Copyright © 2003 by Tracy K. Smith. "Theft," "When Zappa Crashes My Family Reunion," "The Nobodies," and "Duende" from *Duende*. Copyright © 2007 by Tracy K. Smith. Reprinted with the permission of Graywolf Press, Minneapolis, Minnesota, www.graywolfpress.org. *Poetics Statement*: Used by permission of the author.

Spellman, A. B.: "I Looked & Saw History Caught," reprinted by permission of the author. *Poetics Statement*: Statement by A. B. Spellman. Copyright © by 2010 A. B. Spellman. Used by permission of A. B. Spellman.

Spriggs, Edward S.: "For Brother Malcolm," from *For Malcolm*, by Edward S. Spriggs, copyright © 1969 by Edward S. Spriggs. Reprinted by permission of the author. *Poetics Statement*: Statement by Edward Spriggs. Copyright © 2010 by Edward Spriggs. Used by permission of Edward Spriggs.

St. John, Primus: "The Cigar Maker," "Catch and Release," and "Trap a Congo," by Primus St. John. Reprinted by permission of the author. *Poetics Statement*: Reprinted by permission of the author.

Strange, Sharan: "Childhood," "Froggy's Class," and "Last Supper" published in *Ash* (Beacon Press, 2001). Reprinted by permission of Beacon Press, Boston. *Poetics Statement*: Unpublished poetics statement, by Sharan Strange. Copyright © 2010. Printed by permission of the author.

Thomas, Amber Flora: "Chore" and "Dress" from *Eye of Water: Poems*, by Amber Flora Thomas, © 2005. Reprinted by permission of the University of Pittsburgh Press. "Swarm" and "The Killed Rabbit" Copyright © Amber Flora Thomas. Reprinted by permission of the author. *Poetics Statement*: Copyright © Amber Flora Thomas. Reprinted by permission of the author.

Thomas, Lorenzo: "Onion Bucket," from *Black Fire*, copyright © 1968. Reprinted by permission of Aldon L. Nielsen, Literary Executor for Lorenzo Thomas. "Downtown Boom," from *Time Step*, copyright © 2004. Reprinted by permission of Aldon L. Nielsen, Literary Executor for Lorenzo Thomas. *Poetics Statement*: Charles H. Rowell, " 'Between the Comedy of Matters and the Ritual Workings of Man': An Interview with Lorenzo Thomas," *Callaloo* 11, no. 13 (1981): 19–35. © 1981 The Johns Hopkins University Press. Reprinted with permission of the Johns Hopkins University Press.

Tolson, Melvin B.: *from* "Harlem Gallery" and "Chi," from *"Harlem Gallery" and Other Poems of Melvin B. Tolson*, edited by Raymond Nelson, pp.335–41. © 1999 by the Rector and Visitors of the University of Virginia. Reprinted by permission of the University of Virginia Press. *Poetics Statement*: Excerpt from Joy Flasch, *Melvin B. Tolson*, (Twayne Publishers, 1972).

Trethewey, Natasha: "Incident," "Pastoral," "Elegy for the Native Guards," and "Myth," from *Native Guards: Poems*, by Natasha Trethewey. Copyright © 2006 by Natasha Trethewey. Reprinted by permission of Houghton Mifflin Harcourt Publishing Company. All rights reserved. "Letter Home" and "Bellocq's Ophelia," from *Bellocq's Ophelia*. Copyright © 2002 by Natasha Trethewey. "Limen" and "Flounder," from *Domestic Work*. Copyright © 1994, 2000 by Natasha Trethewey. All reprinted with the permission of Graywolf Press, Minneapolis, Minnesota, www.graywolf press.org. *Poetics Statement*: Published in *The New Young American Poets*, edited by Kevin Prufer © 2000 by the Board of Trustees, Southern Illinois University; reprinted by permission of Southern Illinois University Press.

Van Clief-Stefanon, Lyrae: "Lost," "Garden," and "Bop: The North Star," from *Open Interval*, by Lyrae Van Clief-Stefanon, © 2009. Reprinted by permission of the University of Pittsburgh Press. *Poetics Statement*: "To Renovate the House of Living Words," copyright © Lyrae Van Clief-Stefanon. Reprinted by permission of the author.

Walker, Alice: "Revolutionary Petunias," from *Revolutionary Petunias & Other Poems*, copyright © 1972 by Alice Walker, reprinted by permission of Houghton Mifflin Harcourt Publishing Company and the Wendy Weil Agency. "On Stripping Bark from Myself," copyright © 1977 by Alice Walker (first appeared in *American Poetry Review*), from *Good Night Willie Lee, I'll See You in the Morning*, by Alice Walker. Used by permission of Doubleday, a division of Random House, Inc. *Poetics Statement*: "Alice Walker: An Interview," *Interviews with Black Writers*, edited by John O'Brien. Reprinted by permission of the Wendy Weil Agency, Inc. First published by Liveright Publishing Corporation © 1973 by Alice Walker.

Williams, Crystal: "This Parable, This Body" and "Extinction" copyright © Crystal A. Williams, 2009. "Enlightenment" copyright © Crystal A. Williams, 2010. All unpublished. Reprinted by permission of the author. *Poetics Statement*: Statement by Crystal Williams. Copyright © 2010 by Crystal Williams. Used by permission of Crystal Williams.

Williams, Sherley Anne: from *Letters from a New England Negro*: "Mrs. Josiah Harris / August 25, 1867," "Miss Ann Spencer / August 30, 1867," "/ October 22, 1867," "/ November 24, 1867," "/ February 15, 1868," copyright © 1982 by Sherley Anne Williams. First appeared in *Some One Sweet Angel Chile*. Reprinted by permission of the Sandra Dijkstra Literary Agency. *Poetics Statement*: Sherley Anne Williams, "*from* Meditations on History (1980)," *Callaloo* 22, no. 4 (1999): 786–70 © Charles H. Rowell. Reprinted with permission of the Johns Hopkins University Press.

Wilson, Ronaldo: "Serena Williams, Whiteness, and the Act of Writing" and "Brad Pitt, Kevin Bacon, and the Brown Boy's Mother," from *Narrative of the Life of the Brown Boy and the White Man*, by Ronaldo V. Wilson, © 2008. Reprinted by permission of the University of Pittsburgh. "On the C Train the Black Object Ponders Amuzati's Family Eaten in the Congo," from *Callaloo* 27, no. 4. Copyright © Ronaldo Wilson, 2004. *Poetics Statement*: Copyright © Ronaldo Wilson. Reprinted by permission of the author.

Young, Al: "The Song Turning Back Into Itself 3," from *The Song Turning Back Into Itself*, by Al Young. Copyright © 1971, 1992, by Al Young. Reprinted by permission of the author. "A Dance for Ma Rainey," from *Something About the Blues* (2007), by Al Young. Copyright © 1969, 1992, 2007, by Al Young. Reprinted by permission of the author. "Ravel: Bolero," from *Straight No Chaser*, by Al Young. Copyright © 1994, 2007, by Al Young. Reprinted by permission of the author. *Poetics Statement*: From *Interviews with Black Writers*, by John O'Brien, editor. Copyright © 1973 by Liveright Publishing Corporation. Used by permission of Liveright Publishing Corporation.

Young, Kevin: "The Game," from *Black Maria*, by Kevin Young, copyright © 2005 by Kevin Young. Used by permission of Alfred A. Knopf, a division of Random House, Inc. "For the Confederate Dead," from *For the Confederate Dead*, by Kevin Young, copyright © 2007 by Kevin Young. Used by permission of Alfred A. Knopf, a division of Random House, Inc. "Letters from the North Star" and "Eddie Priest's Barbershop & Notary" from *Most Way Home*, by Kevin Young. Published by Zoland Books, an imprint of Steerforth Press. Reprinted by permission of Steerforth Press. "Crowning" copyright © 2010 by Kevin Young, reprinted by permission of the author. All rights reserved. *Poetics Statement*: Charles Rowell, "An Interview with Kevin Young," *Callaloo* 21, no. 1 (1998): 43–54. © 1998 Charles H. Rowell. Reprinted with permission of the Johns Hopkins University Press.

Acknowledgments

An editor is seldom, if ever, alone in the making of an anthology. While it may not always be a group effort, it certainly requires support and assistance—and, sometimes, encouragement from family, friends, and colleagues. Such has been my experience at Texas A&M University in College Station. Janis P. Stout, Karan Watson, and Shona Jackson—the three individuals, friends, and colleagues to whom I dedicate this anthology—have, more than they probably know, in one way or another supported and encouraged me in my efforts to complete this project, as well as to move forward in my work as editor of *Callaloo*. So has my colleague Michael Sibble Collins, who reviewed and critiqued the manuscript of *Angles of Ascent* in its early stages, and who offered me a number of suggestions on how I might improve it. Then, too, there is Antonio Cepeda-Benito, who, as my immediate *jefe,* has demonstrated that he too believes in and supports the work I do.

There are other friends and colleagues who have assisted me in the production of this anthology, some with kind words and others with words not easily transliterated into the politeness required for these pages. There is my friend and colleague Carl Phillips, who offered me suggestions and advice on this anthology in its initial stages. This brilliant working poet knows how necessary such an anthology is to American literature. Marcus Jones, Michael Kahlil Taylor, Melvin White, James Pernell Woodruff—all good friends outside the production of literature and the discourse devoted to it—have not only read and critiqued drafts of what I have written, but, over the years, have also given me an ear and a hand, a place to write, a wake-up call, invaluable advice, etc., as I was assembling *Angles of Ascent.*

In the final stages of the production of this anthology, two members of the *Callaloo* staff literally rescued much of what others assigned to assist me, whom I will not name here, had failed to do. I am referring to Katy Karasek and Eunice McCain-Davis, whose invaluable attention to and selfless engagement in work helped to bring this project to a joyous conclusion. Without their assistance—their organizational and critical linguistic skills, and their willingness to do their work independent of supervision—this project would have taken much longer to complete. It is obvious, then, that I am deeply indebted to each of them for their respective sterling work with me. And to them, as I do my aforementioned friends and colleagues, I want to express my sincere gratitude.

There is much positive to be said about different kinds of student employment in institutions of higher education. Given the kind of work I do, I can always depend on the employment of graduate and undergraduate students at Texas A&M University in support of my work. The kinds and quality of the contributions Oscar Berrio, Dennis Winston, and Brian Yost, three graduate students, made to *Angles of Ascent* recall the work of veterans in the field. Then, too, the work of a host of undergraduate students was necessary. Rashad Aninye, Sarah Bishop, Matthew Broussard (University of Texas), Nancy Garcia, Alysa Hayes, David Johnson, Addison Morris, Daniel Peña, Daniel Robinson, Gabrielle Royal, Andy Sanchez, Aaron Vano, Elizabeth Wells, and others also made important contributions toward the completion of *Angles of Ascent*. I am grateful to them all.

I am also grateful to my editor, Jill Bialosky, and her assistant, Alison Liss, for their patience and understanding. From beginning to end, Jill, herself a poet, believed in and supported this project.

And, finally, again, to all named—and unnamed—supporters of and contributors to *Angles of Ascent,* thank you. This is also your anthology. It bears your mark, too.

—*Charles Henry Rowell*

INDEX

Absentee Landlord, 224

A colored woman stands beside a red dirt road, 455

A dog's bark breaks the December, 224

A dog's sudden slickness slices such raw terror, 398

Adrienne's Poem: On the Dialectics of the Diatonic Scale, 103

A flower in a weedy field, 215

African Dream, 109

Agave water crests, 339

A honeybee queen lays the nettle, 533

Ai, 174–83

Alexander, Elizabeth, 304–10

All day I've listened to the industry, 407

All night long the capitol glows. The Day-Glo day all night long, 315

All She Wrote, 296

All silence says music will follow, 153

All their fences, 317

All Their Stanzas Look Alike, 317

All the new thinking is about loss. Like a diseased lung, 544

Although the sandy soil's already red, 265

always pyrotechnics, 83

Amarillo, 446

American Smooth, 216

American Sonnet (17), 193

American Sonnet (54), 193

AM/TRAK, 36

An Agony. As Now, 33

And I and I / must admit, 114

And the levees crackled, 397

And then I said, That's what it means, 389

Ars Poetica, 191

ascension, 510

As from a Quiver of Arrows, 380

A squeegee blade along your tongue's length, 354

As through marble, or the lining of, 377

A street sweeper rounds, 497

As usual, legend got it all, 212

at best you can say, 130

At Pegasus, 343

At the rest stop on the way to Mississippi, 237

awake at 4 A.M., 483

Baraka, Amiri, 30–41

Barrax, Gerald, 76–79

Battle Report, 106

Because all energy went into making him breathe, 290

[Because we love wrong], 453

BECAUSE WE LOVE WRONG we are no one's daughter. We cannot go, 453

Because women are expected to keep silent about, 158

bed calls, i sit in the dark in the living room, 192

Bedtime Story, 192

Belle's Promenade: Nassau Street, Princeton, 334

Bellocq's Ophelia, 407

Belly Song, 114

Black Art, 31

Black Light, 369

Black Nikes, 296

blind lemon taught me, 461

blk / rhetoric, 68

Blue, 377

Blue jays balance on the chicken wire fence, 531

Blue Light Lounge Sutra for the Performance Poets at Harold Park Hotel, 261

Blue Whale, The, 309

Bop: The North Star, 540

Boston Year, 308

Boy Breaking Glass, 10

Brad Pitt, Kevin Bacon, and the Brown Boy's Mother, 547

Breakthrough, 62

Bridgetower, The, 219

Bright Moments, 315

Brooks, Gwendolyn, 4–11

Brown as a mule, I stomped, 446

Brown, Jericho, 422–26

Bryan, Texas Procession, 431

But He Was Cool, or: he even stopped for green lights, 55

Butte Creek steps out of the canyon, 152

"Can I go back to the top, 319

Cassells, Cyrus, 184–89

Catch and Release, 152

Chi, 21

Childhood, 400

childhood remembrances are always a drag, 45

Children of the Pentecost like moles, 251

Children we have not borne, 120

Chore, 531

Cigar Maker, The, 150

Civilization, 384

Clay Bison in a Cave, 126

Clay-tan, eyeless, 126

Cleaning, 443

Clifton, Lucille, 80–87

Climbing Montmartre, 205

Coal, 119

Coleman, Wanda, 190–94

Coliseum Pool, 1960 (Dream), 96

Collins, Michael Sibble, 427–33

Composition with Guitar and Apples, 245

Conversation, 178

Copyright, 503

Cortez, Jayne, 88–92

couldn't stand to see these new young faces, these, 195

Crossing the Rubicon at Seventy, 131

Crowning, 419

Crows in a Strong Wind, 222

Culture of Near Miss, The, 290

Curious Journey of Ulysses Paradeece After a Hurricane, The, 179

Current Events, 101

Cut the adults. Huck-um dun the chest, 551

Dance for Ma Rainey, A, 169

Dargan, Kyle, 434–38

Daughters, 1900, 301

[Daughters of four generations], 452

DAUGHTERS OF FOUR GENERATIONS of undines, 452

Day 33, 510

Day 36, 511

Day 41, 511

Day 48, 512

Day Before Kindergarten, The: Taluca, Alabama, 1959, 283

Daystar, 214

Dear Ann, 161

dearest cousin, 193

dear grandma, 510

Dear Miss Nettie, 159

Dear Obour, 18

Dear you: the lights here ask, 413

Deep Song, 240

Derrick Poem (The Lost World), 345

Derricotte, Toi, 195–204

Despite his caricatures, 21

Devil Comes on Horseback, The, 265

Discipline, 480

Discovering the Camera, 374

Disguised in my mouth as a swampland, 90

Distance is money just out of reach, 392

Distant Drum, The, 54

Dixon, Melvin, 205–10

do not speak to me of martyrdom, 67

Don Pullen at the Zanzibar Blue Jazz Café, 349

Don't Drink the Water, 398

Don't Explain: A Ballad Played by Dexter Gordon, 98

Don't give me nothing in, 360

Double Dutch, 501

Dove, Rita, 211–20

Downtown Boom, 154

Downtown-Boy Uptown, 51

Downtown-boy uptown, 51

Dress, 532

Drought, 513

Duende, 527

Dungy, Camille T., 439–44

Eady, Cornelius, 221–22

Eagle. Tiger. Whale., 77

Eclogue, 142

Eddie Priest's Barbershop & Notary, 414

[Edges in the rhododendron], 451

EDGES IN THE RHODODENDRON. There is not always enough cloud or, 451

Ego Tripping (there may be a reason why), 47

El Beso, 234

el corazón—toward an ars poetica, 510

elders on their bench upright, 512

Elegies for Paradise Valley, 14

Elegy for the Native Guards, 410

elizabeth cotten / nahum chandler, 492

Ellis, Thomas Sayers, 311–26

Enlightenment, 545

Enter the Dragon, 497

Evans, Mari, 42–44

Everything's a metaphor, some wise, 213

Exchange in greed the ungraceful signs. Thrust, 110

Extinction, 544

Facing It, 260

FADE IN:, 372

Falling, 458

far memory, 84

Fast Skirt Blues, 359

Fire, 459

first diesel came through cuba, 489

First Grade, All Over Again, 321

First time I lay with him, 361

Fishing the White Water, 121

Fish in the Stone, The, 213

Five daughters, in the slant light on the porch, 301

Flash Reverses Time, The, 368

Flounder, 405

For a Young Artist, 12

For Brother Malcolm, 74

Forgive me, I'm no good at this. I can't write back. I never read your, 296

For Malcolm's eyes, when they broke, 35

For me, the movie starts with a black man, 497

For the Confederate Dead, 417

Four Improvisations on Ursa Corregidora, 506

Four weeks have passed since I left, and
    still, 408
Foxes, 241
Francis, Vievee, 445–48
frank ramsay / nancy wilson, 495
Fred Sanford's on at 12, 342
Fretwork, 382
Froggy's Class, 401
from, 367

Game, The, 415
Garden, 536
gayl jones, 488
gigan 63, 469
Gilbert, Christopher, 223–26
Giovanni, Nikki, 45–48
Giscombe, C. S., 227–30
Glenn on Monk's Mountain, 275
God's got his eye on me, but I ain't a
    sparrow, 425
Godzilla's Avocado, 324
Goldsboro Narratives, 329
Goldsboro narrative #4, 329
Goldsboro narrative #7, 330
Goldsboro narrative #28, 331
Gomez, Jewelle, 231–35
Gonna jump   gotta jump up to go
    down in the bottom land, a, 462
Gospel of Barbecue, The, 356
Great Horned Owl, The, 125

Hagar to Sarai, 360
Hairston, Alena, 449–53
Half past eight Don Pullen just arrived,
    349
Hamer, Forrest, 327–31
Hamilton, Bobb, 49–50
Hamilton, Kendra, 332–35
*Hard Rock Returns to Prison from the
    Hospital for the Criminal Insane*, 113
Hard Rock / was / "known not to take
    no shit, 113
Hardy, Myronn, 336–41

Harlem Gallery, 21
Harper, Michael S., 93–99
Harrington, Janice N., 454–60
*Hattie McDaniel Arrives at the Coconut
    Grove*, 217
Having nothing else to do, 431
Having wanted to drive out to the edge,
    right out, 227
Hayden, Robert, 12–20
Hayes, Terrance, 342–48
Headless Saints, The, 339
Heartbeats, 208
he came down the mountain, 191
He did not!, 101
He glides, descending, 125
He is not quite the color of coffee, 150
Henderson, David, 51–53
Here, she said, *put this on your head*, 405
Here the ashtrays smoke, 415
Hernton, Calvin C., 54
Herodotus, woven into his story, 263
Heroes, 215
Hey there poleece, 49
History, 213
Holy Cross Hospital, 195
Homecoming, 66
Homeric Interim, 392
Hoover, Edgar J., 175
Horse in the Dark, 446
How did I believe life would change?,
    337
how i got ovah, 61
How People Disappear, 388
how sad it must be, 70

I, 119
I Am a Black Woman, 43
I am a black woman, 43
I am a Cowboy in the Boat of Ra, 134
I am a cowboy in the boat of Ra, 134
I am five, 257
I am inside someone, 33
I am not a metaphor or symbol, 54

i am seized with the desire to end, 193

I am sitting in a cell with a view of evil parallels, 104

I am the Seventh Son of the Son, 58

"I, as usual, lost what favor I had, 238

i can tell you, 61

Icarus on Fire Island, 391

I could be wrong, but I think my life is half over, 328

Ida Rewrites, 238

Idea of Ancestry, The, 112

If Ezra Pound couldn't make it cohere, 430

If this world were mine, the stereo, 388

If was at the Beginning. If, 219

if you killed me now my legs would walk to another country, 469

[if your complexion is a mess], 297

if your complexion is a mess, 297

i gather up, 70

I guess, 313

i have been a, 66

I have finally learned to speak to God, 467

I Have Folded My Sorrows, 107

I have folded my sorrows into the mantle of summer night, 107

I have no answer to the blank inequity, 299

I know you are not wholly, 164

I learned regret at Mother's sink, 443

I Looked & Saw History Caught, 73

I looked & saw history caught, 73

Images of the stud and the buck have an amorously crafted reso-, 505

I'm going to be just like you, Ma, 169

I'm holding on to you, but you're gone already, 294

I'm old enough to stand, 77

I'm the man behind the man, 175

Inamoratas, with an approbation, 4

in a place beyond, 511

In black core of night, it explodes, 109

Incident, 411

In his knapsack, he tucked a notebook of sketches, 459

In its eye a convex universe, 534

Inland where no seagulls circled, 446

In Memory of Radio, 32

In Millais's painting, Ophelia dies faceup, 407

In the backyard of our house on Norwood, 203

In the dream, I am with the Fugitive, 411

In the Middle, 328

In the middle of an argument I recall a high peak, 285

In the Morning, 90

Invisible Dreams, 199

i remember a useless eyed street busker, twin holes shriveled small, 461

I remember, we walked (we didn't walk), 448

i rose from stiffening, 81

is music   is men, 414

I take my $, buy a pair of very bright kicks for the game, 345

I take two from the sack, 206

It doesn't matter if you can't see, 351

I tell you, 542

I too have turned, 536

It's a slow, slow process, 123

"It's your imagination," said Mama Paradeece, 179

I turn the dress loose—its hand-sewn collar, 532

It was 1963 or 4, summer, 327

I've had tangled feelings lately, 62

I've seen hogs herded for slaughter, 403

I wanted to reflect the sun, 424

I was asleep while you were dying, 412

I was born in minutes in a roadside kitchen a skillet, 507

I was born in the congo, 47

I watch Daddy tear down, 283

I waved a gun last night, 515

I wonder if anyone ever thought, 142
I worked in the icehouse, 95

Jackson, Angela, 236–39
Jackson, Major, 349–55
Jail Poems, 104
Jeffers, Honorée Fanonne, 356–62
Je m'appelle Sally, 184
Jennifer, here are some facts bred by the
    others, 288
Jess, Tyehimba, 461–65
John Cabot, out of Wilma, once a
    Wycliffe, 9
johnny cash / rosetta tharp, 489
Jones, Gayl, 240–49
Jones, Patricia Spears, 250–55
Jordan, A. Van, 363–75
Jordan, June, 100–103

Kaufman, Bob, 104–109
Killed Rabbit, The, 534
King: April 4, 1968, 78
Knight, Etheridge, 110–17
Kocher, Ruth Ellen, 466–70
Komunyakaa, Yusef, 256–67

Last Supper, 403
late, in aqua and ermine, gardenias, 217
lazarus, 81
leadbelly sings to his #1 crew, 462
Leda, After the Swan, 379
leda 1, 82
leda 2, 83
leda 3, 83
Lesson, 327
Letter from Phillis Wheatley, A, 18
Letter Home, 408
Letters from a New England Negro, 159
Letters from the North Star, 413
Light is a distant world, 225
Limen, 407
Lingo, 263
Long after it was, 356

Lorde, Audre, 118–22
Lost, 539
*Love of Travellers, The (Doris, Sandra and
    Sheryl)*, 237
Lying, 483

Mackey, Nathaniel, 268–81
Madhubuti, Haki, 55–56
Major, Clarence, 123–28
Making Stars with Jacob Lawrence, 340
Malcolm, 67
Malcolm X—An Autobiography, 58
Mama's Promise, 299
Man of the Family, 438
martha promise receives leadbelly, 1935,
    464
Martin, Dawn Lundy, 471–81
Maundy Thursday, 334
McElroy, Colleen J., 129–32
Me and Bubble Went to Memphis, 292
Me and Bubble Went to Memphis. I did
    everything I, 292
Meditation on Breathing, 467
Men claim the easiest spots, 121
Merritt, Constance, 482–87
metoika, 490
Microphone Fiend, 436
Minks, The, 203
Miss Ann Spencer / August 30, 1867, 161
Miss Ann Spencer / October 22, 1867, 162
Miss Ann Spencer / November 24, 1867,
    163
Miss Ann Spencer / February 15, 1868, 164
mistress stella speaks, 465
Mixed Couple, 1908, 372
Moss, Thylias, 282–93
Moten, Fred, 488–95
Mr. Dynamite Splits, 319
Mrs. Josiah Harris / August 25, 1867, 159
*Mulberry Breath as Proof of the Wave in
    Form of Question*, 288
Mullen, Harryette, 294–98
Murillo, John, 496–500

Mute Swan, The, 483

My black face fades, 260

My Chakabuku Mama (a comic tale), 232

my daddy drank red soda pop, 488

My Dear Khomeini, 136

My eight aunts titter. *Look at all that hair*. He takes a plate, 523

my father is a retired magician, 146

my father is a retired magician, 146

My Father's Love Letters, 258

My father was an enormous man, 311

My first big love was cosmically correct, 232

My first week in Cambridge a car full of white boys, 308

My husband Mutt backhanded me down the fire, 506

my knees recall the pockets, 84

My shared bedroom's window, 14

My story—hieroglyphics of scuff and blister, 448

Myth, 412

nappy edges (a cross country sojourn), 148

Neal, Larry, 57–60

Negrotizing in Five or How to Write a Black Poem, 472

Nelson, Marilyn, 299–302

Nestor's Bathtub, 212

New York grows, 221

Next it was Austria we, 275

Nikki-Rosa, 45

Nobodies, The, 524

Northernmost Road, The, 227

Not the palm, not the pear tree, 423

Not the white of hard-won cotton, 188

Now that knowing means nothing, 419

Now that she has not come back, 468

Ocean Springs Missippy, 167

[Of a girl, in white], 298

Of a girl, in white, between the lines, in the spaces where nothing, 298

Of course I know the story of the scorpion, 503

Off go the crows from the roof, 222

On a Bench: My Life, 337

On a deserted playground in late day sun, 499

On CNN a girl's fingers slack, empty of weapons. Behind her, shrapnel, 480

One enters an unforgiving, inchoate world. No mold to make, fos-, 472

One for All Newborns, 287

One thousand saxophones infiltrate the city, 106

On Fridays he'd open a can of Jax, 258

Onion Bucket, 153

Only now, in spring, can the place be named, 440

On Stripping Bark from Myself, 158

On the C Train the Black Object Ponders Amuzati's Family Eaten in the Congo, 551

On Watching a Caterpillar Become a Butterfly, 123

Orpheus Plays the Bronx, 387

Oscar Micheaux, 374

Oscar to Sarah, 373

Our bodies cast a shadow of one, 369

Palinode, Once Removed, 437

Pardlo, Gregory, 501–508

Paring Potatoes, 206

Paris Subway Tango, 130

Pastoral, 411

Perhaps, 379

Phillips, Carl, 376–85

Photo of Miles Davis at Lennies-on-the-Turnpike, 1968, 221

Poem for Black Hearts, A, 35

Poem for My Father, A, 70

Poem No. 3, 70

Poems are bullshit unless they are, 31

Poem to a Nigger Cop, 49

Poetry, 430

Polaris sits still in the sky and if I knew, 540

Pope Replies to the Ayatollah Khomeini, The, 136

Practicing Fade-Aways, 499

Prayer of the Backhanded, 423

prep. 1. Starting at (a particular place or time): As in, John, 367

Prologue—And Then She Owns You, 395

Ravel: Bolero, 168

Reed, Ishmael, 133–37

Regina Brown Hears Voices, Kills Son Week Before Christmas, December 18, 1996, 364

Reports are various—, 382

Requiem, 266

Revolutionary Petunias, 157

Riot, 9

Roberson, Ed, 138–45

Rodgers, Carolyn, 61–65

Sally Hemings to Thomas Jefferson, 184

Sammy Lou of Rue, 157

Sanchez, Sonia, 66–71

Science of Wearing a Dress, The, 333

Science, science, science!, 304

Search for Robert Hayden, 434

Self-Portrait As the Letter Y, 515

Self-Portrait: Lilith, Eve, 485

Serena Williams, Whiteness, and the Act of Writing, 549

Several hours past that, 378

Shades of Green: Envy and Enmity in the American Cultural Imaginary, 505

Shange, Ntozake, 146–49

She, 223

She dips the calabash, 151

She eats breakfast, 245

She is merging onto the Edsel Ford Freeway in a car no longer, 545

Shepherd, Reginald, 386–93

she put a statue of a surprise on the windowsill. it was the size of a, 492

Sherman Ave. Love Poem, 497

She Sees What It Sees, 397

She wanted a little room for thinking, 214

She was an old maid, Froggy was, 401

singleton, giovanni, 509–12

Sit In What City We're In, 138

Six Sketches: When a Soul Breaks, 428

Skin Trade, 389

Smith, Patricia, 394–99

Smith, Tracy K., 513–29

Smoke Under the Bale, 448

So, 266

Solo Finger Solo, 88

Some Kind of Crazy, 351

Someone may want, 138

Something there is in every woman, 333

sometimes another star chooses, 83

Song of the Andoumboulou: 16, 269

Song Turning Back Into Itself 3, The, 167

Sound and Severance, 277

Speak Low, 383

Spellman, A. B., 72–73

Sprawled in the pigsty, 12

Spriggs, Edward S., 74

Sticks, 311

Still Life with Summer Sausage, a Blade, and No Blood, 448

St. John, Primus, 150–52

st. louis/ such a colored town/ a whiskey, 148

Strange, Sharan, 400–404

Suddenly two, they sat side by, 277

Summer brought fireflies in swarms, 400

Sundays of Satin-Legs Smith, The, 4

super-cool, 55

Supposing everytime I hit this key, 103

swam alongside the vessel for hours, 309

Swarm, 533

Sweet beats of jazz impaled on slivers of wind, 108

Sylvester, my eight-year-old son, lives in sin, 364

Symbolic Nature of Chaos, The, 477

Take these thousand steps, these up-running shoes, 205

Taped to the wall of my cell are 47 pictures: 47 black, 112

Territorial Claims, 127

Thanksgiving, 254

That moment in church when I stared at the Reverend's black, 354

That time my grandmother dragged me, 198

The austere angels dozing at their posts, 485

The blues calling my name, 240

The brown boy is afraid, because he can't tell, exactly, what his, 549

The child freestyles in the shower, 436

The countryside slides away, elides trees, 238

The cry I bring down from the hills, 259

The earth is dry and they live wanting, 527

[The fathers worked their hands to meat], 450

THE FATHERS WORKED THEIR hands to meat, side by side, tarry mat-, 450

The fish in the stone, 213

Theft, 518

The garage has not been allowed to breathe, 434

The girl from Martinsville sets her eyes on me, 437

The girls are bold, fingering, 162

The girls turning double-dutch, 501

The hydrangea begins as a small, bright world, 513

[Their greatgreatgranddaddies], 452

THEIR GREATGREATGRANDDADDIES were paid in scrip yet thrived a, 452

[The jawbone of an ass. A shank], 265

[The jawbone of an ass. A shank], 265

the need gotta be, 261

The one you hold in your arms is not Maxine (his living wife &, 98

The only cardboard we had was the box, 340

The railroad station is like a big barn, 241

There are many parched lips, 254

There are no gospel singers, 154

There is no darkness like a closed door, 234

there is no memorial site, 74

there is nothing luminous, 82

There's an art, 384

There's a sickness in me. During, 199

There was in Warwick Neck, at, 163

the water by, 510

There were robberies and thieves, deft cutting into and savaging, 477

The river, unrolled bolt of silk, gives, 539

The sail had been drawn into an, 336

These are the last days, 417

The splendid coat that wrapped the favored son, 484

[The tyranny of pig boys], 449

THE TYRANNY OF PIG BOYS: brotherhood of menchildren whose hands, 449

The wind stirred—the water beneath it stirred accordingly . . . , 383

The woman with the microphone sings to hurt you, 422

The world shatters, 518

They are like those crazy women, 343

They kick and flail like crabs on their backs, 287

The young dead soldier was younger, 329

They rise from the dawn and dress, 524

They say, erased, 473

They were dredging, 269

This ink. This name. This blood. This blunder, 347

This is not morning. There is a nasti-ness, 395

This Parable, This Body, 542

Thomas, Amber Flora, 530–35

Thomas, Lorenzo, 153–55

Thought Clouds, 372

Time was a boy, specially a black boy, 330

Timex *Remembered*, 285

Tolson, Melvin B., 21–27

To me, image is any value in the exchange. Pleasure's accidental. In, 230

To My Daughter the Junkie on a Train, 120

Tonight, Prophet, 324

To Put Things Right, 444

Touch, 346

Touching, 225

Towhomitmayconcern, 71

Track 1: Lush Life, 422

Track 4: Reflections, 424

Track 5: Summertime, 425

Trane, 36

Trap a Congo, 151

Trethewey, Natasha, 405–12

Turning Forty in the 90's, 207

1200N Road, Going East, The, 230

Two loves I have, each one, 391

Two Trains, 238

Undertones, 336

Undress, The, 473

Unraveling Ravel is no longer a secret, 168

Unspoken, 294

Up on the Roof, 397

Up on the roof, stumbling slickstep, you wave all your sheets and, 397

Urban Renewal, 353

Van Clief-Stefanon, Lyrae, 536–41

Venus Hottentot (1825), The, 304

Venus's-flytraps, 257

View-Master, 313

viii. Block Party, 353

Violent Space, The (or when your sister sleeps around for money), 110

Walker, Alice, 156–58

Walking Parker Home, 108

Warning Comes Down, The, 455

watch out fo the full moon of sonia, 71

Weakness, The, 198

we are busy and wanting, 511

Wearing My Red Silk Chinese Jacket, 251

we do not know the name, 131

We leave Gulfport at noon; gulls over-head, 410

We made our own laws, 346

We need quarters like King Tut needed a boat. A slave could row, 296

We promised to grow old together, our dream, 207

We smile at each other, 178

We tell the story every year—, 411

We were dancing—it must have, 216

What can't be said, can't be said, and it can't be whistled either. It, 495

What do we do with the body, do we, 380

What I Am, 342

What I saw first was an elephant rising, 444

What to Eat, and What to Drink, and What to Leave for Poison, 440

What Would I Do White?, 101

What would I do white?, 101

When evening goes down into its jelly jelly jelly, 88

When folks caught on to what was hap-pening, 331

When he wakes up out of sleep, the brown boy remembers two, 547

When he was little, 321

When I'm running across the city, 368

When I was a child, 78

When I was ten (*no, younger*, 387

When rice was our nemesis, 188

When she sits at the kitchen table, 223

when your man comes home from
    prison, 464

*When Zappa Crashes My Family
    Reunion*, 523

While walking a narrow path, 127

White Iris Beautifies Me, The, 188

White silence on the water pulls me in
    and under. And I know it is, 483

Who has ever stopped to think of the
    divinity of Lamont Cranston?, 32

Whose broken window is a cry of art, 10

who's gonna make all, 68

Wife of Lot Before the Fire, The, 361

Wild Indigo, Because, 188

Williams, Crystal, 542–46

Williams, Sherley Anne, 159–65

Wilson, Ronaldo, 547–52

Wind in a Box, 347

*Window Cleaner Writes to the Astro-
    naut's Husband, The*, 468

With a full keyring, beach bathtowel, 96

With lengths of string and canted
    chairs, my father, 458

Woman of Color, 484

Woofers stacked to pillars made a disco
    of a city block, 353

Work out. Ten laps, 208

Written by Himself, 507

X, 378

xvi, 354

xxi, 354

Yaddo, Mrs. Ames & Black Men, 95

Years later, the house paid for, the
    church his rock, he was caught sell-
    ing, 428

Yellow Dishes, The, 93

"You and I Are Disappearing," 259

You Mama's son. You, 359

Young, Al, 166–70

Young, Kevin, 413–20

Your sister calls from college to say,
    "There's an asshole in my bed.", 438

You taste the lemon of speech, 93

you think i'm his property, 465